Millennium, Messiahs,

and Mayhem

Millennium, Messiahs, and Mayhem

Contemporary Apocalyptic Movements

Edited by

Thomas Robbins and Susan J. Palmer

Routledge
New York and London

Published in 1997 by

Routledge
29 West 35th Street
New York, NY 10001

Published in Great Britain by

Routledge
11 New Fetter Lane
London EC4P 4EE

Library of Congress Cataloging-in-Publication Data

Millennium, messiahs, and mayhem: contemporary apocalyptic movements
/ edited by Thomas Robbins and Susan J. Palmer.
p. cm.
Includes bibliographical references and index.
ISBN 0-415-91648-8 (hb). — ISBN 0-415 91649-6 (pb)
1. Millennialism—North America—History—20th century. 2. End
of the world—History of doctrines—20th century. 3. Violence—
Religious aspects—History of doctrines—20th century. 4. North
America—Religion—20th century. I. Robbins, Thomas. 1943–
II. Palmer, Susan J.
BL2520.M55 1997   97-12408
291.2'3—dc21   CIP

To Nestlea, Demon Cat of the Apocalypse   And to Susan's tribe

Contents

Section Three: Apocalypticism and the Churches

Section Four: Violence and Confrontation

Acknowledgments

Aside from the editors and the contributors the person most responsible for the actual creation of this manuscript is Jean Peterson. Her work went far beyond mere clerical assistance and has entailed a major responsibility for standardizing contributors' technical formats and computer programs to meet the publisher's needs and manuscript guidelines. Ms. Peterson worked not only with the editors but on occasion dealt directly with several contributors and with the publisher.

The editors are deeply indebted to Marlie Wasserman, erstwhile editor for religion at Routledge, who recognized the potential of the volume proposed by the editors and had faith in the abilities and expertise of the latter. It was largely owing to the support and encouragement of Ms. Wasserman that the editors received a contract on the basis of a detailed prospectus. Marlie Wasserman was succeeded by Maureen MacGrogan, under whose general direction the actual manuscript was completed. The editors wish to give particular thanks to Laska Jimsen, assistant editor for religion at Routledge, with whom the editors have worked closely and upon whom we have relied for advice and for assistance in resolving certain issues.

The editors are indebted to Dr. David Bromley, who gave the editors useful advice and who helped bring the editors' project to the attention of Routledge. The editors acknowledge the helpful comments and criticisms directed to the original prospectus by Dr. E. Burke Rocheford, Dr. Paula Nesbitt, and Dr. Catherine Wessinger.

Patterns of Contemporary Apocalypticism in North America

Introduction

Thomas Robbins, Susan J. Palmer

It was once a common view of historians that as the year A.D. 1000 loomed, a wave of terror swept over Europe as the coming of Antichrist and the Last Judgment were anxiously awaited. "It was," the great historian Jules Michelet asserted, "a universal belief in the Middle Ages that the world would end with the year 1000 from the Nativity" (quoted in O'Brian 1994, 6). Richard Erdoes (1988, 2) writes in *AD 1000*:

Some were certain that the Second Coming of Christ would fall on the last day of the year 999, at the very stroke of midnight. Others were equally convinced that Armageddon would come a little earlier, on the eve of the nativity when "the Children of Light would join in battle with Gog's army of hellish fiends." Some fixed the date on the day of the summer or winter solstice of the thousandth year after our Lord's passion . . . though people quarreled about the exact date and hour, they all agreed, in the words of [the monk] Raoul Glaber that "Satan will soon be unleashed because the thousand years have been completed."

Some recent historians have challenged this notion. They believe that the supposed millennial terrors of the year 1000 have been exaggerated by earlier writers extrapolating a handful of apocalyptic "terror texts" (McGinn 1994).[1] Nevertheless, as one revisionist notes, "Historical fables like the 'Terrors of the Year 1000' have a way of reproducing themselves as real events." Thus, "In all likelihood some will view the approaching year 2000 in terms of such foreboding, perhaps even fearing the imminence of Antichrist" (McGinn 1994, xi).

In recent decades the millennial impetus to apocalyptic imagination has been reinforced by various provocative, "earth shaking" developments. "Messianism is always associated with the presences of 'signs' " (Rapoport 1988, 200). Recent "signs" might include the astonishing collapse of the Soviet "Evil Empire," the terrifying specter of global epidemics such as AIDS;[2] warnings by scientists about imminent climactic and ecological disaster; genocidal horrors in countries such as Cambodia in the 1970s or Rwanda in the 1990s; the development of advanced weapons and the threat of "nuclear holocaust"; the "breakdown of the family" and disorienting flux in gender roles and norms of sexual intimacy; the growth of violent crime; the rapid rise of computer technology; global techno-economic integration; the resurgence of militant Islam; the growth of spiritual pluralism and occultism; the founding, expansion, and continuing peril of the Zionist state of Israel; and the prospect of a united Western Europe. Each of these developments has either been cited by scholars and journalists as helping to stimulate apocalyptic visions or has been identified by Christian prophecy writers such as Hal Lindsey (e.g., 1973a, 1973b, 1981) as representing a significant portent of the approaching "last days."

An example of the attribution of apocalyptic religious meanings to the economic trends of recent decades is afforded by Hal Lindsey's identification of the emerging techno-finance infrastructure of global economic integration as foreshadowing the looming reign of Antichrist (or the Great Tribulation). In this period, "Antichrist will require that all men on Earth worship him as God" and those who refuse to "profess this allegiance by receiving the Antichrist's identifying mark [666] on their forehead or hand will be prohibited from buying or selling":

> The worldwide computer banking system that will allow the Antichrist to accomplish this is already into its fledgling stages as we see more in-home computers and automated tellers with secret access codes springing up all over. Bank of America, the world's largest bank, has already begun penalizing customers monetarily who are not using their automated system in order to quicken the pace of change to a virtual cash-free society. (Lindsey 1973b, 93)[3]

According to another prophetic writer (Relfe 1981), Antichrist's 666 system can be seen emerging through new technological systems such as the electronic bar codes appearing on many products. Exotic extensions of religious pluralism and the growth of occultism and "New Age" mysticism have been seen as anticipating the advent of Antichrist's universal, false religion. "The New Age movement is Mystery Babylon, the last days' worldwide church of Satan" (Marrs 1989, 18). Reverend Pat Robertson hints that Antichrist may arise from the New Age subculture. The emerging "one-world political, economic social system will require a leader. Is it farfetched to think that we could soon see a New Age world leader linked with a New Age prophet?" (Robertson 1990, 122).[4]

Finally, sensational current news events such as the recent Mideast war (Desert Storm) refuel apocalyptic prophecy. Since a pre-apocalyptic gathering of the Jews in Israel is alleged to have been prophesied in Jeremiah 29:14, the founding of the state of Israel in 1948 has been viewed by Lindsey (1973a) and other prophecy writers as a sign of approaching endtimes. The Mideast, which is now a strategically significant source of vital oil supplies, is also the site of original biblical prophecies; e.g., the final battle of Armageddon will supposedly transpire on the actual ancient battleground of Megiddo.[5] Iraqi strongman Saddam Hussein has contributed to the apocalyptic salience of the Mideast by overtly identifying with the ancient Babylonian King Nebuchadnezzar, such that his assertiveness is seen in some quarters as the prophecied reemergence of ancient and wicked Babylon. However, Protestant Armageddon prophecy is not the exclusive source of pronouncements on the apocalyptic significance of Saddam's actions. The latter's invasion of Kuwait in 1990 was interpreted by the Lubavitcher Hassidic (Jewish) movement and its (then) messianic leader Rebbe Menahem Schneerson (Nadler, 1992) as a sign of the

incipient fulfillment of a prophecy from the Book of Isaiah predicting the coming of the Messiah after a terrible war between Persians and Arabs (ancient Persia included parts of modern Iraq). Now deceased, Rebbe Schneerson was
believed by his followers to be *Moshiach* or the Jewish messiah (Horowitz, 1984).

It is our premise that a wave of apocalyptic and millennial ferment has been
washing over American society and culture for several decades, a development
that has elicited scholarly commentary for some time (e.g., Martin 1982; Lifton
and Strozier 1990). A heightening of apocalyptic expectation may indeed represent a worldwide phenomenon, and is discussed as such in the present volume
by James Aho. Aho sees apocalyptic fundamentalism as well as postmodern
"linguistic" perspectives arising to fill a vacuum created by the diminished
plausibility of liberal universalist ideologies. "Decentering" trends in culture
lead to apocalypticism as the waning of the cultural center stimulates a perception of the imminent end of culture. Millennialist fundamentalist visions look
toward an ultimate postapocalyptic recentering of culture. However, the
American apocalyptic excitation cuts across sectarian differences and can be
discerned in Protestant, Catholic, Jewish, Islamic, and Mormon contexts.
Additionally it transcends the increasingly ambiguous boundary between
"sacred" and "secular" realms. As Philip Lamy points out in his contribution
to the present volume, a "millennial myth" of biblical origin is deeply
ingrained in American culture and represents a major cultural resource for the
interpretation of unsettling events and trends. Various groups and movements,
sometimes volatile and potentially violent, are now drawing upon as well as
reconstructing and reshaping the millennial myth (Lamy 1996). The purpose of
this collection of original papers is to explore the present apocalyptic ferment
transpiring in North America as the end of the second millennium approaches,
and to examine some of the movements that are emerging to respond to unsettling developments and a popular mood of anxiety and expectation.

Views of Apocalypticism

Apocalypticism is a form of *eschatology*. The latter refers to divinely revealed
teachings about the final events of history. "Apocalyptic eschatology, or apocalypticism, is the form of eschatology believing that these events are in some
sense imminent" (McGinn 1994, 2). "Eschatology interprets the historical process
in the light of the final events" (McGinn 1994, 13; see also O'Leary 1994, 61). Its

apocalyptic variety, in Bernard McGinn's (1994) view, emphasizes a "deterministic view of history," in which things are viewed in terms of a model of *crisis-judgment-reward*: a persecuting tyrant (e.g., Antichrist) oppresses the faithful and is destroyed by divine forces, after which there is divine judgment involving retribution for the wicked and a (possibly utopian) reward for the deserving.

Bernard McGinn sees apocalyptic eschatology as central to Judaic, Christian, and Islamic traditions. Arguably his conceptualization is somewhat westernized. Apocalyptic eschatology is inseparable, McGinn clearly implies, from a *linear* and purposive model of history. In contrast, Catherine Wessinger argues in this volume that forms of apocalypticism can occur without linear temporality and have occurred in Asiatic contexts where a *cyclical* conception of time prevails.[6] McGinn's construction also assumes that apocalypticism is necessarily *catastrophic*; that is, the apocalypse or future historical terminus is explosive—a kind of "big bang"—as well as violent and harshly retributive. This is a common view, but Catherine Wessinger demurs. Within a cyclical view of time, chaotic, catastrophic, and apocalyptic phases of the cosmic cycle (e.g., the Hindu *Kali Yuga*) that somewhat resemble linear, Western apocalypses, may be awaited with foreboding. But there may also be visions of a more positively toned apocalyptic phase such as the contemporary New Age or Age of Aquarius, which is also redemptive. The Western linear conceptions of apocalypse merge the demonic chaos and oppression of the catastrophic "down" phase of cyclical conceptions (e.g., the *Kali Yuga*) and the eagerly awaited and optimistic quality of the "up" phase. One sequence of final historical events is both dreaded as terrifying and joyously anticipated as ultimately salvific or redemptive.

The apocalyptic imagination, as McGinn and other writers have noted, bestows meaning on current events. Present events and tensions are seen as an image or prototype of the ultimate decisive struggle between good and evil and its final resolution at the end of time. Current vicissitudes thus have eschatological meaning. They are "signs" of the final crisis to come. The "last days" are thus experienced as *psychologically* (if not always chronologically) imminent.

The apocalyptic view is *deterministic*. The future is resolved into deterministic scenarios that might be viewed as *scripts*. As such they can occasionally become dangerous when actual events appear markedly convergent with the anticipated scenarios of zealots. Persons and groups who adhere to apocalyptic visions and are under stress may perceive scripted catastrophic scenarios being actualized and may themselves become volatile and prone to violence.

This dynamic operated at Waco, as Anthony and Robbins (this volume) and others have noted. An attempted "dynamic entry" by federal agents into the Branch Davidian compound appeared to the sectarians therein as a manifestation of the anticipated endtime assault of the demonic "Babylonians" against the Lamb of God (i.e., David Koresh, their messianic leader) and his disciples. A shoot-out ensued followed by a siege and then what appeared to be a final assault by the FBI and (probably) subsequent collective Davidian suicide. Anthony and Robbins quote Michael Barkun on the danger of authorities allowing themselves to "become co-participants in millenarians' end-time scripts" (Barkun 1994, 48). Barkun extrapolates on this point further in his contribution to the present volume.

Apocalypticism is *historicist*—salvation is tied to history and therefore must also be this-worldly and largely collective. What matters is not individual afterlife but the eschatological destiny of a collectivity. Salvation unfolds through history. Apocalypticism is also, at least in its catastrophic manifestations, decidedly *dualistic*. Absolute good and evil contend through history such that there is no room for moral ambiguity—no shades of gray. Apocalyptic symbolism "admits no ambiguity in its figures of good and evil, the Lamb and the Beast, The Bride of Christ and the Whore of Babylon" (O'Leary 1994, 71). Historicism and extreme dualism often combine. "The great temptation of apocalyptic eschatology is to externalize good and evil in terms of present historical conflicts" (McGinn 1994, 32). In this connection Anthony and Robbins (this volume) delineate a volatile apocalyptic orientation that they term *exemplary dualism*, a perspective that identifies powerful political and religious forces as exemplars of absolute polarities in terms of morality, eschatology, and the millennial destiny of humankind.[7] They argue that exemplary dualism may appeal to persons with "split selves" who may attain a provisional sense of wholeness through identification with a messianic leader and his perceived heroic virtues. Disvalued elements of self are dissociated and projected onto demonized "enemies" of the leader, his vanguard movement, and humanity. Cultural fragmentation is said to have presently rendered several split-self conditions such as "narcissistic" and "borderline" syndromes somewhat ubiquitous. Manipulative prophets and gurus exploit the vulnerability of persons exhibiting these patterns.

"Apocalypses," argues McGinn, are essentially "a genre of revelatory literature—that is, texts in which a message from the divine world is given to a believing community" (McGinn 1994, 11). Recently the construction of apocalypticism as a narrative literary form and mode of communication has produced an influential formulation by Stephen O'Leary (1994), whose seminal treatise *Arguing the Apocalypse* analyzes apocalyptic meanings as patterns of *persuasive rhetoric*.

O'Leary sees apocalypticism as a mode of persuasive communication that articulates a *symbolic theodicy* or general resolution of the "problem of evil." In particular, apocalypticism articulates a "temporal resolution of the problem of evil." *Temporal* resolutions of the problem of evil generally entail claims that evil will be neutralized or justified in the fullness of time, which will unfold the ultimate destiny of creation. The temporal resolution operates through *narratives*—stories about what is going to happen. Such narratives are rhetorical in the sense that they aim to persuade believers that their lives do have meaning and purpose in the face of life's apparent meaningless parade of suffering and evil.

The apocalyptic form of temporal resolution of evil entails the notion that there will be an *end of history* when all things will be sorted out and everyone will get what they deserve ("justification"). Apocalyptic theodicies thus acknowledge the pervasiveness of evil in the world; indeed, it is often claimed that the present is the *time of greatest evil*—everything is going to get worse for awhile until the situation more or less explodes, after which evil will dissipate. Rampant present evil is thus carefully positioned in a cosmic drama.

Apocalyptic narratives "view events as parts of a cosmic pattern," and apocalyptic discourse of interpretation "imposes a dramatic pattern onto historical time" (O'Leary 1994, 63). Drawing on dramaturgical theory, O'Leary identifies two frames of apocalyptic drama: *tragic* and *comic*. The former is deterministic—an inexorable fate leads to a decisive, retributive denouement—as well as catastrophic and radically dualist. The comic apocalyptic frame is less deterministic—there is more room for the free will of human agents to determine ultimate outcomes. It is also less catastrophic. The conflict of good and evil is a continuously recurrent element of life that is rooted in human frailty. It will not be extinguished in a spectacular denouement that resolves all issues and ties up all of the loose ends. Radical dualism is thus somewhat mitigated. To illustrate the comic apocalyptic mode, O'Leary discusses St. Augustine's writings, particularly *City of God*, in which some of the apocalyptic symbols of the Book of Revelation are interpreted allegorically in terms of the moral struggle of the soul such that "the radical dualism of the original mythic narrative is undercut" (O'Leary 1994, 74). There seems to be some confusion, however, as O'Leary refers to "Augustine's anti-apocalyptic eschatology" while also seeming to treat Augustinian discourse as a comic or non-tragic variant of apocalypticism. The ambiguity in the notion of the "comic apocalypse" muddies the picture a bit as to whether apocalypticism must necessarily be catastrophic. Wessinger (this volume) comments on this confusion.

It is worth noting that O'Leary's development of his "rhetorical theory of apocalypse" in *Arguing the Apocalypse* is preceded by a sharp critique of sociological and psychological perspectives on apocalypticism that feature social science concepts such as "deprivation." However, the currently influential literary-narrative-communicational approach, which may reflect the preoccupation of postmodern scholarship with "texts," may itself elicit a counterreaction. The latter may be exemplified by David Bromley (this volume), who attempts to formulate a more sociological conceptualization of apocalypticism.

Bromley proposes to detach "apocalypticism from its traditional theological moorings and to analyze it more generically and sociologically as a radical form of social organization." He sees apocalypticism as an extreme form of the *prophetic method,* which challenges, deconstructs, and sometimes demonizes received interpretations of reality and promotes an alternative vision of social order. The transcendental realm and the phenomenal world, which are seen as continuously interrelated by the conformist "priestly method," are seen as increasingly discontinuous and divergent in the prophetic mode. "Apocalypticism pushes the prophetic method to its logical limit, asserting an impending fusion of the two realms that will result in a radical restructuring of the phenomenal world to bring it into accord with the larger purpose represented in the transcendental realm."

While the priestly method evaluates and legitimates the present in terms of the past, the prophetic mode evaluates the present in terms of the preordained future. Apocalypticism is distinguished by the greater *imminence* of the future such that "the present is reduced to simply a gateway moment leading to the future." One consequence "is to create temporal liminality as the present is ending while the future is yet to be born. This creates inherent marginality for adherents who feel themselves to be standing poised on the brink of time." This is in turn linked to the "anti-structural" and antinomian motifs of prophetic milieux and to the exaltation of charismatic leadership. The latter reflects "the extraordinary claimsmaking capacity" created by the prophetic method and often leads to the radical devaluation of persons outside of the movement and even of the devotees themselves vis-à-vis the leader, as well as to "totalistic" organization and heightened internal solidarity (see also Anthony and Robbins, this volume). Intensive ritual and the cultivation of altered states of consciousness enable adherents to directly experience both transcendental agency and a vision of a new order and to become more distanced from the existing order. Although the final apocalypse may be in the future it may be partly experienced in the present.

Bromley's view of apocalypticism operates within a sort of occidental framework in which the transcendental and phenomenal realms (or, more traditionally, "creator" and "creation") are ontologically separate and distinct though variably interrelated. Bromley also notes that the sacred narratives of apocalyptic groups focus mainly on the *period of apocalyptic transformation* and "there is little charting of the future order that would serve as a plan for reordering life on the other side of the apocalypse." The editors are reminded here of the distinction made by Martha Lee (1995 and this volume) between *apocalyptics*, who focus mainly on the catastrophic apocalypse, and *millenarians*, who are more concerned with a utopian postapocalyptic order. Similarly Michael Barkun (this volume) identifies a continual tension within the racist Christian Identity belief system between an optimistic millenarian vision in which the believers will attain inevitable victory and then rule the world as a divinely appointed elite, and a dark expectation of an apocalyptic race war including the specter of imminent genocide perpetrated against the white race. For Lee and Barkun it is the apocalyptic focus that is more closely related to possible violence.

Millenarianism has generally referred to the belief in a final endtime with a compensatory or retributive significance. Such beliefs may have first originated in Zoroastrianism in ancient Persia and impacted prophetic Judaism and early Christianity (Cohn 1993). Millennialism is often more or less equated with millenarianism, but has a special biblical reference to the postapocalyptic thousand-year kingdom to be established on earth under the rule of Christ. (Adolph Hitler's notion of the "1000-year Reich" represented a secularization of the traditional Christian millennial vision.) In the last few centuries two Christian millennial orientations have competed in the United States: *postmillennialism*, which envisions the return of Christ transpiring after the millennial kingdom has been ushered in largely by human agency in terms of the gradual Christianization of culture; and catastrophic *premillennialism*, which sees humanity as incapable of creating the kingdom or even of blocking the coming reign of Antichrist (or Great Tribulation), such that Christ must arrive with a heavenly host and vanquish Antichrist at Armageddon before the millennium can unfold. These concepts are discussed here by Catherine Wessinger and by

Massimo Introvigne, whose contribution delineates varying patterns of apocalypticism and millennialism in early and contemporary (particularly heterodox) Mormonism. The fierce contemporary debate in conservative, Protestant evangelical circles between fundamentalist premillennialism and new, triumphalist neo-postmillennialist mystiques such as Christian Reconstructionism and Dominion Theology (Cox 1995) is delineated here by Anson Shupe, whose lively "blow-by-blow" account will reinforce O'Leary's conception of apocalypticism as a pattern of rhetoric. Issues of passivity and Armageddonist fatalism versus the imperative of Christian activism to bring in the millennial kingdom are highlighted. However, Wessinger (this volume) urges that scholars replace the received Protestant terminology of pre- versus postmillennialism with a more generalizable distinction between *catastrophic* and *progressive* millenarianism.

Premillennialist fundamentalism arose almost a century ago as evangelical protestants confronted what they saw as an increasingly degraded modernist culture. The contemporary impetus for neo-postmillennialism has come from a reaction to the *fatalism* of premillennialism that is arguably out of sync with growing voluntaristic political activism among conservative evangelicals (Shupe, this volume). Why fight politically against abortion or pornography if Antichrist will shortly become dictator and make things worse? Ammerman (1987) and O'Leary (1994) see possibilities for reconciling premillennialism and Christian politics. O'Leary has described how in the 1980s conservative evangelical prophets such as Hal Lindsey, Pat Robertson, and Ronald Reagan superimposed a "comic gloss" on tragic-fatalist "Armageddon theology" to reconcile the latter with political mobilization.[8] Nevertheless, as one of the editors has written, "contemporary American biblical evangelicism appears to waver between an apocalyptic vision in which a hopelessly depraved culture will shortly be destroyed as the world was destroyed 'in the days of Noah' . . . and a contrary triumphalist vision in which evangelicals and their allies will purify the world through political activism" (Anthony and Robbins 1990, 498).

In any case, notwithstanding its fatalism, the apocalyptic drama of premillennial dualism may in fact be vital to the legitimation of the political mobilization of the Christian right. The catastrophic premillennial vision confers cosmic significance on contemporary cultural conflict and political work in behalf of cultural reconstruction. "Apocalyptic religions have given many average, twentieth-century Americans an arena of significant action in the world" (Moore 1986, 148).

Contemporary American premillennialism is subdivided according to the issue of whether the "saints" or faithful Christians will have to endure the Tribulation, in which Antichrist will reign as a brutal tyrant and his "false prophet," the "lesser beast" of Revelation (McGinn 1994), will lead the churches into apostasy and unite them in a universal false religion worshipping the Antichrist. Most American fundamentalists might be said to be *pretribulationists* who look to the Rapture, in which the saints will be "caught up in the clouds" and taken to Jesus right before the onset of the Tribulation. The notion of the "secret rapture," grounded in Thessalonians 4:16–17, provides a number of rhetorical advantages as noted by O'Leary (1994, 134–143). These include a promise to the faithful that they *will not have to endure the Tribulation.* At the same time, since the Rapture can come at any time (and is often assumed to be imminent), believers are keyed up and motivated to purify their lives to be part of the "Gathered Remnant." Nevertheless, because the timing of the Rapture is not made explicitly clear and precise, a "comic" ambiguity prevails and fervent expectation does not entail a risk of empirical disconfirmation. As long as the Rapture has not transpired, the nonappearance of the scripted events of the coming Tribulation will not denote a failure of premillennial prophecy. The doctrine of the Rapture keeps the apocalypse always on the horizon of the future (O'Leary 1994).

The possibility of "failed prophecy" such as the "Great Disappointment" of the Millerites (prefundamentalist American premillennialists who believed in the imminent end of the world) in the 1840s (O'Leary 1984, 92–133), haunts apocalyptic movements, particularly those that embrace the tragic vision of premillennialism, which anticipates a sensational, discontinuous apocalyptic process. Since the famous study by Festinger, Riecken, and Schachter (1964) there has been substantial research on responses to apparent prophetic failure in millenarian groups (Balch, Farnesworth, and Wilkins 1983; Zygmunt 1972; Palmer and Finn 1991). In the present volume, the report by Balch, Mahnke, Dimitrovich, and Morrison analyzes the responses to a sequence of nonactualized prophecies in a deviant offshoot of the Baha'i religion.

In contrast to the pretribulationist vision, *posttribulationists* expect to have to survive the hostile environment of the Tribulation. According to Barkun (1994, this volume) a defensive "survivalist mentality" crystallizes among some posttribulationist groups, which puts a premium on weapons and military training (see also Lamy, this volume, and 1996) and enhances the likelihood of violence. While those pretribulationists who view the Rapture as imminent live, as it were, on the threshold of sacred or apocalyptic time, post-tribulationists may live *in* apocalyptic time such that any opposition or persecution that they experience may be identified literally with the catastrophic events of endtimes. The same may hold for *midtribulationists,* who expect to have to endure part (e.g., half) of the Tribulation before being either slain or raptured and then returning with Jesus to fight at Armageddon. The Branch Davidians at Waco, as Anthony and Robbins point out here, were midtribulationists who were led by the military raid on their compound on the part of federal agents to identify the latter with the demonic "Babylonians" who will menace the messianic Lamb of God (i.e., David Koresh) in the last days.

SECULAR AND RELIGIOUS APOCALYPTICISM

Apocalyptic excitation in contemporary North America, in our view, transcends the increasingly indeterminate boundary between religious and secular realms of meaning. Secular movements such as environmentalism and feminism often seem to wax apocalyptic while other phenomena such as survivalism-paramilitarism, radical feminism, or antiabortion advocacy appear to have both religious and secular dimensions. Supernaturalist and nonsupernaturalist apocalyptic notions often, as Lamy points out (this volume, 1996), appear to interpenetrate or meld into each other in various social movements.

"Concern for the environment," notes Martha Lee (this volume), "is at its core, a concern for the fate of the Earth. . . . Many environmentalist ideologies are therefore marked by millenarian themes." In her analysis of the evolution of the millenarian worldview of the Earth First! movement, Martha Lee shows how the radical environmentalist movement espoused a quasimillenarian ideology that became unstable (as millenarian orientations, according to Lee, often do). An extremist faction lost interest in a postapocalyptic vision of a more gentle and environmentally aware human community, and increasingly appeared to welcome a catastrophic destruction of much of the human population, which was deemed inevitable (since humans are incapable of changing their behavior to avert disaster) and was, moreover, not to be deplored since humans have no privileges over other species. A more humanist group of newer recruits believed that a disaster, while inevitable, could be significantly mitigated in its effects by environmentalist proselytizing leading more persons to "awaken to the simple joys and wisdom of environmental living." Dr. Lee contrasts the moderate *millenarian* outlook that focuses on a favorable postapocalyptic milieu with the *apocalyptic* concentration on the catastrophic transformational event, which characterized the more extreme faction. It appears (to the editors) that O'Leary's distinction between tragic and comic frames of apocalyptic rhetoric is applicable here. The tragic and harshly retributive vision of the extremist faction appears in some ways to evoke the catastrophic, rigid, and retributive vision of fundamentalist premillennialism.

In his interesting contribution, "Secularizing the Millennium," Philip Lamy notes that "secular millenarian movements" tend to represent evil "not by supernatural forces but by human ones, generally those who persecute them." By "adopting apocalyptic imagery and ideas to frame their beliefs," some secular movements can "instill a fervor in their followers that closely approximates that of the classical millennialist." Survivalists studied by Lamy "often speak of the imminent collapse of civilization and 'nuclear Armageddon' with the zeal of a doomsday prophet."

As noted by O'Leary, "Apocalyptic myth functions in our culture as a well of metaphor, a subterranean spring of symbolic resources drawn on by those who seek to define and construct their own historical epoch" (O'Leary 1994, 218). In a similar vein Philip Lamy (this volume) delineates a biblically based "millennial myth" at the core of American culture, "a symbolic form of belief that acts as a powerful metaphor for real human events." The millennial myth "provides a context in which to interpret current events and give meaning and direction to people's lives. The myth is like a floating framework for explaining the 'big picture' for both religious and secular millenarian movements and all manner of 'intermediate groups.' " Drawing on the Book of Revelation, Lamy evokes the images of *Babylon, Beast, Tribulation, Redemption, Armageddon, Revelation,* and *Millennium* and shows how these themes play out today in terms of the rhetoric of the Unibomber's manifesto, Christian Identity racists, *Soldier of Fortune* magazine, David Koresh, and other exemplars of contemporary apocalyptic "survivalism."

Lamy's reference to "intermediate groups" refers to the interaction and melding of religious and secular millennial elements within social movements. Thus some paramilitarists are overt Christian fundamentalists and some are not. Some apocalyptic antiabortion activists are more overtly supernaturalist than others (Kaplan 1995). Different environmentalist groups and individual participants are variably involved in supernaturalist New Age ideas. In contemporary American culture, notes Lamy, "elements from the classical apocalyptic tradition merge with modern and secular forms such as survivalism, producing a strange array of 'postmodern' millennial phenomena."

Contemporary feminism represents a key area in which secular and supernaturalist elements interpenetrate and in which explicitly supernaturalist and "pagan" theistic (e.g., evocations of the "Goddess") elements coexist with overtly secular themes that are nevertheless sometimes tinged with apocalyptic fervor and quasimessianic claims concerning the superior quality and messianic role of women. Susan Palmer's paper on the "feminization of the millennium" describes the striking prominence of feminine imagery in contemporary millennial visions (particularly on the margins of American religious life). Although it is not entirely unprecedented, this situation is particularly interesting in light of the many "male-oriented millenarian visions that have largely dominated Western history."

In contrast to the dark, tragic visions of the most extreme environmentalist activists (Lee 1995, and this volume) or the hyper-violent fringe of the antiabortion movement (Kaplan 1995), feminist millenarians are inclined to envision optimistic and voluntaristic scenarios (in O'Leary's terms, comic), which anticipate a forthcoming higher mode of culture to be permeated by "feminine" qualities of spiritual sensitivity, empathy, and pacificism (Palmer, this volume). In this respect feminist millenarianism is convergent with the techno-scientific millenarian movements discussed in this volume by John Bozeman. Apocalyptic mystiques of eugenics, cryonics, and space colonies look forward to a positive qualitative transformation in the parameters of human life through applications of advanced science and technology. Such movements ultimately shade into pervasive "forms of 'scientized' millennial faiths such as Scientology, UFO worshippers, and segments of the New Age that rely upon science . . . as a source of vocabulary and legitimating mythic paradigms." The constant emergence of quasireligious scientism and "techno-scientific religions" (Bainbridge 1987) in America reflects the "millennial myth" that Philip Lamy sees operating in American culture and that is continually being reshaped and reconstructed through new movements and visions of the millennium.

The fascinating currents of secular apocalypticism notwithstanding, the primary focus for millenarian visions remains in organized religions. Here again the torrent of contemporary apocalyptic and millenarian ferment sweeps across religious and secular borders and also crosses church and denominational boundaries as well as the line that separates institutionalized churches from esoteric "cults." One difference between the prophetic visions of the marginal sects and those of more conventional churches is that the latter groups are likely to allow for some element of *indeterminacy* that insulates their vision from empirical disconfirmation; i.e., they evade the trap of predictive specificity. Marginal groups are somewhat more likely to stress the immediacy of their prophetic vision in such a way that maximizes the fervor of devotees but also risks the eventuality of something akin to the Great Disappointment experienced by the Millerites. Robert Balch and his associates probe the effects of several apparent disconfirmations on the evolution of a deviant offshoot of the Baha'i religion. They note a divergence between the reactions of leaders and followers.

The distinction between deviant and nondeviant movements is not always clear. Ronald Lawson's paper here examines potentially schismatic apocalyptic ministries on the margins of the Seventh-Day Adventist Church, which is itself an offshoot of the original Millerite movement. The SDA Church's persisting commitment to a prophetic vision combined with its otherwise conventional church structure and style may frustrate some members who become intensely involved with prophecy. (The notorious Branch Davidians were descended from an earlier schism in the SDA Church.) Massimo Introvigne discusses apocalyptic fringe groups within contemporary Mormonism. Dr. Introvigne speaks of the "routinization of millenarian charisma," which frequently generates "countermovements." If we accept Bromley's notion of apocalypticism as constituting a distinctive pattern of religious organization, then we might expect tensions to arise when millenarianism is encapsulated within a conventionally institutionalized church structure.

Protestant fundamentalist churches represent the best-known institutionalized locus of apocalyptic prophecy. Indeed, the doctrine of Dispensational Premillennialism has been identified, along with biblical literalism and separatism, as a defining attribute of Protestant fundamentalism (Ammerman 1987). Recently, however, in conservative evangelical circles premillennial orthodoxy has been challenged by Christian Reconstructionism and other neo-postmillennial currents, which affirm that *Christians can build the millennial kingdom*. The heated rhetoric of Reconstructionist critics of fatalistic Armageddonist orthodoxy and the defensive rejoinders of premillennial loyalists are analyzed by Anson Shupe (this volume). The rise of neo-postmillennial mystiques such as Reconstructionism and Dominion Theology has also recently been discussed by Harvey Cox (1995), who identifies an ironic convergence between rightwing Reconstructionism and left-wing Catholic Liberation Theology. On opposite ends of the political spectrum, both movements envision Christian activists battling to bring in the kingdom of God on earth.

Evangelical Protestantism is the best-known but not the only locus of apocalyptic prophecy. In his paper, "The Vengeful Virgin," Michael Cuneo explores
apocalypticism among overtly schismatic and borderline Catholic fringe groups.
The visions of these groups somewhat resemble Protestant fundamentalist models. Interestingly, some of these groups also "incorporate elements of secular apocalypticism into their belief systems . . . expatiating on the debacle at Waco or the
machinations of the FBI or the specter of one-world government . . ." To some
degree, Protestant fundamentalist prophecy has created a model to which
Catholic, Mormon, and other varieties of American millennialism partly conform.

APOCALYPSE AND VIOLENCE

The relationship between apocalypticism and violence is presently receiving
attention from social scientists (Barkun 1996). Since institutionalized culture and
its norms are perceived by apocalyptics as doomed, apocalyptic movements have
an antinomian potential. A group that sees itself as a prophetic vanguard at the
approach of endtimes may also expect to face hostility and persecution for which
they must prepare (Anthony and Robbins 1995). For these and other reasons
nearly all of those religious "cults" that have become involved in spectacular
violent episodes have manifested distinctly apocalyptic outlooks (Anthony and
Robbins 1995). It is also noteworthy that enhanced acceptance of violence on the
part of intense activists in initially secular social movements (e.g., environmentalists, antiabortionists) has tended to be associated with increasing apocalyptic
dualism (Kaplan 1995; Lee 1995, and this volume). On the other hand, only a
small minority of apocalyptic movements have been (or are likely to become)
involved in violence; moreover, the symbolic meanings of the nonviolent majority of apocalyptic-millennial movements and the violent minority are often
rather similar and may overlap (Boyer 1993; Robbins and Anthony 1995).
Significant lines of inquiry are now opening with respect to why apocalyptic
groups are sometimes volatile and what characteristics of such movements tend
to increase the likelihood of violence (Anthony and Robbins 1995, this volume;
Barkun 1994, this volume; Robbins and Anthony 1995; Rosenfeld 1995).

In a recent formulation coauthored by one of the present editors (Robbins
and Anthony 1995), violent episodes involving religious movements are seen as
emerging from an interaction of *endogenous* factors implicating the leadership,
beliefs or organization of the group with *exogenous* or environmental factors

often involving some kind of hostility or persecution in the movement's environment. Violent incidents often (though not necessarily) appear to require the involvement of several endogenous factors interacting with an external influence that often involves some kind of provocation. However, particular violent episodes involving specific groups may differ from each other in terms of the relative weight of internal or predispositional volatility and external provocation.[9] Thus Anthony and Robbins (1995, and this volume; Robbins and Anthony 1995) maintain that the amount of provocation necessary to precipitate violence at Waco in 1993 (a military raid by federal agents and later a seeming FBI assault with armored vehicles and gas) was greater than the provocation at Jonestown, Guyana, in 1979 (a visitation by an unarmed congressman and his party who planned to return to the United States with a handful of defectors). The implication drawn by Anthony and Robbins is that David Koresh and the Davidians at Waco were really less volatile than Jim Jones and the Peoples Temple in Guyana. On the other hand, the role of external provocation, while not entirely absent, seems even less significant with respect to the Japanese Aum Shinrikyō sect, which appears to have gotten away with a lot of violent behavior before authorities belatedly intervened (Mullins, this volume; Sayles 1995). Violence gradually escalated from actions against individual defectors and enemies to mass subway mayhem in which more than 500 persons were exposed to lethal poison gas. As Mullins shows, in the years leading up to violent episodes, the apocalyptic vision of the leader, Asahara, became increasingly tragic in the sense of an inescapable, all-pervading catastrophe looming on the horizon.

The case of the Order of the Solar Temple is particularly interesting. Hall and Schuyler (this volume) emphasize the perception on the part of the self-conceived spiritual elite that they faced an apocalyptic "war" of persecution in addition to an imminent ecological catastrophe for Earth. Humiliated by a mundane firearms arrest, the leaders may have accelerated their timetable for the anticipated "transit" of their core members to a higher (nonbody) state. The situation was further complicated by a conflict involving a number of apostates and one apostate family in particular who were perceived as traitors and whose child was denounced as the living Antichrist.

Conflicts involving apostates are, in John Hall's (1996) view, particularly stressful for close-knit apocalyptic sects with authoritarian leadership, and have actually played a key role in precipitating sensationally violent episodes involving notorious groups such as the Peoples Temple, the Branch Davidians,

Aum Shinrikyō, and the Order of the Solar Temple.[10] The issue was particularly conspicuous with regard to the Solar Temple, in which the first persons to die (they were brutally murdered) were an apostate couple and their infant son in Quebec. The child had actually been designated as Antichrist by one of the sect's leaders, Joseph DiMambro, who had also conferred messianic status on his own female "cosmic child" (Hall and Schuyler, this volume; Palmer 1996, and this volume). Although the prospect of apostasy may be stressful to the leadership of any totalist and close-knit "cult," the salience of these conflicts may be greater for apocalyptic and messianic movements where apostasy may call into question the validity of the group's prophetic vision and the messianic claims of the inspired leader.

One model that interrelates endogenous and exogenous factors, with particular stress on the latter, might be termed the interpretive model. In the most general terms this approach focuses on how volatile groups are affected by their interpretations of the actions and dispositions of those entities whom they perceive as their enemies. In the present volume, the paper by Anthony and Robbins represents a variant of this conception. The authors present a psychological model which delineates an endogenous condition that heightens group volatility, but also heightens a sect's impressionability in terms of the impact on its own behavior of its perception of the behavior of these entities it demonizes. Much of the analysis of the Waco tragedy has thus focused on the blunders of officials and their impact on the perceptions (and thus on the actions) of volatile messianic believers (Anthony and Robbins, this volume; Barkun 1994; Wright 1995). There has also been attention directed to the simplistic and stereotypical perceptions of authorities that interact with the interpretations of apocalyptics to escalate a confrontation (Aho 1994). In his paper on the racist Christian Identity network for this volume, Michael Barkun applies the model of "Deviance Amplification" that has sometimes been previously employed to analyze cult-state conflicts.

The interpretive model may be susceptible to exaggeration in terms of a conception of violent millenarians or militant racists as mainly *reacting* to the dynamic countermobilization of their opponents. Jeffrey Kaplan's stimulating recent analyses of the apocalyptic, violent fringe of the antiabortion "rescue community" (1995), of the partly symbiotic relationship between racist movements and anticult "watchdog" groups (1993), and of the impact of Jewish countermobilization on (partly anti-Semitic) paramilitarist militias (1996) depict racist or violent extremist groups being pushed in a more extreme direction by strident opposition, stigmatization, and legal controls. On the other hand, Barkun's present contribution notes that Christian Identity racists employ "pseudo-validation" strategies to deliberately elicit through their own provocative behavior confirmation of their racist conspiracy visions.

As emphasized by Robbins and Anthony (1995), explanations of violent outbreaks must balance endogenous and exogenous variables. The stimulating interpretive (our term) approach may sometimes appear to place primary emphasis on exogenous factors and to downplay internal sources of racism, "paranoia," and dangerous volatility (Robbins, 1997). The goal of this approach, however, is to interrelate endogenous and exogenous conditions. The paper by Anthony and Robbins (this volume) attempts to combine a depth psychology (endogenous) analysis with an emphasis on the Branch Davidians' interpretation of the provocative behavior of federal agents (see also Anthony and Robbins 1995). However, the authors' psychodynamic model, though arguably reductive, affirms the essentially *voluntary* quality of devotees' commitment to "totalist" apocalyptic sects. The authors reject the analysis of totalistic "cults" in terms of "brainwashing" or an overwhelming psychological coercion sufficient to annihilate personal responsibility, an approach that the authors have criticized elsewhere (Anthony and Robbins 1992; Robbins and Anthony 1995). On the other had, as Mark Mullins's report on Aum Shinrikyō (this volume) indicates, occasionally an authoritarian sect may actually employ crude *physical* coercion to discourage defection.

Various other pertinent endogenous conditions possibly related to violence are worth considering, including whether premillennial sects expect to have to survive the Great Tribulation. Posttributionists, notes Barkun in his chapter on racist Christian identity believers, tend toward survivalism and paramilitarist preparedness. It is also significant whether prophetic groups see the present as actual apocalyptic time or whether the final events are, as most fundamentalists believe, *imminent but not right now* (Robbins and Anthony 1995; Barkun 1994; Rosenfeld 1995). Do apocalyptic believers feel that their actions can actually help bring in the millennium? One may predict an imminent apocalypse but "no action will ensue unless the believer also thinks that he can influence messianic events." (Rapoport 1988, 201).

Other factors may implicate patterns of leadership: Is there one absolute leader who totally embodies prophetic or messianic authority or is dissent legitimated (Robbins and Anthony 1995; Rosenfeld 1995)? In this connection, *charismatic authority* represents an ensemble of endogenous factors related to volatility and violence in apocalyptic or "world-rejecting" sects (Robbins and Anthony 1995; Wallis and Bruce 1986). Charismatic leadership, which is legitimated in terms of the leader's perceived exemplary qualities, probably enhances the antinomian potential of apocalypticism. Indeed the combination of charismatic leadership and an apocalyptic worldview may create a kind of tinderbox, although much will depend on the particular qualities of the visionary leader. Apocalyptic and millenarian beliefs are thus "most likely to be associated with volatility when they are embodied in charismatic 'messianic' leaders who identify the millennial destiny of humankind with their own personal vicissitudes and demonize any opposition to their aspirations and personal aggrandizement" (Robbins and Anthony 1995, 244). Asahara, the leader of Aum Shinrikyō, is an obvious example (Mullins, this volume; Sayles 1996), as is David Koresh, who "identified *himself* as the Lord's anointed and saw the standoff at Waco as the literal fulfillment of an intensifying campaign of demonic earthly rulers to destroy the righteous remnant" (Boyer 1993, 30, emphasis in original).

Arguably there is a kind of "fit" between apocalyptic visions and charismatic leadership, notwithstanding numerous fundamentalist churches that manage to combine doctrinal commitments to prophetic, premillennial visions with institutionalized structures of (suprapersonal) authority. But prophecies generally presuppose prophets, and world-rejecting sects manifest a stance of total rejection of or detachment from the broader society that may require the legitimating authority of a revered charismatic prophet with a compelling vision (Wallis and Bruce 1986). The relationship of charismatic leadership and apocalyptic movements is discussed in David Bromley's contribution here.

It is understandable that institutionalized churches that manifest a posture of accommodation to the environing culture and society while maintaining a definite commitment to an apocalyptic vision tend to be prone to defection by volatile congregants who are attracted to new charismatic prophets (who may become schismatic leaders). Koresh and the Branch Davidians (Wright 1995) were descendants (via several splits and schisms) of Victor Houteff's original Davidian split from the Seventh-day Adventists. The SDA today are saddled with a number of troublesome quasischismatic or borderline ministries, often deeply apocalyptic and, moreover, sometimes anti-Catholic. Such groups and the problem they pose for the prophetic but otherwise conventional and conformist SDA Church are discussed by Ronald Lawson in the present volume. Similarly, the Mormon Church, which has given up some of its early millenarianism and its practice of polygamy (which originally had deep eschatological significance), is faced with a plethora of partly or fully heterodox "fringe Mormon" groups, some of which are polygamous and/or deeply apocalyptic. In effect, the cultures of Mormonism and Adventism extend beyond the doctrinal and institutional boundaries of the SDA and Mormon Churches and include apocalyptic splinter groups. Apocalyptic currents in contemporary and early Mormonism are discussed here by Massimo Introvigne.

Charismatic authority is associated with group volatility because it is inherently *precarious* (Wallis and Bruce 1986). The charismatic leader operates in a vacuum in the sense that there is a relative absence of institutionalized restraints to curb the whimsy of the leader, a situation that facilitates violence, sexual excesses, and financial irregularities. There is also a dearth of institutionalized *supports* that the leader can fall back on to stabilize his authority, which is legitimized in terms of the leader's perceived extraordinary qualities. (Robbins and Anthony 1995). The charismatic leader must always look out for challenges to his leadership and will often tend to "simplify" his milieu by reducing internal pluralism and normative diversity and forcing out of the group those who are either potential rivals or who have inhibitions against unconditional obedience. Charismatic authority is antithetical to fixed rules and administrative procedures such that the leader may seek to maintain fluidity and relative chaos. He or she may "crisis monger" or provoke constant challenges and crises (Bird 1993) such that the threat of disruption will both enhance group solidarity and accentuate the indispensability of the inspired leader. Tension at the "boundary" of the group may be promoted and an external "threat" thereby evoked to heighten internal solidarity and the group's sense of dependence on the inspired leader. This can be a rather dangerous tactic, as boundary conflicts may get out of hand, and the minority sect or its leader may be destroyed. (For example, Joseph Smith, the controversial founding Mormon prophet, was lynched.)

Challenges to the charisma of an apocalyptic movement leader are sometimes viewed as contributing to a violent crisis. Aging, incontinent Joseph DeMambro of the Solar Temple, who venerated his daughter as the savior but perceived the child of an apostate couple as a satanic rival, may be a case in point (Hall, this volume; Palmer 1996). Interestingly, a number of charismatic leaders were actually in declining physical (and possibly mental) health prior to the spectacular violence that erupted within their movement or at its boundary. This list includes Asahara of Aum Shinrikyō, Jim Jones of the Peoples Temple, and DiMambro (David Koresh may have been healthy before the initial shoot-out with federal agents, but he had a painful bullet wound during the subsequent fifty-one-day standoff and the climactic crisis). Physical debility may threaten charisma, although debility and pain may also affect judgment directly, particularly in a context of absolute power, adulation, and the presumed sacredness of the leader's person. If one sees oneself as the center of the universe and also perceives oneself as dying, is not the universe then ending?

PLAN OF THIS BOOK

Our introductory essay has often commented on a particular contribution under more than one rubric. Many of the papers in this book are pertinent to more than one of the editors' thematic concerns. Nevertheless, our volume must have an organizational structure that assigns contributions to particular topical subdivisions, even though the papers in any one topical subdivision are likely to also contain elements bearing on the thematic issues highlighted in other sections.

Our initial section features papers that make contributions to theoretical issues in the study and basic conceptualization of apocalypticism and millenarianism. Essays in this section are by David G. Bromley ("Constructing Apocalypticism: Social and Cultural Elements of Radical Organization"), Catherine Wessinger ("Millennialism With and Without the Mayhem"), James A. Aho ("The Apocalypse of Modernity"), and Robert W. Balch et al, ("Fifteen Years of Failed Prophecy: Coping with Cognitive Dissonance in a Baha'i Sect").

The second section deals with the contemporary secularization of millenarianism and the interplay of "religious" and "secular" elements in particular movements and activist milieux. Papers included here are by Philip Lamy ("Secularizing the Millennium: Survivalists, Militias, and the New World Order"), Martha F. Lee ("Environmental Apocalypse: The Millenial Ideology of Earth First!"), and John M. Bozeman ("Technological Millenarianism in the United States"), plus Susan J. Palmer's paper on contemporary messianic feminism ("Woman as World Savior").

Section Three explores apocalyptic and millenarian ferment across the spectrum of American institutionalized religion. Included in this section are papers by Michael W. Cuneo ("The Vengeful Virgin: Case Studies in Contemporary American Catholic Apocalypticism"), Anson Shupe ("Christian Reconstructionism and the Angry Rhetoric of Neo-Postmillennialism"), Ronald Lawson

("The Persistence of Apocalypticism Within A Denominationalizing Sect: The Apocalyptic Fringe Groups of Seventh-Day Adventism"), and Massimo Introvigne ("Latter Day Revisited: Contemporary Mormon Millenarianism").

Our final section looks at issues of violence and confrontation. Contributors to this section are Michael Barkun ("Millenarians and Violence: The Case of the Christian Identity Movement"), Dick Anthony and Thomas Robbins ("Religious Totalism, Exemplary Dualism, and the Waco Tragedy"), John R. Hall and Philip Schuyler ("The Mystical Apocalypse of the Solar Temple") and Mark R. Mullins ("Aum Shinrikyō as an Apocalyptic Movement"). The latter paper deals with a sensational Asian group that has electrified American scholars and media. All of the other papers deal with North American groups, although the Solar Temple deaths transpired in both Quebec and Western Europe.

The papers in this volume, unfortunately, do not add up to a fully comprehensive delineation of contemporary millennial ferment in North America. We had hoped to present a paper on contemporary Jewish movements. We particularly regret the absence of a contribution dealing with black messianism (Lee 1988), which has been so prominent in the history of American millenarianism. A paper on Native American movements would also have been welcome. Nevertheless, we do hope that the issues, ideas, and case studies examined here will prove valuable and stimulating.

Notes

1. McGinn cites the study by Focillon (1969), *The Year 1000,* to the effect that expectations increased before and *after* A.D. 1000 but were not narrowly focused on one year. As McGinn (1994, 7) notes, some other modern writers have seen "the terrors of the year 1000" as a quintessential historical myth.

2. Palmer (1997) analyzes the response of contemporary apocalyptic sects and ministries to the AIDS pandemic, which has sometimes been incorporated into groups' millennial meaning systems in interesting ways. "Messianism," notes Rapoport (1988, 200), "is always associated with the presence of 'signs' . . . the 'Last Days' emerge in the context of world catastrophe." Biological, ecological, demographic, and violent catastrophes have abounded in recent decades and a global network of modern media ensures that we are aware of them.

3. Lindsey (1973b) is "convinced that we're living in the closing days of the world's history" in part because the emergence of the European Economic Community. "There is not doubt in my mind that it's the [pre-apocalyptic] fore-

runner of the Revived Roman Empire which the prophet Daniel spoke about with such certainty" (Lindsey 1973b).

4. A 1991 article in the same evangelical journal in which Robertson's 1990 article appeared suggested that "Gog" and Magog" from Ezekiel and Revelation, which Hal Lindsey and others have interpreted as referring to Russia or Russia-China, may refer to an imminent *Islamic* confederation whose military forces may fulfill the biblical prophecy (Revelation 16:16) of a great army entering the valley of Armageddon in the last days (Otis 1991).

5. According to one popular prophecy writer (Walvoord 1990, 12), "The providential presence of oil explains why the Bible makes the Middle East the center of world attention. It will be the scene of the Battle of Armageddon and the end of Western civilization as we know it."

6. Messianic and millenarian movements existed in China long before Christian influence was manifested there; see Smith, Green, and others. (1995, 718–720) and Spence (1996, xx–xxiii). "Messianic" movements tended to erupt in China in periods when dynastic decline and sociopolitical chaos suggested that the reigning dynasty had lost the "Mandate of Heaven." Messianism in Chinese religion "can thus be seen as an extreme manifestation of a broadly accepted principle, the difference being that instead of claiming the mandate, the leader of a messianic movement would proclaim that civil authority as such was about to be swept away and replaced by a new era of direct theocratic rule" (Smith, Green et al. 1995, 221–222).

7. Anthony and Robbins have related this apocalyptic orientation to the messianic beliefs of the Unification Church (Anthony and Robbins 1978), Jim Jones's Peoples Temple (Anthony and Robbins 1995; see also Jones 1989) and the Branch Davidians at Waco (Anthony and Robbins 1995, this volume).

8. Hal Lindsey (1973) seems not to have anticipated the surge of evangelical political activism in the 1970s. Later on he modified his fatalist premillennial and Armageddonist scenario to allow for a vital role for Christian activists in making a "last stand" against Satan that will effectively defend Christian culture until Christians are "raptured" (or sort of beamed up to heaven to join Christ) after which Antichrist can temporarily seize control of Earth (see O'Leary 1994, 172–193).

9. Robbins and Anthony (1995) acknowledge that exogenous and endogenous variables not only interact with each other but may be difficult to clearly separate from each other. Conflicts with apostates and defectors might be classified as either an endogenous or exogenous source of violence.

10. In 1994, an apostate family was murdered by a small "cult" led by Jeffrey Lundgren, a former (expelled) Temple guide and teacher in the Reorganized Latter Day Saints Church (McPherson 1993).

REFERENCES

Aho, James A. 1994. *This Thing of Darkness: A Sociology of the Enemy*. Seattle: University of Washington.

Ammerman, Nancy T. 1987. *Bible Believers: Fundamentalists in the Modern World*. New Brunswick, NJ: Rutgers University.

Anthony, Dick, and Thomas Robbins. 1990. "Civil Religion and Recent American Religious Ferment." In *In Gods We Trust*, edited by Thomas Robbins and Dick Anthony. New Brunswick, NJ: Transaction.

———. 1992. "Law, Social Science and the 'Brainwashing' Exception to the First Amendment." *Behavioral Sciences and the Law* 10 (1): 5–30.

———. 1995. "Religious Totalism, Violence and Exemplary Dualism." *Terror and Political Violence* 7 (3): 10–50.

Bainbridge, William S. 1987. "Science and Religion: The Case of Scientology." In *The Future of New Religious Movements*, edited by David Bromley and Phillip Hammond. Macon, GA: Mercer University.

Balch, Robert, Gwen Farnsworth, and Sue Wilkins. 1983. "When the Bombs Drop: Reactions to Disconfirmed Prophecy in a Millennial Sect." *Sociological Perspective* 26 (2): 137–158.

Barkun, Michael. 1994. "Reflections After Waco: Millennialists and the State." In *From the Ashes: Making Sense of Waco*, edited by James Lewis. Lanham, MD: Rowman and Littelfield.

———. 1995. "Understanding Millennialism." *Terrorism and Political Violence* 7 (3): 1–9.

———, ed. 1996. *Violence and the Millennium*. London: Frank Cass. Originally a special issue of *Terrorism and Political Violence* (1995) 7 (3).

Bird, Frederick. 1993. "Charisma and Leadership in New Religious Movements." In *Handbook of Cults and Sects in America*, vol. 3A, *Religion and the Social Order*, edited by David Bromley and Heffrey Hadden. Greenwich, CT: JAI Press.

Boyer, Paul. 1993. "A Brief History of the End of Time." *New Republic* (May 17): 30–33.

Cohn, Norman. 1993. *Cosmos, Chaos, and the World to Come: The Ancient Roots of Apocalyptic Faith*. New Haven, CT: Yale University.

Cox, Harvey. 1995. "The Warring Visions of the Christian Right." *Atlantic* (Nov.): 59–69.

Erdoes, Richard. 1988. *AD 1000: Living on the Brink of the Apocalypse*. New York: Barnes and Noble.

Festinger, Leon, Samuel Schachter, and Henry W. Rieckan. 1964. *When Prophecy Fails*. New York: Harper.

Focillon, Henri. 1969. *The Year 1000*. New York: Frederick Unger.

Hall, John R. 1996. "Apostasy, Apocalypse and Religious Violence: A Comparison of the Peoples Temple, the Branch Davidians and the Solar Temple." Different versions presented to the American Sociological Association, New York, August, and to the Society for the Scientific Study of Religion, Nashville, November.

Horowitz, Craig. 1994. "Holy War." *New York Magazine* (Feb. 4): 26–34.

Jones, Constance. 1989. "Exemplary Dualism and Authoritarianism at Jonestown." In *New Religions, Mass Suicide and the Peoples Temple*, edited by Rebecca Moore and Fielding McGee. Toronto: Edwin Mellen.

Kaplan, Jeffrey. 1993. "The Anti-cult Movement in America." ZYZYGY 2 (3-4): 267–296.

———. 1995. "Absolute Rescue: Absolutism, Defensive Action and the Resort to Force." *Terrorism and Political Violence* 7 (3): 128–163.

———. 1996. "The Politics of Rage: Militias and the Future of the Radical Right." *The Christian Century* 113 (20): 657–662.

Lamy, Philip. 1996. *The Millennium Rage: Survivalists, White Supremacists, and the Doomsday Prophecy*. New York: Plenum.

Lee, Martha F. 1988. *The Nation of Islam: An American Millenarian Movement*. Lewiston, NY: Edwin Mellen. Reprinted by Syracuse University Press, 1995.

———. 1995. "Violence and the Environment: The Case of 'Earth First.' " *Terrorism and Political Violence* 7 (3): 109–127.

Lifton, Robert J., and Charles E. Strozier. 1990. "Waiting for the Apocalypse." *New York Times Sunday Book Review Magazine* (Aug. 15): 1, 24–25.

Lindsey, Hal. 1973a. *The Late Great Planet Earth*. New York: Bantam.

———. 1973b. *There's a New World Coming*. Irving, CA: Harvest House.

———. 1981. *Countdown to Armageddon*. New York: Bantam.

Marrs, Wanda. 1989. *New Age Lies to Women*. Austin, TX: Living Truth Publications.

Martin, William. 1982. "Waiting for the End: The Growing Interest in Apocalyptic Prophecy." *Atlantic* (June): 31–37.

McGinn, Bernard. 1994. *Antichrist: Two Thousand Years of the Human Fascination with Evil*. San Francisco: Harper.

McPherson, Sandra B. 1992. "Death Penalty Mitigation and Cult Membership." *Behavioral Sciences and the Law*. 10, 1: 65–74.

Moore, R. Laurence. 1986. *Religious Outsiders*. New York: Oxford.

Nadler, Allan. 1992. "Last Exit to Brooklyn: The Lubavitchers of Crown Heights and Their Powerful, Preposterous Messianism." *The New Republic* (May 4): 27–33.

O'Brian, Conor Cruise. 1994. *On the Eve of the Millennium*. New York: The Free Press.

O'Leary, Stephen D. 1994. *Arguing the Apocalypse: A Theory of Millennial Rhetoric.* New York: Oxford.

Otis, George, Jr. 1991. "The Threat of a New Islamic Alliance." *Charisma & Christian Life* (April): 53–60.

Palmer, Susan J. 1996. "Purity and Danger in the Solar Temple." *Journal of Contemporary Religion* (October) 11 (3).

Palmer, Susan J., and Natalie Finn. 1992. "Coping with Apocalypse in Canada." *Sociological Analysis* 53 (4): 397–415.

Rapoport, David. 1988. "Messianic Sanctions for Terror." *Comparative Politics.* 20 (2): 195–213.

Relfe, Mary Stuart. 1981. *When Your Money Fails.* Montgomery, AL: Ministries.

Robbins, Thomas. 1997. "Religious Movements: A Friendly Critique of the Interpretive Approach." *Nova Religio* 1 (1), in press.

Robbins, Thomas, and Dick Anthony. 1995. "Sects and Violence: Factors Enhancing the Volatility in Marginal Religious Movements." In *Armageddon in Waco*, edited by Stuart Wright. Chicago: University of Chicago.

Robertson, Pat. 1990. "Breaking Counterfeit Religion." *Charisma & Christian Life* (Sept.): 120–124.

Rosenfeld, Jean E. 1995. "Pai Marire, Peace and Violence in a New Zealand Millenarian Tradition." *Terrorism and Political Violence* 7 (3): 83–108.

Sayles, Murray. 1995. "Nerve Gas and the Four Noble Truths." *New Yorker* (April 1): 56–71.

Smith, Jonathan Z., William S. Green, et al., eds. 1995. *The Harper Collins Dictionary of Religion.* San Francisco: Harper.

Spence, Jonathon D. 1996. *God's Chinese Son: The Taiping Heavenly Kingdom of Hong Xiuquan.* New York: Norton.

Strozier, Charles E. 1994. *Apocalypticism: On the Psychology of Fundamentalism in America.* Boston: Beacon.

Tabor, James P., and Eugene V. Gallagher. 1995. *Why Waco? Cults and the Battle for Religious Freedom.* Berkeley, CA: University of California.

Wallis, Roy, and Steven Bruce. 1986. "Sex, Violence and Religion." In *Sociological Theory, Religion and Collective Action*, edited by Roy Wallis and Steven Bruce. Belfast: Queens University.

Walvoord John W. 1990. *Armageddon, Oil and the Mideast Crisis.* Grand Rapids, MI: Zondervan.

Wright, Stuart A. 1995. *Armageddon in Waco.* Chicago: University of Chicago.

Zygmunt, J. F. 1972. "When Prophecies Fail: A Theoretical Perspective on the Comparative Evidence." *American Behavioral Scientist* 16: 245–267.

Theories of Apocalypticism

Constructing Apocalypticism
Social and Cultural Elements of Radical Organization

1

David G. Bromley

Apocalypticism is a fascinating social form given its inherently radical nature. The wonder of a group utterly convinced that historical time is at an end, warning their fellows that the day of reckoning is at hand, and assiduously preparing themselves for the climactic events looming on the horizon engages the imagination of social scientists and laymen alike. There is no shortage of current scholarship describing the nature of specific apocalyptic groups (e.g., de Silva 1992; Kumar 1995; Mullins 1995; Palmer and Finn 1992) and dissecting the essence of apocalypticism as a social form (Bergoffen 1982; Bull 1995; O'Leary 1994; Wagar 1982; Zamora 1982). The present historical moment may offer a particularly propitious occasion to revisit the concept as the imminence of the new millennium augers a proliferation of such groups (Kumar 1995).

One major problem confronting social scientists employing apocalypticism as a theoretical concept is that it is a borrowed term. Like a number of other concepts in the sociology of religion, it is analytically constrained as a result of having been drawn from theology in the Judeo-Christian tradition. The heritage of the concept makes it more difficult to apply it in analyzing other religious traditions; it becomes conflated with or overlaps other concepts, such as millennialism, doomsday, and utopianism; and its applicability in understanding various nonreligious counterparts, which bear a strong family resemblance, becomes problematic. I am therefore proposing that apocalypticism be considered more generically, as a radical form of social organization (Lippy 1982).

In this chapter I analyze religious apocalypticism, that is, a type of radical religious organization. This moves the study of apocalypticism in both narrowing and broadening directions. On the one hand, to focus on religious apocalypticism is not to dispute the broader significance of analogous secular forms, such as nuclear or environmental catastrophe scenarios that have received substantial attention of late (e.g., Barkun 1990; Lamy 1992); it is merely to delimit the argument. Much of the analysis developed here can be transferred to secular forms of apocalypticism, but religion is a distinctive social form requiring separate analysis. On the other hand, to interpret apocalypticism as a social as well as cultural form is to expand the scope of inquiry. A number of scholars have defined apocalypticism specifically in cultural terms—as a genre of literature, narrative, or rhetoric (e.g., O'Leary 1994; Wagar 1982). The perspective I propose connects the symbolic formulation of apocalypse through narrative to the organizational forms through which an apocalyptic reality sense can be constructed. This is not an argument to create a deterministic relationship between cultural and social forms. Obviously the cultural and social forms may be constructed independently. There are apocalyptic narratives rendered both as fiction and scientific prediction. Likewise, organizations characterized by a high degree of social mobilization or totalism do not require an apocalyptic ideological base (Hillery 1969; Kanter 1972; Lofland and Richardson 1984).

To summarize the argument briefly, I shall contend that apocalypticism is constructed through extreme implementation of the *prophetic method* (Bromley

1994). It is a social form that has occurred historically during moments of crisis. In the strongest form in which it has been constructed, apocalypticism creates structural liminality. Apocalyptic groups unequivocally reject the social order in which they reside and invest their loyalty and identity in a new order whose arrival they view as imminent and inevitable. The result is a collective existence located between the old order, whose demise is presumed imminent, and the new order, which has yet to be born. Preserving this position of structural liminality requires intensive social and cultural effort. The emphasis here is *how* apocalypticism as a radical form, incorporating both social and cultural elements, is created through the processes of deconstruction/reconstruction and destructuring/restructuring work.

APOCALYPTICISM AND THE PROPHETIC METHOD

It is most productive to explore how apocalypticism in its religious form is created by grounding the discussion in a specific perspective on the nature of religion and in assumptions about the social sources of apocalypticism. I begin with the sociological axioms that the reality humans inhabit is socially constructed and that religion is a key element in the human project of reality-construction. Religion involves the creation of the ultimate form of social authorization for social relations. In the Judeo-Christian tradition, at least, this has typically taken the form of the creation of the transcendent—variously envisioned as realm, domain, plane, force, principle—that is juxtaposed to empirical counterparts in the phenomenal world. The creation of a transcendent reality reconstitutes the phenomenal world as what now becomes part of a larger whole. Constructing the transcendent domain as the largest symbolic context for authorizing social relationships, the source of ordering forces that ultimately structure the everyday world, and the locus of independent agency (i.e., spiritual agency) makes religion a source of power. Further, I proceed from the assumption that Western societies are characterized by a high degree of social differentiation and inequality that yields a hegemonic power structure. If the level and kind of religious authorization groups construct are shaped by their social locations, then it follows that one important dimension of religious authorization will be confirmation of or resistance to the existing structure of social relations.

I pursue this line of analysis by distinguishing between two distinctive *methods* for building religious authorization, *priestly* and *prophetic* (Bromley

1994). Through the first, religion attains its power by creating *continuity* between the transcendent realm and the phenomenal world. Positing fundamental congruence between the two domains creates authorization for the existing structure of social relations, thereby energizing and orienting groups and individuals by aligning them closely with the ultimate ordering of the cosmos. Through the second, religion achieves power by creating *discontinuity* between the two domains. The incongruence between the two realms energizes and orients individuals and groups in the direction of contesting the legitimacy of the existing social order and distancing themselves from it. Defining priestly and prophetic as methods conceptually allows acknowledgment of the active construction efforts of specific groups in the social order as well as structural conditions favoring one method or the other, without predetermining or overdetermining either.

Apocalypticism is a radical form of organization that is most likely to be elected by groups in social locations experiencing crisis. Crisis episodes may be defined as historical moments when individuals/groups experience major elements of a structure of social relations, which are accorded a high level of moral priority and generate institutionally central lines of action, as standing in opposition to one another and therefore yielding contradictory behavioral imperatives (Fuchs and Ward 1994; Moaddel 1992; Swidler 1986). At the most basic level, the problem that groups in contemporary Western societies that are caught up in crisis and seek to mobilize resistance confront is that the existing social order is encountered as incorporating natural, or at least neutral, rules that are requisite for civilized social life (see Reiman 1996). The dominant social order thus presents itself as isomorphic with transcendent ordering logic. Likewise, in their own sectors, dominant institutions construct themselves as reflecting, representing, and incorporating transcendent ordering logic through which the larger social order is recreated (Crippen 1988).

Groups facing historical moments of crisis challenge this preemptive program. The apocalyptic position culturally involves repudiation of the foundational elements of the dominant ideology; the strategy is to assert that the contemporary order does not constitute what is and must be but rather that it embodies an unremitting denial of what is and must be. Socially the apocalyptic response is to distance from the existing social order and create an alternative order that models social relations on a vision of the new world to come. Apocalypticism is thus revolutionary but not revolution; it proposes much more than a transfer of power and a replacement of regime. And it is not a vision of doomsday. Catastrophe may be imminent, but the apocalypse is a cataclysm with meaning, one that has as its final purpose not destruction but creation.

Religious apocalypticism involves a dramatic reconstruction of reality.[1] In its religious formulation apocalypticism entails both cultural and organizational work. Culture work centers on symbolically recasting relationships of time, space, and logic between the transcendent realm and the phenomenal world, primarily through reconstructing sacred texts and narratives. Organizing for the apocalypse calls for destructuring and separation, enhanced charismatic claims, and extensive dramatization and ritualization of group life.

APOCALYPTIC CULTURE WORK

Religious work in the priestly mode is necessarily pragmatic to some degree. In highly differentiated societies there are multiple principles that orient both organizational and individual activity patterns to which priestly guided institutions adjust. This means that there is ongoing conflict, compromise, and change both within the religious institution and with respect to other organizations in the institutional field. Because the religious institution is isomorphic with other central institutions, however, the priestly method involves only moderate cultural reconstruction/deconstruction of symbolic patterning as various organizational actors seek to bolster or weaken their institutional claims. The prophetic method, by comparison, employs *radical* deconstruction/reconstruction that challenges, and sometimes demonizes, official interpretations of reality and offers an alternative vision of a social order.

In Western religion the cosmos often is conceived "spatially" as consisting of the phenomenal world and transcendent realm. In the priestly method separation of the two realms acknowledges that human activity and transcendent purpose are not identical, but the stability of that separation signifies that transcendent reordering is not mandated. There is relatively limited boundary crossing of various kinds (e.g., prayer) as humans seek periodic guidance and renewal of purpose. The prophetic method involves a changing relationship between the realms with greater initiative and intervention occurring from the transcendent domain. The discontinuity between the two realms mandates greater intervention in human affairs. Apocalypticism pushes the prophetic method to its logical limit, asserting an impending fusion of the two realms that will result in a radical restructuring of the phenomenal world to bring it into accord with the larger purpose represented in the transcendent realm. In the moment of the apocalypse the two domains are reduced to one. This vision of the future destabilizes the viability and meaningfulness of space in the everyday world, which becomes transitional rather than permanent terrain. Adherents of apocalyptic groups frequently search out and interpret catastrophic events in their environments as evidence of external intervention that presages the ultimate cataclysm.

Religious myth in the Western tradition arrays the flow of events in a temporal sequence (i.e., the social construction of time) and creates categoric organization of this temporal sequence, typically past, present, and future. In the priestly tradition the present is linked to and legitimated through the past, which adds temporal to spatial stability. By contrast, in the prophetic tradition the present is linked to and legitimated by a predicated future, and so the value of the past as a guide to behavior is depreciated. The world is to be understood in terms of what is to come rather than what has been. What distinguishes apocalypticism is that the future is given greater eminence, and both past and present recede in importance. In the limiting case where an imminent date for the apocalypse is set, the present is reduced to simply a gateway moment leading to the future.

Apocalyptic intensity can be maintained through predictions that are imminent but indeterminate, which then necessitates and legitimates a constant state of readiness. The effect is to create temporal liminality or intermediacy as the present is ending while the future has yet to be born. This creates inherent marginality for adherents who feel themselves to be standing poised on the brink of time.

The priestly method involves constructing a basic concordance between the phenomenal world and transcendent realm such that there is a continuity of order and purpose between the two domains. Prophetic religious workers, by contrast, assert a vast chasm and a basic antithesis of ultimate purpose between sacred cosmos and existing social order that accounts for both personal and collective troubles. From a prophetic perspective, both the social order and its inhabitants have become morally corrupted to the point that the very essence of each has been compromised. The prophetic method therefore emphasizes transformation, through some combination of transcendent and human agency, in order to restore the ordering priorities of the transcendent realm. To the extent that human agency is required, this process may entail either transforming the social order as a means of liberating true human nature or transforming individuals as a means of liberating the social order. But in either case humans bear significant responsibility for their separation from ultimate purpose. Apocalypticism alters the balance of human/transcendent agency toward the latter. Humans have fallen to such a level of depravity that unilateral, reorienting transcendent intervention is mandated. In some versions preparatory effort by humankind may be requisite, but in others human activity is deemed inconsequential. Transforming the social order becomes largely irrelevant unless a group assumes responsibility for issuing warnings of impending cataclysm and for gathering the faithful. The focus of activity becomes attending to revelations concerning the timing of the apocalypse, preparing for endtime events, and reorienting expectations and organization toward the world that is to come.

The prophetic method thus deconstructs and delegitimates the ultimate understandings established by the priestly method to authorize organizations and relationships in the existing social order and to connect human and transcendent purpose (Bourdieu 1991; Fuchs and Ward 1994). Apocalypticism simply extends this process. Its assertions—that the organizing logic of the dominant social order is so antithetical to transcendent purpose that unilateral intervention is mandated; that there will be a fusion of the transcendent and phenomenal realms, which will sweep away the latter; and that the apocalypse will transpire imminently—mount a challenge to the established social order that is direct, total, and on highest authority. A vision of the future that can be juxtaposed to the fatally flawed current social order is central to authorizing resistance and withdrawal. Indeed, as Rorty (1991, 16) notes, "it is not much use pointing to the 'internal contradictions' of a social practice, or 'deconstructing' it, unless one can come up with an alternative practice—unless one can at least sketch a utopia in which the concept or distinction would be absolute." In most cases the shape of the future is little more than a sketch, as apocalyptic groups strive to catch glimpses of the new order through revelatory activity.

One of the key processes in the prophetic method is deconstruction/reconstruction of sacred texts, since these are a basic source of religious authorization and contain the initial formulation of time, space, and logic relationships. Whereas priestly religious work involves ongoing modification of received tradition through reinterpretation of sacred texts (e.g., apologetics), the prophetic method is premised on revelation. The method therefore involves a reformulation of sacred texts, often involving drastic revisions of traditional meanings or production of new texts that expand upon existing ones, as new revelations

are received. The base upon which established religion rests, the true rendering of the nature and purpose in the cosmos, is directly undermined by these
revelations. Apocalypticism deconstructs the practical meaning of traditional
texts through its erosion of the spatial/temporal stability of the phenomenal
world; everyday life can no longer be taken for granted. The imminence and
totality of impending change renders priestly method interpretations not just
irrelevant but counteradaptive. Apocalyptic revelations are particularly likely
to enunciate unitary, overarching principles as a response to the compromise
and corruption within the social order that has precipitated the current crisis.
These principles are used as emblems of the purity of the apocalyptic group
and thematize its organization.

ORGANIZATION FOR THE APOCALYPSE

There is a substantial body of work in social science that distinguishes between
more moderate and radical forms of organization (Bittner 1963; Hillery 1969;
Kornhauser 1962; Lofland and Richardson 1984) and that details organizational
attributes of the latter (Bromley and Shupe 1979; Coser 1974; Kanter 1972). The
organizational attributes of what are here termed priestly and prophetic structured groups correspond in some respects to this distinction.

Priestly religious workers buttress and preserve existing social differentiation, which means integration and coordination with other established institutions. They are therefore pro-structural in the sense that they sanctify official
interpretations of reality and seek to harmonize the various types of differentiation that are integral to any structure of social relations and that also are an
ongoing source of tension and conflict. This involves more than accommodation; priestly guided institutions are constitutive of the established social
order. Organizational energy is generated through positive integration and
social continuity with other institutions.

Consistent with its emphasis on cultural deconstruction, the prophetic
method sweeps away the sources of social differentiation in the prevailing structure of social relations. It is anti-structural in the sense that it is antinomian; it
challenges official interpretations of reality; exposes sources of contradiction,
compromise, and corruption; and promotes de-differentiation. Prophetically
structured organizations derive their energy from a negative relation to institutions in the existing social order. This means more than simply separation;

it entails rejection of and resistance to established institutions. Groups employing the prophetic method often publicly decry the persecution and repression they elicit, for these groups require distancing and intense solidarity, both of which are enhanced by heightened internal-external tensions. The prophetic method moves toward collectivism organizationally and relationally, at least for a time, as the group mobilizes itself. This entails both a reduction in status differences within the group and a totalistic environment through which the ideology is sustained and confirmed. In contrast to the more limited charismatic authority involved in priestly religious work, the prophetic method creates extraordinary claimsmaking capacity. The morally elevated status of prophetic figure(s) and the morally degraded status of adherents means that mutual pledges of commitment between prophetic leader and followers are accompanied by weighty sacrifice and obligation as well as stringent testing of loyalty and commitment for both leaders and followers.[2] The process of prophetic religious work fashions a sharp break in individual biographies, between generations, and among elements of the social order. Individuals and the social order both must have a new beginning. Movement adherents assume new identities, create a social structure that models the future order, and may even begin a new lineage. Adherents gain biographical continuity and salvation by assuming charter membership in the tradition that is about to be born.

Apocalypticism accentuates these attributes. Given the extremity of the apocalyptic vision and the totalistic organization, the ingroup interaction intensifies and the apocalyptic organization segregates itself from conventional society. It is a profoundly antinomian form. The more imminent the projected apocalypse, the more inaccessible the organization and its adherents become to social control. Particularly as apocalyptic groups create their own space organized as part of the new order that they construct to authorize ongoing social relations within the group, they inevitably leave themselves in a position of spatial liminality. The community they create is specifically constructed, both to be part of an order that does not yet exist and to be distanced from the existing social order.

Through the priestly method, ritualistic observances are constructed that are designed to reintegrate the prevailing structure of social relations by transcending the inevitable concommitants of social differentiation—divisions created by the rules, statuses, inequalities, and conflicts. Ritual observances therefore naturalize existing structural arrangements, as well as the constituent inequalities and conflicts. Narrowly bounded ritualization and spiritual agency are sufficient to achieve such reaffirmation and repair of social relations. Breaches of the prevailing social order can be interpreted in aesthetically distanced ritual enactments that allow participants simultaneously to experience emotionally and reflect cognitively on the complexity of forces creating tension and conflict in their world. These aesthetic dramas can then offer object lessons around which the group can organize its agenda for progressive change.

In the prophetic method, religious workers create ritualistic observances that protest and resist the reality presented by the prevailing structure of social relations; this is achieved through disassembling and invalidating the sources of differentiation in the dominant social order while simultaneously creating means for adherents to experience directly an alternative reality. The countervailing vision of reality is sustained and the massive influence of conventional realities is neutralized in part through extensive ritualization. Ritualized interchanges with members of conventional society, on the one hand, maintain distance despite contact and, on the other hand, engage adherents in the *symbolic transformation of the environment*. Active transcendent agency is created through "trance" states—defined as being connected and oriented to and having a desire to fulfill transcendent purposes (Swanson 1978, 254)—that simultaneously distance individuals from the conventional social order and maintain active integration with the transcendent realm.

The great discontinuity experienced through the prophetic method yields a social drama of the first order. Those employing the prophetic method become participants rather than simply participant-observers in an agonic drama, a confrontation between protagonist and antagonist forces. Prophetic revelations depict a cosmic struggle in which the group and individual adherents have decisive roles to play, with the result that a great part of day-to-day activity is orchestrated as scenes in this drama. Because the drama involves agency located in the transcendent realm, there cannot be an end to the crisis until restoration of the appropriate relationship between the two realms is achieved.

In apocalyptic groups ritualization pervades group life. Given that the moment of cataclysm is imminent, group activity is riveted on determining what form transcendent intervention will take, when the apocalyptic moment will occur, what responsibilities human actors bear, and how the future order will unfold. This requires extensive *boundary-crossing activity* in the form of prophecy, revelation, trance, possession, and related states. Such activity, of course, further distances apocalyptic groups from the larger society; interaction is reduced to warnings and condemnations from one side and accusations of mental aberration and "religious extremism" from the other. The drama in which the group perceives itself to be a participant is heightened to the ultimate level, and the narrative plot is simplified. There are two forces, good and evil; two domains, transcendent and worldly; two moments, the fleeting present and the expansive future. The role of human agents is reduced as a result of transcendent intervention, but proper performance of this more limited role remains vital, for it is the passport to the future.

CONCLUSIONS

In this chapter I have proposed detaching apocalypticism from its traditional theological moorings in the Judeo-Christian tradition and analyzing it more generically and sociologically as simply a radical form of organization—incorporating specific cultural and social elements—that occurs during moments of crisis in particular locations. To argue for a structural source of apocalypticism is not to advocate structural determinism. Apocalypticism as a social form is the product of active social and cultural work through what I refer to as the prophetic method. Culturally, apocalypticism deconstructs the symbolic order created and sustained by the dominant social order. The deconstruction process involves reconceptualizing the shape of the cosmos as reflected in relationships of time, space, and logic between the transcendent and phenomenal realms. Apocalyptic reconstructions are designed to destabilize the present as a time period by forecasting an epochal transformation, the everyday world as site of human activity by predicting its imminent destruction, and the logic of the existing order by auguring a paradigmatic shift through unilateral intervention from the transcendent realm. The corresponding social process is destructuring. This process involves a rejection of and separation from the conventional social order and the heightened internal solidarity and totalism of collectivist organization. Group life is ritualized extensively as the group constructs itself as a participant in an agonic drama of cosmic proportions and as the group strives for ongoing interaction and integration with transcendent reality.

These cultural and social strategies reinforce one another. The deconstruction process places apocalyptic groups at the edge—of time, space, and order.

The destructuring process takes these groups out of the organizational matrix of conventional social life and leaves them on the edge—between a world that they reject and one that has yet to be born. The result is *structural liminality* (Turner 1967, 93–111). Apocalyptic groups socially and culturally construct themselves a liminal position that literally is between worlds. At the same time there is little reconstruction or restructuring work. It is true that apocalyptic groups do reformulate sacred narratives, but most of this work is directed at describing the apocalyptic period. There is little charting of the future order that would serve as a plan for reordering life on the other side of the apocalypse. In fact, the narratives specifically disempower them at this point. Correspondingly, there is little restructuring. Apocalyptic groups may model their social relations after their limited vision of the new order but they do not attempt to erect that order. It is this combination of withdrawal from the existing order and eschewing of creating an alternative that characterizes the apocalyptic form. It is group life in suspended animation.

Viewing apocalypticism from this perspective allows some further insights. First, it involves a peculiar kind of confrontation with the host society. Apocalypticism directly challenges the symbols of cultural legitimation and outflanks institutionalized control systems. At the same time, these groups do not usually engage in a struggle for power; they present themselves as messenger not adversary. While paving the way for intervention by transcendent forces may call for confrontation with the existing order, there does not appear to be any necessary connection between apocalypticism and group-sponsored violence. Second, this analysis suggests that apocalypticism is not inherently "pathological," as many writers on the subject have implied. The public rantings against conventional society and the extensive ritualization of social life, replete with ecstatic forms, can easily be misinterpreted. By contrast, if apocalypticism is viewed as a group-constructed line of action that creates structural liminality, these activities can be understood simply as radical forms of organization. Finally, apocalypticism is more likely to constitute a moment in a group's history rather than a stable, long-term form of organization. The central reason for the ephemeral nature of apocalypticism is that it is extremely costly. Enormous energy is required to sustain the liminal state these groups create; the rejection of and by conventional society, maintaining a conviction of imminent transformation indefinitely in the wake of failed expectations and counterevidence, and the absence of any institutionalized order through which life can be lived in the long run all exact a high price. In fact, the most likely course appears to be the gradual emergence of reconstruction and restructuring. I would argue, however, that such efforts signal a transition out of the apocalyptic moment. The formation of apocalyptic groups itself constitutes a statement that this moment is, from their perspective, the beginning of the end. If these fledgling groups long persist and commence the process of cultural reconstruction and social restructuring, I would argue that moment constitutes for apocalyptic groups the end of the beginning.

Notes

1. For a discussion of drama in social movement ideology, see Bromley (forthcoming).
2. The charismatic authority associated with the prophetic method does not imply that such authority is automatically vested in a single individual or small circle of leaders. Although this pattern is relatively common, it may also be the case that leaders of prophetic groups are symbolic centers of the group and have limited influence. Further, leaders of prophetic groups may be the objects of charisma-building activities and demands for heightened charismatic performances.

References

Barkun, Michael. 1990. "Racist Apocalypse: Millennialism on the Far Right." *American Studies* 31: 121–140.

Bergoffen, Debra. 1982. "The Apocalyptic Meaning of History." In *The Apocalyptic Vision in America*, edited by Lois Zamora. Bowling Green: Bowling Green University Popular Press.

Bittner, Egon. 1963. "Radicalism and Radical Movements." *American Sociological Review* 28: 928–940.

Bourdieu, Pierre. 1991. "Genesis and Structure of the Religious Field." In *Comparative Social Research: A Research Annual*, volume 13, edited by Craig Calhoun. Greenwich, CT: JAI Press.

Bromley, David. Forthcoming. "The Social Construction of Subversive Evil: The Contemporary Anti-Cult and Anti-Satanism Movements." In *Social Movements of the Eighties and Nineties*, edited by Jo Freeman. Boulder: Westview Press.

Bromley, David. 1994. "A Sociological Narrative of Crisis Episodes, Collective Action, Culture Workers, and Countermovements." Presidential Address, Association for the Sociology of Religion, Los Angeles.

Bromley, David, and Anson Shupe. 1979. *Moonies in America: Cult, Church and Crusade*. Beverly Hills: Sage Publications.

Bull, Malcomb. 1995. *Apocalypse Theory and the Ends of the World*. Cambridge: Blackwell Publishers.

Coser, Lewis. 1974. *Greedy Institutions*. Glencoe: Free Press.

Crippen, Timothy. 1988. "Old and New Gods in the Modern World: Toward a Theory of Religious Transformation." *Social Forces* 67: 316–336.

de Silva, David. 1992. "The Revelation to John: A Case Study in Apocalyptic Propaganda and the Maintenance of Sectarian Identity." *Sociological Analysis* 53: 375–395.

Fuchs, Stephan, and Steven Ward. 1994. "What is Deconstruction, and Where and When Does it Take Place? Making Facts in Science, Building Cases in Law." *American Sociological Review* 59: 481–500.

Hillery, George. 1969. "The Convent: Community, Prison, or Task Force." *Journal for the Scientific Study of Religion* 8: 140–151.

Kanter, Rosabeth. 1972. *Commitment and Community: Communes and Utopias in Sociological Perspective*. Cambridge: Harvard University Press.

Kornhauser, William. 1962. "Social Bases of Political Commitment: A Study of Liberals and Radicals." In *Human Behavior and Social Processes*, edited by Arnold Rose. Boston: Houghton Mifflin.

Kumar, Krishan. 1995. "Apocalypse, Millennium and Utopia Today." In *Apocalypse Theory and the Ends of the World*, edited by Malcomb Bull. Cambridge: Blackwell Publishers.

Lamy, Philip. 1992. "Millennialism in the Mass Media: The Case of *Soldier of Fortune* Magazine." *Journal for the Scientific Study of Religion* 31: 408–24.

Lippy, Charles. 1982. "Waiting for the End: The Social Context of American Apocalyptic Religion." In *The Apocalyptic Vision in America*, edited by Lois Zamora. Bowling Green: Bowling Green University Popular Press.

Lofland, John, and James Richardson. 1984. "Religious Movement Organizations: Elemental Forms and Dynamics." In *Research in Social Movements, Conflict and Change*, edited by Lewis Kriesberg. Greenwich, CT: JAI Press.

Moaddel, Mansoor. 1992. "Ideology as Episodic Discourse: The Case of the Iranian Revolution." *American Sociological Review* 57: 353–379.

Mullins, Mark. 1995. "Aum Shinrikyō as an Apocalyptic Movement: A Review of Recent Japanese Responses." Paper presented at the annual meeting of the Society for the Scientific Study of Religion, St. Louis, MO.

O'Leary, Stephen. 1994. *Arguing the Apocalypse: A Theory of Millennial Rhetoric*. New York: Oxford University Press.

Palmer, Susan, and Natalie Finn. 1992. "Coping with Apocalypse in Canada: Experiences of Endtime in la Mission de l'Esprit Saint and the Institute of Applied Metaphysics." *Sociological Analysis* 53: 397–415.

Reiman, Jeffrey. 1996. "A Radical Perspective on Crime." In *Deviant Behavior*, edited by Delos Kelly. New York: St. Martin's Press.

Rorty, Richard. 1991. *Objectivity, Relativism and Truth*. Cambridge: Cambridge University Press.

Swanson, Guy. 1978. "Trance and Possession: Studies of Charismatic Influence." *Review of Religious Research* 19: 253–278.

Swidler, Ann. 1986. "Culture in Action: Symbols and Strategies." *American Sociological Review* 51: 273–286.

Turner, Victor. 1967. *The Forest of Symbols: Aspects of Ndembu Ritual*. Ithaca: Cornell University Press.

Wagar, W. Warren. 1982. *Terminal Visions: The Literature of Last Things*. Bloomington: Indiana University Press.

Zamora, Lois. 1982. *The Apocalyptic Vision in America*. Bowling Green: Bowling Green University Popular Press.

Millennialism With and Without the Mayhem

Catherine Wessinger

Here today, and gone tomorrow;
there's a better world than this.[1]

INTRODUCTION

As far as we know, humans are the only animals who rebel at life's finitude. We do not accept suffering and death, and we create religious systems with the goal of attaining the ongoing experience of well-being. We want to have continued well-being that extends even beyond death. The religious pattern that has been termed "millennialism" is audacious human belief that suffering and death, i.e., evil, will be eliminated, so that collective (not simply individual) salvation is accomplished on earth. The audacity of this expectation lies in the conviction that finitude can be overcome in the here and now rather than in an undisprovable afterlife.

Millennialism has been a pattern in many religious traditions at least since the prophetic visions of Zarathustra (perhaps circa 2000 B.C.), who was possibly the great-grandfather of Western and Eastern millennialism (Cohn 1993; Basham 1954, 274; Overmyer 1976, 1). The approaching year A.D. 2000 in the Gregorian calendar has already as of 1995 stimulated increased millennial expectations, and will not mark the cessation of the millennial imagination. In this essay I propose the following points to enhance understanding of millennialism: (1) recent violent episodes involving millennial groups highlight the need for scholars to communicate with the general public about millennialism. To communicate clearly, scholars need to abandon the obscure terms premillennialism and postmillennialism for terms whose meanings are more readily apparent; I suggest catastrophic millennialism and progressive millennialism; (2) most studies of millennialism are actually studies of catastrophic millennialism; therefore the scholarly literature perpetuates inaccurate assumptions about the characteristics of the type of millennialism that entails belief in progress; (3) because most studies of millennialism have focused on Western religions, it has been assumed erroneously by some scholars that millennialism requires a linear view of time and history. A small but growing body of literature on Asian and Asian-derived millennial movements indicates that both catastrophic and progressive millennialisms are compatible with cyclical views of time.

Millennialism Terminology

The term "millennium" originally referred to a period of one thousand years foretold by the New Testament Book of Revelation (Apocalypse) to be the period of Christ's reign on earth. In scholarly usage, "millennialism" refers to belief in an earthly salvation, and no longer implies belief that the kingdom of God will last one thousand years. The term millennialism has its origins in the study of Judaism and Christianity, but scholars now use this term to refer to similar movements in non-Western religious traditions. Millennialism in its most general definition refers to the expectation of an imminent and collective earthly salvation accomplished according to a divine or superhuman plan.

The terms premillennialism (premillenarianism) and postmillennialism are used by scholars to refer to the Christian belief that Christ will come either before or after the millennium. Scholars have applied these terms to non-Christian forms of millennialism (see Sponberg 1988, 295). Premillennialism is used by scholars to denote a pessimistic expectation of universal catastrophe caused by divine intervention to destroy the world as we know it and then subsequently to establish the millennial salvation. The term postmillennialism is used to refer to the optimistic expectation that human effort working progressively according to a divine plan will bring about the millennium. In 1980, Sandeen expressed disappointment that "more dynamic categories" have not been devised by scholars, and observed that the categories of premillennialism and postmillennialism possess "little explanatory power" (165, 167). I suggest below that it is time for scholars to develop more readily understandable terminology in order to communicate about millennialism to the general public.

Catastrophic Millennialism

The historically predominant and most commonly studied form of millennialism has a pessimistic view of humanity, society, and history. Evil is seen as being rampant, and things are believed to be getting worse all the time. Therefore, to eliminate evil and achieve the earthly collective salvation, the world as we know it has to be destroyed and created anew by God (or a superhuman power).[2] Further, it is believed that the catastrophic destruction is *imminent* (Cohn 1962, 31; Talmon 1966, 159). When the sense of urgency conveyed by belief that the current world can end at any moment weakens, then the religion is no longer millennial. The millennial expectation fades, or is pushed into the background by clerics anxious to protect their worldly authority (Landes 1988), and other ultimate goals come to the fore—such as salvation in the afterlife.[3] This religious pattern is not confined to Christianity, nor to now-obscure arguments over whether Christ will return before or after the millennium. Therefore, I suggest that this type of millennialism be called "catastrophic millennialism." The term catastrophic millennialism more clearly conveys this perspective's expectation of how the millennium will be accomplished, and can be applied readily to non-Christian forms of millennialism.

The term "apocalypticism," meaning revelation of what has been veiled, has most often been applied to catastrophic millennialism. Apocalypse is the name of the last book of the New Testament known in English as Revelation. "Apocalypticism" has acquired the connotation among scholars and the general public of the expectation of imminent catastrophe that will destroy the current world and thus accomplish the millennium (Landes 1988, 207). Since this term was widely popularized in 1993 by the events at the Branch Davidian community near Waco, Texas, dubbed "Ranch Apocalypse," I suggest that apocalypticism is a readily recognizable and useful synonym for the millennialism that expects catastrophe. Apocalypticism has become so synonymous with universal cataclysm, that scholars tend to create confusion instead of clarity when they use the term in its neutral sense of revelation and apply it to the form of millennialism that expects progress (see O'Leary 1994).

Catastrophic millennialism is rooted not only in a pessimistic evaluation of human nature and society, but also in the pervasive human tendency to think in dualistic categories. Cohn (1993) suggests that the first formulations of the catastrophic millennial expectation developed out of ancient western Asian "combat myths" of good and evil. This dualistic thinking, the "us versus them" mentality, which leads to belief in the necessity of battling evil located in the demonized "other," is the conceptual basis of warfare, and also provides the standard plot of most cartoons, not to mention adult dramas. The 1993 violent confrontation of the Branch Davidians and United States federal law enforcement agents involved dualistic thinking on both sides—the Branch Davidians regarded their attackers as agents of satanic "Babylon," and the ATF and FBI agents regarded David Koresh as a demonic criminal and con man (Tabor and Gallagher 1995). As in most wars, it was the good guys versus the bad guys, with each side convinced it was the good.

Progressive Millennialism

The millennialism that entails belief in progress, or what I suggest be termed "progressive millennialism," has a much briefer history than catastrophic millennialism. The pervasive outlook until recent centuries has been that things will get worse before they can get better. But with significant increases in scientific understanding and accelerated technological invention, belief in progress in the Western developed world dates to about the eighteenth century and was strong in the nineteenth century (Tuveson 1949; Olson 1982; Bury 1921). Belief in progress combined with the expectation of a collective terrestrial salvation was widespread among early-nineteenth-century American Christians, whose perspective has been termed postmillennialism. But the optimistic belief that the collective earthly salvation will be accomplished by humans working in harmony with a divine (or superhuman) plan is also found in religious traditions not shaped primarily by Christianity. In these cases, the belief that the millennium will arrive noncatastrophically by means of human cooperation with divine (or superhuman) will has nothing to do with whether Christ comes after or before the millennium. I suggest that the term "progressive millennialism" more readily expresses the expectation of how the millennium will be accomplished in this religious pattern.

After the 1859 publication of Darwin's *Origin of the Species,* progressive millennialism often has been understood in evolutionary terms. This is what Stephen Jay Gould calls "spin doctoring" the theory of evolution (1995a, 1995b). Darwinian natural selection is full of the pain and death against which humanity rebels. Extinction of individuals and species, according to the scientific view, is random and contingent upon chance factors. But the millennialism that believes in progressive evolution sees humanity as overcoming contingency according to divine will to achieve a collective terrestrial salvation.

Summary

I suggest that we drop the terms premillennialism and postmillennialism, because they are no longer adequate to communicate about millennialism. I suggest that the term catastrophic millennialism more clearly conveys the premillennial expectation, and that "apocalypticism" can continue to serve as a synonym for the type of millennialism that anticipates catastrophe. I also recommend dropping the term postmillennialism and using instead the term progressive millennialism. I suggest below that the term postmillennialism has perpetuated significant misconceptions about this millennial pattern.

I recommend this new terminology to enhance clarity of communication between scholars, and between scholars and the general public; I am not claiming that these are the "correct" terms for these phenomena.

I am not suggesting that catastrophic millennialism and progressive millennialism are mutually exclusive. In fact, it is likely that a religious tradition will contain resources that can be utilized to support either perspective. It is well known that the Christian tradition in recent centuries has manifested a shifting interplay between these pessimistic and optimistic views of humanity and history. A recent study of Baha'i millennialism reveals the same phenomenon. Catastrophic millennialism was predominant in the precourser of the Baha'i movement, which focused on the messiah known as the Bab ("gate"). The Baha'i second messiah, known as Baha'u'llah, made progressive millennialism dominant in Baha'i, but he also predicted imminent upheaval as a precursor to global unification. Progressive millennialism is now the norm in Baha'i, but there are also small groups of excommunicated Baha'is who expect catastrophe (Collins 1995, 1996; Balch, Farnsworth, and Wilkins 1983; see Balch et al., this volume). Similarly, Joel Elliott's study of the Jehovah's Witnesses, a group strongly committed to catastrophic millennialism, reveals elements that tend toward progressive millennialism. He highlights the Witnesses' "proleptic rhetoric," in which they cite their international and interracial church as prefiguring the earthly millennium. The Jehovah's Witnesses have not refrained from institution-building just because they believe that the current world will imminently be destroyed. Jehovah's Witnesses are having to give up their belief that Armageddon will occur within the lifetimes of people alive in 1914, and there may be further accommodation in the direction of progressive millennialism (Elliott 1996). I expect that future comparative studies (example Rosenfeld 1995) will elucidate the dynamics of this interplay between these two polarities of millennial expectations.

The Sensational Elements of Catastrophic Millennialism and Resulting Scholarly Misconceptions About Progressive Millennialism

Catastrophic millennialism has most often captured the attention of scholars, news reporters, and the general public. The "doomsday cult" led by an authoritarian charismatic leader has become ubiquitous in news reporting. Millennialism with the expectation of mayhem does not necessarily have to result in violence, but it sometimes does (Cohn 1957; Burridge 1969; Wallace 1956; Naquin 1976; Underwood 1993). Catastrophic millennialism does not necessarily require leadership by a dominating individual, but it appears to be an excellent vehicle for persons who relish authoritarian control (Wessinger 1993, 1994).

Both catastrophic millennial and progressive millennial movements can be characterized by "ideological" or "open-access" leadership (Eichler 1971, 1983), in which every believer has access to the source of authority—often sacred literature or, alternatively, mystical experience—and the teachings of the leaders are considered valid by the followers only to the extent that they conform to the source of legitimation. An unarmed millennial movement with ideological leadership does not provide scope for leaders to exercise authoritarian control over followers and will not initiate violence.[4] Catastrophic millennial movements, even when their leadership is ideological, have been prone to the folly of setting specific dates for the millennial transition that will be disconfirmed.

The catastrophic millennial expectation, when combined with charismatic and authoritarian religious leadership and arms, has produced occasionally volatile episodes that have riveted the attention of the general public and scholars. "Charismatic leadership" here means having direct access to the superhuman — usually intangible — source of authority. When the charismatic source of legitimation is believed to be accessible only to the leader ("closed-access" authority) (Eichler 1971, 1983), and there are armed subordinates willing to enforce control, then there is greater likelihood of highly authoritarian control of followers. Catastrophic millennial groups possessing arms and a charismatic leader who monopolizes revelation and exercises control over followers have sometimes committed violent attacks to bring about the millennium. Or, such groups have been attacked by government agents threatened by the alternative millennial authority.[5]

Since most studies of millennialism are actually studies of catastrophic millennialism (this book bears out this trend), scholars have made assumptions about progressive millennialism that are not borne out in case studies. It has been assumed that progressive millennialism lacks the sense of urgency and imminence of the arrival of the millennium that is found in catastrophic millennialism (see O'Leary 1994). Following the postmillennial model of nineteenth-century Western Christianity, scholars have assumed that what I term progressive millennialism does not involve belief in a "messiah," defined as an individual with divine or superhuman powers who will bring about the millennium. Scholars have assumed that messianism is a possible, but not a necessary, feature of only catastrophic millennialism (premillennialism).

My study of Annie Besant's Theosophical millennialism (Wessinger 1988) revealed the inadequacy of these standard scholarly assumptions. Annie Besant (1847–1933) preached with great urgency the imminent and noncatastrophic coming of the millennium, and urged people to participate in the transformation to the "New Civilization." Annie Besant had a "postmillennial" (progressive millennial) view of history and humanity, *but* she also promoted her own messiah. Much of Besant's progressive millennial and messianic expectations were passed to the contemporary New Age movement via the Theosophical writings of Alice Bailey (1880–1949); however, the contemporary New Age movement also contains thinkers who expect catastrophic "earth changes" or nuclear destruction prior to the millennium. In the late twentieth century, Benjamin Creme promotes progressive millennial expectations in the Theosophical tradition with a great sense of the imminence of the millennium. If only we will indicate our readiness for him, the World Teacher will reveal himself to the entire earth at any moment via supernatural means and communications technology (Share International 1995). Even late-eighteenth- and nineteenth-century American Christian postmillennialists fervidly believed and worked for the accomplishment of the earthly collective salvation through evangelism and good works, and their sense of imminence equaled those who expected divine catastrophic intervention (Moorhead 1984, 527–528; Davidson 1977, 275, 281).

More case studies are needed of progressive millennial groups and thinkers. I suggest that progressive millennialism is characterized by a keen sense of imminence of the millennium and, often, messianism.[6] At this point, it appears unlikely that progressive millennialism is compatible with authoritarian charismatic leadership and violence initiated by the millennial group, but more studies will indicate whether this is indeed the case.

MILLENNIALISM IS NOT TIED TO A LINEAR VIEW OF HISTORY

Because most studies of millennialism have been made by Western scholars of the Abrahamic religious traditions, sometimes it has been assumed that millennialism requires a linear view of time and is not found in traditions with cyclical views of time (see DeHaas 1994). This is totally incorrect.

Both catastrophic and progressive millennialisms are fully compatible with cyclical views of time, as the South and East Asian Buddhist millennial movements (Sponberg and Hardacre 1988), Chinese Buddhist and Taoist millennial movements (Overmyer 1976; Seidel 1970; Naquin 1976), as well as Theosophical and Hindu millennialisms bear out. Within the Hindu tradition, Maharishi Mahesh Yogi teaches the progressive evolutionary view that the practice of transcendental meditation will bring about Ram Rajya (the rule of God) on earth (1995/1963). Also within Hinduism is the doctrine that a final *avatar* (divine incarnation) of Vishnu named Kalkin will catastrophically destroy this degenerate world to accomplish the transition to the golden age (O'Flaherty

1976). There is currently a new religious movement focused on an Indian man who claims to be this Kalki Avatar (Narayanan 1995).

If there is focus on the improving movement of the cycle of time, an optimistic progressive millennialism may be produced. If the focus is on the degenerative movement of the cycle, the result may be the pessimistic catastrophic millennialism. Since millennialism addresses the perennial human concern to overcome finitude and ongoingly experience well-being, linear or cyclical conceptions of time are not the determinants of whether millennial expectations manifest. The average person is concerned with achieving well-being in the here and now, so whether there is a linear or cyclical conception of time is beside the point.

CONCLUSION

Recent violent events involving millennial groups and the approach of the year 2000 indicate that it is time that scholars adopt readily understandable terminology to communicate to the general public about the primary categories of millennial expectations. In order to adequately educate the general public, scholars must first educate themselves about the two primary patterns of millennialism. Millennialism does *not* require a linear view of time. More case studies of optimistic noncatastrophic millennialism are needed. I believe that such case studies of what I term progressive millennialism—the millennialism involving belief in progress—will reveal that this millennial pattern is just as likely to involve a sense of imminence and expectation of a messiah as catastrophic millennialism.

Future studies of millennialism need to address the following key issues: how and why individuals and groups shift between the optimistic and pessimistic patterns of millennialism; the process by which the sense of imminence of the millennium becomes diminished and attention turns to salvation in the unseen world, i.e., highlighting doctrines such as heaven or ascension; the grey area between ideological leadership and authoritarian charismatic leadership that is represented by the charismatic leader who monopolizes access to revelation but who does not exercise authoritarian control over followers; and further exploration of Sandeen's observation (1980) that millennial movements in industrializing or industrialized cultures have different characteristics than millennial movements in preliterate and/or preindustrial cultures.

Obviously, typologies are useful only to the extent that they accurately reflect and order the data. The catastrophic millennial pattern has existed for several millennia, and the progressive millennial pattern (in the West) for only several hundred years. In the late twentieth century, we have seen how political expediency can prompt convinced catastrophic and dualistic millennialists such as Ronald Reagan and Pat Robertson to renounce, at least temporarily, their expectation of imminent cataclysm (Boyer 1992, 138, 142). Many late-twentieth-century optimists, who prefer to hope for a noncatastrophic and progressive movement into the new age, are acutely aware of present suffering in the world and potential for global catastrophe (for example, the subject interviewed in Daniels 1995). It may be that the total optimism of progressive millennialism is difficult to sustain in the late twentieth century, and that instead millennialists who want to believe in progress—for example, the Church Universal and Triumphant—may opt for a "cautious millennial optimism,"[7] believing there is the possibility of imminent catastrophe but utilizing spiritual techniques to avert the mayhem. This type of millennial pattern is found also in some of the Japanese new religions (Reader 1995).

Recent catastrophic events may indicate the practical significance of millennialism studies, which in any case represents a fascinating area for pursuing a greater understanding of human nature and the human religious imagination.

Notes

1. Hazel Dickens, vocalist. *The Stained Glass Hour: Bluegrass and Old-Timey Gospel Music*. Compact disc.
2. I keep stressing "superhuman" in addition to "divine" because a number of contemporary millennalisms rely on the superhuman, but not supernatural, agents of UFOs and extraterrestrials.
3. The "amillennialism" of Augustine was not progressive millennialism because in Augustine's day there was no belief in earthly progress. Augustine's doctrine that the millennium was synonymous with the institution of the Church was an attempt to eliminate the catastrophic millennial fervor of the masses.
4. It is possible that an armed catastrophic millennial movement with open-access authority can become violent. The dualistic worldview and expectation of catastrophe combined with arms is potentially volatile.

5. I will explore with greater nuance the characteristics of millennial groups involved in violence in a future essay comparing Jonestown, Branch Davidians, Aum Shinrikyō, and Solar Temple.

6. In 1988 I suggested a new category, "progressive messianism," to make sense of Annie Besant's combination of a postmillennial view of history with messianism (Wessinger 1988). I no longer think the category of progressive messianism is necessary. Instead, scholars need to recognize that progressive millennialism is just as likely to involve belief in a messiah as catastrophic millennialism.

7. The promotional literature of the Church Universal and Triumphant states that CUT's members are "cautiously optimistic" about the future. They work for the establishment of the millennium that they term the "Golden Age," but their charismatic leader, Elizabeth Clare Prophet, has also predicted dangerous periods in which nuclear war is possible. CUT members practice the ancient spiritual technique of chanting, which they term "decreeing," to transmute the negative karma that they believe is descending during these dangerous periods. (Field trip to the headquarters of Church Universal and Triumphant, Montana, in summer 1993.)

BIBLIOGRAPHY

Balch, Robert W., Gwen Farnsworth, and Sue Wilkins. 1983. "When the Bombs Drop: Reactions to Disconfirmed Prophecy in a Millennial Sect." *Sociological Perspectives* 26 (2) (April): 137–158.

Basham, A. L. 1954. *The Wonder That Was India*. New York: Grove Press.

Boyer, Paul. 1992. *When Time Shall Be No More: Prophecy Belief in Modern American Culture*. Cambridge, MA: Harvard University Press.

Burridge, Kenelm. 1969. *New Heaven New Earth: A Study of Millenarian Activities*. Oxford: Basil Blackwell.

Bury, J. B. 1921. *The Idea of Progress: An Inquiry into Its Origin and Growth*. London: Macmillan.

Cohn, Norman. 1957. *The Pursuit of the Millennium*. London: Secker and Warburg.

———. 1962. "Medieval Millennialism: Its Bearing on the Comparative Study of Millenarian Movements." In *Millennial Dreams in Action: Essays in Comparative Study*, edited by Sylvia L. Thrupp. The Hague: Mouton.

———. 1993. *Cosmos, Chaos and the World to Come: The Ancient Roots of Apocalyptic Faith*. New Haven: Yale University Press.

Collins, William. 1995. "The Millerites and Time Prophecy: Their Function as Millennial Themes in the American Baha'i Community." M.S.Sc. thesis. Syracuse University.

————. 1996. Personal e-mail communication dated April 15.

Daniels, Ted. 1995. "Interview: Channeling Freedom." *Millennial Prophecy Report* 4: 33–36.

Davidson, James West. 1977. *The Logic of Millennial Thought: Eighteenth-Century New England*. New Haven: Yale University Press.

DeHaas, Jocelyn. 1994. " 'Apocalyptic' Prophecy and the Notion of Non-linear Time in the Church Universal and Triumphant." Paper presented at the Society for the Scientific Study of Religion.

Eichler, Margrit. 1971. "Charismatic and Ideological Leadership in Secular and Religious Millenarian Movements: A Sociological Study." Ph.D. diss., Duke University.

————. 1983. "Leadership in Social Movements." In *Leadership and Social Change*, edited by William R. Lassey and Marshall Sashkin. San Diego: University Associates.

Elliott, Joel. 1996. Personal e-mail communication dated April 25.

Gould, Stephen Jay. 1995a. "Spin Doctoring Darwin." *Natural History* 7: 6–9, 70–71.

————. 1995b. "Boyle's Law and Darwin's Details." *Natural History* 8: 8, 10–11, 68–71.

Landes, Richard. 1988. "Lest the Millennium Be Fulfilled: Apocalyptic Expectations and the Pattern of Western Chronography 100–800 c.e." In *The Use and Abuse of Eschatology in the Middle Ages*, edited by Werner Verbeke, Daniel Verhelst, and Andries Welkenhuysen. Leuven: Leuven University Press.

Maharishi Mahesh Yogi. 1995/1963. *Science of Being and Art of Living: Transcendental Meditation*. New York: Meridian.

Moorhead, James H. 1984. "Between Progress and Apocalypse: A Reassessment of Millennialism in American Religious Thought, 1800–1880." *Journal of American History* 71: 524–542.

Naquin, Susan. 1976. *Millenarian Rebellion in China: The Eight Trigrams Uprising of 1813*. New Haven, CT: Yale University Press.

Narayanan, Vasudha. 1995. Personal communication.

O'Flaherty, Wendy Doniger. 1976. *The Origins of Evil in Hindu Mythology*. Berkeley: University of California Press.

O'Leary, Stephen D. 1994. *Arguing the Apocalypse: A Theory of Millennial Rhetoric*. New York: Oxford University Press.

Olson, Theodore. 1982. *Millennialism, Utopianism, and Progress*. Toronto: University of Toronto Press.

Overmyer, Daniel L. 1976. *Folk Buddhist Religion: Dissenting Sects in Late Traditional China*. Cambridge, MA: Harvard University Press.

Reader, Ian. 1995. Personal communication.

Rosenfeld, Jean. 1995. "Pai Marire: Peace and Violence in a New Zealand Millenarian Tradition." *Terrorism and Political Violence* 7 (3) (Autumn), special issue on Millennialism and Violence, ed. Michael Barkun, 83–108.

Sandeen, Ernest R. 1980. "The 'Little Tradition' and the Form of Modern Millenarianism." In *The Annual Review of the Social Sciences of Religion,* edited by Joachim Matthies, Bryan R. Wilson, Leo Laeyendecker, and Jean Séguy. The Hague: Mouton.

Seidel, Anna K. 1970. "The Image of the Perfect Ruler in Early Taoist Messianism: Lao-Tzu and Li Hung." *History of Religions* 9: 216–47.

Share International. 1995. Internet gopher address is shareintl.org port 7004. World Wide Web address is http://www.hooked.net/shareint.

Sponberg, Alan. 1988. "Epilogue: A Prospectus for the Study of Maitreya." In *Maitreya, the Future Buddha,* edited by Alan Sponberg and Helen Hardacre. New York: Cambridge University Press.

Sponberg, Alan, and Helen Hardacre, eds. 1988. *Maitreya, the Future Buddha.* New York: Cambridge University Press.

Tabor, James D., and Eugene V. Gallagher. 1995. *Why Waco? Cults and the Battle for Religious Freedom in America.* Berkeley: University of California Press.

Talmon, Yonina. 1966. "Millenarian Movements." *Archieves Européènes de Sociologie* 7: 159–200.

Tuveson, Ernest Lee. 1949. *Millennium and Utopia: A Study in the Background of the Idea of Progress.* Berkeley: University of California Press.

Underwood, Grant. 1993. *The Millenarian World of Early Mormonism.* Urbana: University of Illinois.

Wallace, Anthony. 1956. "Revitalization Movements." *American Anthropologist* 58: 264–281.

Wessinger, Catherine Lowman. 1988. *Annie Besant and Progressive Messianism.* Lewiston, NY: The Edwin Mellen Press.

Wessinger, Catherine. 1993. "Annie Besant's Millennial Movement: Its History, Impact, and Implications Concerning Authority," with "Epilogue on David Koresh and the Branch Davidians." *Syzygy: Journal of Alternative Religion and Culture* 2: 55–70.

———. 1994. "Varieties of Millennialism and the Issue of Authority." In *From the Ashes: Making Sense of Waco,* edited by James R. Lewis. Lanham, MD: Rowman and Littelfield.

The Apocalypse of Modernity

3 James A. Aho

We begin by distinguishing between earth and the world. The first is the physical ground of being-in-a-world. The second refers to a coherency of ideal, material, and social objects into which we find ourselves thrown. While the earth may be written as a "gift" to the human species—the gratuitous making-possible of human existence—worlds are social projects, human creations (Berger and Luckmann 1967). This chapter concerns our shared world, the world of modernity.

All worlds have "centers" relative to which truth claims are assessed, actions morally judged, and beauty ascertained. In the ancient world, these centers were represented vividly and geographically. The classic example is Babylonia's world *omphalos* or navel (tower of Babel), the familiar baked-mud brick ziggurat linking heaven and earth, atop which the New Year Festival (each spring) was conducted, involving the death and resurrection of the god-king. Facsimiles of this symbolic architecture have been uncovered in Tenochtitlan, Mexico, and in the Forbidden City, heart of the Flowery States of the classic Chinese world.

Although the modern world has had its own geographic center, indeed a series of contending centers—Paris, Berlin, London, and today New York—following the train of military victories and commercial preeminence, the primordial center and unchanging measure of modernity—relative to which all else is marginal—has become Man(kind) Itself: its interests and its outlook. Our era, in other words, is one of *anthro*-centrism, or as it is more popularly known, humanism. The argument of this chapter is that the human center of modernity has destabilized and collapsed. Its fragmentation has opened a space for new revelations. We call this space the apocalypse of modernity.

It is not necessary to conduct an archaeology of modernity to determine its origins with any precision. According to some, the approximate time of the birth of modernity was 1500 A.D., its paternity being multiple: Francis Bacon, Martin Luther, Rene Descartes, John Calvin, Thomas Hobbes. Others claim to find progenitors of modernity in medieval Christianity, and this in either Hebraic prophecy (Max Weber) or in Greek philosophy (Martin Heidegger). However this question may eventually be answered, there is virtual consensus that as God slowly receded from the world of everyday practical concerns in Western civilization (Freidman 1995), finally to "die" altogether—the deity's obituary first being announced by Nietzsche's prophet, Zarathustra (Nietzsche 1954, sec. 123)—Mankind has expanded to fill the void. Man Itself has become the center of the modern world.

There is what might be named an "anthrocentrism of the left," which posits the proletariat as humanity's embodiment and true center. Then there is "anthrocentrism of the right," which insists, on the contrary, that the folk, nation, or tribe is the unparalleled standard relative to which all things must be measured. But the plausibility of these two collectivist anthrocentrisms, as compelling (and deadly) as they occasionally have been, pales in the face of still another anthrocentric doctrine: the individual self (*Seele* [German], soul).

In the modern era, God has been superseded not by class or race, but by self, the rational, willful ego. It is the sanctity and believability of universal self-hood that today is imperiled. This has occasioned the apocalypse of modernity.

THE APOCALYPSE OF MODERNITY

Around A.D. 1800 a localized debate between free-thinking English gentlemen and their French counterparts (the Founding Fathers) produced what today are celebrated, respectively, as the American Creed and the Declaration of the Rights of Man. Both doctrines announced as "self-evidently true" for all individuals that insofar as they are human, each has a claim to certain inalienable rights: life, liberty, and happiness.

Slavery and imperialism posed a dilemma to the Founding Fathers (Myrdal 1944). If, on the one hand, human essence were granted to Africans (or to Native Americans, Hindus, Polynesians, Chinese, Arabs, and Aborigines) then there would be no moral basis for their exploitation, exclusion, or excision. On the other hand, if life, liberty, and happiness were denied them, this would require the "acceptance of a principle obnoxious to the evidence of daily life," to wit, that they are beasts (Lemert 1994, 107).

The consequences of the second of these two choices are amply documented in libraries of infamy throughout Euro-America. They are summarized in a phrase still heard in extremist enclaves today: "Not everything that walks on two legs is human." Instead they are coons, rats, dogs, cats, goats, pigs, or worse. That is, they are "mud people," denizens of darkness, frequenters of garbage heaps, the "dregs" (*Dreck*), refuse of the world, and excrement, to be dealt with accordingly.[1]

Only that which is *essentially* human warrants individual rights, so the argument of the Founding Fathers went. But humanity is incumbent upon the display of reason: it is to think. *Cogito: sum.* Man's distinctiveness from animals is said to reside in the capacity to reason. The center of modernity, in other words, is pictured as a calculator incarnate in a two-legged body, serenely detached from life's passions. As for lesser hominids, they are relegated in maps of early modern geographers to terra incognita, the earth's unexplored periphery. They are silent monster-men, craven, lust-filled, savage.

The denial of humanity to non-Europeans was just one response to contact with human variety. The second, and as it turns out inestimably more important historically, has been liberalism. This is the conviction that non-Europeans are themselves human. They are not simply objects of nature to be overcome, used, and then discarded. They are thinking, knowing selves in their own right, hence worthy of freedom.

The possibility of humanity was granted first to non-Europeans inhabiting the remnants of civilizations as majestic as Europe, with their own monuments, cities, temples, and artworks. These in turn rested on multivolumed *dharmashastras* and Mahabharatas, Spring and Autumn Annals, codices of poetry and myth, and hieroglyphed papyra.

Confrontation with civilized non-Europeans constituted an intellectual challenge of massive proportions to westerners. How could peoples so different from ourselves in language, confession, folkways, and above all, appearance, be so . . . "human"? The most attractive answer was to deny the actuality of their difference by insisting that beneath the variety of alien tastes, mores, and appearances resided "essential man," man-as-knower, as described above. Given this answer, the center of modernity held.[2] Regarding the Hindus, Pakastanis, Afghans, and Persians, for example, an elaborate saga was concocted, demonstrating that (with the Nordic, Germanic, Celtic, and Greco-Roman peoples) they all derived from the same, racially superior, Indo-Aryan stock (Poliakov 1971). In the case of the Aztec, Mayan, and Peruvian peoples, chroniclers argued that in truth they were descendants of the legendary Lost Tribes of Israel, and thus their civilizations were merely bizarre offshoots from European tradition.[3]

Needless to say, this way of handling human variety was considerably less credible when applied to China and Japan, to the preliterate folk of Africa, Australia, and America, or most pointedly, to females. Once having admitted *these* others into the realm of humanity, the liberal was compelled to entertain the possibility that being human might mean infinitely more than Descartes' *cogito*: hence, the rise of multicultural identity politics and the so-called "displacement" of essential Man. Modernity's allegedly universal self ruptured into a plurality of parochial selves, each with their own style of mindedness and body life: African, Muslim, Native American, etc. (cf. Asante 1987).[4] Universal Man, that is, Euro-American male perception, reasoning, and emotional sensibility, was shown to be merely one more situated identity, as biased and partial as the rest.

Following the disintegration of Man into a plurality of men, there arose Woman with *her* own "her-story," *her* own nonmasculine way of being-in-the-world (de Beauvoir 1949). Then, within two decades essential Woman (meaning college-educated, middle-class Caucasian Euro-American female experience generalized to all females) exploded into a profusion of lower-case women of different races, classes, and tribal allegiances, each with their peculiar differences, each demanding recognition (Spelman 1989). Finally, homosexuals began railing against "compulsory heterosexual hegemony," insisting that human sexual difference could not be encompassed in two clumsy categories, man and woman. There exist instead three and maybe more sexualities, each of which has equal moral standing to the others (Rich 1983).

In short, as modernity's imperial destiny has unfolded it has been "decentered by difference," to paraphrase Jacques Derrida. Its center has lost plausibility. This is one reason why, instead of being enthusiastically embraced as a "victory of freedom over tyranny," as it has by some (Bloom 1989), news of modernization is received even in Euro-American circles with glowering faces and cynicism. Might our era be "the End of History?" asks Francis Fukuyama (1992). Might it be "the End of the World?" ask those affiliated with the American Study Group, a consortium of John Birch Society, Eagle Forum, and Freemen Institute activists (Idaho State Journal 1991). Might this be "Jesus and the End of History: Coming Soon?" ask Christian fundamentalists (ISU Ecumenical Ministry 1996). The very triumph of modernity has occasioned apocalypticism.

Crises shatter what is taken for granted as natural, inevitable, and right (from the Greek *krinein*, to split). In doing so, crises engender space, room wherein are glimpsed and spoken new revelations. When posed in prophetic words these "in-flashings" give rise to new worlds. This simultaneous "birthing-at-death" is encompassed in the Greek term "apocalypse" (*apo* = reversal + *kalyptein* = to cover). An apocalypse is not simply an end. It is also and more importantly a beginning, an uncovering, an illumination unveiled precisely at the very moment of the greatest darkness and danger. As Martin Heidegger would say, with all its accompanying anxiety and terror, the fracturing *is* the saving power "inasmuch as it brings the saving power out of its . . . concealed essence" (Heidegger 1977, 42).[5]

In the void left after God's erasure in the nineteenth century, prophets announced the Age of Man(kind). In our era, Man has come to an end (Clifford 1989).[6] In the space occasioned by Man's erasure, two new revelations have displayed themselves. The first, we call the Linguistic Turn, the second Fundamentalism; or, if we wish, postmodernism and millenarianism. The Linguistic Turn calls us to step, eyes open, into the emptiness left after Man's disappearance.

Fundamentalism urges us to flee the emptiness, to fend off its harbingers, to build impregnable fortresses that might keep chaos at bay.

REVELATIONS

The Linguistic Turn

With the repetition of situated, equally parochial identities—Afrocentric, homocentric, Islamic, femicentric, and so on—the suspicion has begun to spread among some academics that perhaps the whole idea of an essential center in the first place is nonsense. All that really exists is "the repetition itself," to quote Derrida: talk, discourse, language games, words (Derrida 1978, esp. 78–82). To use his rather stilted phraseology, in the postmodern age "linguistics invades the universal problematic."

What before was a unitary whole, a concrete world experienced alike by all sane people, in our era has become just one of a number of "world*views,*" that is, language games. Reality, once believed to have an ontological existence independent of its knowers, has evolved into a *linguistic construct,* less what words describe than what words "accomplish." Time, one of reality's dimensions, heretofore thought to be given in the nature of things themselves, is now but a *notion,* a localized theory. There is, for example, Hopi cyclical time and English linear time. Race, until recently considered an indisputable biological fact, is now disclosed as little more than a "*trope* of the world," a quaint (if dangerous) figure of speech invented by Portuguese explorers, a form of talk, a conversation piece. Finally, just as God (according to Nietzsche) was "murdered," in our era Man has been "killed." In place of a living, physical being, all that remains is a "*concept* of man." Even the human core, which Freud called the Id, the It, a cesspool of lubricious sexuality and destructiveness, has now devolved into words. To Freud's postmodern translator, Jacques Lacan, Freud's libidinal energy is "dream *language,*" with a structure analogous to puns and double entendres.[7]

"All that is solid melts into the air" (Berman 1982). In postmodernism, everything that before had provided a ground on which to stand has been "de(con)structed" into linguistic conventions, points of view produced by so-called subjects promoting their own interests in the course of talking.

"Subject" is a term from grammar. In postmodern jargon it is the substitute both for Descartes' rational self (*cogito*) and for its postcolonial replacement, the situated identity. Contrary to self or identity, however, the subject is not a concrete substance. It is, instead, a sentence fragment. More specifically, "subject" refers to the infinite void about which anything in principle may be said (or "inscribed"—another grammatical inflection).

Postmodernism advocates a stance of openness to the fundamental emptiness of subjectivity, both our own and that of others. Instead of objectifying them by fitting them into preset categories, we are admonished to yield, to "let beings be," "to give them ear," to let them reveal themselves to us (Levinas 1981). This is one revelation showing itself at the "moment of greatest danger" today.

Fundamentalism

Without question, surrender to the mystery of subjectivity can be exhilterating, even liberating. But for those already residing in chaos, the thought of further immersion in "Being and Nothingness" can only instill terror. The Linguistic Turn, as we have called it, appeals primarily to comfortably ensconced individuals who take moral civility and order for granted. That is, it finds audience among those whose outward indifference to a centered existence is founded on the security of knowing that "after all, most people are generally decent chaps anyway." This is far from the life experience of most human beings. To the latter, an attitude of easy-going, live-and-let-live tolerance, if not madness, is at least a kind of sentimentality bordering on stupidity. It calls for its own corrective in doctrines equally extreme, doctrines of theocentricism.

The mass of people today consists of two sorts. A large portion live in urban areas attempting to escape rural poverty. There, they are confronted daily with the necessity of devising a semblance of order amidst an ambiance of greed, violence, corruption, and filth. The balance remain in the countryside, where they face the destruction of local communities growing from the assimilation of their economies into the global market. To both types of late-modern displacees the ideology of free market capitalism, if not considered the immediate cause of their plight, is viewed as irrelevant to solving it. Not only does capitalism undermine customary folkways and moral restraints by means of its emphasis on the bottom line, it also seems to encourage indifference to the plight of the less fortunate. Above all, it is based on the very object that today has been dismantled, the universal self.

Into this vacuum a second revelation has moved—fundamentalism. By this, we mean the global-wide appearance of "back to basics" movements, each headed by messiahs, each preaching a brand of thousand-year egalitarian utopia of peace, each occasionally inspiring armed mayhem. In Latin America, there are Roman Catholic and Protestant fundamentalisms; in the Middle East, Sunni, Shiite, and Zionist equivalents; and in the Orient, Hindu and Sikh, Buddhist, Confucian, and Shinto parallels. To a handful of academics at elite Euro-American universities the end of Man means the rise of words. To millions, if not billions, of others Man's erasure signals the resurrection of the Word, the rebirth of a transcendent center—this, either in the form of a personal deity or an impersonal force.[8]

To be sure, religiously inspired reform is nothing new. The considered opinion of contemporary experts, however, is that fundamentalist enthusiasm is "gaining momentum in our time" (McNeil 1993). This, because today the disruptive consequences of modernization noted above affect people nearly everywhere on earth. Contact with strangers and with strangeness has become planetary, and with it the unsettling sense of being knocked off center, of losing footing and plunging into anomie. And for every action, there is an opposite and equal reaction. In response to the discomfiting extremity of cognitive and moral vertigo has been an equally extreme, global-wide call to go "back to the fundamentals," or to use our terminology, "back to the center," back to an originary source and immutable standard.

Revolutionists, Crane Brinton once wrote, are not children of despair, but offspring of hope (Brinton 1965). One of the paradoxes of political sociology is that radical reform and reactionary movements alike originate not among the most downtrodden, but in the discontents of those who have recently experienced improvement in their condition. One explanation for this is that elimination of certain abuses draws people's attention to others that now appear more galling. Another explanation is that those who are relatively advantaged can afford to luxuriate in inflicting their morality on others. Whatever the case, the theory of rising expectations, as it is known, finds considerable support in the area of fundamentalist recruitment. In the United States, fundamentalist Christian political activists are drawn from those whose positions in the world are advancing, not retreating. They are white, technically trained suburbanites living in the southeastern, Sun Belt, and Rocky Mountain states (Simpson 1983). Anecdotal information suggests an analogous pattern in Central America and in the Middle East. Indeed, the relationship between social betterment and fundamentalist appeals is so obvious as to have inspired hypothesis contrary to the theory of rising expectations. It is that the ascetic requirements of fundamentalism—its insistence on frugality, appetite control, hard work, and obedience—cause fundamentalists to be upwardly mobile, not the reverse.

However this question is eventually answered, it is a mistake to see fundamentalism merely as a revival of traditional beliefs. Reflecting the fact that fundamentalist cadres are not just passive victims of modernization, but are beginning to enjoy the benefits of urbanization, bureaucratic administrative rule, and technology, "fundamentalism" in reality weds a romantically idealized, largely fictitious past to carefully selected features of modernity. Thus, while each fundamentalism condemns the relativism and demythologizing of modernity, and while each attacks modernity's emphasis on reason, modernity's defense of Man, and its advocacy of individual rights, each also appropriates the latest communication and other tools to disseminate messages and to neutralize opponents. Among these tools are instruments of mass destruction: artificially produced germs, poison gases, and, some critics fear, nuclear weapons.

The ultimate task of all fundamentalisms is to delineate a center, to mark off boundaries relative to which persons and peoples can identify themselves. But, to pervert an old saying of Jacques Maritain, "we must *distinguish* in order to unite." To know who I am, to grasp who we are, we must first learn who we are *not*. Locating oneself in the center, in other words, is predicated on identifying who resides on the periphery in (what Islam, for example, calls *dar al-harb*) the abode of ignorance and sin. Every fundamentalism thus posits the existence of an *op-posite*, a Great Satan or Evil Empire: "Amerika, Amer-the-Reich, the rich, whose Hollywood imagists and Madison Avenue ad-men serve as agents of moral corruption; Russia, the so-called horde of Slavs, slaves, clumsy, slow-witted, vicious." However it is characterized, it is a demonic specter that narcoticizes dissenting voices or crushes them outright. This is the *Erbfiende*, the "enemy from birth," the recipient of a perversely delicious hatred, every bit as visceral as the psychological insecurity that feeds it.

At the end of this century, then, the glimmer of two prophecies shows through the fractures of modernity. The first is an-archic and ex-centric. It takes the deconstructionist project of modernity to its logical conclusion, denying ultimate origins altogether. Life is revealed as an illusion, something to be smiled at benignly, toyed with, and played: a language game. Having no place from which to draw energy and conviction, this revelation is politically limpid, impotent in the face of thrusts from those standing on solid ground, fundamentalists.

One irony of our age is that numbered among the enemies of fundamentalists East and West are those to whom the Linguistic Turn has such great appeal. These have been the advocates of "giving ear to" and "willing the freedom of" all voices equally, including those who now fill fundamentalist ranks. In doing so, these allies of the downtrodden have not only precipitated the end of Man, but inadvertently their *own* erasure. For like Alice's Cheshire cat who grasps the illusory nature of reality and thus grinningly imagines itself bodiless, the linguistic reductionists smugly claim themselves to be but ciphers, sentence fragments, subjects. In the most excruciatingly vivid (if necessary) bloody way, fundamentalists across the planet intend to display to this cat the foolishness of its pretension.

NOTES

1. In Euro-American demonology, these commonly represent, respectively: Negroes, Jews, homosexuals, witches, satanists, and again, Jews. A common German pejorative for Jew is *Schweinhund* (swine-dog). For further analysis, see Aho 1994, 108–12.
2. Until recently, this historiographic style enjoyed immense popularity in Euro-American intellectual circles (cf. McNeil 1963).
3. This the basis of *The Book of Mormon*, one of the holy documents of the Church of Jesus Christ of Latter-day Saints.
4. Each of these lesser essences in turn has splintered into smaller units. For the classic example, see Edward Said's critique of Oriental identity (1978).
5. That is, by definition one can not make out the light without there being darkness. Hence, the paradoxical figure Lucifer, light-bringer, who serves his purpose of enlightenment through his role as archangel of darkness.
6. The death of Man was first announced by Michel Foucault (1983, 208–9).
7. Even the body and sexuality are said to be "texts" (Halberstam and Livingston 1995).
8. The planned six-volume Fundamentalism Project out of the University of Chicago constitutes recognition of the worldwide significance of such movements in our era. The first volume was published in 1991 by the University of Chicago Press. (Cf. Lawrence 1989; Caplan 1987.)

REFERENCES

Aho, James. 1994. *This Thing of Darkness: A Sociology of the Enemy*. Seattle and London: University of Washington Press.

Asante, Molefi. 1987. *The Afrocentric Idea*. Philadelphia: Temple University Press.

Berger, Peter, and Thomas Luckmann. 1967. *The Social Construction of Reality*. Garden City, NY: Doubleday-Anchor.

Berman, Marshall. 1982. *All That is Solid Melts into the Air*. New York: Simon and Schuster.

Bloom, Allan. 1989. "Response to Fukuyama." *National Interest* (Summer): 19–21.

Brinton, Crane. 1965. *Anatomy of Revolution*. Englewood Cliffs, NJ: Prentice-Hall.

Caplan, Lionel. 1987. *Studies in Religious Fundmentalism*. Albany: State University of New York Press.

Clifford, Michael. 1989. "Postmodern Thought and the End of Man." In *The Question of the Other,* edited by Arleen Dallery and Charles Scott. Albany: State University of New York Press.

de Beauvoir, Simone. 1949. *The Second Sex*, H. M. Parshley, trans. New York: Vintage Books.

Derrida, Jacques. 1978. *Writing and Difference*. Chicago: University of Chicago Press.

Foucault, Michel. 1983. "Afterword: The Subject and Power." In *Michel Foucault: Beyond Structuralism and Hermeneutics*, edited by Hubert Dreyfus and Paul Rabinow. Chicago: University of Chicago Press.

Friedman, Richard. 1995. *The Disappearance of God*. Boston: Little, Brown and Co.

Fukuyama, Francis. 1992. *The End of History and the Last Man*. New York: Free Press.

Halberstam, Judith, and Ira Livingston. 1995. *Posthuman Bodies*. Bloomington: Indiana University Press.

Heidegger, Martin. 1977. "The Turning." In *The Question of Technology and Other Essays*. William Lovitt, trans. New York: Harper and Row.

Idaho State Journal. 1991. "End's in Sight, Group Insists." September 3.

ISU Ecumenical Ministry. 1996. "Jesus and the End of History: Coming Soon." March 10.

Lawrence, Bruce. 1989. *Defenders of God: The Fundamentalist Revolt against the Modern Age*. San Francisco: Harper and Row.

Lemert, Charles. 1994. "Dark Thoughts about the Self." In *Social Theory and the Politics of Identity,* edited by Craig Calhoun. Cambridge, MA: Blackwell.

Levinas, Emmanuel. 1981. *Otherwise Than Being: Or Beyond Essence*, Alphonso Lingis, trans. The Hague: Martin Nijhoff.

McNeil, William. 1993. "Fundamentalisms and the World of the 1990s." In *Fundamentalisms and Society*. Chicago: University of Chicago Press.

———. 1963. *The Rise of the West*. Chicago: University of Chicago.

Myrdal, Gunnar. 1944. *The American Dilemma*. New York: Harper and Brothers.

Nietzsche, Friedreich. 1954. "The Gay Science." *The Portable Nietzsche*, Walter Kaufman, trans. New York: Vintage Books.

Poliakov, Leon. 1971. *The Aryan Myth*. New York: Basic Books.

Rich, Adrienne. 1983. "Compulsory Heterosexuality and Lesbian Existence." In *Powers of Desire*, edited by A. Sitnow, C. Stanwell, and S. Thompson. New York: Monthly Review Press.

Said, Edward. 1978. *Orientalism*. New York: Vintage Books.

Simpson, John. 1983. "Moral Issues and Status Politics." In *The New Christian Right*, edited by Robert Liebman and Robert Wuthnow. New York: Aldine.

Spelman, Elisabeth. 1989. *Inessential Woman*. Boston: Beacon Press.

Fifteen Years of Failed Prophecy
Coping with Cognitive Dissonance in a Baha'i Sect

Robert W. Balch, John Domitrovich,
Barbara Lynn Mahnke, Vanessa Morrison

On April 29, 1980, members of the Baha'is Under the Provisions of the Covenant (BUPC) entered fallout shelters to await a nuclear holocaust that they believed would fulfill the prophecies of Revelation. In the first hour, they expected a third of the world's population to perish, and they claimed that over the next twenty years, the planet would be ravaged by starvation, disease, revolutions, and natural disasters. They believed that by the year 2000

God's kingdom would be established on earth and a thousand years of peace would ensue.

This prediction was only the first in a long series of failed prophecies that would test the faith of the BUPC. Between 1980 and 1995 the group's leader, Dr. Leland Jensen, set twenty dates for the battle of Armageddon or lesser disasters that would lead up to the Apocalypse. In this paper we will examine the long-term effects of these failed prophecies on the BUPC.

Our analysis is based on the theory of cognitive dissonance, which Festinger, Riecken, and Schachter (1956) used to analyze reactions to failed prophecy in a millennial flying saucer cult. The group's leader, Marian Keech, was a medium who claimed an extraterrestrial being named Sananda had warned her that much of the Midwest would be inundated by a catastrophic flood on December 21, 1954.

Paradoxically, Festinger et al. predicted that the failure of Mrs. Keech's prophecy would result in increased conviction and heightened efforts to recruit new believers. They argued that Mrs. Keech and her followers would experience severe cognitive dissonance when the prophecy failed, but that it would be extremely difficult for them to abandon their beliefs because they had made numerous public and private commitments to the prediction. To reduce the dissonance they would invent rationalizations to explain away the disconfirmation, and more importantly they would try to gain social support for their beliefs by increasing their efforts to recruit new believers.

The study by Festinger et al. supported these hypotheses. Mrs. Keech responded to the failure of her prophecy by proclaiming that the catastrophe had been called off because her group "had spread so much light that God had saved the world from destruction" (1956, 169). She eagerly granted interviews to reporters and invited curiosity seekers into her home to explain Sananda's latest revelation. Most of her followers were equally enthusiastic about publicizing Sananda's message, which was remarkable because the group had never shown much interest in proselytizing.

Festinger et al. specified five conditions that must be met before prophetic failure will be followed by increased conviction and vigorous proselytizing:

1. Belief in the prediction must be held with deep conviction.
2. Members must have committed themselves to the prediction by engaging in important actions that are difficult to undo.
3. The prediction must be specific enough that it can be clearly disconfirmed.

4. There must be undeniable evidence that the prediction was wrong.

5. Members must have social support from fellow believers.

The BUPC clearly met these conditions in 1980, but less so when Jensen made his second prediction a few years later. By the 1990s, when Jensen made a flurry of predictions, hardly anyone in the BUPC except for Jensen and a few members of his inner circle met the first condition of deep conviction, and the commitments specified in the second condition were minimal compared to those that members had made in 1980. Our data suggest that the diminishing relevance of the Festinger et al. theory reflects the emergence of an underground *culture of dissonance-reduction* consisting of disclaimers and *post factum* rationalizations that reduced the impact of the predictions and subsequent disconfirmations. This culture enabled members to dismiss the predictions and move on with their everyday lives while still claiming allegiance to Jensen and the Baha'i faith. The goal of preparing for the holocaust ultimately was displaced by more immediate, mundane concerns, despite the fact that the group's rhetoric remained as apocalyptic as ever.

DATA COLLECTION

Our data on the BUPC come from four participant-observer studies we conducted between 1980 and 1996. Besides taking part in numerous group activities, including potluck dinners, teaching sessions, and weekly meetings, we conducted forty-seven formal interviews with members, three group interviews with six ex-members, three individual interviews with high-ranking defectors who left in 1994 and 1996, and a lengthy interview with Jensen in 1980. Balch and two students also spent the night of April 29, 1980, in three BUPC fallout shelters. In addition, we have studied the group's press releases and BUPC newsletters pertaining to the predictions.[1]

AN OVERVIEW OF THE BUPC

The BUPC are a small Baha'i sect based in Missoula, Montana. Their founder, a chiropractor named Leland Jensen, was expelled from the mainstream Baha'is in 1960. During a doctrinal dispute following the death of Shoghi Effendi, the

Guardian of the Baha'i faith, Jensen aligned himself with a schismatic leader named Mason Remey who claimed to be the second Guardian. However, Remey died a few years later and his followers split into rival factions, each proclaiming a different Guardian. In 1964, after becoming disillusioned with the infighting, Jensen and his wife, Opal, moved to Missoula where they opened a chiropractic clinic. Although Jensen once had been a highly acclaimed Baha'i missionary, he had stopped teaching the Faith by the time he got to Montana.

Then in 1969 Jensen was convicted of sexually molesting a fifteen-year-old patient. During the trial, several women testified against him, and he was sentenced to twenty years in the Montana State Prison. Shortly after his imprisonment, Jensen had a revelation:

> I felt a presence only. I saw nobody. I saw no dove, no burning bush or anything of this nature. It talked to me—not in a physical voice but very vividly expressing to me that I was the Promised Joshua (prophesied in Zechariah 3).

After studying the Bible and Baha'i writings, Jensen understood that his mission was to establish the Baha'i Universal House of Justice after the world was cleansed of evil and apostasy by a nuclear holocaust.[2]

Jensen immediately began tying together diverse strands of Bible prophecies, Baha'i teachings, and pyramidology to substantiate his claims. He recruited many followers in prison, and after being paroled in 1973 he founded the BUPC in Missoula. By the end of the 1970s Jensen also had attracted followers in Wyoming, Colorado, and Arkansas.

Since 1980 membership in the BUPC has fluctuated considerably, but it probably has never exceeded 200 nationwide despite Jensen's claims of having thousands of followers around the world. In 1994, the last year for which we have a membership list, there were only sixty-six members in Montana and fewer than twenty in other states. The Wyoming and Arkansas contingents disbanded after the 1980 disconfirmation, but new groups were formed in Minnesota and Wisconsin.

Over the years, about a third of the members have had college degrees, and the group has always stressed the importance of reading and research, so members tend to be exceptionally well informed about the Bible, Baha'i teachings, world religions, and international politics.

One of the most significant events in the history of the BUPC was the recruitment of Neal Chase, a spiritual seeker from Wisconsin who proved to be brilliant at synthesizing Jensen's teachings with other prophetic beliefs. Chase's most notable contribution was to bolster the "proofs" for Jensen's mission by incorporating the prophecies of George Williams, leader of an obscure nineteenth-century Mormon sect known as the Morrisites (Anderson 1988; Chase 1990). According to Chase, Williams predicted that Christ would return in Montana's Deer Lodge Valley where the Montana State Prison is located. The anticipated date of Christ's return, August 9, 1969, happened to be the first full day that Jensen spent in the prison, which Chase claims bears a striking resemblance to Ezekiel's temple described in the Bible.[3] By 1990, Jensen, then 76, had turned much of the responsibility for interpreting the scriptures over to Chase.[4]

THE PREDICTIONS

Between 1979 and 1995 Jensen and Chase made twenty specific predictions. The first time Jensen set a date for the apocalypse was in 1979, when he proclaimed that a nuclear war would begin on April 29, 1980. Jensen's second prediction came in 1985, when he claimed that Halley's comet would crash into the earth the following year, triggering catastrophic upheavals that would culminate in the battle of Armageddon. All eighteen predictions in the 1990s were made by Chase, although each had Jensen's approval. Unlike Jensen's two predictions in the 1980s, which foretold worldwide catastrophes, Chase's predictions pertained to small-scale disasters that he claimed would lead step-by-step toward the apocalypse. Some of his predictions focused on upheavals caused by meteors, asteroids, and comets, but most pertained to the destruction of New York City by a nuclear bomb that would be planted by Middle Eastern terrorists.

REACTIONS TO PROPHECY FAILURE IN THE BUPC

Two predominant patterns emerged in response to the BUPC's failed prophecies. Jensen and Chase reacted in a manner that for the most part supports dissonance theory, whereas their followers generally did not. Therefore, it is important to treat these patterns separately.

The Reactions of Jensen and Chase

Before and after each prophesied date, Jensen and Chase behaved much like Marian Keech. Prior to every date they made strong public commitments by

issuing strident press releases, and in the 1990s Chase made numerous unequiv-
ocal proclamations on the BUPC's public-access television show, "Baha'i Phone-
In Live." Before the 1980 date, Jensen urged his followers to build fallout
shelters and stock them with food, water, and survival gear, and he allowed his
own shelter to be photographed for a front-page story in the local newspaper.
Jensen also proclaimed in one of his books that any religion that cannot predict
the exact moment of the apocalypse "lacks Divine Guidance" (1979, 61–62).

Jensen and Chase also reacted like Mrs. Keech when their predictions were
disconfirmed. In light of the hypothesis that proselytizing should increase
after disconfirmation, their most notable response was to heighten efforts to
spread the BUPC message. After each failed prediction they quickly issued more
press releases in which they insisted they had been right all along. These
releases were sent as far away as the Vatican and the United Nations, and frequently they were hand delivered to politicians and media executives. Jensen
and Chase eagerly granted interviews to newspapers and radio talk shows, and
they urged BUPC members to take advantage of each reprieve by renewing their
efforts to recruit the 144,000 who would enter God's kingdom.

Renewed proselytizing, however, required plausible explanations for each
prophecy failure. Throughout the fifteen-year period, at least seven types of
explanations were used: (1) the prediction was fulfilled spiritually rather than
physically; (2) the prophecy was fulfilled physically, but not in the manner
expected; (3) the date was off because of a miscalculation; (4) the date was a
prediction, not a prophecy; (5) the leaders had a moral responsibility to warn
the public despite the date's uncertainty; (6) God had given the world a
reprieve; and 7) the predictions had been tests of members' faith.

1. Jensen relied heavily on the notion of a *spiritual fulfillment* in 1980. He
claimed that the seven-year Tribulation described in Revelation had commenced on April 29 and that the four winds of destruction (Revelation 7:1)
were being held back until the 144,000 had been recruited. He offered a similar explanation in 1986 after Halley's comet failed to crash into the earth:

> The spiritual fulfillment [of the prophecy] did take place. A spiritual stone hit
> the earth. This stone is the message of the messiahship that only the [true]
> Baha'is understand. The spiritual stone crushes and destroys what the Christians
> claim, and what the covenant breakers [mainstream Baha'is] claim.

When a meteor collision and massive earthquakes failed to occur as predicted
in 1991, Jensen claimed the prediction had been fulfilled by a "spiritual

earthquake" caused by the defection of one of his most important followers. "Everything," he said, "happens on the spiritual plane before it manifests in the physical plane."

2. More often, Jensen and Chase claimed their predictions were *physically fulfilled by other events* that happened on or around the dates or shortly thereafter. In 1980, Jensen cited numerous phone calls from reporters as far away as Australia to prove that he had fulfilled the prophecy that the Seventh Angel would pour his "bowl of wrath" into the air (Revelation 16:17–18). He claimed this referred to the worldwide media coverage his message received on April 29. When Mt. St. Helens erupted nineteen days later, Jensen proclaimed the volcanic ash that inundated Missoula was a warning of what would happen when Portland and Seattle were bombed.

A more recent instance of claiming a physical fulfillment occurred in 1994 after Chase made the following prediction about the bombing of New York City:

> On March 23, 1994, the veils will be rent asunder with the fiery holocaust of New York City's millions of inhabitants! Forty days later will come the Battle of Armageddon, in which one third of mankind will be killed in one hour of thermonuclear war. (Press release, November 1, 1993)

In fact, on March 24, 1994, a gas pipeline exploded in Edison, New Jersey, across the Hudson River from New York. To buttress his claim that the prophecy had been fulfilled, Chase quoted an eyewitness who compared the explosion to a nuclear blast.

3. Jensen and Chase frequently claimed to have made a *miscalculation* when they missed the mark. After the prophecy failure in 1980, Jensen immediately set a second date and then a third. Chase used this strategy continuously in the 1990s. For example, Chase's first prediction about New York was that the city would be bombed on November 29, 1992. Nothing happened until the World Trade Center was bombed three months later, although not with a nuclear weapon. Chase subsequently cited Daniel 7:12, which says, "their lives were prolonged for a season and a time," to prove that his prediction had been correct. Claiming that "a season" is three months, he announced that the November 29 date "plus the prophesied season of three months brought us to February 26, 1993, the day, the minute, the hour, the second that the World Trade Center was bombed" (press release, August 4, 1993).

4. The admission of human error was rationalized by making a sharp distinction between a *prediction* and a *prophecy*. Prophecies came directly from

God, whereas the BUPC's predictions were based on research and logic, which are subject to human fallibility. As Chase put it: "We can't be false prophets because we don't claim to be prophets. We simply *interpret* what is already there in the Bible." Jensen had always made this distinction, but it became increasingly important in the 1990s. According to this reasoning, Jensen and Chase were only human and they could make mistakes like everyone else.

5. Despite the uncertainties caused by human failings, Jensen and Chase claimed they had a *moral responsibility* to warn the public because so many "signs" had suggested that catastrophes were imminent. The signs were synchronistic events that converged around a particular date. For instance, Chase claimed that numerous events had pointed to November 26, 1992, as the date for the bombing of New York:

1. Thousands of covenant-breaking Baha'is would be gathering on this date in New York, a city marked for destruction in the prophecies of Nostradamus.
2. Comet Swift-Tuttle, which supposedly heralded the founding of the Baha'i faith in 1863, would reach its closest distance to earth on December 18.
3. During a lunar eclipse on December 9, the moon would turn blood red as foretold in Revelation 6:12 and Joel 2:31.

To ignore these signs would have been morally irresponsible because the BUPC had a "mandate from God to warn the people" about the apocalypse. If New York had been destroyed while they kept silent, because they only *suspected* something might happen, then "the blood of the people" would have been on their hands.

6. With each disconfirmation, Jensen and Chase claimed that God had granted the BUPC a *reprieve*. After the 1980 prediction, Jensen claimed that God had given the BUPC more time to recruit the 144,000. The same explanation was offered in 1986. After both the Trade Center bombing and the Edison pipeline explosion in the 1990s, Chase claimed that God in his mercy had spared New York, but that the predictions were "wake-up" calls for the city's residents.

7. Finally and most consistently, Jensen and Chase repeatedly claimed that the predictions were *tests*. After the 1980 prediction, Jensen pointed out that Matthew 24:37 says that the "coming of the Son of Man [Jensen] will repeat what happened in Noah's time," which according to Baha'i teachings is that

Noah predicted the flood several times (Baha'u'llah 1931). Noah's first predictions separated the "sheep from the goats" so that when the flood finally happened only the pure-of-heart remained. By the 1990s, Jensen was referring to the 1980 prediction as "God's fire drill" and a "practice run."

The explanations offered by Jensen and Chase are examples of what Lyman and Scott (1968) call *accounts*. These are face-saving strategies intended to reduce embarrassment after a discrediting situation has occurred. In the BUPC these accounts enabled Jensen and Chase to claim they had been right all along: "We didn't make a mistake," Chase proclaimed after two failed attempts to predict the nuclear destruction of New York, "not even a teeny eeny one!" (press release, November 1, 1993). Almost a year later, after five more failed prophecies, Chase claimed that the BUPC had "a 100 percent track record!" (press release, October 9, 1994).

At first glance, the way Jensen and Chase reacted to the failure of their predictions seems to be entirely consistent with cognitive dissonance theory. However, the theory does not consider the effects of *repeated* prophecy failures.

Before the 1980 date, Jensen encouraged his followers to build fallout shelters and store food to prepare for the holocaust. Yet by the time of the second prediction in 1986, Jensen no longer emphasized physical preparedness and the group's fallout shelters, including his own, had been dismantled. Instead he claimed that Missoula would be safe because of its remote mountainous location, as well as the fact that the "Promised One" lived there. In the event that shelters might be needed, Jensen said that the BUPC would be able to occupy an extensive network of tunnels under the university and city center, and he claimed his followers could stockpile all the provisions they would need in just three days.

By downplaying the need for building, stocking, and maintaining shelters, Jensen eliminated one of the most important commitments members had made in 1980. This is significant because, following the reasoning of Festinger et al., the fewer commitments members make before a prediction, the less the dissonance should be when a prophecy fails.

Perhaps more important are two changes that occurred in the 1990s. First, the nature of the predictions changed from apocalyptic global catastrophes to small-scale disasters heralding the nuclear conflagration. Chase explained that prophecy fulfillment is not a discrete event but a continuous, unfolding process. This had the effect of diffusing the impact of any particular prophecy failure.

Second, beginning in 1993 Jensen and Chase began making *disclaimers* before their predictions. Disclaimers are face-saving strategies that are used to head off *anticipated* embarrassment (Hewitt and Stokes 1975). For example, one of the dates for the bombing of New York was September 4, 1993, the third anniversary of Opal Jensen's death. Even before the day was over Jensen was speculating that the real date might be September 8, the anniversary of his wife's burial. Before the next date Chase clearly hedged his bets by saying:

> I don't really care if the bombing is today, tomorrow, or next year. I only know that it is part of God's plan, and it *will* happen as prophesied. Nothing can alter the plan of God.

Because severe dissonance is likely to occur only when a prediction is believed with deep conviction, the use of disclaimers should reduce the dissonance caused by prophecy failure. What is most interesting about these disclaimers, however, is that ordinary members had been using them for years before Jensen and Chase.

The Reactions of Ordinary Members

The responses of ordinary BUPC members to the failed predictions were considerably more complicated than those of Jensen and Chase. Not only were their reactions less consistent with the hypotheses proposed by Festinger et al., but their reactions changed considerably over time. By "ordinary members" we refer to everyone in the BUPC except Jensen and Chase. It will help to divide the fifteen-year period into three phases: 1980–1981, before and after the original prediction; 1986–1987, before and after the second; and 1990–1995, when Chase made a flurry of predictions about lesser events that would culminate in Armageddon.

1980-81. The first prediction provided the clearest test of dissonance theory because the BUPC met all the conditions specified by Festinger et al. (Balch, Farnsworth, and Wilkins 1983).

The prediction was specific down to the minute, and members had made substantial commitments based on their belief that it would come true. The most important commitment was the construction of fallout shelters, but members also wrote numerous pamphlets and books using Bible prophecies and pyramidology to prove the prediction was correct. Several members sent letters to the local paper warning people to prepare for the holocaust, and the BUPC organized a nuclear-preparedness group called SAFE (Safety and Fall-Out

Education), which distributed thousands of leaflets urging Missoulians to prepare for nuclear war. The disconfirmation was painfully obvious to everyone, but, consistent with Festinger et al.'s fifth condition, members had the support of a close-knit community of fellow believers.

However, there was no increase in proselytizing after the date. In fact, proselytizing stopped altogether, which is significant because the BUPC had been heavily committed to teaching the Faith before April 29. During the first BUPC meeting after the prophecy failure, Jensen gave an emotional speech in which he exhorted his followers to capitalize on the reprieve: "Rise and Shine!" he shouted. "Establish the kingdom! Teach as you never have before!" Although he had brought a large box of books for members to distribute, not one was taken. The BUPC were extremely confused and demoralized, and attendance at meetings dropped precipitously. These reactions clearly contradict dissonance theory.

On the other hand, it took six months before anyone openly defected, and when members left, their stated reasons usually had no direct connection to the failed prophecy. Instead their leaving usually was prompted by doctrinal disputes or interpersonal conflicts within the group. The prophecy failure may have contributed to their disillusionment but it was not emphasized by any of our informants. The members who stayed were able to sustain their faith by claiming that the prophecy was only a test, which had given them more time to prepare. The Noah analogy was quickly adopted throughout the group. However, rather than redoubling their efforts to prepare for the holocaust, most members seemed burned out by the group's apocalyptic fervor. They claimed they had become so wrapped up in the prophecy that they had lost sight of the basic Baha'i teachings. As a member explained: "I think we all made a mistake. We got too caught up in the physical. We weren't ready for the war because spiritually none of us were strong enough."

1986-1987. Since Jensen claimed the seven-year Tribulation began on April 29, 1980, he had committed himself to a second prediction for 1987. Halley's comet, which was due to arrive in 1986, provided the rationale. Jensen predicted that on April 29, 1986, the comet would get pulled into an orbit around the earth and begin breaking up, pelting the planet with debris that would strike with the force of nuclear warheads. The gravitational pull of the comet would produce massive earthquakes and a convulsive shifting of the earth's crust. This would continue for one year until April 29, 1987, when the remainder of the comet would plummet to earth, producing tidal waves thousands of feet high and earthquakes more devastating than any before.

The prediction rekindled the group's millennial enthusiasm. The comet dominated practically every meeting as members eagerly discussed books, articles, TV documentaries, and biblical prophecies about comets. On March 22, 1986, the group finally went public with the prediction by issuing a press release proclaiming Halley's comet as the herald of the new kingdom.

However, the activities of the BUPC prior to the 1986 prediction differed from those in 1980 in two important ways. First, this time members made hardly any personal preparations to survive the coming destruction. Missoula presumably would be safe from the tidal waves and earthquakes that would devastate coastal cities.

The second difference was that members began hedging their bets with disclaimers before the 1986 date. The group's self-taught comet expert suggested that God might be using the comet to distract mankind from the real threat, which he speculated might be asteroids. Others speculated that God might be using the comet to test their faith, much as they had been tested in 1980. Still others claimed Jensen could be mistaken because, despite his identity as the "Promised One," he was "only a man" with failings like everyone else.

On the evening of April 28, 1986, the BUPC had a potluck dinner. Unlike a similar meeting the night before the 1980 date when Jensen delivered a fiery speech and members had talked excitedly about the impending holocaust, Jensen did not address the group and nobody even mentioned the comet.

The morning after the disconfirmation members quietly resumed their lives by going to work, attending school, or taking care of their children, as if it were just another day. As in 1980 there was no increase in proselytizing and members offered accounts to explain the failed prophecy, the most common being the parallel with Noah's predictions. But unlike 1980 there was no apparent confusion or disillusionment, perhaps because members had not committed themselves to the same extent and because they already had prepared themselves for the prophecy failure. The expression "business as usual" is a good description of the aftermath of the disconfirmation. Although some members continued to profess belief that Armageddon would happen by April 29, 1987, others appeared to have lost interest in Jensen's date setting.

By August of 1986 the emphasis had shifted away from the new date to being spiritually prepared for the end, whenever it might occur. Reports by ex-members indicate that the 1987 date was ignored by virtually everyone. Jensen began ridiculing the Tribulation as a misguided concept promoted by "the Christian sects," and his followers quickly followed suit.

1990–1995. Prior to the 1980 and 1986 predictions, members had sought confirming evidence to prove the accuracy of the prophecies, and that pattern continued in the 1990s. The evidence marshalled to support the predictions included Hopi prophecies, planetary conjunctions, dreams, numerological coincidences, the prophecies of Nostradamus, and predictions made by psychics and other religious leaders, such as Jeane Dixon and Elizabeth Clare Prophet.

However, as in 1986, the BUPC made few public commitments to the dates. The members who had weathered the disconfirmations of the 1980s were the least likely to take the predictions seriously. They made virtually no preparations. Some of the newer members attended civil defense workshops and stored survival gear, but these were isolated individual efforts. No maps of the city's civil defense tunnels were distributed to the BUPC and members did not make an effort to warn the public as they had with SAFE in 1980. On two occasions members boxed up their possessions and camped in parks or their back yards when earthquakes were expected, but these commitments were minimal compared to those in the shelter-building days of 1979 and 1980.

Members also used disclaimers more often than ever before. Significantly, these face-saving strategies were extensions of the accounts that had been offered to explain past prophecy failures. Even members of Jensen's inner circle used these disclaimers. For example, one of Jensen's staunchest supporters started telling prospective members "not to lay any stock in the predictions Neal made [because] the real sign would be the entrance of the 144,000." She added that "the truth is that people would have really preferred for Neal to knock off his prophesying."

After each failed prediction, life for the BUPC continued on course. There were few traces of disillusionment among either new or old members. The BUPC provided the usual accounts in an offhanded manner: Jensen and Chase had to warn the public whether they were sure or not; God gave the BUPC more time because they were not ready yet; the prediction had been just another test. Some members did not even bother to offer accounts for the failed predictions. "I didn't get too concerned about these predictions," one said, "because a number of them had not materialized in the past." Proselytizing continued unabated, but few members stressed the predictions when teaching the Faith. Instead they focused more on Jensen's mission and the importance of being spiritually prepared when the prophecies of Revelation ultimately would be fulfilled. Even the World Trade Center bombing and Edison gas explosion failed to rekindle the group's apocalyptic enthusiasm.

Instead of focusing on Armageddon, members became increasingly absorbed by everyday life in the BUPC. In addition to the traditional round of weekly and monthly events, new group activities developed. These included a public-access television show, information tables at the university, Sunday church services, song writing and a choir, and demonstrations against the U.S. government's treatment of Iraq. The demonstrations are significant because prior to the 1990s the BUPC had never shown an interest in changing political events, only monitoring them for warning signs.

In 1991, Jensen established a twelve-person governing body called the Second International Baha'i Council (IBC) whose stated purpose was to lay the foundation for the Universal House of Justice, which Jensen expected to govern the world after the apocalypse.[5] The IBC quickly came to dominate the lives of its members as its meetings steadily became longer and more frequent. IBC members engaged in endless wrangling over administrative details, writing projects, plans for establishing the world government, and discussions of other members' personal affairs, including martial problems, homosexuality, drug use, and gambling.

In contrast to the informality of previous years, the BUPC took on an increasingly bureaucratic character despite the fact that by 1990 the group probably had fewer than one hundred members nationwide. The IBC elected officers passed numerous "laws" governing the conduct of BUPC members, and conducted its meetings according to Robert's Rules of Order. To deal with more mundane matters, local BUPC "councils" were formed in Montana, Colorado, and Wisconsin. City and county councils were established in Missoula, each with its own officers and formal responsibilities.

We found no evidence that these changes were prompted by the spate of failed prophecies in the 1990s. Instead, former IBC members attributed them to the death of Jensen's wife in 1990 and the growing irrelevance of the predictions. According to their first hypothesis, Opal Jensen's death compelled Jensen to consider his own mortality and the need for an administrative structure to carry on his mission after he died. The second hypothesis was that the new councils, offices, and activities were created to keep members motivated as the predictions lost their grip on the BUPC.

In addition to the structural changes that occurred in the BUPC, the defection rate accelerated in the 1990s. However, this too seems unrelated to the failed prophecies. Instead members were leaving because of doctrinal disputes[6] and resentment over the intrusion of the IBC in their private lives.

By 1996 we found only one member who still placed much emphasis on the predictions. He admitted to "feeling stupid" when they failed and he claimed he would leave if the nuclear war did not happen by the year 2000. For the others, the date setting had become irrelevant even though they continued to believe in Jensen's mission. The IBC's former vice president explained the general attitude this way:

> I think we're immune to it now. We've been desensitized. [The dates] come and they go and they come and they go and they come and they go. I think that's . . . why there isn't much preparedness. I think people mostly really don't believe them. I think mostly people would be really shocked [if a prediction came true].

Conclusion

When reviewing the reactions of the BUPC to repeated prophecy failures, two major patterns emerge: the behavior of the BUPC leaders generally supports the theory proposed by Festinger et al., but the responses of ordinary members do not. Jensen and Chase maintained their enthusiasm for the predictions and never seemed disheartened when their prophecies failed. This was not true for their followers. After the 1980 debacle, Jensen's followers became disillusioned and for a while they stopped proselytizing altogether. Over the next fifteen years Jensen's predictions became less and less important for the average member. The BUPC made fewer preparations and they showed little disappointment when the prophecies failed. By the mid-1990s the predictions had become largely irrelevant.

The long-term responses of the ordinary members reflect the emergence of a *culture of dissonance-reduction* within the BUPC. The key ingredients of this culture are accounts and disclaimers that were disseminated in BUPC meetings, press releases, newsletters, and conversations among members. The origins of this culture can be traced to the accounts Jensen used to explain the 1980 failure. Following subsequent predictions, the ordinary members began turning these accounts into disclaimers to reduce the *possibility* of dissonance even before it could occur.

Eventually even Jensen and Chase began to conform to the culture of dissonance-reduction. Not only did they start using disclaimers themselves, but they reduced the magnitude of the dissonance caused by their failed prophecies by making predictions about relatively minor events instead of a global catastrophe. They also demanded fewer commitments to their predictions.

The trends between 1980 and 1995 illustrate the process of *goal displacement*. Goal displacement occurs when an organization's original goals are supplanted by more achievable ends. Group members "retreat from the initial program to a more moderate and conservative program in the interest of maintaining the strength of the organization" (Blau and Scott 1962, 229). In goal displacement the means of achieving organizational goals become ends in themselves as members focus their attention on mundane administrative jobs, and the group's original ideals become increasingly irrelevant to members' everyday lives.

The concept of goal displacement describes what happened in the BUPC. In 1980 the group's primary goal was preparing for the holocaust, but by the 1990s this objective had been supplanted by the more immediate goal of creating an administrative structure for ushering in God's kingdom. The first hints of goal displacement occurred after the failed prophecy in 1980 when members began downplaying the importance of physical preparedness in favor of getting back to the basics of the Baha'i faith. The back-to-the-basics movement reemerged after the second disconfirmation in 1986. By 1995 the culture of dissonance reduction had become so entrenched in the BUPC that hardly anyone was concerned about the imminence of the Apocalypse.

Our study of the BUPC, like all case studies, is more suggestive than conclusive. However, the data reveal two important weaknesses in Festinger et al.'s dissonance theory of prophecy failure. First, the theory ignores a fundamental structural distinction between leaders and followers: the leaders who make prophecies may respond to their failure quite differently than their followers. Second, the theory fails to address the long-range effects of prophecy failure. Our findings suggest that repeated failures cause a decline in both the fervor before the predictions and the disappointment afterward, until the goal of preparing for the apocalypse is finally displaced by more ordinary and achievable objectives.

NOTES

1. Balch observed the BUPC over an eight-month period before and after the 1980 prediction. Mahnke (1987) spent eight months with the group in 1986 when

members expected Halley's comet to collide with the earth. Domitrovich took part in BUPC activities between 1990 and 1995 when most of the failed prophecies occurred, and Morrison observed the group for almost twelve months in 1995 and 1996.

2. The development of the BUPC is a classic example of the psychopathological model of cult formation, in which religious founders assume a messianic role to compensate for a devastating collapse of their self-image and social world (Bainbridge and Stark 1979).

3. Leroy Anderson, the leading expert on the Morrisites (Anderson 1988), disputes Chase's claims about Williams's Deer Lodge prophecy. In a personal conversation, Anderson told Balch that Williams never specified August 9, 1969, as the date for the Second Coming of Christ. The date simply happened to be the day of the last annual Morrisite gathering.

4. Jensen died unexpectedly on August 6, 1996. Chase has taken the helm and members seem to be taking the transition in stride. Neither the group's apocalyptic rhetoric nor its routine activities appear to have changed. However, Jensen's death is likely to have serious repercussions because Chase is disliked by some influential longtime members.

5. The first IBC was established by Shoghi Effendi, the Guardian of the Baha'i Faith. The BUPC's IBC was an exact replica of the first.

6. These disputes usually revolved around the Guardianship. Ever since the 1970s, Jensen had claimed that Mason Remey's son, Pepe, was the Guardian, but Pepe steadfastly refused the title. After Pepe died in 1994, Jensen began hinting that Chase might be the next Guardian, but many members disagreed.

References

Anderson, C. Leroy. 1988. *Joseph Morris and the Saga of the Morrisites*. Logan, UT: Utah State University.

Baha'u'llah. 1931. *The Book of Certitude*, translated by Shoghi Effendi. Willmette, IL: Baha'i Publishing Trust.

Bainbridge, William Sims, and Rodney Stark. 1979. "Cult Formation: Three Compatible Models." *Sociological Analysis* 40: 283–295.

Balch, Robert W., Gwen Farnsworth, and Sue Wilkins. 1983. "When the Bombs Drop: Reactions to Disconfirmed Prophecy in a Millennial Sect." *Sociological Perspectives* 26: 137–158.

Blau, Peter M., and W. Richard Scott. 1962. *Formal Organizations: A Comparative Approach*. San Francisco: Chandler.

Chase, Neal. 1990. *Ezekiel's Temple in Montana*. Private publication: Baha'i Center, 1830 South Avenue, Missoula, MT.

Festinger, Leon, Henry Riecken, and Stanley Schachter. 1956. *When Prophecy Fails*. Minneapolis: The University of Minnesota.

Hewitt, John P., and Randall Stokes. 1975. "Disclaimers." *American Sociological Review* 40: 1–11.

Jensen, Leland. 1979. *The Most Mighty Document*. Private publication: Baha'i Center, 1830 South Avenue, Missoula, MT.

Lyman, Sanford M., and Marvin B. Scott. 1968. "Accounts." *American Sociological Review* 33: 46–62.

Mahnke, Barbara Lynn. 1987. *Prophetic Failure: A Re-Testing of the Festinger, Riecken and Schachter Study of Disconfirmed Prophecy in a Millennial Cult*. Unpublished thesis. Missoula, MT: The University of Montana.

Secularizing the Millennium

Secularizing the Millennium
Survivalists, Militias, and the New World Order

 Philip Lamy

Timothy McVeigh and Terry Nichols, arrested in connection with the April 19, 1995, bombing of the Alfred P. Murrah Federal Building, are purported to be responsible for the deaths of 168 people, including nineteen children, in one of the worst acts of domestic terrorism the United States has experienced. The bombing in Oklahoma City magnified attention on paramilitary extremists of the far right, including the so-called "militia movement" with which

McVeigh and Nichols allegedly had been associated in Kingman, Arizona. In the next few weeks Americans learned a lot about the militia movement and a growing paramilitary, antigovernment subculture that had literally exploded in the country. These extremists were armed and angry at the U.S. government for eroding the rights of American citizens; they espoused a "patriotic" and separatist philosophy; they practiced survivalism, or disaster preparedness, and predicted the collapse of civilization; and they feared that a conspiracy to create a socialist one-world government and a "new world order" was unfolding.

Militia leaders and supporters pointed to Ruby Ridge, where in 1992 a white supremacist named Randy Weaver had resisted arrest on illegal weapons charges, and so had been "attacked" by United States marshals. During a shoot-out and subsequent standoff, Weaver's wife, his fourteen-year-old son, and a U.S. marshal were killed. There also had been the tragic events in Waco, Texas, in the spring of 1993, where an apocalyptic sect called the Branch Davidians, led by David Koresh, a man who claimed to be the messiah, came into fatal contact with federal law enforcement agencies of the FBI and the Bureau of Alcohol, Tobacco and Firearms (ATF), once again over the alleged possession of illegal firearms. "Ruby Ridge" and "Waco" became rallying cries for a millenarian movement comprised of Americans who were losing patience with their government and federal law enforcement and were taking up arms, joining paramilitary organizations such as the militias, and practicing survivalism in preparation for the Apocalypse.

For "secular" millennialists the Apocalypse will most likely be man-made—brought about by social, economic, or industrial collapse, environmental degradation, race war, civil war, or nuclear war. Salvation may not be in the hands of a messiah but in the preparations of the individual. Survivalism—the philosophy and practice of disaster preparedness—is an example of secular millennialism. To survivalist-oriented individuals and groups such as the militias, the Patriot Movement, *Soldier of Fortune* magazine, and the Unabomber, evil is represented by the government and big business, the mass media, technology, the entire complex industrial society, and the greatly feared emerging "new world order." The mix of survivalism with apocalypticism—as doomsayers take up arms, hide out in the country's hinterlands, and start throwing bombs at the "system"—reflects a secularization of millennialism, an increasingly popular and combustible mix.

Secularizing the Millennium

Today millennial expressions are found not only in revitalized messianic movements like the Branch Davidians, but in groups that appear, at least on the surface, not to be religious in orientation. Secular millennialism is principally a nonreligious set of prophecies that have been identified in a wide variety of political and revolutionary movements throughout history (Cohn 1957; Hobsbawm 1959; Hyams 1974; Bellah 1967; Lamy 1992; Greil and Robbins 1994). In an important book on millenarian movements entitled *Primitive Rebels* (1959), historian Eric Hobsbawm outlined the basic differences between religious and secular millenarian movements. The classic religious movements, best represented by those that have periodically developed in the history of Christianity, have three main features. First, there is a total rejection of the present evil world and a belief in its imminent demise and replacement by a more humane and just one. Second, religious millennialists believe a messiah will return to build the new utopian world through supernatural action. Third, there is a fundamental vagueness concerning how the new world will come about, including the actual timing and sequence of events, since most of this will be caused by supernatural intervention.

Hobsbawm contrasts the religiously inspired millenarian movements with the more secular forms, which primarily lack supernatural elements, especially the belief that the Apocalypse will be engineered by God and that the millennium will be ushered in by the Second Coming of Christ. Instead, secular millennialists build an organization of ideology, politics, and an alternative plan for society. They also view the collapse of civilization as imminent, and hope to hasten its demise so as to institute a new historic period. For secular millenarian movements evil is represented not by supernatural forces but by human ones, generally those who rule or persecute them. Secularists, however, can adopt apocalyptic imagery and ideas to frame their beliefs and actions, thus instilling a fervor in followers that closely approximates that of the classical millennialist. For example, survivalists often speak of the imminent collapse of civilization and "nuclear Armageddon" with the zeal of a doomsday prophet. On the other hand, religious movements can adopt secular ideas by interpreting current events through the prism of the classical myth that Revelation, for example, provides. Some Christian fundamentalists confidently predict that the millennium will be ushered in by nuclear war, economic collapse, environmental destruction, or a combination of them all, "if that's God's will." Likewise, the Branch Davidians stockpiled weapons and food in a survivalist fashion in anticipation of the tribulations and Armageddon. Hobsbawm also suggests that between the "pure" or classical millenarian movement and the more secular kind, all manner of intermediate groups are possible.

This appears to be the case in American culture today, where elements from the classical apocalyptic tradition merge with modern and secular forms such as survivalism, producing a strange array of "postmodern" millennial phenomena. Survivalism is a "practical" approach to disasters—natural, man-made, or supernatural—because it addresses the physical survival of nuclear war, economic collapse, environmental degradation, race war, or some other major societal disaster, through crisis relocation, the stockpiling of food and weapons, and the practice of survival strategies. Most survivalists are convinced that the current social, ecological, and industrial world order is corrupt and moribund. Furthermore, many believe that the U.S. government and United Nations are controlled by an international elite set to create a slave-like, "socialist" new world order. Survivalists have taken steps to prepare for the collapse of civilization and the subsequent wars, economic and environmental degradation, and other "tribulations" that are likely to ensue.

Survivalism provides a modern site where the millennial myth has "fractured"—its symbols and meanings reproduced and redefined through the beliefs and experiences of a militant right-wing millennialism. In certain ways survivalism reflects the severe downside of the millennial myth. The survivalist philosophy speaks of mass destruction and mass death. It is not interested in reforming the system; the collapse of civilization is imminent. However, it does offer a plan of action—a kind of personal redemption or self-salvation—in the manner of surviving the great destruction of the current order and living on to build a new and better one.

THE MILLENNIAL MYTH

Perhaps the most famous example of apocalypticism is the Christian Apocalypse or Revelation of John. The final book in the Bible, Revelation was probably written in the Roman Emperor Domitian's reign in A.D. 95, when Christians were being persecuted for their unpatriotic refusal to worship the deified governor. John of Patmos, Revelation's author, saw Rome as the Antichrist, and he wrote to strengthen the faithfuls' resistance to engaging in public rituals that honored the emperor's divinity. Written in a literary style that only the initiated (presumably the author's original audience) would fully understand, Revelation is the least understood and most misinterpreted book in the Bible. However, it is also one of its most influential.

Like Jewish apocalypticists of the Greco-Roman era, John saw the Messiah appearing amid a series of catastrophic events culminating in the near success of the Antichrist, the evil false prophet who, during the final days, rises in leadership to deceive the world. The Messiah destroys the Antichrist, brings redemption for the chosen, and establishes a new spiritual world beginning with the millennium. Revelation presents the Roman persecutions of Christians as the beginning of a universal war between the forces of good and evil. While Revelation has no single indisputable meaning, its very ambiguity has left it open to numerous interpretations and has imbued it with the power and persistence of myth.

While a great number of volumes have interpreted the vast complexities of Revelation, some of the more outstanding visions and striking symbols can be summarized under the following themes: Tribulation; the Dragons, Beasts, and Antichrist; Babylon; Redemption; Armageddon; and Millennium. Plagues of famine, disease, earthquakes, and war visited on humankind by God or other supernatural forces represent the Tribulation that will accompany the endtimes. Revelation is also populated by demonic beasts, dragons, and the Antichrist—different personifications of Satan that plague and corrupt humankind. Armageddon expresses the militaristic and moral imagery of great battles and final war with the demonic hosts. Babylon is the metaphor for the ancient city, reflected in Revelation as the rich, sinful, and corrupted whore (and people) who had fallen away from God. Redemption refers to the belief that a savior or messiah (Jesus Christ) will return to redeem the chosen and damn the cursed. The last feature is the promise of the millennium, a new utopian world transformed by supernatural action.

The millennial myth is a symbolic form of belief that acts as a powerful metaphor for real human events. It provides a context in which to interpret current events and give meaning and direction to people's lives. The myth is like a floating framework for explaining the "big picture" for both religious and secular millenarian movements and all manner of "intermediate groups." By examining the paramilitary and survivalist subculture as expressed through *Soldier of Fortune* magazine, the militia and Patriot movements, and the "Unabomber's Manifesto," I will demonstrate how elements of the millennial myth take secular forms in adaptation to the current age. In contrast, I will show how religious millennial groups, such as the Branch Davidians or the Christian right, adapt their beliefs to the current events of the day, often taking forms similar to the secularists.

TRIBULATION: FEAR AND LOATHING IN LAS VEGAS

The age-old battle against tyranny raged on at the 1995 *Soldier of Fortune* Convention and Exposition held at the Sands Hotel and Casino in Las Vegas in the fall of 1995.[1] Celebrating its twentieth anniversary, *Soldier of Fortune Magazine: The Journal of Professional Adventurers* (*SOF*) brings together an odd assortment of characters, including mercenaries, survivalists, militiamen and women, and all manner of paramilitary patriots, antigovernment zealots, and would-be Rambos. For five days and four nights more than 500 conventioneers, many in fatigues or other military dress, attended seminars on combat weaponry and survival strategies in the morning, fired machine guns and discussed "Grass Roots Activism" in the afternoon, and debated the politics of the "new world order" over drinks and blackjack in the evenings. Gun enthusiasts competed in "the world's premier three gun shooting match," while other conventioneers competed in pugil-stick fighting, a pool-side paintball gun shoot-out, or explored "The Warrior's Way." At the *SOF* Exposition Center more than one hundred exhibitors hawked paramilitary and survivalist weaponry, equipment, literature, videos, services, even "isolated rural properties." Paladin Press, publishers of "the Action Library," displayed dozens of their best-selling books and videos, including *Fallout Survival, New I.D. in America, The Ultimate Sniper,* and *State of the Art Survival Caching.*

The temper of the 1995 *SOF* Convention seemed quieter than the patriotism and bravado displayed at the 1990 Convention, held during the Persian Gulf War, but it also seemed angrier and more bitter (Lamy 1992). In April there had been the Oklahoma City bombing, and the intense focus it had brought on the militia movement and related organizations like *Soldier of Fortune*. A congressional hearing was currently underway regarding possible FBI abuses in the 1992 shoot-out at Ruby Ridge, Iowa. And there had been Waco; the April 1993 tragedy is viewed by many on the survivalist right, including many at the *SOF* Convention, as a vicious and murderous attack on a small, independent American church by fascist law enforcement agents of the American government.

For the past twenty years it was tyrants like Idi Amin, Moammar Gadaffi, the Ayatollah Khomeini, Saddam Hussein, and the former Soviet Union that infected the world, according to *Soldier of Fortune*. And while international tyrants still exist, *SOF* has turned it sights increasingly inward—at the U.S. government and federal law enforcement agencies, especially the FBI and the now-infamous ATF. Distrust, anger, and fear of the government was evident throughout the convention. It was in every conventioneers' packet in a warning from publisher Robert K. Brown that "the ATF and the Clinton Administration are bitterly and dangerously hostile to the law-abiding gun owners of this country. At Waco and elsewhere they have demonstrated an entire lack of concern for legality and the Constitutional rights of the ordinary citizen." Brown fears that the *SOF* Convention may be seen by government as an ideal setting for a sting or entrapment. Brown admonished conventioneers to "Always, always, always keep in mind that the person with whom you are talking may be an employee of a federal or other law-enforcement agency. You don't have to explain what you didn't say. Just because you're paranoid doesn't mean that they aren't plotting against you."[2]

A seminar called "The Militarization of Law Enforcement" focused on a possible military takeover of law enforcement agencies. *SOF* reporter Jim Pate (who briefly negotiated with the antigovernment Montana Freemen during the spring 1996 standoff) pointed to the collapse of the Soviet Union and America's large, expensive, and outdated military as the root of the problem. A defense lawyer for the surviving Branch Davidians presented photographs of the Waco fire allegedly taken by FBI helicopters ("and never before seen by the public"), which purported to show military vehicles methodically tearing down the Branch Davidian compound in a "seek and destroy" military mission. Panelists concluded that at Ruby Ridge, Waco, and elsewhere paramilitary police groups have routinely used military tactics to handle domestic crime and order situations with disastrous results. Said one member of the audience, "Our law enforcement agencies have turned on the American people. Along with gun control this is the next step in the emergence of an American police state."

At a seminar entitled "Regaining the Pioneer Spirit," survivalist and radio talk show host Bob Speer said that "the U.S. government had become the new Evil Empire, and it looks to me like the entire social order is going to unravel." This is why he had taken on the "ministry" of talk radio to teach survival skills and values. Called *The Preparedness Hour*, Speer's radio show is carried on the USA Patriot Network. At the exposition center, the Militia of Montana had an exhibit featuring an extensive book, pamphlet, and video library. Books included *The New World Order: Takeover America, Blueprint for Survival,* and *Citizen Soldier*. For videos, one could buy *The Countdown has Begun, The True Story of Waco,* and *Millennium 2,000*. There were Militia of Montana baseball caps with the signature "MOM—the Mother of all Militias." And there were MOM T-shirts—including one that stated simply, "Angry White Guy." Bumper stickers proclaimed, "Don't let Clinton Gore your Gun Rights," "I Love my Country, but I Hate my Government," and "The U.N.—Peace through Terror."

Claiming more than one million subscribers worldwide, *Soldier of Fortune* is the most popular periodical in the industry and subculture of survivalism (Coates 1987; Lamy 1992; Gibson 1994).[3] Published out of Boulder, Colorado, *SOF* is a venture begun by Robert K. Brown. A former Army special forces team leader during the Vietnam War and a lieutenant colonel in the Army Reserve, Brown is an active member of the National Rifle Association and an ardent American nationalist and anticommunist. His magazine reflects these interests. Blending state-of-the-art weapons with military action, espionage, survivalism, and right-wing politics, *SOF* now dominates an extensive paramilitary and survivalist literature and has become a main player among gun magazines. In addition, it has infused new energy into the subculture of American survivalists.

The paramilitary and survivalist "market" that *Soldier of Fortune* caters to is more than a catalog for American gun enthusiasts and military-minded doomsayers. Like the survivalist subculture from which it grew, *SOF* expresses a unique American view of the world, where soldiers of fortune fight the never-ending battle against international and domestic "tyranny," and where citizen soldiers practice survivalism in defense of the "American way" and in preparation for social collapse, foreign invasion, or "nuclear Armaggedon." While *Soldier of Fortune* is not generally mistaken for a religious tract, apocalyptic symbols and images permeate its pages. Through reports of military conflicts around the world, advertisements and classifieds, and most recently the *SOF* home page on the Internet, the world as seen by *SOF* is a world caught in a "cosmic war," on the brink of massive destruction and death.

In Revelation (Revised Standard Edition) the classic image of the tribulations that are to accompany the endtimes is the "Four Horsemen of the Apocalypse" (Revelation 6:1–8). Bearers of conquest, slaughter, famine, and death, the Four

Horsemen often ride through the pages of *SOF*. Especially in advertisements and on T-shirts and posters, the symbols and images of the apocalypse provide the millennial message of *Soldier of Fortune*. One popular T-shirt from over the years shows the Fourth Horseman (Death) cloaked in a hooded black robe and clutching a smoking Uzi: "Liberty or Death" the caption reads. Another *SOF* T-shirt image shows Death galloping up behind a soldier of fortune clutching an AK-47. The right hand of Death is outstretched and guiding the head of the soldier. The caption reads "Death Rides a Pale Horse." Fragments of the American millennial myth, the paramilitary "Horsemen" provide a symbolic context for *SOF* to express its unique mythology of world conflict and American destiny.[4]

Soldier of Fortune focuses on the dark side of the millennial myth, the part that speaks of war, destruction, and death. But it also sees America as the primary defender of freedom in the world, whose crusade is the battle against tyranny and the preservation and benevolent expansion of the American way of life. Ultimately, redemption for Americans will come in fighting the great tyrants and evil forces in the world and surviving into the next millennium, where every individual fends for himself in a world dominated by "survival of the fittest" values and practices. If a new world order is to be built, it will be the "fit" who will build it.

While less overtly religious than millenarian groups like the Branch Davidians or the Aryan Nations, the survivalist worldview in *Soldier of Fortune* is tribulationist. According to *SOF*, domestic and international instability is likely to increase in the near future and military and paramilitary conflicts will continue into the new world "disorder." At home, poverty, crime, and disease will persist and intensify as long as welfare and immigration continue unabated. Government intrusion into the lives of ordinary citizens, through the steady erosion of gun rights, will further undermine the domestic order and Americans' faith in the nation's leaders. There's a bad time ahead, *SOF* tells its readers, and you must be prepared to survive it. In these ways *Soldier of Fortune* and the survivalist subculture it reflects can be read as part of a secular apocalyptic movement in the United States.

DRAGONS, BEASTS, AND THE NEW WORLD ORDER

The August 1992 gunfight and standoff between white supremacist and survivalist Randy Weaver and federal authorities at Weaver's Ruby Ridge, Idaho, ranch, was a key event in the recent growth of the militia movement. The actions of the FBI, federal marshals, and the ATF were viewed by many right-wing gun owners as "Gestapo"-like, designed to disarm Americans and take away individual rights in the name of law and order. For years, voices on the right had been warning of increasing government powers and intrusion into Americans' lives. The "attack" on Ruby Ridge showed just how far federal law enforcement was willing to go in order to disarm gun-owning Americans, even to the point of murdering innocent women and children. Less than eight months later the sensational incident at Waco involving the Branch Davidians and David Koresh confirmed fears, if Ruby Ridge hadn't already, that the U.S. government and law enforcement agencies especially were out of control and had become downright tyrannical. In the aftermath of Ruby Ridge and Waco, the survivalist and paramilitary subculture responded. In protests, editorials, letters to their representatives, in calls to radio talk shows, and over the Internet, survivalists and paramilitarists attacked government law enforcers as brutal thugs who were stomping on the rights of American citizens.

Calls to "abolish" and "disarm" the ATF and to investigate the motives and actions of federal authorities, including those of Janet Reno, came from all quarters on the right. The FBI and ATF are particularly loathed by the gun-toting paramilitary culture. Because it must enforce laws that many American gun owners find abhorrent, including the Brady Bill requirement for a five-day waiting period before purchasing a gun, the ban on assault rifles, and legislation in many states forbidding concealment of weapons—federal law enforcement has come to be demonized as an evil agent of larger sinister forces conspiring in government and, indeed, the world, to take away Americans' most basic rights.

In the rhetoric and imagery of the survivalist subculture, the U.S. government and particular agencies have acquired the persona of the evil demons who populate Revelation. In Revelation, the dragons, beasts, and Antichrist are symbolic representatives of the arch-opponents of Christianity. Of particular interest is the seven-headed dragon: a composite of apocalyptic beasts who persecutes a pregnant women dressed in the sun, moon, and the stars, presumably those faithful to Christ (Revelation 12:1–17). The creature's multiple heads reflect the many deceivers who serve Satan. The beast with "ten horns and seven heads" probably symbolized Rome to first-Century Christians, the earthly focus of Satan's power (Revelation 13:8). Another beast is identified as the "serpent of old" and the "red Dragon" (Revelation 12:9; Genesis 3:1,

15–15). A third, two-horned beast (Revelation 13:11–17) may represent the Roman priesthood that persecuted early Christians and helped enforce emperor worship among them.

To those who plug into the millennial myth, the U.S. government is the secular equivalent of the seven-headed dragon. Its several heads are reflected in the ATF, FBI, IRS, EPA, and the whole alphabet soup of federal agencies that feed the ravenous appetite of the government beast. Some on the militant right have likened federal law enforcement to "jack-booted thugs," as the NRA did, or to "fascists" and "Gestapo," as the militias, *Soldier of Fortune* magazine, and former Watergate burglar and conservative radio personality G. Gordon Liddy have.[5] The red dragon and the two-horned beast are demonic metaphors too, for international organizations like the World Bank and the United Nations, who right-wing conspiracy theorists believe are set on undermining the power of the U.S. in order to impose upon it the dictates of a world government.

The belief in the international conspiracy to build a new world socialist order is a central feature of the so-called Patriot movement, which has existed on the margins of American society for decades, but came to the surface in the wake of Ruby Ridge, Waco, and Oklahoma City. These and other recent events have brought the ideas of the Patriot movement into the mainstream and before a larger audience, attracting militias, survivalists, and other antigovernment groups like the Montana Freemen. Providing a Christian-based "constitutional" philosophy, it offers an alternative plan for rebuilding American society "after the collapse." Through networks created on the Internet, via an extensive literature that includes all manner of desktop-published books, pamphlets and newsletters, videos, and cassette tapes, and through talk radio programs and grassroots organizations, Patriots, militia members, and white supremacists (who want to preserve white Christian American racial and cultural purity) are finding common ground.

While Patriot leaders condemned the attack on innocent people in the Oklahoma City bombing, many intimated that they weren't surprised by the event, given the viciousness of federal law enforcement actions in recent years. To them, the bombing demonstrated just how far Americans were going to be pushed. As its name implies, the Patriot movement espouses a strong nationalist philosophy, and reflects the views of "super"-patriotic Americans, who see America as a Christian land promised to God-fearing Americans by the Almighty. Older and more broadly based than the militias, but organized in the same loose fashion, the Patriot movement has reached out in recent years to the emerging militia movement.

Some Patriots fancy themselves "Constitutionalists" and latter-day Thomas Jeffersons, employing legal and constitutional analysis of the nation's founding documents, including the Constitution and its amendments, which they believe to have been inspired by God. The Montana Freemen tried to use constitutional analysis and "common law" procedures and courts to sanction their flouting of local, state, and federal laws, in their attempt to create a separatist and autonomous "township," resulting in the spring 1996 standoff with the FBI. Linda Thompson, a lawyer and the leader of a Patriot organization in Indiana, gained national headlines in 1994 with her "Declaration of Independence," sent out over the Internet and mailed to hundreds of sympathetic individuals and groups that comprise the growing survivalist movement. Like the Declaration of 1776, "the Declaration of Independence 1994" is a call for revolution. Because the current American government had usurped and abused its powers and had become destructive to the rights of citizens, Thompson writes, "It is the Right of the People to alter or to abolish it, and to institute new government" (1994, 1).

Many in the Patriot movement fear that America has reached a dangerous crossroads. The values that have made this nation a beacon to the world have weakened and are dangerously close to unraveling. America is becoming seduced by the values of a God-less secular humanism, with its values of multiculturalism, globalism, and cultural relativism, which survivalist and militia group members believe will dilute and even obliterate (white, Christian) American culture. In different versions of the new world order conspiracy theory weaved by militias, Patriots, and survivalists, the proponents of this new world government are centered in the United Nations and other international organizations, such as global think tanks, multinational corporations, and cultural or humanitarian organizations. The aim of the conspiracy is to build a new global order controlled by a cadre of powerful economic, political, and cultural elites, bent on creating a global socialism. Global socialism will require Americans to share their wealth and resources more equitably with the rest of the world, inevitably resulting in the lowering of the living standards of Americans to those of the Third World. The laws and rules that govern the global order and are instituted by the new world government will take precedence over the federal government of the United States, and Americans will be taking orders from foreigners.

The terms "globalism" or "globalization" strike terror into the hearts of right-wing conspiracy theorists. They maintain that these "internationalists" are comprised of elites who believe it is necessary for highly educated and "globally aware" individuals from all nations to rule the new world order. International organizations like the Trilateral Commission, the World Bank, and the United Nations comprise the tentacles of the dragons and beasts of Revelation "set forth to deceive the nations" by creating a one-world government and a new world Babylon. Further down the road of the survivalist right are racist and neo-Nazi paramilitary groups, who see Jews behind the conspiracy to create a one-world government and a new global socialist order. It is the Jewish Antichrist, or ZOG (the Zionist Occupation Government), that rules in Washington, taking its orders from internationalist Jews in Israel, the United Nations, and the Fortune 500.[6]

BABLYON THE GREAT IS FALLEN

In Revelation, the group of "deceived" or "fallen away" people, who become the followers of the Antichrist, and the seat of the devil's realm on earth, is often referred to as Babylon. The destruction of Babylon is the metaphor for the final destruction of the world, which ushers in the millennium (Revelation 14:8, 16:19, 18:2, 18:21). While Rome, primarily, had been identified as Babylon by early Christians, millenarian movements throughout history have likened Babylon to the nation and culture of their oppressors. In the subculture of survivalism Babylon takes on various guises; America, Western culture, and most recently, the new world order. For the Unabomber, it is the vast industrial and technological system that is the Babylon of modern humanity, whose demise, he predicts, is imminent.

The Unabomber first struck on May 26, 1978, when a suspicious package addressed to an engineering professor at Northwestern's Technological Institute in Washington was turned over to local police, who opened it, detonating a bomb that injured a police officer. Until the arrest of alleged Unabomber Theodore Kaczynski on April 10, 1996, a series of package bombs had been sent to eight states from California to Connecticut, killing three individuals and injuring twenty-three others, some severely. Each bomb was delivered to a well-known scientist or corporate executive for their supposed role in helping to advance the decadent modern world. According to the Unabomber, the current industrial and technological "system" reflects the modern Babylon. The "Manifesto," a 35,000-word analysis of the state and fate of the modern technological and industrial society, is a most intriguing piece of the secular apocalypse. While the Unabomber does not include a great deal of discussion of Christianity, religion, or other supernatural elements in his visions of the decay of Western civilization, the apocalyptic metaphor for Babylon can be seen in the modern technological society, "which has led to wide-spread psychological suffering," has "inflicted severe damage on the natural world," and "will probably lead to greater social disruption, and psychological suffering . . . even in 'advanced' countries" (1995, para. 1).[7]

The Unabomber attacks much of medical science, genetic engineering, and biotechnology. He also attacks computers, mass communications, government and corporate bureaucracies, and the modern scientific and technological culture. He calls the activities of the scientist and technologist, like those of the university professor, "surrogate" activities—work with no meaningful purpose or value, but engaged in for the "personal" fulfillment the scientist or engineer receives from the work. The "benefit to humanity" explanation, the Unabomber says, does not hold water, because the only benefit scientists get out of their work is in seeing their theories put into practice. Like those who believe in a cabal of internationalists, corporations, and Jews who conspire to control nations through the creation of a slave-like new world order, the Unabomber paints a picture of technocrats, scientists, and "leftists" conspiring to advance the destructive and controlling forces of modernization, development, and political correctness.

As with the Luddites of the early nineteenth century, a movement of English handicraftsmen who rioted against and destroyed the new machinery of the Industrial Revolution that was replacing them, the Unabomber rails against modern society and the institutions of science and technology that are replacing an older and better way of life. Much like the rural survivalist, the Unabomber idolizes nature and living interdependently with it. He also believes that individualism, autonomy, and the development of the abilities to survive by one's own wits comprise the "right" way to live, in comparison to working as a cog in the machine run by the power elite's system. The Unabomber calls for a return to nature and a more natural way of life. "Nature takes care of itself," says the Unabomber, suggesting that in the end nature will get its way. Nature was a "spontaneous" creation, he reasons, and it existed long before any human society. When humans finally evolved, many different kinds of human societies coexisted with nature for centuries without doing it much harm. But with the Industrial Revolution the effect of human society on nature was devastating.

The Unabomber calls for a revolution against the industrial system and outlines the ways to do it. He emphasizes that the revolution is not a "political" revolution: "Its object will be the overthrow not of governments but the economic and technological basis of the present society" (para. 3). Still, he employs apocalyptic language when he speaks of the collapse of society and when he creates evil and demonic characters out of the scientists, "technophiles," bureaucrats, and other cultural elites who perpetuate technological progress and the "psychology of leftism," and who most benefit from the existing social order. He calls on revolutionaries to increase the stress within the social system so that it will break down or be sufficiently weakened that a revolution against it becomes possible. He argues that revolutionaries will be unable to bring the system down unless it is already in deep trouble, which he believes it is. While there's a good chance that it will collapse sooner or later, he argues that the bigger the system grows the harder it will fall, and the more disastrous it will be for the planet's ecosystem and the survival of the human race. "So," he concludes, "it may be that revolutionaries, by hastening the onset of the breakdown, will be reducing the extent of the disaster" (para. 168).

In the meantime, he advises, it will be necessary to develop and propagate an ideology that opposes technology and the industrial society so that when the system is teetering on the brink, many will herald its ultimate collapse. Similar to the classical millennialist, the Unabomber believes the collapse of the current (industrial) world order is necessary to save humanity and bring on a new and better world. Hence the letter and package bombs, which the Unabomber believes further add to the chaos of a civilization on the eve of destruction. In the end, the collapse of civilization will be a good thing and we will all be cleansed by the event—at least those who are able to survive.

The Unabomber makes an interesting and pointed argument about the state of modern society regarding the effects of rapid social change and the transformation and fragmentation that advanced industrial society seems to be creating or contributing to. But why does the Unabomber kill? Quite simply, to be heard. Through large and complex political and economic organizations, the mass media and "information industry" are under the control of the system, says the Unabomber. They will never hand over control to the people. While anyone with a little money can have something printed, or can distribute it on the Internet, it will be swamped by the volume of material already there and multiplying hourly. Most Americans aren't even paying attention, he laments, mesmerized by TV, materialism, and a decadent way of life created by a mass entertainment culture. Revolution is easier than reform, argues the Unabomber, but "In order to get our message before the public with some chance of making a lasting impression, we've had to kill people" (para. 96). The only way out is by a revolution, says the Unabomber, though not necessarily an armed uprising. The radical and fundamental change in the nature of society will come about with the collapse of the industrial-technological system.

The Unabomber sees parallels between the current global situation and Babylon of Revelation and so many other civilizations in history that have collapsed during the advanced stages of their development. "History shows that leisured aristocracies tend to become decadent . . . aristocracies that have no need to exert themselves usually become bored, hedonistic and demoralized, even though they have power" (para. 34). The Unabomber is quite explicit about the problems caused by the propagandistic and manipulative mass media and popular culture. Throughout the "Manifesto" the Unabomber employs a form of social and cultural criticism called the mass culture critique. It is an argument that has been made by many critics of modernization in the past. The critique has focused on mass culture as a combination of elements corroding the cultural diversity essential to a pluralistic society. Mass (and popular) culture is seen as a form of social decay, the "bread and circuses" of a culture in decline. The mass culture critique can be viewed as an apocalyptic idea that continues to inform theories about our modern society and its way of life.

In his book, *Bread and Circuses: Theories of Mass Culture as Social Decay* (1983), Patrick Brantlinger traces the history and persistence of literary and social criticism regarding mass culture and shows that this form of "negative classicism"—the idea that mass culture and mass society lead to the decay of civilization—is both apocalyptic mythology and political ideology. It is an apocalyptic philosophy that pervades all levels of public consciousness today, from scholarly and intellectual writing to the mass media themselves. Mass culture is a metaphor of Babylon, behind which lies a concern for the preservation of civilization as a whole. While Rome, the Catholic Church, and Western civilization in general have been past symbols of Babylon, today the American government, the new world order, and the industrial and technological system have become the secular equivalents of the sinful harlot whose fall has been prophesied since ancient times.

REDEMPTION: SALVATION THROUGH SURVIVALISM

Redemption generally refers to the Second Coming of Christ. Also called messian-ism, this belief holds that a savior or "messiah" will bring salvation for the chosen and damnation for the wicked. In the mix of militant right-wing politics and fun-damentalist apocalyptic lore, there was bound to arise a messiah—or at least someone who claimed to be the messiah. Among the Christian fundamentalist churches the expectation for Christ's Second Coming is still an expectation. How-ever, for others steeped in right-wing Christianity and the survivalist right, a messiah, or at least a martyr, had come, and he was David Koresh. To them, Koresh was crucified for his religious beliefs, and he has become a martyr for the cause of government-fearing militias, Patriots, white supremacists, and other survivalists.

Koresh and his church's view of the larger world rested on classical pillars of the millennial myth, which provided not only a frame of reference for current events but a guide for members' behavior. For example, the FBI, ATF, and the aggregate of American government were seen by Koresh and his followers as symbols of Babylon. Even while many survivalists saw Koresh as deluded, he still was the head of a church in America. Yet because his church was different from others—they were Christian survivalists who stockpiled food and weapons, presumably in anticipation of Armageddon—they lost their church and their lives because of government intrusion on their most basic rights.

Some Patriot and militia leaders pointed to the ways the Branch Davidian tragedy reflected the Jewish defenders at Masada in A.D. 71, who committed mass suicide rather than surrender to the Romans, by executing women and children and then killing themselves. This has happened in other times as well and was common to the early Christian martyrs, who willingly chose death rather than capitulate to their Roman persecutors. In the case of the Branch Davidians it may never be known whether they committed mass suicide, were killed to give that impression, or whether the fire was caused by accident. But the results did reflect a phenomenon of millennial history, as well as the apoca-lyptic fears of Americans on the militant right. In this way David Koresh and his followers became martyrs for survivalism, whose rights were violated by a vicious militarist government and their goon squads, the FBI and ATF. "Remember Waco" was the most frequently seen bumper sticker at the 1995 *Soldier of Fortune* Convention and Exhibition.

In the aftermath of the tragedy at Waco, the federal government, the ATF, and the FBI took a lot of heat from the public, the media, and Congress. ATF director Steven Higgins and five other top-ranking officials resigned from the agency in the political aftermath. Many Americans not connected to the militant right began to take a second look at the actions of their government and wondered if there wasn't something to all the right-wing paranoia. On April 19, 1995, exactly two years from the day the Branch Davidian church at Mount Carmel went up in flames, the Oklahoma City bombing happened. A note recovered at the scene pointed to the Waco tragedy and the conspiracy of the federal government to destroy the Davidians as the reason for the bombing of the downtown federal office building that morning—an explosion that killed 168 people.

Although there are many examples of millennial Christian symbolism in the subculture of survivalism, the notion of a messianic savior who holds salvation for the true believer does not appeal to many. David Koresh may not have been the messiah as prophesied in the Bible, but he has become a prophet and martyr to the survivalist right of a more secular apocalypse, in which the federal government stands for an American Babylon. In the absence of a messianic savior, a more practical form of "self-salvation" through survivalism has replaced it. In survivalist ideology, salvation comes to the individual through personal defense and disaster preparedness. The other-worldly savior has been transformed into a this-worldly survivor.

ARMAGEDDON: FIGHTING THE GREAT COSMIC EFFORT

In Revelation 16:16, Armageddon is the name of the place where the kings of the earth are to be gathered together by the Dragon, the Beast, and the Antichrist to make war upon God at the end of world history. A Greek translation of the Hebrew *Har Megiddon*, or "Mountain of Megiddo," refers to a famous battlefield in the Plain of Jezreel in Palestine, where many battles of the past were fought. Like Babylon, the physical site of Armageddon is less important than the metaphor for Armageddon as the "spiritual battlefield" and the place where the final showdown takes place between the armies of the Messiah and those of Satan—the forces of light and the forces of darkness. More generally, Armageddon refers to the conflict itself, both the military and ideological battles that mark the endtimes.

Soldier of Fortune is a major site in the survivalist subculture where Armageddon has its fractured expressions. In *Soldier of Fortune* the battle of

Armageddon has been commonly expressed in the symbolism of crusades and holy wars. From the start *sof* was "pro-American" and "anticommunist." Its analyses of the political and military conflicts around the world were framed by its patriotism and American cultural values. It was also framed by the American millennial myth, which saw America as the world's primary defender of freedom and democracy in the world. International military conflict was easily defined by *sof* as a simple philosophical dualism that marked the forces of good from the forces of evil—the secular equivalents of the "forces of light" and the "forces of darkness."

For *Soldier of Fortune* the forces of evil in the world can be lumped under the umbrella heading "tyranny." The *sof* motto is "Death to Tyrants." "International terrorists," "cartel drug lords," "tin-horn dictators," and the "communist monolith" are the labels that *sof* journalists and readers apply to the evil that America and her allies must resist and destroy in the coming battles. It was, of course, the Soviet "Evil Empire" that had been the leading force of tyranny in the world according to *Soldier of Fortune*. For most of *sof*'s history the "Battle of Armageddon" was generally defined in terms of an American-Soviet showdown. The apocalyptic rhetoric in *sof* was especially sharp throughout the 1980s, when Ronald Reagan was in the White House and American covert military actions, such as those exposed in the Iran-Contra affair, became familiar occurrences in the American battle against worldwide communism.

During the closing months of the 1980s, millennial fever peaked in the United States and in other parts of the world. For many Americans the breaching of the Berlin Wall signaled the end of the cold war and the collapse of authoritarian communism. For the truly optimistic it heralded the birth of a new age of peace, freedom, and international cooperation—a "new world order." *sof* also reflected these momentous changes in a positive light. For *sof*, however, these events did not mean the end of war or the start of a utopian new world order. In light of the revolutionary changes that continue to sweep through Eastern Europe, *sof* has had to look elsewhere for the sources of evil in the world. Fortunately for them, there is no shortage of tyrants in the world and *sof* maintains a long and ever-changing list of them: Islamic fundamentalists, Marxist-Leninist revolutionaries, and "tin-pan dictators" battle it out with "freedom fighters" on the world stage that *sof* provides. Into the 1990s the "communist monolith" and the "battle against tyranny" have continued to be planks in *sof* ideology. And these battles will continue, warns *sof*, until the world is made safe for democracy and the "American way."

"It's only appropriate," begins Robert K. Brown in the twentieth-anniversary issue of *Soldier of Fortune*, "that I find myself on the Bosnian border preparing to take a *SOF* team into Sarajevo under the murderous guns of the barbaric Serbs" (Brown 1995, 3). As he had so often done in the past in the name of "participatory journalism," Colonel Brown, editor of *SOF* magazine, was in the midst a murderous international conflict. Fighting the "good fight" with the soldiers and citizens of Sarajevo, the mission of Brown and his *SOF* team was "to hump Scot Air-Pacs — breathing gear for firemen — through Serb lines over Mount Igman, and deliver them to the Sarajevo Fire Department." Brown continues, "Our current operation sums up much of what *SOF* is and has been about over the past 20 years: slashing away at tyrants both foreign and domestic and at the same time not ignoring our 'humanitarian' mission to alleviate some of the world's suffering" (ibid.).

Brown goes on to list all those tyrants with whom *SOF* has "crossed swords," from the now defunct "Evil Empire" to the "politically correct frauds" in Washington to the "barbaric Serbs" in the former Yugoslavia. "For the past 20 years we've tromped with the good guys and the bad guys," writes Brown, "in our quest to get the story first hand. . . . We've been fired upon and fired back . . . and paid a price" in the deaths to *SOF* comrades serving "the cause of freedom." In a nod to "our loyal readers," Brown concludes with an apocalyptic flourish and a reference to the battle of Armageddon: "Without you we would not have been able to forge the swords necessary to gut the dragons we've taken on. Stand by us for the next 20 years and we'll continue to march — sword in hand" (ibid.).

As transfigured in *Soldier of Fortune*, Armageddon is represented by the great cosmic battles against the forces of tyranny that threaten America, its spiritual allies, and "our" way of life. For *SOF*, the future will be a world where peace and democracy and the "American way" thrive, preserved and protected from tyranny by the world's crusaders of light and right — the soldiers of fortune. Like classical Christian millennialists and like the more secular Unabomber, *Soldier of Fortune* rarely expresses its apocalyptic worldview outside of its clarion call for vigilance toward the enemy and its ethic of survival preparation. *SOF* focuses on those areas of the myth that express a near-future of death, war, and survival (Apocalypse, Armageddon, Salvation). More likely, the *SOF* millennium will be a world of domestic and international conflict, where Americans are threatened by foreign and domestic tyrants — "a never-ending battle against tyranny and terrorism" (ibid.).

APOCALYPSE NOW

There is a strong relationship between millenarian movements, especially secular ones, and nationalist movements. While their aspirations may be purely political, nationalist movement leaders often evoke doomsday predictions or a utopian millennium in order to provide a credo and motivation for followers, as well as to bring legitimacy to the sometimes questionable words and actions of their leaders or members. From George Bush's clarion call to preserve the new world order in the Gulf, to Patrick Buchanan's anti-new world order speeches, American forms of nationalism continue to be fueled by millennial rhetoric. Supported by the Christian Coalition and many on the survivalist right, Buchanan's "America First" presidential campaign underscores how the classical, or more clearly religious, forms of millennialism have adapted secular elements in adaptation to current social and political issues.

This is the way the millennial myth works, by providing the stories of apocalyptic texts and interpreting current events through them. When Christian fundamentalists like Jerry Falwell or Pat Robertson suggest that nuclear war, environmental degradation, or AIDS may be God's way of fulfilling scripture, as in the "plagues" unleashed by the Seven Seals of Revelation, a rational understanding of these important social issues and problems becomes challenged by a supernatural or apocalyptic one. Similarly, when militias, survivalists, or *Soldier of Fortune* enthusiasts ascribe apocalyptic language and imagery to their interpretation of current events, they are also transforming the secular into the sacred. In the process a melding of apocalyptic scenarios of the classical religious groups with those of secular millennial types has occured, creating the "intermediate" forms of millennialism we see in the Christian survivalism of the Branch Davidians and the Aryan Nations and in the American "civil millennialism" of George Bush and Patrick Buchanan.[8]

In important ways survivalism represents the downside of the millennial myth, the part that predicts decay, mass destruction, and mass death. But it also prophecies "redemption" in the manner of surviving "the great cosmic battle" and the collapse of civilization and living on to build a new world where independence, individualism, small communities, and greater autonomy will be their rewards—such as the postindustrial world envisioned by the Unabomber. Like the classical myth, this important dual nature is always present. In Revelation we see the terrible side of the myth in the decay of the Tribulation and the destructive war of Armageddon. But we also witness the hope of salvation in the return of the Messiah and the dream of a utopian kingdom in the millennium. This duality provides flexibility for the myth and allows for a wide range of interpretive meaning and staying power. It is also important to point out that the millennial myth is not "monolithic," with a single meaning influencing all in the same way. The power of the millennial myth rests in its protean adaptation to change and its ability to mirror the experiences of many different groups, as the American version of the millennial myth has done throughout American history.

The survivalist ethic is a part of the American millennial myth, the myth of the "individual" and of the pioneer who leads and holds in his hand the destiny of the nation, expanding the "rim of Christendom," by carving a civilization out of the wilderness. Through the millennial myth, many survivalists, militiamen, Patriots, and Christian survivalists see America as the "Redeemer nation"—the primary defender of freedom, democracy, and Christian heritage in the world. When used to justify or legitimate a cause, as in the case of the war with Iraq, the millennial myth becomes a tool for ideological and social control. When used to bomb a federal office building in an act of antigovernment terrorism, it becomes a form of social and political revolt.

Both the paranoia of the survivalist right to the new world order and George Bush's embrace of it during the Persian Gulf War in 1990 reflect the often contradictory nature of contemporary expressions of the millennial myth. With the help of the mass media, which further distort its history and meaning, the myth is freed up; its meaning goes up for grabs, to be manipulated by certain individuals and groups as they see fit, or to be lodged in other sites in the culture, as in Hollywood movies, popular music, best-selling books, and elsewhere in our mass culture.[9] In any case, Americans are receptive to the symbols and images of the millennial myth, if only in fragmented, obscured, or secularized expressions. Indeed, as we have seen with messianic sects like the Branch Davidians, in the Unabomber's secular analysis of global collapse and revolution, and in the antigovernment bombing in Oklahoma City, the effects of apocalyptic thinking can blow up, quite literally, on the rest of society.

NOTES

1. Data were collected at the 1995 *Soldier of Fortune* magazine Twentieth Anniversary Convention and Exposition held at the Sands Hotel and Casino, Las Vegas, Nevada, from September 27 to October 1.

2. Robert Brown, Comments, 1995 *Soldier of Fortune* conventioneers packet, September 27, 1995.

3. *Soldier of Fortune Magazine: The Journal of Professional Adventurers* is published by Omega Group Publications, Boulder, Colorado. While SOF claims more than one million readers worldwide, data collected from ULRICH'S *International Periodical's Directory*, 3rd edition, 1996, list circulation figures of 104,593.

4. According to *Soldier of Fortune* assistant editor Susan Max (SOF field notes, September 15, 1990), SOF art director from 1979 to 1989 was Craig Nunn, a "born again" Christian whose religious values strongly influenced the graphic look and feel of the magazine. Many of the apocalyptic images and symbols in advertisements, T-shirts, and posters were Nunn's creations. A member of a Christian motorcycle club, Nunn was killed in a motorcycle accident in 1989.

5. In light of all the media attention on the militant right after Ruby Ridge, Waco, and Oklahoma City, many old faces on the right reappeared on the national stage as if on cue, including James "Bo" Gritz, ex-Green Beret colonel and Sylvester Stallone's model for Rambo, and G. Gordon Liddy, former Watergate burglar, part-time actor, and host of his own radio talk show. Liddy is another American "patriot" who was "reading the signs" in American society and has become one of the more well-known spokesmen for the militant right; he fans the flames of public discontent on his own talk radio program, one of a growing number on the Patriot Network.

    The USA Patriot Network is a loosely organized group of radio stations, many on shortwave bands linked via satellite to a wider audience, that promotes the agenda of the Patriot movement and has become a beacon to militias, survivalists, and other like-minded individuals and groups. Other new stars in the Patriot constellation include Bob Speer—survivalist, author, *Soldier of Fortune* convention regular, and host of the *Preparedness Hour*. And there's Mark "from Michigan" Koernke; questioned by authorities in the aftermath of the Oklahoma City bombing and later released, Koernke believes that foreign troops stationed in America and allied with the United Nations are ready to take over the United States. Koernke broadcasts on his shortwave radio program, *The Intelligence Report*.

6. For the many groups who hold to this worldview, the plan for these actions—and, it may turn out, for the bombing in Oklahoma City—is contained in the novel *The Turner Diaries*, which was written in 1978 by William Pierce, a member of the neo-Nazi National Alliance. Beginning in 1991, so the story goes, white supremacists start a guerrilla war against ZOG (the Zionist Occupation Government), which rules in Washington. After several years of antigovernment activities, including the destruction of public utilities and the assassination of federal officials, lawmen, and politicians, the rebels eventually overthrow ZOG.

They purge the country of all Jews and other minorities and destroy Israel with ZOG's own nuclear arsenal. As crazy as it sounds, federal authorities believe that *The Turner Diaries* may, in part, have provided both motive and method in the bombing of the federal building in Oklahoma City. The incident bears a striking resemblance to parts of the storyline in *The Turner Diaries*, in which the separatists bomb a federal building in a manner similar to the Oklahoma City blast.

7. In June 1995, the "Unabomber's Manifesto" was sent to the *New York Times* and the *Washington Post*. The Unabomber claimed that unless the "Manifesto" was published, he would continue to kill. FBI agents in charge of the investigation later said that along with the "Manifesto" the Unabomber included a list of potential bombing targets. On the advice of the FBI, who had sought the Unabomber since 1979, the *Post* printed the "Manifesto," with financial support from the *Times* (it can also be found on the Internet), in the hope that it might turn up some leads. While many criticized the *Times,* the *Post,* and the FBI for "giving in" to terrorism, the decision to publish the "Manifesto" in September 1995 appears to be a key event leading to Kaczynski's arrest. Reading the "Manifesto" caused Kaczynski's brother David to link it to writings attributed to Ted that had been discovered by the family at their Lombard, Illinois, home in January 1996. David then alerted the FBI. The complete text of the Unabomber's "Manifesto" as reviewed here appeared on the Internet. The document is referenced by paragraph number.

8. The secular millennial thesis has been adopted by Nathan Hatch (1974, 1977), who applied Robert Bellah's (1967) civil religion thesis to the study of millennialism and thus spoke of "civil millennialism."

9. In *Bread and Circuses: Theories of Mass Culture as Social Decay* (1983), Patrick Brantlinger shows how the apocalypticism of the mass culture critique transcends the specific ideologies and literary content of numerous great thinkers and writers through the ages, including Aristotle and Heraclitas; Marx and Engles; the existentialists Kierkegaard and Nietzsche; the literary critics Arnold, Eliot, Ortega y Gasset, and Mark Twain; "cyclical historians" such as Oswald Spengler; Freud, Jung, and the psychoanalysts; the Frankfurt School theorists; and sociologists Christopher Lasch and Daniel Bell.

REFERENCES

Bellah, Robert N. 1967. "Civil Religion in America." *Daedalus* (Winter 1996): 1–21.
Brantlinger, Patrick. 1983. *Bread and Circuses: Theories of Mass Culture as Social Decay*. Ithaca: Cornell University Press.

Brown, Robert K. 1995. "Two Decades of *Soldier of Fortune.*" *Soldier of Fortune* (October): 3.

Coates, James. 1987. *Armed and Dangerous: The Rise of the Survivalist Right*. New York: Hill and Wang.

Cohn, Norman. 1957. *The Pursuit of the Millennium*. Fairlawn, NJ: Essential Books.

Gibson, William. 1994. *Warrior Dreams: Violence and Manhood in Post-Vietnam America*. New York: Hill and Wang.

Greil, Arthur L., and Thomas Robbins. 1994. "Between the Sacred and the Secular: Research and Theory on Quasi-Religion." *Religion and the Social Order* 4: 1–23.

Hatch, Nathan O. 1974. "The Origins of Civil Millennialism in America: New England Clergymen, War with France, and the Revolution." *William and Mary Quarterly* 31: 417.

———. 1977. *The Sacred Cause of Liberty in Republican Thought and the Millennium in Revolutionary New England*. New Haven: Yale University Press.

Hobsbawm, E. J. 1959. *Primitive Rebels: Studies in Archaic Forms of Social Movements in the Nineteenth and Twentieth Centuries*. New York: Norton.

Holy Bible. 1952. Revised Standard Edition. New York: Harper and Brothers.

Hyams, Edward. 1974. *The Millennium Postponed: Socialism from Sir Thomas More to Mao Tse-tung*. New York: Taplinger.

Lamy, Philip. 1992. "Millennialism in the Mass Media: The Case of *Soldier of Fortune* Magazine." *Journal for the Scientific Study of Religion* 31 (4) (December): 408–424.

Pate, James L. 1995. "Waco Hearings: Somebody's Lying." *Soldier of Fortune* (October): 92.

Pierce, William L. (alias Andrew MacDonald). 1978. *The Turner Diaries*. Hillsboro: National Vanguard Books.

Thompson, Linda. 1994. "Declaration of Independence 1994." Patriot Archives, Internet.

"Unabomber's Manifesto." 1995. *Washington Post*, September 19.

Environmental Apocalypse
The Millennial Ideology of "Earth First!"

6

Martha F. Lee

Concern for the environment is, at its core, a concern for the fate of the earth. Many environmental ideologies are therefore marked by millenarian themes; they understand the planet to be in such danger that species life is threatened, and typically, a transformation of human thought and behavior is perceived as the means through which the world can be reborn. These themes are present in such mainstream documents as the 1972 Club of Rome report, which threatened that "[if] the present growth trends in world population, industrialization, pollution, food production, and resource depletion continue unchanged, the limits to growth on this planet will be reached some time within the next one hundred years" (Meadows et al. 1972, 23). Similarly, Greenpeace was once explicitly millennial. Its image of "the Rainbow Warrior" was drawn from an aboriginal legend that

> there would come a time . . . when the earth would be ravaged of its resources, the sea blackened, the streams poisoned, the deer dropping dead in their tracks. Just before it was too late, the Indian would regain his spirit and teach the white man reverence for the earth, banding together with him to become the Warriors of the Rainbow. (Brown and May 1989, 9)

After experiencing the environmental apocalypse, human civilization will be altered in such a way as to be more environmentally responsible, and often, we are told, more equitable and peaceful. These themes mark virtually all environmental philosophies. They are, however, most concentrated, and therefore most evident, in the ideologies and activities of radical environmental groups.

This article examines one such group in detail. Earth First!, an American movement that began in early 1980 and continues to exist today, provides an excellent example of the coincidence of millenarianism and environmentalism. This article considers the origins of the Earth First! movement, as well as its doctrine and historical development. It finds that although Earth First!'s brand of radical environmentalism initially supported a millenarian belief system, ultimately the two proved incompatible. When pushed to their extreme, radical environmental ideologies understand human beings to be at best the equal of other species, and unable to predict or control the impact of their behavior on the planet. Millenarian belief systems, however, must understand humans to be superior beings, for they are the directors of history. Earth First!'s development illuminates this tension.

THE ORIGINS OF EARTH FIRST!

Millenarian ideologies posit an imminent end to history, and promise that from its ashes, a perfect postapocalyptic world will emerge. The origins of millenarian movements are therefore typically found among the poor and oppressed, who often suffer both multiple and relative deprivation. Such individuals have little to lose from the demise of the present world. As Talmon has pointed out, however, millenarian beliefs may also develop among those who live in "post-political" states, where individuals believe that they have no effective means to voice their political claims and grievances, and among those who are searching for a new social and cultural identity (Talmon 1968, 355). In these cases, millenarian beliefs provide an alternative source of meaning and identity. Earth First! emerged from a situation that was marked by these latter characteristics.

Earth First! began in April of 1980, when five conservationists spent a week hiking together in Mexico's Pinacate Desert. Dave Foreman, Ron Kezar, Bart Koehler, Howie Wolke, and Mike Roselle were experienced environmental activists, and among them had acquired a significant amount of experience working with mainstream environmental groups such as the Sierra Club and the Wilderness Society.[1] They had recently become convinced, however, that the earth was facing an environmental crisis that threatened all species life, and that traditional political methods could not prevent it.

The event that galvanized the five men was the 1978–79 United States Forest Service Roadless Area Review and Evaluation II (RARE II), a policy initiative that reviewed the sixty-two million acres of American territory that up until that time were classified as wilderness (a status that protected them from commercial development). During the review, the mainstream conservation lobbyists had asked that only one-third to one-half of that territory remain protected land (a tactic that Foreman and his colleagues believed was intended to preserve the groups' congressional support). In the end, RARE II released thirty-six million acres of land to commercial development, thus reducing the American wilderness by more than 50 percent (Manes 1990, 62, and Foreman 1991, 13–14).

For the founders of Earth First!, RARE II was more than just a destructive government policy. It was evidence that the people's representatives were in league with big business, and thus unable or unwilling to pursue the public good. In effect, the United States government had become a tyranny, and as a result, the American wilderness was being destroyed. The emergence of Earth First! was thus partly a response to what was perceived as the corruption and tyranny of the American government. The movement's founders were convinced that such a system compromised individual freedom and the public good. They remained patriotic, but argued that their government was in a state of moral decline, a process that had begun when Hamilton's vision of America achieved hegemony, and "[t]he business of America became business" (Foreman

1992). The rejuvenation of American political life would recognize the importance of wilderness preservation. In the words of Dave Foreman, "Wilderness is America. . . . We will be Americans only as long as there is wilderness. Wilderness is our true Bill of Rights, the true repository of our freedoms, the true home of liberty" (Foreman 1981a, 1).

Earth First!'s founding myth reflects these themes. In it, the five men are said to have wandered in the desert for a week, during which time they became increasingly convinced of the evils of government and industrial society, and the need for a radical new environmental group. Those who participated tell different variations of the story: in some, the founding occurs during their drunken return to civilization (Scarce 1990, 61); in others, it occurs in a Mexican whorehouse (Brower 1988, 40). All of their accounts, however, emphasize a spiritual and physical rebellion against the industrial and technological order that they believed was destroying the wilderness. These stories advocate adherence to a higher law—the intrinsic good of wilderness—and they emphasize the importance of a community of shared beliefs in the fight against industrial civilization. Earth First!'s original adherents were disillusioned with the American government and the lack of what they termed a true "political community" within the United States. Rampant greed and self-interest were tearing apart American society and destroying the environment. Earth First!'s doctrine addressed those problems by creating an alternative political community, and by advocating moderate consumption and respect for all species.

The foundation of the new movement's doctrine (its motto was to be "No Compromise in the Defense of Mother Earth") was decided on the desert journey. Following their rejection of "tyrannical" political authority, however, Earth First!'s founders decided that instead of setting out the details of the movement's belief system themselves, they would call a meeting of like-minded individuals, and determine the movement's doctrine through discussion and consultation. Soon after their return from the New Mexican desert, they contacted sympathetic friends and colleagues from the conservation movement, and called the movement's first general meeting, which came to be known as the Round River Rendezvous.[2] More than sixty people attended the gathering in DuBois, Wyoming. Most were from the western states and Washington, D.C. (Anonymous 1983, 11), and the group was relatively homogenous. The majority were in their mid-thirties, had a university education, and held employment related to their environmental concerns. They had been drawn to environmental issues in their youth, and that interest had led to a life-long dedication to wilderness conservation (Zierenberg 1992). Like the movement's founders, they were convinced that industrial society's destruction of the environment would end in an environmental crisis, and they were skeptical of the American government's ability to protect wilderness (Foreman 1980).

At the Round River Rendezvous, both organizational and doctrinal issues were discussed. Those who attended were determined to avoid what they felt was the hierarchical and authoritarian structure of the state, an attribute that they felt was partly responsible for its corruption. For this reason, they declared that they were "Earth First!ers," not members of Earth First! As well, although Dave Foreman emerged from the first Rendezvous as the movement's *de facto* leader, its formal structure was limited: "[W]hen you take on the structure of the corporate state, you develop the ideology and the bottom line of the corporate state. So what is the one kind of human organization that's really worked? The hunter/gatherer tribe" (Foreman 1992). As a result, it had only two organizational bodies: the "Circle of Darkness," its national coordinating committee, and "La Manta Mojada" ("the wet blanket"), a secret group of advisors to the Circle. The movement's lack of organization was also intended to facilitate flexibility and diversity, two themes that were also reflected in its ideology (Foreman 1992).

THE ORIGINAL EARTH FIRST! BELIEF SYSTEM

Earth First!'s original adherents claimed that their beliefs were rooted in their experience as environmentally aware individuals: "Most people in Earth First! are not dependent on books to explain their own views of things" (Draffan 1991). An analysis of their belief system, however, reveals that their millenarian beliefs were closely related to a doctrine known as "deep ecology." Arne Naess first used the term "deep ecology"[3] to distinguish between what Devall and Sessions termed "reform environmentalism" (an approach to environmental issues that remains within traditional political parameters) and a perspective that argues for a reevaluation of humankind's role in the world (Naess 1973, 95–100; Devall and Sessions 1985, 2–3; Sessions and Naess 1984, 19). Its precepts are not explicitly millennialist, but they provide an ideological framework conducive to the development of an eschatological doctrine. Deep ecology argues that since the Copernican revolution, humans have understood the world anthropocentrically—they have believed themselves to be the planet's most important species. Deep ecology contends, however, that human beings do not hold such a privileged position. For deep ecologists, all species life holds intrinsic worth, and as a result, the whole of nature is part of the moral community. Humans, therefore, should more properly see the world "biocentrically." They should respect all species, and dedicate themselves to maintaining the earth's full complement of species. Some deep ecologists, and many of the original Earth First!ers, took this belief one step further. They also advocated biocentric equality, the belief that all species are intrinsically equal and therefore have an equal right to life. Earth First! transplanted these ideas from the realm of philosophical speculation to the realm of political action, adding to them the urgency of a belief in an imminent apocalypse. It is this millenarian transformation that directly motivated Earth First!'s actions and determined its development.[4]

Earth First!ers believed that Western society's anthropocentrism had resulted in a "spiritually sick" civilization. Its citizens pursued their own interests at the expense of each other, and at the expense of other species. Earth First!ers therefore argued that "[i]f we take the tenets of civilization, psychic, social, sexual and spiritual, and stand them on their head, then we would have a decent basis for a respectable and creative existence. . . . " (Reserve (Reverse) [pseud.] 1981, 1). Further magnifying this problem was the fact that industrial civilization could (but only in the short term) support human populations in excess of the earth's natural carrying capacity. As a result, Earth First!ers argued that "the human race resembles a cancer, which is rapidly destroying the Earth and Her community of life" (Dustrud 1982, 6).

Earth First!ers believed that although the United States contained some of the planet's last great wilderness areas, the American government was willfully and deliberately destroying those regions by encouraging the spread of industrial civilization. Ronald Reagan's administration provided particularly clear evidence of this (Foreman 1981b, 1): James Watt advocated "anti-environmental policies"; Interior and Agriculture Department appointees had close ties to the resource industry (Manes 1990, 79, 209); and national conservation groups had been "seduced by promises of establishment respectability" (Foreman 1980, 2–3). Every day that this situation continued brought the end of industrial civilization nearer. A crisis was therefore inevitable and imminent:

I don't have any specific number of years that I would set, but I think it's pretty clear from recent events that total economic collapse, the cessation of the infrastructure of our current civilization is only a heartbeat away. . . . I'm not sure which event will actually be the breaking point, but it's certain that things cannot continue as they are. (Winguard 1991)

Many Earth First!ers were unwilling to set a specific date for this crisis, but those willing to engage in prediction usually argued that it would occur when the world's oil supply was exhausted. At that point, the eastern United States would run out of food, farmers would no longer be able to depend on irrigation or fertilizer, and steel production would cease (Draffan 1991). For Earth First!ers, this situation was desirable. With each day industrial civilization continued, more irreplaceable wilderness was lost. Thus, "the sooner the system collapses, the better" (Foreman 1992).

The growth of industrial civilization was also responsible for an imminent ecological catastrophe. The impending "biological meltdown" was a mass extinction so severe that it would destroy one-third to one-half of the planet's species and therefore result in the probable extinction of an "exponentially greater number of animal species" (Manes 1990, 26). This mass extinction would be far worse than any that preceded it. Previous extinctions occurred among higher-order species, and thus did not significantly disrupt evolution. The current crisis, however, was destroying plant species and entire habitat, and thus threatening the very origin and foundation of species life. As well, the demise of so many plant species would hinder the restoration of biodiversity for thousands of years (Manes 1990, 25–26). This crisis also differed in character from earlier mass extinctions because it was the result of human beings taking upon themselves the task of governing evolution (Draffan 1991). Their intervention in the earth's ecosystems cast doubt on the planet's ability to recover.

Earth First!ers therefore believed that they were among the most important generation to inhabit the earth. They understood the importance of wilderness preservation and had a specific role to play in the resolution of these crises:

The Earth is our first love, our first concern . . . a recognition of the significance of *our* role leads to even greater dedication. . . . [Earth] must live Her healthy, tumbling life, free from a dread of infestation and misdeed. As Her seed, we become embassadors [sic], emissaries in the final drama, and our mission is indeed grand! (Tir Eriaur Aldaron [pseud.] 1981, 5)

The limited time available prior to the biological meltdown meant that educating human beings about environmentally responsible behavior was a waste of valuable time and resources. Earth First!ers' primary role was to protect what remained of the American wilderness, so that after the apocalypse, the planet's biodiversity could be restored. Earth First!ers were "Antibodies against the Humanpox," and their role was "to fight and destroy that which would destroy the greater body of which they are a part, for which they form a warrior society" (Foreman 1991, 55–58).

In response to these crises, which together constituted the apocalypse, Earth First!'s original political platform demanded that the American government create forty-one wilderness areas, totalling over 137 million acres of land (including the entire state of Hawaii), all of which were to be protected from commercial development.[5] Where the specified territory was already in commercial use, development was to be "obliterated by the same implements of technology that had put [it] there. We aim to help nature reclaim the earth" (Foreman and Wolke 1980, 2). The Earth First! manifesto, which Dave Foreman compiled after the group's initial gathering, reflects the movement's radical interpretation of deep ecology, and helps to explain its political demands. It asserted that wilderness was the primary political good, and that all species "from virus to the great whales" had an inherent and equal right to existence. These principles were to be the measure of all human activity. Any action that protected wilderness was good, and any action that harmed it was evil. The manifesto concluded that "[p]olitical compromise has no place in defense of Earth" (Foreman 1980, 2–3). These principles reflect both a biocentric perspective and an emphasis on biodiversity and biocentric equality, and they demand radical action.

In this respect, the first generation of Earth First!ers were inspired by Edward Abbey's 1975 novel *The Monkey Wrench Gang*. Abbey's novel was dedicated to "Ned Ludd or Lud" (Abbey 1975, 5), and told the story of four friends who traveled across the American Southwest, defending the American wilderness by damaging or destroying commercial development. They removed survey stakes, destroyed heavy machinery, and plotted to explode bridges. Their ultimate goal, however, was the destruction of Glen Canyon Dam, long a symbol of the American government's destruction of the American wilderness.[6] Thus, on the morning of the spring equinox in 1981, when Earth First! chose Glen Canyon Dam as its first major protest site, it signaled its affiliation with Abbey's fictional characters and their tactics.

Earth First!ers believed that the severity of the environmental crisis necessitated the use of sometimes desperate tactics to preserve wilderness areas.

While they used a variety of means to achieve their goals, their most publicized and controversial tactic was ecological sabotage, or "monkeywrenching." Following in the tradition of Luddism and Abbey's Monkey Wrench Gang, monkeywrenching usually involved damaging or destroying private property. It was used to "defend" wilderness where all other efforts had failed, discouraging development by exponentially increasing its cost. It included such relatively innocuous actions as the removal of survey spikes but also more dangerous and potentially violent operations, such as road spiking, arson, and the movement's trademark tactic, tree spiking (Foreman and Haywood [pseud.] 1993).[7] Its ultimate goal was to insure that

> When the floundering beast [industrial civilization] finally, mercifully chokes in its own dung pile, there'll at least be *some* wilderness remaining as a seed bed for planet-wide recovery. (Wolke 1989, 29)

Earth First!ers insisted that monkeywrenching was not mindless vandalism, but strategic protection of the environment. Properly performed, monkeywrenching activities were nonviolent, targeted, dispersed, and elegantly simple. In *Hayduke Lives*, Edward Abbey outlined the Code of the Eco-Warrior: "Rule Number One is nobody gets hurt, Rule Number Two is nobody gets caught, and Rule Number Three is if you do get caught, you're on your own" (Abbey 1990, 110). Earth First!'s lack of formal structure facilitated its adherents' use of monkeywrenching. Because such tactics were often illegal, they could not be centrally organized or performed by groups; such direction would invite discovery and/or infiltration. To openly discuss specific monkeywrenching actions was also to invite arrest. Monkeywrenchers were therefore discouraged from discussing their activities in detail at Earth First! gatherings or informing local newsletter contacts of their activities (Draffan 1991).

Monkeywrenching was not supported by all Earth First!ers, but most understood its motivation. When asked their opinion on such matters, a common response of such individuals was the reply, "I deplore the necessity of the tactic" (Winguard 1991). In the stories that Earth First!ers told around their campfires, however, monkeywrenchers were heroes, and the activity itself gained a glorified symbolic status. Monkeywrenchers believed their activity was of practical value (Draffan 1991),[8] but it also symbolized their apocalyptic battle against the military industrial state. It was not just a political tactic; it was also a religious act that required "using the tools of the devil against the devil" (Bradley 1990, 4). It thus reveals much about the religious and political character of Earth

First!'s millenarian belief system. Foreman often identified monkeywrenching as "a sacrament" and "a form of worshipping the earth" (Foreman 1992). In the context of Earth First!'s millenarian ideology, that sacrament was especially important: "I don't use violence but there's a war being waged upon us and upon the planet. . . . I am a warrior, and I will continue to defend myself and the planet as best I can" (Cherney 1991).

Earth First!ers' vision of the postapocalyptic world reflected their critique of the American government and industrial civilization. In it, a significantly smaller population of human beings would live in bioregional communities that were self-sustaining (Draffan 1991), and would be organized in the form of the hunter/gatherer tribe (Foreman 1992).

THE FRAGMENTATION OF EARTH FIRST!

Earth First!'s original doctrine therefore exemplifies the five characteristics of millenarian belief systems. Its believers awaited an imminent apocalypse, in the form of industrial society's self-destruction. Earth First!ers, who understood the vital importance of wilderness, would prepare the earth for the impending apocalypse by preserving what little wilderness remained. The fall of industrial civilization would usher in the ultimate, or final, stage of human history, a period wherein balanced species life would be restored, wilderness would reemerge, and where humans would live in harmony with their environment.

Earth First!'s original doctrine, however, was to some degree contradictory, and as a result, it contained the seeds of the movement's eventual fragmentation. Its founders insisted that to be an Earth First!er all that was needed was to "put the earth first." Following that, all manner of individual was welcome within the movement, from "animal rights vegetarians to wilderness hunting guides, from monkeywrenchers to followers of Gandhi . . . from bitter misanthropes to true humanitarians" (Foreman 1985, 16). For the original Earth First!ers, however, putting the earth first necessarily meant adherence to a belief in both biocentrism and biocentric equality. This assumption was problematic for two reasons.

First, when pushed to the extreme, biocentric equality undermines a millenarian belief structure because it denies human beings an important or privileged role in the planet's evolution. Earth First!ers were not troubled by this contradiction during the movement's early history; indeed, it is unlikely that

they were even aware of it. During those first years, the movement was relatively free of internal discord and experienced a number of political successes.
As will be seen, however, both internal and external pressures eventually
brought the contradiction to the fore. As a result, the movement's first generation of adherents transformed its millenarian ideology into an apocalyptic
belief system. They still believed they were to play a critical role in bringing
about the appropriate conditions for the apocalypse to occur, but they no
longer believed that they, or any human beings, would necessarily be a part of
the new millennium.[9]

Second, while the founders of Earth First! assumed that putting the earth
first meant biocentrism and biocentric equality, that assumption became problematic as Earth First!ers came to number in the thousands.[10] In a movement
that emphasized its adherents' freedom and diversity, doctrinal differences
were bound to emerge. When the movement's founders began to abandon their
millenarian beliefs, and became increasingly apocalyptic, dissension became
inevitable. Within a relatively short period of time, a significant proportion of
Earth First!ers came to define the movement's core belief system in a new way.

During the first year of its existence (1980–1981), Earth First! focused its
energies not only on wilderness preservation, but also on recruitment, and it
was successful in its efforts. Media attention, coupled with the proselytising
efforts of Foreman and the other founders, saw the group's size more than
triple during this period. By early 1982, Earth First!ers numbered close to two
thousand (Anonymous 1981, 1). This momentum continued into early 1983,
supported by successful direct actions, media attention, and further proselytizing efforts. In the mid-1980s, this trend resulted in a major demographic
change within the movement.

As noted above, Earth First!'s original adherents were primarily drawn from
the mainstream environmental movement in the southwestern United States.
The movement's message, however, fell on particularly fertile ground in Oregon and California. Its radical stance was especially attractive to a group of
people who might be termed "career activists," individuals who regularly participated in a variety of political action groups (for example, women's health
care and antinuclear protest groups) (Reed 1991; Cherney 1991). Those individuals linked environmental issues to the larger and more broadly defined goal of
"social justice": "[I]f you can believe that there's good and value in a muskrat,
or a squirrel, or a plant, it's really easy to believe that there's good and value in
your neighbour, another culture, another colour, another religion" (Reed

1991). They believed that human nature could be changed to appreciate the importance of the natural environment:

> [A]s the Bhopals, Chernobyls, Love Canals and Space Shuttles accelerate our understanding that modern centralized civilization is a death trip, more and more people will reawaken to the simple joys and wisdom of ecological living. (Sayen 1987, 36)

They still believed that an environmental apocalypse was imminent, but they also believed that if enough people could be warned of its effects and persuaded to change their way of life, its effects could be limited. For them, proselytism and education became as important as directly saving wilderness. This belief system contrasted markedly with the first generation's primary concern of wilderness preservation and their insistence that human beings deserved no more attention than plant species. Earth First!'s policy of accepting diversity, however, allowed the two groups to coexist within the movement for approximately three years, during which time the movement continued to grow. Earth First!ers of both factions participated in hundreds of protests, and through monkeywrenching activities, committed millions of dollars worth of damage to commercial development (Anonymous 1981).[11]

Between 1983 and 1987, the first generation of Earth First!ers became discouraged by their lack of absolute achievement; most often, their efforts stalled wilderness development, but did not prevent it. As a result, they became convinced that most human beings were incapable of properly appreciating wilderness. During the late 1980s, this mistrust of human nature was magnified by their concern over the growth of the human population. These forces caused them to conclude that neither they, nor any other human beings, would or should have an important role in the millennium. They abandoned their millenarian beliefs, and hoped only for an apocalyptic end to industrial civilization.

Their concern regarding population growth was transformed into the assertion that it was not important that any human beings survive the biological meltdown. They repeatedly debated this issue with their social justice colleagues in the movement's journal, but the two factions could not reconcile their divergent beliefs. The argument culminated in a notorious 1987 article entitled "Population and AIDS." Its pseudonymous author, "Miss Ann Thropy," suggested that AIDS was an environmentally beneficial epidemic because if it infected and killed 80 percent of the human population, it could cause the industrial infrastructure to crumble: capital would "dr[y] up, governments lose authority, power fragmen[t] and devolve. . . ." (Miss Ann Thropy 1987a, 32).[12] It promised to hasten the apocalypse and preserve wilderness by reducing population pressure. The article concluded that "if the AIDS epidemic didn't exist, radical environmentalists would have to invent [it]" (Miss Ann Thropy 1987a, 32).

Miss Ann Thropy's article brought the dispute between Earth First!'s two factions to a head. Those who advocated social justice were horrified by the article's content (Miss Ann Thropy 1987, 22; Sayen 1987b, 22). Although they supported Earth First!'s biocentrism, they did not advocate biocentric equality. The article's suggestion that the AIDS virus was of equal moral status to human beings, and thus the answer to an environmentalist's prayer, was too much for them. Their faith that human nature could change led them to believe that all human beings were intrinsically valuable, and conceivably part of the millennial community. They interpreted Miss Ann Thropy's article as both cruel and "fascist." Their anger was further increased by an article by Edward Abbey in the *Bloomsbury Review*, which suggested that in the interests of limiting population growth in the United States, American borders should be closed to all immigrants (Alien Nation [pseud.] 1987, 17).

The movement's 1987 Round River Rendezvous provided the occasion for a direct confrontation between the two groups. At a violent direct action protest that followed that meeting, Foreman claimed he had "lost his stomach" for tolerating those within Earth First! who felt they could change human nature, as well as with their civil disobedience tactics, which he felt achieved little noticeable change in the system (Foreman 1992). He and many of the other "biocentrists" then slowly drew back from the movement.

Following this confrontation, two events occurred that shaped the movement's final fragmentation. In late 1988, the FBI concluded a two-year infiltration of an Earth First! Arizona cell group. Five individuals, including Dave Foreman, were arrested for attempting to cut electrical power to a nuclear power plant. Foreman, although not directly involved in the monkeywrenching action, eventually pled guilty, and he was released on probation. Soon after the trial, he disassociated himself from Earth First! He argued that the majority of Earth First!ers were no longer focused on ecology. They had abandoned biocentrism in favor of humanism (Foreman and Morton 1990, 5). As a result Earth First! had become simply another "Leftist group."

The second influential event occurred in California, among the Earth First!ers who advocated social justice. In early 1990, many Californian Earth

First!ers attempted to form an alliance with West Coast logging unions. To facilitate that goal, they publicly renounced Earth First!'s trademark monkey-wrenching tactic, tree spiking (Scarce 1990, 83–84). Following that denunciation, Judi Bari, a Californian Earth First! leader, planned a mass demonstration in California for the summer of 1990. Called Redwood Summer, it was intended to parallel 1960's Mississippi Summer, and draw activists from across the United States to preserve the West Coast Redwoods.[13] In the end, however, Bari herself was unable to participate fully in that demonstration (Gabriel 1990, 62). On May 24, 1990, a bomb exploded in her car while she was driving; she was seriously injured and hospitalized for several months.[14] Following the bombing, Earth First!'s social justice faction approached its goals with renewed vigor, and after Dave Foreman's withdrawal from the movement, they assumed leadership of Earth First!.

Since that transformation, Earth First! has pursued both environmental and social justice issues. Like the original Earth First!ers, current adherents understand themselves to be "the most important generation" in human history. They foresee an imminent biological crisis, but they believe and hope that smaller, environmentally sensitive human communities will exist after the crash of industrial civilization. They understand their goals to be the protection of American wilderness and the creation of a community that can stand as a model of social justice and environmental sensitivity after the apocalypse.

As a result of this transformation, in September of 1990 many prominent Earth First! biocentrists publicly left the movement, decrying its new social justice agenda (Davis 1990, 2).[15] They now independently pursue the fight to preserve American wilderness. They maintain their belief that a biological meltdown is imminent, but they hold little hope that human society can reduce its patterns of growth, overproduction, and overconsumption. Their goal is to protect as much wilderness as possible before the system collapses. Their beliefs are truly apocalyptic in nature (Davis 1991).

CONCLUSION

In the summer of 1980, Earth First!'s founders came together in fear and anticipation of an imminent environmental apocalypse. Their goal was to preserve a significant proportion of American wilderness prior to that event, and they understood virtually all activities aimed at achieving that goal to be both necessary and justifiable. They believed that they were the most significant group of individuals in the most important generation in human history, for they were responsible for the continued existence of the planet's biodiversity.

To hold such a faith in the face of an unchanging world is a precarious endeavor. It is difficult to remake the world in the image of one's dreams. For this reason, millenarian belief systems are inherently unstable. Within Earth First!, the conflict between dream and reality led to internal instability, and ultimately produced two factions: a group that reinterpreted the movement's original doctrine, and continued to hope for the millennium, and a group that hoped only for the apocalypse, and the fall of industrial society. Both factions remain determined to preserve wilderness, but as a result of their different understandings of human nature and the direction of human history, their visions of the future are radically different. Those Earth First!ers who returned to millenarianism focus their energies on education and wilderness preservation. They envision a future wherein reeducated human beings are able to live in harmony with the environment. Those Earth First!ers who became apocalyptic focus their energy on preserving as much wilderness as possible prior to the apocalypse. They hope only that after the fall of industrial civilization, the planet's biodiversity—which may or may not include human beings—can be restored.

Earth First!'s evolution has serious implications for society at large. It suggests that the most radical of environmental doctrines may initially support, but cannot sustain, a millenarian faith. The biocentric beliefs of Earth First!'s apocalyptic faction deny the human species a pivotal role in history. When it is pushed to its limits, this belief system provides a justification for any action undertaken in defense of the wilderness, regardless of whether or not human beings are harmed. Individuals who hold such beliefs are capable of wreaking significant havoc on the human civilization in which they live.[16]

NOTES

1. Foreman had just resigned his position as the chief Washington lobbyist for the Wilderness Society. Kezar was affiliated with the Sierra Club, Koehler had worked for the Wilderness Society, and Wolke had worked for the Friends of the Earth. Roselle was a longtime activist for such groups as the Yippies and the Zippies (Manes 1990, 65–69; Scarce 1990, 58–61).

2. The gathering was named to recall Aldo Leopold's essay, "The Round River, A Parable," which compared Paul Bunyan's round river to the functioning of the planet's ecosystem. For those in Earth First!, "round river" symbolized the interconnectedness and equality of all elements of the ecological cycle (Leopold 1953, 158–163). The term "rendezvous" was meant to convey the spirit of the Old West (Scarce 1990, 62).

3. See, for example, George Sessions and Arne Naess, "The Basic Principles of Deep Ecology." This article popularized the formal precepts of deep ecology among Earth First!ers.

4. It should be noted that many deep ecologists criticize the movement's peculiar interpretation of the doctrine because they claim it misinterprets deep ecology's precepts (Eckersly 1992; Bookchin in Chase, 1991).

5. Foreman defined wilderness as areas that were large enough to support a complete ecosystem, and that were free from human influence.

6. The 1956 construction of Glen Canyon Dam is often identified as a critical point in the history of the American conservation movement. David Brower claims that this is because until that point, the amateur conservationists who lobbied for such groups as the Wilderness Society had assumed that the government would not violate the national park system. The dam's construction violated that trust, and according to Brower, resulted in the professionalization of the American conservation movement (Brower 1990, 328).

7. Tree spiking is the insertion of metal or ceramic spikes into the trunks of trees that are scheduled for cutting, an act of sabotage that threatens the lives of loggers cutting the tree and mill employees responsible for cutting it into planks. As well, should a chainsaw or mill blade hit a spike, it would result in significant damage to the equipment concerned. After spiking a stand of trees, Earth First!ers notified the company that owned the forest. From that point on, they claimed, it was the moral responsibility of the company not to cut the trees and endanger its employees (Foreman and Haywood [pseud.] 1993).

8. The practical value of monkeywrenching was a source of continued debate within the movement. Many Earth First!ers argued that the cost of monkeywrenching, in terms of public approval, rendered it an ineffective tool. This was a charge often made against tree spiking (Draffan 1991).

9. While the eventual split in Earth First! to some degree parallels the more typical distinction between premillennial and postmillennial ideologies, these terms are arguably too closely tied to their religious origins to be useful here. Apocalypticism, with its focus on the present world and its ultimate demise, is the most appropriate term to describe a radical, secular biocentrism, wherein human beings are not the most important historical actors. This distinction is discussed in greater detail in Lee 1995.

10. Earth First!'s lack of organization and refusal to compile a "membership" list makes it difficult to assess the number of its adherents at any given moment. Likewise *Earth First!*'s subscription numbers do not provide an accurate estimate. Many Earth First!ers did not subscribe to the journal, choosing the more environmentally responsible option of sharing a single issue with their friends and colleagues. In this article, estimates of Earth First!'s size are based on the leadership's estimations, and journalists' reports; given the circumstances, these are the most accurate assessments available.

11. Forestry executives in Washington State, for example, estimated the average annual damage done by monkeywrenching in their state alone to be over two million dollars. They admit that they publicly underestimate that damage in order that Earth First!ers not be "encouraged." Their spokesmen request anonymity in order that they not be targeted by Earth First! (Anonymous 1981).

12. Evidence suggests that Miss Ann Thropy was in reality Christopher Manes, the author of *Green Rage*.

13. By the end of August 1990, more than 3,000 individuals had participated in the event, and 150 of them had been arrested (Gabriel 1990, 62).

14. Bari and Darryl Cherney, who was her passenger, were originally charged with transporting the pipe bomb that injured them. Those charges were later dropped. American law enforcement agencies have not yet determined who was responsible for the bombing (Bishop 1990, A8).

15. Among those individuals were John Davis, the journal's editor; Paul Watson (a founder of Greenpeace and head of the Sea Shepherd Conservation Society); and Howie Wolke, one of Earth First!'s original founders (Davis 1990, 2).

16. This analysis appears to be supported by recent evidence that suggests that Theodore Kaczynski, the alleged Unabomber, attended Earth First! gatherings and read the movement's literature. Although the vast majority of Earth First!ers would likely deplore his actions, the biocentric faction's belief system (if pushed to its limits) would support such activity (Chavez 1996, 11A).

References

Abbey, Edward. 1990. *Hayduke Lives!* Boston: Little, Brown and Company.
———. 1975. *The Monkey Wrench Gang.* New York: Avon Books.
Aldaron, Tir Eriaur [pseud.]. 1981. "Ele! Mellonkemmi Greetings Earthfriends!" *Earth First!* 1 (5) (Beltane): 5.
Alien Nation [pseud.]. 1987. "Dangerous Tendencies in Earth First!" *Earth First!* 10 (13): 17.

Bishop, K. 1990. "Militant Environmentalists." *New York Times*, June 19, A8.

Bradley, Ed. 1990. "Earth First!" *Sixty Minutes* 22 (24) (March 4).

Brown, Michael, and John May. 1989. *The Greenpeace Story*. London: Dorling Kindersley.

Brower, David. 1990. *For Earth's Sake*. Layton, VT: Peregrine Smith.

Brower, Kenneth. 1988. "Mr. Monkeywrench." *Harrowsmith* (Sept/Oct.): 40.

Chase, Steve, ed. 1991. *Defending the Earth*. Boston: South End Press.

Chavez, Linda. 1996. "Want Motive for Unabomber?" *U.S.A. Today*, April 10, 11A.

Cherney, Darryl. 1991. Interview with the author. Ballard, Washington, April 10.

Davis, John. 1990. "Editorial." *Earth First!* 10 (8): 2.

———. 1991. Interview with the author. Canton, NY, December 4.

DePaul, Tony. 1989. "Earth First!" *Sunday Journal Magazine* (March 26): 8.

Devall, Bill, and George Sessions. 1985. *Deep Ecology*. Salt Lake City: Peregrine Smith Books.

Draffan, George. 1991. Interview with the author. Ballard, Washington, April 8.

Dustrud, Pete. 1982. "Dear Reader You Now Have a New Editor" *Earth First!* 2 (7): 2.

"Earth First!: The First Three Years." 1983. *Earth First!* 4 (1): 1.

Eckersly, Robin. 1992. *Environmentalism and Political Theory*. Albany: State University of New York Press.

Federal Bureau of Investigation file, F.O.I.P.A. #344,522/190−71269. Washington, D.C.: FBI.

Foreman, Dave. 1980. "Memorandum regarding Earth First Statement of Principles and Membership Brochure," (Sept. 1): 2−3.

———. 1981. "The Hounds of Hell are Howling High." *Earth First!* 1 (6): 1.

———. 1985. "Welcome to Earth First." *Earth First!*. 5 (5): 16

———. 1991. *Confessions of an Eco-Warrior*. New York: Harmony.

———. 1992. Interview with the author. Tucson, Arizona, January 24.

Foreman, Dave, and Bill Haywood [pseud.], eds. 1993. *Eco-Defense, a Field Guide to Monkeywrenching*, 3rd ed. Chico: Abbzug Press.

Foreman, Dave, and Nancy Morton. 1990. "Letter of Resignation." *Earth First!* 10 (13) (Sept. 22): 5.

Foreman, Dave, and H. Wolke. 1980. Memorandum Regarding Earth First. (Sept.)

Gabriel, Trip. 1990. "If a Tree Falls in the Forest, They Hear It." *New York Times Magazine* (Nov. 4): 62.

Kane, Joe. 1987. "Mother Nature's Army." *Esquire* (February): 33−38.

Lee, Martha F. 1995. *Earth First! Environmental Apocalypse*. Syracuse: Syracuse University Press.

———. 1995. "Violence and the Environment: The Case of Earth First!" *Terrorism and Political Violence* 7 (3): 107−127.

Leopold, Aldo. 1953. *Round River, From the Journals of Aldo Leopold*. New York: Oxford University Press.

Manes, Christopher. 1990. *Green Rage: Radical Environmentalism and the Unmaking of Civilization*. Boston: Little Brown.

Meadows, D. H., et al. 1972. *The Limits to Growth*. New York: Universe Books.

Miss Ann Thropy [pseud.]. 1987a. "Population and AIDS." *Earth First!* 7 (5) (May 1): 32.

———. 1987b. "Miss Ann Thropy Responds to 'Alien Nation.'" *Earth First!* 8 (2) (Dec. 22): 22.

Naess, Arne. 1973. "The Shallow and the Deep, Long Range Ecology Movement, A Summary." *Inquiry* 16: 95–100.

Reed, Renee. 1991. Interview with the author. Seattle, Washington, April 10.

Reserve (Reverse) [pseud.]. 1981. "We've Got to Do Some Motherin." *Earth First!* 1 (8) (Oct. 31): 1.

Robbins, J. 1988. "The Environmental Guerrillas." *Boston Globe Magazine* (March 27): 14.

Sayen, Jamie. 1987. "Grow Up Leftists." *Earth First!* 8 (2) (Dec. 22): 22.

Scarce, Rik. 1990. *Eco-Warriors: Understanding the Radical Environmental Movement*. Chicago: Noble.

Sessions, George, and Arne Naess. 1984. "The Basic Principles of Deep Ecology." *Earth First!* 4 (6) (June): 19.

Shute, Nancy. 1989. "Dave Foreman Meets the Feds." *Outside* (Sept.): 15.

Talmon, Yonina. 1968. "Millenarism." *International Encyclopedia of the Social Sciences*, vol. 10. New York: Macmillan.

"The Tucson Eco-Raiders." 1987. *Chicago Tribune*, August 2, section 1, 21.

"Two Hundred Celebrate the 4th of July with Earth First." 1981. *Earth First!* 1 (7) (Lughnasad [sic]): 11.

Wilson, Helen. 1992. Interview with the author. Tucson, Arizona, January 26.

Winguard, Greg. 1991. Interview with the author. Seattle, Washington, April 10.

Wolke, Howie. 1989. "Thoughtful Radicalism." *Earth First!* 10 (2) (Dec. 21): 29.

Zakin, Susan. 1989. "Earth First!" *S.M.A.R.T.* (Sept./Oct.): 88–94.

Zierenberg, Nancy. 1992. Interview with the author. Tucson, Arizona, January 26.

Technological Millenarianism in the United States

7 John M. Bozeman

"It is essential to be absolutely modern."

—*Rimbaud*

INTRODUCTION

Commentators have noted that widespread frustration within a culture frequently gives rise to revitalization movements (Wallace 1956). Such revitalization movements may take any of a variety of forms, such as a move toward fundamentalism (i.e., a "back-to-basics" or *ad fontes* approach); alternatively, if enough of a society's basic presuppositions are called into question, sectarian groups and new religions may emerge or, if present already, may experience radical growth. Such revitalization movements are frequently accompanied by notions of millenarianism, the idea that a new, more perfect age is beginning, breaking radically from the past—and/or chiliasm, the belief that the movement is a divinely ordained and assisted harbinger of the arrival of a literal heaven on earth. Participants may also expect to inherit a privileged place in the new order, while opponents will be humbled or destroyed.

Many, perhaps most, religous revitalization movements have historically been triggered by the existence of intolerable levels of corruption and moral breakdown within the dominant faith, as well as the growth of feelings of nationalism and changes in the notions of human rights and sovereignty. However, by the late 1600s western Europe was facing a new cultural force: the Enlightenment, and its new attitudes toward the authority of science. The interaction of western European Christendom produced a number of interesting syntheses over time, giving rise to such movements as Swedenborgianism, Comptian Positivism, Freemasonry, and various occultic groups.

In America, too, new faiths emerged that attempted to deal with the increasing authority of science. Some, such as Unitarianism and Felix Adler's Ethical Culture Society, tried to formulate more rational, less supernaturally oriented religious systems. Others have attempted a more direct synthesis. Mary Baker Eddy, for example, formed the First Church of Christ, Scientist. This faith incorporated aspects of the newly discovered science of hypnotism and auto-suggestion to effect cures; it also asserted the proposition that matter is completely subservient to spirit. Joseph Smith, on the other hand, tried a different approach, suggesting that spirit is but a special form of matter, and thus subject to scientific laws. Attempts at dealing with scientific advances continue to the present day, with Christian Fundamentalists, as well as new religions such as Scientology, the New Age movement, and psychic and UFO-worshiping groups, each presenting their own interpretations of the meaning of scientific endeavor (Lewis 1995).

Yet if we examine the groups above, we find that despite their attempts to make some sort of accommodation to science, relatively few were founded by persons with extensive scientific training. The scientific establishment, for its part, appears to have relatively little interest in synthetic religio-scientific endeavors. Part of this reason is historical: during much of the 1800s, most American natural philosophers and scientists had achieved what they thought was "an impregnable synthesis of faith and reason" that allowed science and

orthodox Christian theology to support each other. Later, the professionalization of both science and theology during the early twentieth century, along
with science's growing prestige, did not encourage efforts at reconciliation on
the part of the scientists. Books such as Andrew Dickson White's *History of the
Warfare of Science with Religion* (1896) tended to generate a myth of perpetual
conflict between dogmatic religious obscurationism on the one hand, and
value-free scientific truth on the other (Marsden 1989).

But was this "value-free" search for truth as neutral as has traditionally
been portrayed? Recent work in the history of science suggests that social factors have had at least as much effect upon the direction of scientific endeavor
as has simple technical feasibility. Such sociological studies have also tended to
focus more upon the inner workings of the scientific establishment than upon
the interaction of this establishment with the larger culture. Closer examination reveals that scientific and technological movements are often undertaken
for reasons other than the simple search for abstract knowledge; often, the
investigators may be laboring under a scientized faith with convictions that
border on the millennial or chiliasm. Furthermore, once begun, such efforts
may generate and/or ride an unacknowledged tide of public sentiment to
unforseen conclusions. We turn now to one such case, that of eugenics.

EUGENICS: BETTER BABIES FOR A BETTER TOMORROW

While eugenic notions can be found in the culture of Sparta and the writings
of Plato, the rise of modern eugenic thought in the West is usually credited to
the Englishman Francis Galton. Inspired by the work of his cousin, Charles
Darwin, Galton first published his ideas in 1865; this work, "Hereditary Talent
and Character," laid the groundwork for modern hereditarian thought. Galton's premises were simple: character traits of all types are inherited, with
nature favoring adaptive traits and destroying maladaptive ones. The same
process is at work, Galton felt, in the human animal; observation indicated
that some families were "good," populated with morally virtuous, hard-working,
healthy, and long-lived individuals, while some were "bad," i.e., given to vice,
sloth, and poor health. In this view, character was as much inherited as height,
so generalizations could be made about entire races as well. Native Americans,
for example, were generally "naturally cold, melancholic, patient, and taciturn,"
though patriotic and possessing an "astonishing" sense of personal dignity.

West Africans, on the other hand, were perceived by Galton as "impulsive," "warm-hearted," and "eminently gregarious, for [they are] always jabbering, quarrelling, tom-tom-ing, or dancing." These traits were thought to be transmitted "as truly as physical forms," even if the children were raised by stepparents.

Galton was, of course, merely echoing many of the racist and imperialist stereotypes of his day, which maintained that the Anglo-Saxon race was at the peak of biological and cultural evolution. What made Galton noteworthy was his interest in mathematical and biological statistics—fields to which he made several valuable contributions—and his interest in applying this knowledge to contemporary social problems. However, his work toward the implementation of a more biologically desirable social structure was necessarily delayed until eugenic and genetic science achieved a better understanding of cellular science and human anatomy.

By the turn of the century, however, both the scientific and social climates were changing. Lamarckian theories of the inheritance of acquired characteristics fell from favor, replaced by Weismann's "germ plasm" theory. Rediscovery of Mendel's work, coupled with improvements in microscopy, allowed better understanding of the mechanisms of genetics. Eugenic science could also point proudly to its proponents, who included such notables as polymath Alexander Graham Bell (who had done substantial work in the field of audiology in addition to his better-known career as an inventor), biologist David Starr Jordan, plant breeder Luther Burbank, and Harvard biologist Charles Davenport. Similarly, eugenicists received public support from such notables as Theodore Roosevelt, Harvard president Charles Eliot, and British writers George Bernard Shaw and H.G. Wells (Bozeman 1993).

A turning point was reached, however, in 1907. This year marked the passage of the first involuntary sterilization law in the United States, in Indiana. Surgical sterilization in the form of vasectomy had recently become practical. (Castration had generally been seen as needlessly cruel and debilitating, and the cutting of women's Fallopian tubes was at this time a serious operation that resulted in the death of the patient in 2–3 percent of all cases.)

Armed now with a measure of scientific respectability and a tolerably safe surgical technique, the eugenicists were now ready to make war on the causes of racial degeneration. Societies began to form to popularize the eugenic message. The sizable American Eugenics Society (AES), for example, tried to promote eugenic thought by publishing a popular magazine, *Eugenics: A Journal of Race Betterment*. Other AES efforts included running large displays at fairs (including "Fitter Families for Future Firesides" contests, in which family pedigrees were examined for eugenic merit and trophies then awarded), and conducting contests in which clergymen competed for cash prizes by preaching pro-eugenics sermons in their churches.

But could the eugenics movement be called chiliastic or millennial? If we examine the writings of both amateur and professional proponents of eugenics, the answer appears to be at least a qualified "yes." Even before Galton had published "Hereditary Talent" and his follow-up book, *Hereditary Genius* (1869), Horace Bushnell had stated in the 1863 edition of his classic work *Christian Nurture* that the kingdom of God would come not only through preaching and conversion, but also through the superior "populating force" of sanctified puritan stock (Bozeman 1994). Galton's own writings may have inspired John Humphrey Noyes's famous late-nineteenth-century experiment in "stirpiculture" (regulated human breeding) in the perfectionist Oneida colony; persons participating in the program signed statements offering to become, if necessary, "martyrs to science" and regarded themselves as "living sacrifices to God and true Communism" (Parker 1935).

Indeed, such statements—odd as they may sound to persons living in the 1990s—became increasingly common during the early twentieth century. A woman writing on the topic of "Building a Better Race" in the mainstream magazine *World's Work* could write:

> the better race is being builded [sic]. . . . And a new people, who shall be born right in the homes that have been made right of fathers and mothers who have been educated right [in eugenics, home economics, and scientific motherhood], shall be fashioned once more in the image of God from which the generations have so far departed. . . . The American woman is now engaged in the transcendent creative task. And the world awaits her work. (Daggett 1912)

Such views extended to some degree to the credentialed scientists and professionals involved in the leadership of the movement. Charles Davenport, for example, went so far as to compose an essay entitled "Eugenics as Religion." In it Davenport suggested that the highest aim of the human species was to develop a social order of the highest and most effective type—an order in which each person would be physically fit, mentally well endowed for some kind of useful work, calm, cheerful, and possessing such inhibitions as to allow him to control his instinctive reactions and conform to community mores. Davenport went on to propose a "eugenics creed," which affirmed, among other things, a belief in the need to take such "sanitary measures" as necessary to protect the offspring of carefully selected matings from "accidental and unselective mortality" (Davenport 1916[?]).

Only after several decades of popularity did eugenics enter a period of uneven decline. The movement probably achieved its height of scientific respectability from around 1900 to the early 1920s; after this time the new science of genetics quietly began to dissociate itself from eugenics and its social programs. With the coming of the Great Depression, organizations promoting eugenics suffered; however, eugenic philosophies become accepted by persons charged with the operation of state asylums and the number of surgical sterilizations experienced a considerable increase. Eugenic sterilizations in the U.S. only began to decline toward the end of World War II as American surgeons were pressed into the war effort. Public realization of Nazi atrocities (some carried out in the name of eugenics), combined with opposition from the Roman Catholic Church, prevented sterilizations from returning to their prewar levels; however, some programs were active as late as 1976. All told, the U.S. witnessed between 60,000 and 70,000 eugenic sterilizations between 1907 and 1973. Many of these were done without the consent of the patient, and some with varying degrees of coercion (Reilly 1991).

CRYONICS: WAKING UP IN A BETTER TOMORROW

Of course, it is also true that a young, potentially revolutionary science does not necessarily entail coercion. Such is the case of cryonics, the science of freezing persons with the intent of later revival.

Early experiments in this area were carried out by the British surgeon John Hunter. After unsuccessfully trying to freeze and revive fish in 1766, Hunter mentioned that he had originally hoped that the procedure might be useful for freezing people. In America, the earliest expression of a desire for preservation of the self for revival in the future was voiced by Benjamin Franklin. Franklin claimed to have found three drowned flies in a container of wine; after being removed and allowed to dry out, two of the flies revived and flew away. The statesman expressed regret that such a procedure could not be performed on himself, so that he could see what would become of his country in a hundred years (Perry 1990a; Perry 1991a; Perry 1991b).

Serious talk about freezing humans began in 1962, when Evan Cooper privately published a book called *Immortality Physically, Scientifically Now* (Perry 1990b). The year 1963 witnessed a conference dealing with the subject, as well as the formation of the Washington, D.C.-based Life Extension Society. Cryonics began in earnest, however, with the publication of *The Prospect of Immortality* (1964). Written by Robert Ettinger, a physicist who occasionally wrote science fiction, *Prospect* presented a brief review of the science of cryobiology (the branch of biology dealing with life at low temperatures) and suggested that such research might be extended to humans. While presenting a rather optimistic view of the future, the author presented a thorough overview of both the technical and social challenges yet to be overcome. The core problem was, of course, obvious: in spite of some promising research, nobody had yet frozen a higher organism and revived it. In the face of this difficulty, Cooper, Ettinger, and others agreed it was better to follow a "path of least regret": a frozen person might have low chances of revival, but (Christian resurrection notwithstanding) a person who is buried or cremated has absolutely no chance of revival whatsoever. Cryonics researchers thus developed a freezing regimen that could be carried out at reasonable cost while minimizing freezing damage as much as possible. Revival would have to be carried out sometime in the future when thawing technology would be more advanced.

During the 1960s a number of cryonics clubs and groups formed in New York, Michigan, Florida, and California. After several false starts, the first person, a college professor named James Bedford, was frozen in 1967, with others following. Cryonics, however, was still in its infancy and did not yet have a stable physical or legal infrastructure. The result was that many of the early attempts at suspension failed, either due to legal challenges from surviving family members, lack of funds, inability to procure facilities, or unscrupulousness and fraud on the part of facility providers.

In spite of these early difficulties, the movement as a whole survived. After the mid-1970s, suspension failure became the exception rather than the rule as the different cryonics groups gained experience both in freezing clients and in maintaining financial solvency. Standard freezing procedures were devised and trust funds were established to ensure that maintenance costs for the frozen "patients" could be met. Furthermore, the movement's legal battles and the ensuing publicity also had the salutary effect of garnering increased toleration and cooperation from the medical community. Part of this change in attitude was probably due to the cryonicists' increased legal clout; it also appears, however, that the passage of time and the establishment of stable institutions caused physicians to see cryonics less as a field populated by con artists and crackpots, and more as a speculative but sincere form of alternative medical practice.

Even more than eugenics, cryonics has an optimism about the future that includes millennial expectations. Part of this optimism focuses upon expectation of scientific advancement; the technology for revival (known as "reanimation" among cryonicists) does not yet exist, and so is dependent upon assumed future discoveries. More interesting, though, are the social assumptions behind cryonics. Clients assume that the present economic system will remain stable in the ensuing decades and perhaps centuries until reanimation takes place. They also assume that members of future society will in fact wish to revive persons from the past, repair the damage caused by freezing and original cause of death, and make the effort to retrain and socialize them.

Indeed, if the cryonics movement could be called a culture, then one of its primary components is the revival scenario. Ettinger, in *The Prospect of Immortality*, suggests that the future will be a "Golden Age" that will include intelligent robots, ectogenesis (human children carried to term in artificial wombs), lifelong sexual virility, climate-controlled cities, and unlimited wealth. Presumably the aging process will also be conquered, allowing time for artistic and philosophical speculation. Finally, persons will have the ability to improve themselves through genetic enhancement and prosthetic augmentation—people will have the ability to become even "better than new." Ettinger extended these themes in even more fanciful directions in a later book, *Man into Superman* (1972), detailing such possibilities as cybernetically enhanced sex and zero-residue foods that would obviate the need for bowels.

This joyful speculation continues to the present day. Alcor Life Extension Foundation, one of the largest companies to offer cryonic services, includes a "speculative scenario for recovery" in its promotional literature (Alcor 1993). Written in the form of a first-person narrative, the story begins with a man in great pain dying in a hospital in 1997. He awakens, cured, some decades later aboard a space colony to see the same Alcor representative who oversaw his case on earth; his wife (now remarried) is waiting to see him, and his children are now grown up and enjoying successful careers in high-tech fields. There is no mention made of any social or political problems. Such attitudes appear to be consonant with the expectations of Alcor clients themselves. For example, a woman whose husband had recently been suspended immediately after dying from a malignant brain tumor spoke of her feelings of loss, but also of hope for the future:

Today's technology sheds a bright light on the very realistic possibilities of tomorrow's technology. Those who "check it out" can share in the wonderful vision of rejoining loved ones in a future bearing abundance of both time and resources. Time enough for love; time enough to live. (Glennie 1992)

SPACE COLONIES: THE HIGH FRONTIER

Cryonics practitioners tend to believe that human destiny will reach its fulfillment, probably through technological means, sometime in the future. Others believe that this destiny lies in another direction: space exploration. A number of alternative religious groups have focused upon space as an arena of salvation or inspiration. Eric von Daniken's best-seller, *Chariots of the Gods?* (1970), for example, popularized the notion that much of the religious iconography and many ancient texts are really records of visitors from other planets; this book inspired several sequels and prompted a tremendous outpouring of books, television shows, and movies.

A more direct form of veneration of technology is found in various flying-saucer and UFO-worshipping cults. One international group with some 20,000 followers, the Raelian movement, is dedicated to building a landing pad and embassy in preparation for the UFOs' apocalyptic return (Palmer 1995); the group also promises immorality to select followers through being cloned by the aliens. Some New Age psychics have also published works telling of an "earth evacuation plan" that will be carried out by friendly extraterrestrials in the event of an earth-threatening disaster or a nuclear conflagration.

Such beliefs tend to focus upon the salvation of humans through alien intervention rather than collective human technological achievement. Others, however, have chosen a more "humanistic" approach, in which humans, rather than aliens, are the primary source of activity. Indeed, the concept of human space travel has captured the imaginations of writers for centuries, with novels (some of which were social commentaries disguised as fantasy) written by H.G. Wells and others. By the early twentieth century, however, such concepts were no longer the exclusive domain of fantasy; Konstantin Tsiolkovsky of Russia, Robert Goddard of the United States, and Hermann Oberth of Germany were beginning to do serious theoretical work on rocketry. Tsiolkovsky and Goddard, however, spent most of their careers in obscurity. Oberth, who had been inspired by Jules Verne's *From Earth to the*

Moon, actually popularized the notion of interplanetary flight in his 1923 book, *The Rocket into Planetary Space* (Winter 1990). This book inspired a number of other books and magazine articles and turned amateur rocketry into a German national hobby.

The German lead in rocket science was further developed under the Nazi regime. After World War II this knowledge and expertise was divided between the U.S. and the U.S.S.R., where it was used by both power blocs in the development of ICBMs and, in the form of the space race, the fruition of the dream of flight in space. This race was a curious cold war phenomenon. On the one hand, it allowed each superpower to display publicly its missile-launching capacity, a technology that could be easily adapted to the delivery of nuclear weapons. However, the race might also be described as a sort of technological Olympic competition, with Americans and Soviets competing for national prestige through the display of technological prowess in space while simultaneously honoring the peaceful pursuit of scientific knowledge. A crescendo was reached with the race for the Moon, an effort that culminated with the success of the Apollo Moon landing, an event labeled by Walter Cronkite as "the greatest day since Creation."

The Moon effort was actually something of a mixed success, in which each side tended to spend at least as much time pursuing theatrical successes as it did on long-range program building. Thus, while the U.S. national goal of a lunar landing had been accomplished, budget cuts under the Nixon administration had made the space effort appear to be something of a one-way trip. Rather than building a broad-based space infrastructure—NASA had originally hoped for a space shuttle and/or space station from which to base its manned venture—the decision was made instead to build a special-purpose launcher dedicated solely to the lunar expedition. With the successful completion of the program and the near-term Soviet decision not to pursue manned activity beyond low earth orbit (not to mention domestic unrest over the Vietnam conflict), the U.S. government no longer had a political motive to fund expensive manned missions. Scientific exploration was largely shifted to unmanned probes, which were less expensive, did not risk human life, and comprised a branch of space exploration in which the Soviets were still active.

Not all Americans were pleased with this choice of policy. Many, particularly those with a penchant for science fiction, saw space exploration as something of an end unto itself, an expression of a fundamental human need to explore the unknown. In addition, space offered both natural resources and unlimited room for human expansion. To these people it appeared that humans had become a spacefaring race only to lose collective nerve.

In the wake of this disappointment, various persons and groups began to try to formulate alternatives to overly hesitant NASA plans. One such group was the Committee for the Future (CFF), documented by William Bainbridge (1976). The CFF was founded by a visionary couple, Barbara and Earl Hubbard, who saw existence as driving toward two goals: the integration of all humanity into a unified body of Mankind (Roman Catholic theologian Pierre Teilhard de Chardin's "Convergence"), and "transcendence of the human condition through evolution into a 'universal species' " (Bainbridge 1976, 160). The CFF chose to try to realize these goals in part by sponsoring a program called the Harvest Moon Project, in which an international expedition would travel back to the Moon on board a surplus Saturn V rocket in order, among other things, to leave a robotic lunar rover, deploy a telescope, and set up a garden, complete with animal life, under a plastic dome. While the CFF did manage to establish some congressional contacts for its space project, the technical details for Harvest Moon tended to be romantic and impractical. Eventually the project was abandoned, and the group began to lose interest in space while devoting increasing attention to occultic interests.

Not all of the space enthusiasts were so mystically inclined (Michaud 1986). Gerard K. O'Neill, for example, was an accomplished physicist. During his early career he had distinguished himself by developing a new cyclotron configuration that later became a standard in the field. Later he entered the U.S. astronaut training program but was rejected during the final selection process. Returning to academia in the late 1960s, O'Neill began teaching introductory engineering-track undergraduate physics at Princeton. Presented with the task of organizing an informal seminar *cum* discussion group for especially talented and inspired students, O'Neill chose a sample problem that he felt would interest both himself and his students: space colonies.

As a teaching tool the subject was a success, offering enough challenges to occupy the students for the entire year. In the course of the study, though, O'Neill made a discovery: most plans for space colonies started with the assumption that such colonies would be constructed on planets, with space stations serving mainly as way stations and routing points. Such colonies, not surprisingly, would be complex and expensive to build. However, if one were to reverse this scenario—making the planets the way stations and depots and placing the bulk of a colony in orbit, colonization of space became much more feasible, perhaps even practical. The physicist soon began making calculations in earnest and started giving talks on the subject. Eventually, a small conference was held and—after five years of effort—O'Neill's ideas were published in 1974 as a cover story of the professional journal *Physics Today*.

In spite of his revolutionary views, O'Neill was a practical man. His plans were backed up with equations, and his plans made only modest demands on future technological development. He also submitted his ideas for scrutiny to the physics and engineering community for criticism and correction, with good results. Perhaps most importantly of all, he realized that governments needed pragmatic, rather than ideological, reasons for space exploration. As a result he and his followers devoted an extensive amount of time working on such potentially lucrative projects as the development of solar power satellites. O'Neill also set up GEOSTAR, a commercial space-based venture offering global tracking services to clients; a large percentage of the profits were donated to the space colonies effort.

Behind all of this activity, however, lay O'Neill's vision for the future (Michaud 1986; O'Neill 1976, 1981). O'Neill felt that the human population is increasing in size at an exponential rate. This increase, however, was not accompanied by a similar increase in resources. Furthermore, increasing industrialization and crowding resulted in both rising levels of pollution and increasing disparities between rich and poor nations; the latter problem, especially, could lead to a "war of redistribution" and a nuclear exchange. The alternatives were clear: humanity could continue on its path until growth is halted by famine, pollution, economic collapse, or nuclear conflagration. Or, humanity could reorganize into a highly structured, regimented, and intellectually static steady-state zero-sum economy, as described in the Club of Rome's "Limits to Growth" project.

Or humanity could do what it had often done in the past. It could seek out a new frontier—space—which O'Neill saw as a source both of unlimited resources and, like the American frontier, a place of health, wealth, and great personal freedom. O'Neill's economic projections suggested that the average space-dwelling family of the year 2100 could have, in 1975 dollars, an income of more than $300,000 per year. These families would live in enormous spherical or tubular colonies with low population densities; the internal environment of these structures would be pollution-free, "optimized for good health," and beautifully landscaped, with residents enjoying longer lives and lower accidental death rates than on earth. O'Neill also suggested that heavy "smokestack" industry could be transferred to space, thus removing its earthly environmental impact.

Most important, however, would be the social opportunities that colonies could offer. While O'Neill felt that colonies would be more or less politically and culturally autonomous and tend to resemble a "specialized university town" containing a "similar proliferation of drama clubs, orchestras, lecture series, team sports, flying clubs—and half-finished books," he was quick to point out that such colonies would not be "free of sadness." However, he did feel that

> there is reason to hope that the opening of a new, high frontier will challenge the best that is in us, that the new lands waiting to be built in space will give us a new freedom to search for better governments, social systems, and ways of life. . . .(O'Neill 1981)

Life in the Datasphere: Better Living Through Programming

We have now looked at several groups that have blended empirical science with millenarian vision, i.e., groups strongly holding the opinion that technology will bring about a new golden age in the near future that will create a substantial, and permanent, fundamental improvement in the human condition. If we examine these groups we find that such movements have the following characteristics: first, participants perceive a widespread threat—for example, imminent social collapse, personal extinction, or stagnation and boredom; second, a new technology beckons in which recent progress has been made, but also in which the social significance is as yet unclear—genetics, cryobiology, and space. Such fields have a certain numinous quality, holding both great promise coupled with unknown perils. Paralleling Wallace's scenario for a revitilization movement, the stage has been set for the emergence of a prophetic figure who can articulate both the current hopes and the fears of the audience and then connect them to the technology at hand in both a plausible and an inspirational manner. We thus have the following "equation":

Push Factors + Pull Factors + Social and/or
Technical Plausibility —— Social Movement

In the case of eugenics we see a series of technological prophets, first Francis Galton and then Davenport and others, speaking of a threat (racial degeneration through poor breeding stock, national bankruptcy from support of a growing indigent population) but offering a positive alternative vision as well (social stability and Anglo-Saxon cultural supremacy). Here, the plausible means of solving this problem was a program of "positive eugenics," i.e., interbreeding of superior stocks, to be encouraged through the education of children on the need for proper mate selection and possibly through grants or tax exemptions to "eugenically deserving" families; and "negative eugenics," that is, segregation or sterilization of inferior stocks. Scientific plausibility was derived from recent advances in genetic/eugenic science, while social credibility appears to have come from a popular sense of unease about increasing numbers of immigrants and "feebleminded" persons in society, but perhaps also springing from doubts about one's *own* self-worth; examination of literature produced by some eugenics-friendly religionists of the day suggests an increasing preoccupation of human personal worth being determined more by social Darwinian "fitness" and social utility than by more traditional notions of intrinsic human worth.

Note, too, that both social *and* technological plausibility were not always necessary for the movement to continue; while the eugenicists enjoyed broad-based support within the scientific community in the early 1910s, this eroded during the next decade. Nevertheless, the number of surgical sterilizations peaked *after* doubt was increasing about the value of sterilization to the cause of "racial hygiene," apparently due to institutional momentum within state asylums. Only a profound change in the social environment—the reassignment of surgeons out of asylums into the pressing World War II war effort, plus a later reluctance to reinstitute eugenic measures in the wake of the war and on the eve of the civil rights movement—resulted in the decline of such programs.

We find a similar pattern in the cryonics movement. Here we find a rather universal "push" factor: that of personal physical death. Cooper, Ettinger, and others looked to cryobiology, extended to humans, to solve this problem; the "pull," on the other hand, came from a sense of optimism about the future of humanity—human society would become better, both socially and technologically. Technical plausibility, in this case, came from recent advances in cryobiology and cryosurgery. Social plausibility, on the other hand, appears to have been drawn from two sources: first, the growth of "science fiction" culture; the movement was founded by a science fiction author, and ALCOR recruits a number of clients at science fiction conventions. Second, the movement also appears to draw support from increased secularity in American culture; a very high percentage of people involved in the early movement were agnostics or atheists with little expectation of a supernatural afterlife (Sheskin 1979), a trend that appears to continue to the present day. Again, it may be noted that social plausibility may overcome technical plausibility—while early cryobiologists gave a cautious approval to the cryonics movement, they have since rescinded it, giving rise to (in the words of one cryonicist) a "cold war" between the two groups (Perry 1991b). This debate does not appear to have greatly affected the cryonics movement, however, which now has some 1,000 clients presently in or signed up for cryonic suspension.

Within the American space colony movement, we find the same pattern once again. The push factor here was a vision of social stagnation derived from works such as "Limits to Growth," and punctuated by events such as the energy crisis and the emergence of environmental awareness; the pull was offered by a vision of boundless expansion and endless resources. O'Neill served as the charismatic leader who synthesized the initial vision and who also worked out the technical plausibility of the scenario; social plausibility was supplied by recent space achievements by NASA. The continuing social plausibility of the space movement is also demonstrated by the periodic reemergence of both technical and lay-oriented efforts toward space colonization, as well as continued efforts by small companies to produce viable, low-cost launch vehicles with which to commercialize space.

Other patterns emerge as well. Each of the groups that we have examined above began, roughly speaking, with a decade-long period of "prophetic" proclamation and ferment, followed by a period of stabilization and consolidation. Each was also a curious blend of radical and conservative elements; while each promised to completely overturn the social order and bring about a new, more perfect era, this greater perfection was actually the preservation and magnification of the existing, perhaps endangered, present order. Galton, for example, saw eugenics as a way to preserve the British aristocracy against the onslaught of crass industrial plutocracy; in America the science was perceived as a way to shore up a faltering white Anglo-Saxon middle-class cultural imperium faced with the dual threats of immigration and an increasingly visible proletariat. Cryonics, on the other hand, assumed that the future will be like the present, only better—with greater personal wealth, longer lives, and better sex. The space colonies movement, too, claimed to give American energy-intensive industrial capitalism a new, indefinite, lease on life in the face of recessions, nuclear war, and energy crises.

And what of the future? Will Americans continue to view new technologies in a salvific light? The answer would appear to be "yes." Even as old groups stabilize, new groups continue to appear. Presently the trend seems to be to cast computers as the new road to humanity's ultimate destiny; books such as Gregory Stock's *Metaman* (1993), for example, suggest that mankind has now become interlinked into a giant superorganism, "metaman," thanks to the emergence of the "datasphere"—the electronic equivalent to the organic biosphere of the natural world. Others, taking the myth of the "information super-highway" to a further extreme, have proclaimed the emergence of a new subculture called "Cyberia" (Rushkoff 1994). The emergence of such thought is not surprising; the desire for "thinking machines," both autonomous and as a form of human mental augmentation, has existed for decades. However, the explosive growth of personal computers and, soon after, computer networks, has made them at once ubiquitous and, to many, mysterious. Religious and quasi-religious groups have formed around them, as well. One example of this is the "Zippie" movement, a small group led by ethnobotanist and concert promoter Frasier Clark; this group combines elements of pagan religion, computer use, drugs, and some aspects of the hippie way of life into a new techno-shamanistic lifestyle. The watchword of this movement supposedly is the word "pronoia," defined as "the unreasonable assumption that forces are conspiring to help a person" (Marshall 1994; Huffstutter 1994).

A more tough-minded, but equally millennarian, group is the Extropian movement. Led by Max More, this group is dedicated to the discussion and development of "transhumanist" philosophy—a philosophy rooted in the belief that the human state is only a first step, and that human destiny is to become more than human through technologies such as genetic engineering, space colonies, cryonics, intelligence-increasing drugs, nanotechnology, and artificial intelligence. Aggressively secularist and politically libertarian (Morrow and More 1988; More 1994), the Extropians are particularly fascinated by the prospect of direct human-machine interfacing; such a development would not only allow for cybernetic mental and physical enhancements, it could also allow "uploading"—transference of one's memories and personality into a computer. Such an action could conceivably result in a form of effective immortality, either in a robotic body or perhaps in a virtual reality setting in a computer memory bank. Perhaps not surprisingly, the Extropians have their own vision of the apocalypse called the "information singularity" (a concept much discussed on the Extropian internet newsgroup). Evoking images of black holes (the heart of which is also called a singularity), the information singularity may occur within the next twenty to forty years and be the result of the continued exponential growth of data and computer technology. At some point the rate of information increase will become virtually vertical, meaning that information will be accruing at an infinite rate. While the word "singularity" implies a complete, unimaginable break with the past, many assume that this event will entail a fundamental reordering of both the consciousness of individuals and of the greater society.

TECHNOLOGICAL MILLENNIALISM IN AMERICAN CULTURE

Technological millennialism is an American phenomenon that has existed for decades, and will probably continue in decades to come. For many people it appears to serve as a secular religion for a technological age; as such it offers various forms of group and individual salvation, up to and including eternal life. While there may be an initial impulse to dismiss such groups as cranks and/or eccentrics (particularly by more "establishmentarian" scientists and technologists), to do so would be a mistake for a number of reasons. First, the existence of such quasi-religious groups tell us at least as much about our personal and social values as our organized religions do. Eugenics, for example, posits that a person's worth is not intrinsic but rather a function of one's social utility, while cryonics shows that a strong desire continues to exist for personal immortality, even though this desire has become unfashionable to admit in modern secular society.

Furthermore, American culture is perfused with technological millenarianism; while most members of society would not be so bold as to argue that technology is the key to some form of eternal life, many would say that technological progress will lead to a better quality of life. Arguably, this quest to bring forth a better future beginning here and now is one of the forces that have made the United States a leader in both technological production and in popular culture and that have also given Americans a characteristic thirst for novelty. At the same time, technology offers hope for inevitable improvement: problems such as AIDS, or a declining standard of living, are simply temporary afflictions that will pass away in the near future.

Finally, there is the question of the process of technological innovation itself. Science is frequently portrayed as a rational process in which hypotheses are tested and discarded in an orderly process. While occasional breakthroughs do occur (as per Kuhn's *Structure of Scientific Revolutions* [1970]), it is usually assumed that such revolutionary events occur after the slow buildup of counterevidence that undercuts a prevailing paradigm. At the outset of this overturning process, however, no counterevidence exists; furthermore, it may take a great deal of time and effort before any counterevidence is discovered. Often, however, ideas may have no clear precedent upon which to build and/or no clear market to exploit, as in the case of airplanes, electric lighting, rocketry, telegraphy and telephony, and, more recently, the search for gravity waves and neutrino decay. Technological millennialism may provide that element of faith—the belief in the reality of things yet unseen—that allows a visionary to carry his or her ideas through to a perhaps uncertain fruition.

Such visionary conviction seems to stand in an undefined space between avant-garde science and wishful thinking. On the one hand, it may attract professional scientists attempting simply to expand the edifice of science in an anticipated, if not yet proven, manner. Alternatively, such movements also share something in common with some forms of "scientized" millennial faiths such as Scientology, UFO-worshipping, and segments of the New Age movement which rely upon science not so much for providing objective confirmation or disconfirmation, but as a source of vocabulary and legitimating mythic paradigms.

REFERENCES

Alcor Life Extension Foundation. 1993. *Cryonics: Reaching for Tomorrow*, 4th ed. Scottsdale, AZ: Alcor.

Bainbridge, William Sims. 1976. *The Spaceflight Revolution*. New York: John Wiley and Sons.

Bozeman, John M. 1993. "The Popular Rhetoric of the American Eugenics Movement." Unpublished paper.

———. 1994. "American Eugenics and the Liberal Clergy, 1929–1939." Paper presented at the annual meeting of the Society for the History of Technology, January 19, 1995, Charlottesville, Virginia.

Bushnell, Horace. 1861. *Christian Nurture* (reprint of revised ed.). Grand Rapids: Baker.

Daggett, Mabel Potter. 1912. "Building a Better Race." *World's Work* 25 (Dec.): 228–234.

Davenport, Charles. 1916[?]. "Eugenics as Religion." Unpublished typescript, 1–5. Charles Davenport papers. File: Eugenics as Religion. Philadelphia: American Philosophical Society.

Ettinger, Robert. 1964. *The Prospect of Immortality*. Garden City, NY: Doubleday.

———. 1972. *Man into Superman*. New York: St. Martin's.

Galton, Francis. 1865. "Hereditary Talent and Character." *Macmillan's* 12: 157–166, 318–327.

———. 1869. *Hereditary Genius*. London: Macmillan.

Glennie, Mary M. 1992. "A Well-Loved Man." *Cryonics* (Sept.): 8–13.

Huffstutter, P. J. 1994. "We're Not In Woodstock Anymore." *L.A. Times/Calendar*. (Aug. 7): 5, 78–79.

Kuhn, Thomas. 1970. *The Structure of Scientific Revolutions*. Chicago: University of Chicago.

Lewis, James R., ed. 1995. *The Gods Have Landed*. Albany: SUNY.

Marsden, George. 1989. "Evangelicals and the Scientific Culture: An Overview." In *Religion and Twentieth Century American Intellectual Life*, edited by M. Lacey. New York: Cambridge.

Marshall, Jules. 1994. "Here Come the Zippies!" *Wired* (May): 78–84, 130–131.

Michaud, Michael A. G. 1986. *Reaching for the High Frontier*. New York: Praeger.

More, Max. 1988. "Morality or Reality?" *Extropy* 1 (on-line edition) (Fall): 7–10.

———. 1994. "On Becoming Posthuman." On-line at http://www.c2.org/~whitaker/becoming_posthuman.html.

Morrow, Tom, and Max More. 1988. "Introduction." *Extropy* 1 (on-line edition) (Fall): 1–7.

O'Neill, Gerard K. 1976. *The High Frontier*. New York: William Morrow.

———. 1981. *2081*. New York: Simon and Schuster.

Palmer, Susan J. 1995. "Women in the Raelian Movement." In *The Gods Have Landed*, edited by J. Lewis. Albany: SUNY.

Parker, Robert A. 1935. *A Yankee Saint*. New York: G.P. Putnam's Sons.

Perry, Mike. 1990a. "John Hunter, Cryonics Forerunner." *Cryonics* (Nov.): 12.

———. 1990b. "The First Cryonics Newsletter." *Cryonics* (Dec.): 10–11.

———. 1991a. "Franklin As Pioneering Immortalist." *Cryonics* (Jan.): 10–11.

———. 1991b. "Cyrobiologists vs. Cryonicists: Roots of the Cold War." *Cryonics* (Dec.): 6–7.

Reilly, Philip R. 1991. *The Surgical Solution*. Baltimore: Johns Hopkins.

Rushkoff, Douglas. 1994. *Cyberia: Life in the Trenches of Hyperspace*. New York: Harper San Francisco.

Sheskin, Arlene. 1979. *Cryonics: A Sociology of Death and Bereavement*. New York: Irvington Publishers/John Wiley and Sons.

Stock, Gregory. 1993. *Metaman: The Merging of Humans and Machines into a Global Superorganism*. New York: Simon and Schuster.

von Daniken, E. 1970. *Chariots of the Gods?* New York: Putnam.

Wallace, Anthony F. C. 1956. "Revitalization Movements." *American Anthropology* 58: 264–281.

White, Andrew Dickson. 1896. *A History of the Warfare of Science with Theology in Christendom*. New York: D. Appleton.

Winter, Frank H. 1990. *Rockets into Space*. Cambridge: Harvard.

Woman as World Savior
The Feminization of the Millennium in New Religious Movements

8 Susan J. Palmer

The millennial dreams of contemporary apocalyptic movements in America, when carefully surveyed, reveal an overwhelmingly feminine presence. This situation might be described as the "feminization of the millennium." Rosemary Reuther (1988) used the term "feminization"—once a daring neologism—to convey the increasing influence and expanding role of women in Protestant denominations in nineteenth-century America. She observed that in the wake of the disestablishment of mainline denominations, women began to outnumber the men in most congregations. Ministers no longer ran the town councils or main businesses as church and state drifted farther apart. Churches, by now marginalized in the political arena, had begun to function as an extension of the domestic sphere. Christian virtues were associated with what were perceived as the quintessentially feminine virtues of piety, humility, compassion, and sacrifice. Victorian women, therefore, were considered to be somehow natural, effortless Christians, whereas men were perceived to be more inclined toward sin, and drawn to the competition and fleshpots of secular life.

Today this "feminizing" process seems to be occurring in religions outside the mainstream. A wealth of utopian literature has appeared in the 1980s and 1990s that exalts women as world saviors and rulers of the future. The eschatologies of many marginal religions feature goddesses as well as gods presiding over the new age, or the earth as a pregnant planet contracting in birth spasms, and women warriors defeating all-male armies. A close look at the authority patterns of new religious organizations reveals an abundance of female messiahs, mediums, and sybils, and feminine leadership has become surprisingly common. Even among the rank-and-file members there seems to be a prevailing notion that their women will play a key role in the endtime — as midwives assisting the birth of a new age, as mothers of a future *homo superiorus*, or as usherettes in a cosmic theater.

WOMEN IN THE HISTORY OF HERESY

Apocalyptic women are unexpected — perhaps unprecedented — if one considers the male-oriented millenarian visions that have dominated Western history: the Jewish Messiahs, the Muslim Mahdis, the Christian Son of Man. These traditions envisage equestrian sky gods, male demons erupting from earth, and cosmic battles starring warrior-heroes. This situation has been somewhat mitigated within the American Protestant prophetic tradition by a "genderless" Bible-based "number-crunching" — as in the case of mathematically minded prophet William Miller of the Millerites in the 1840s, who kept adjusting his endtime countdown.

Apocalyptic dramas starring women have been comparatively rare and usually confined to esoteric circles. Within orthodox religions — even in our supposedly postfeminist society — women are still absent or prudently keeping a "low profile." They may receive negative publicity, as the Whore of Babylon, the Fallen Eve, or the Bride of the Antichrist. As one moves through the history of heresy, however, one finds that many women prophet-founders have frequently flourished on the margins of American religion (Wessinger 1993).

The prominence of women in marginal religions has often been interpreted by church fathers as a clear sign of heresy—or at least of immorality. The early Gnostics were criticized for their creation myth that emphasized the feminine force of Sophia. Simon Magus, a Gnostic leader of the first century who claimed to be the "first god," shocked Irenaeus and Justin Martyr by wandering around with a former prostitute called Helena, discovered in a Phoenician brothel, whom he claimed was the *ennoia*, or "God's first thought," and a reincarnation of Helen of Troy (Rudolph 1987, 294). Mother Ann Lee of the eighteenth-century Shakers was condemned by her contemporaries as a *virago*, and rumored to be a man in disguise (Foster 1981). Even the Goddess venerated by Wiccans is suspect, according to Wanda Marrs, wife of the Christian evangelist Texe Marrs. She postulates in her book *New Age Lies to Women* (1989) that the Goddess is really the Bride of the Antichrist, who sets the stage for Armageddon and Christ's return.

SEXUAL SOLUTIONS TO SOCIAL DISORDER

Since myths must mirror their social worlds, one would expect the apocalyptic myths of budding religions to reflect current trends and cultural tensions. Utopian communities of the nineteenth century, for example, expressed the Victorians' deep concern for reconstructing family life and clarifying gender roles (Foster 1981). The Oneida Perfectionists, whose founder, John Humphrey Noyes, held himself to be the *Third* Coming, rejected monogamous marriage and procreation and considered woman to be a "female man." The Shakers who followed Mother Ann Lee sought to purify their brothers and sisters from sin through ritual shaking, a celibate life, and egalitarian gender roles. The early Mormons built their kingdoms in heaven through "celestial marriage," polygamy and procreation. All these groups considered their utopian forms of "ordered love" (Kern 1981) to offer spiritual solutions to the decline and fragmentation of the lineage family in the antebellum period.

The suspenseful eschatologies of new religious movements (NRMs) reflect our own preoccupations with issues of sexual identity, women's power, and the disintegration of the nuclear family. For many new religions, reconstructing relations between the sexes in correct alignment to the divine cosmos is an essential step in preparing for the millennium. There are groups that exalt woman as world savior, humanity's only hope for averting nuclear destruction. Other groups are resigned to the prospect of a worldwide holocaust, but see women as the builders of a new society, or rulers in the golden age, as in the case of the Brahmakumaris, founded by Dada Lekraj, who foresee women reigning as goddesses in the *satyug* after the present world has been destroyed (Babb 1986). Radical lesbian spirituality advocates a rejection of and separation from male hegemony so that women can bond in a just and loving sisterhood and excavate their true metaphysical identity. At the other extreme are neo-conservative groups and racialist religions that tell woman to return to her rightful place as wife and mother, "covered" by her husband in order to prepare her children for the Second Coming, or to breed and rear a new, sinless, wholly human race.

GENDER, GENESIS, AND ECOFEMINISM

Some feminist theologians and scholar-critics of patriarchal religions have challenged misogynistic extrapolations on the doctrine of original sin and struck a rich millenarian vein in their writings. Mary Daly, who describes herself as a "post-Christian feminist," redefines "original sin" as a "state of complicity in patriarchal oppression . . . socially transmitted disease involving psychological paralysis . . . horizontal violence, and a never-ending conviction of one's own guilt" (Daly 1987: Word-Web One). Daly finds the "original sin of sexism" wreaking its destructive effects upon women throughout history and proposes a "Fall into freedom" as the only means whereby Eve will learn to "name herself, to become all she can be" (Daly 1974).

Daly's millenarian vision depicts a psychic war between the sexes based on their metaphysical proclivities. She regards males as "gynaecidal" and life-hating, in contrast to women, whom she defines as "biophilic" and creative. In a dazzling poetic passage she warns women that men are on the verge of blowing up the planet:

> Clockocracy is marked by male-ordered monotony that breaks Bio-rhythms, preparing the way for the fullness of fathered time, that is, doomsday. . . . It is

marked by measurements that tick off women's lifetimes/Lifelines in tidy tidbits. It is he world of dismembered time, surgically sewn together to mimic and replace Tidal Time. . . . The fathers' clocks . . . are nuclear time, doomed time. (Daly 1987, 281)

Daly awards women the salvific role of subverting the threat of the man-made nuclear holocaust through their intuitive magical connection to nature, and their shamanic power of sight:

Raging/Be-Laughing Websters unwind these bindings that would numb us, dumb us. With Eyebiting Eyes/I's we See through and Name man's interconnected atrocities. . . . We Proclaim that the primary product of man's civilization/snivilization is toxic waste. Lusty women, in tune with the Moon . . . look toward the madmen and turn them to stone. (Daly 1987, 282)

Also speaking from the margins of radical feminism is Sonia Johnson, an ex-Mormon radical feminist. In her recent book, *Wildfire* (1989), she preaches a message of lesbian apocalypticism.

Another genre of feminist apocalypticism is found in NRMs that venerate the powers in Nature, such as neo-shamanic healing circles, Wicca, and various schools of ecotheology. Gaians espouse the notion of the planet as an integral, living, maternal organism. Wiccans have adopted Margaret Murray's mythologized history of witchcraft as the original religion of the human race, which went underground to withstand the onslaught of Christianity and other "patriarchal" religions and survive in fragmented covens of Goddess worshippers who continued to re-enact the parthenogenic birth and violent death of the vegetation deity in order to stimulate the agricultural cycle. Starhawk, a famous witch, author, and ecological activist, orchestrated protest demonstrations in the late eighties to pit women's natural magic against the marauding masculine forces of industry and war, as when in 1987 her witches in Vancouver saved up their menstrual blood for two years in freezers, then gathered, chanting, to throw it against nuclear reactors.

Other large, international, and well-known NRMs have evolved their own idiosyncratic "sexual solutions" to pollution or the nuclear threat that almost *parody* trends in the feminist movement. Profeminist prophets Rajneesh, Rael, and Ramtha are striking examples of this.

Bhagwan Shree Rajneesh, Indian-born eclectic philosopher and founder of Rajneeshpuram, a communal utopian city in Oregon that lasted from 1981 to

1985, proclaimed: "My own vision is that the coming age will be the age of woman. . . . Feminine energies must be released!" (Krishna 1984; see 'Woman'). In Rajneeshpuram he appointed women as leaders, "the pillars of my commune," and they filled more than 80 percent of executive positions. He explained that woman is "a female Buddha," more receptive and spiritually advanced than man, and less inclined toward aggression and "power trips." In 1983, Rajneesh emerged from a vow of silence and announced that after the world was decimated by AIDS in 2000, women would take over and build a new age based on love, harmony with nature, meditative consciousness, and superior technology (Krishna 1984).

Rael, a former race car driver from France who founded the Raelian Movement after he was contacted by extraterrestrials in 1973, has announced that "the Age of Apocalypse will be the age of women!" He urges men to develop the feminine qualities of love, peace, tolerance, and empathy so that our species can avoid self-destruction through nuclear weapons. The inner circle of male and female Guides grow their hair long to increase their telepathic powers, and avoid procreation in favor of being cloned. Humanity must learn to "make love, not war" in the Raelian Movement's fun-loving international, multiracial, "quadrasexual" community, and to prepare for the descent of the extraterrestrials around the year 2035 by building an intergalactic space embassy in Jerusalem, and spreading the message that the "elohim" created us in test tubes from their own DNA.

The Ramtha Foundation also espouses a feminist apocalyptic theory. J.Z. Knight, a petite blond businesswoman, began in 1977 to function as the mouthpiece for Ramtha, the invisible eight-foot, 40,000-year-old "Lemurian" warrior. Based in Yelm, Washington, Knight has traveled across the country renting hotel ballrooms to hold weekend "dialogues" wherein Ramtha takes over her body, expounds his Gnostic philosophy, and dispenses advice. In a manner reminiscent of nineteenth-century female mediums (Moore 1977), J.Z. Knight channels an entity that defends the rights of women and challenges male hegemony. Ramtha condemns males for their omnivorous sexual appetite and encourages the empowerment of women:

> Men defile your women. Men molest one another. You brutalize sex, eroticize violence. . . . And men, you don't have to go out and copulate everything to impregnate the whole world! . . . You don't have to spill your seed every day! . . . See women as equals, as brilliant gods, just as you are. That *changes* the shadow,

the destiny; that allows you to go forward in harmony with Nature. (Ramtha
1987, 138)

Ramtha describes our planet as a "living entity" regularly visited by space
brothers, and on the verge of irresistible "evolutionary processes"—and
paints an unusual vision of an earth "laced with zippers" about to explode
into volcanic eruptions, tidal waves, and earthquakes (Ramtha 1987, 30–35).
He recommends survivalist preparations—put your money in gold, move to
the Pacific Northwest, stockpile a two-year food supply, and cultivate veg-
etable gardens. Real estate agents have watched with interest the migration
into Washington State of "Ramsters," "many of whom are middle-aged
women" (Montreal *Gazette* 1984).

A "Comic" Ending

While these leaders promote what Reuther calls a "radical romantic feminism,"other groups emphasize cooperation and harmony between the sexes,
and in all these groups the notion of reconciling the sexes and achieving the
"right" balance of power as a prerequisite for ushering in a successful millennium is importantly present. Messiahs and prophets often form a charismatic
duo with their wives or mistresses, for androgyny is a potent ingredient that
enhances the charisma, not only of shamans and rock stars, but of charismatic
leaders as well. Bo and Peep, the founders of a UFO religion, were a charismatic
duo composed of a homosexual choir director and an unhappily married
nurse, who wore identical clothing, ate off the same plate, finished each other's
sentences, and prepared their followers for the extraterrestrials' descent when
they would all become immortal, flying androgynes (Balch 1982). The younger
consorts of male prophet-founders occasionally take over the reins of leadership upon their death. Reverend Moon and his wife represent the male and
female aspects of God, the "One True Parent of Mankind" for members of the
Unification Church, and Moon has anointed Mrs. Moon to preside over the
movement in the future. Women have always assisted the dying, and in their
proximity to dying gurus seize the opportunity to ask favors, manipulate
mythologies, and mould the succession so as to create more egalitarian or
"uxor-friendly" patterns of authority. Another notable example is David Berg,
the "Lord's Endtime Prophet" and founder of the The Family who, before his

"homecoming" in 1994, anointed his consort, Maria, to succeed him as the "Endtime Prophetess."

David Berg always awarded equal opportunity to women. Since the early 1980s when this Christian communal movement was known as the Children of God, their "shepherdesses" have pioneered new missionary fields and administered the international communes, while at the same time contributing to the group's high birth rate. The demands of marriage and motherhood have not impeded Family women in their executive careers, due to communal childrearing patterns and a free love ethic. Berg's "Law of Love" rebelled against the Christian church's "prohibitory and condemnatory attitude towards sex," encouraged women's partial nudity inside the homes, and advocated "sharing" outside matrimony between consenting heterosexuals (Melton 1994). While this development simply "Christianized" the sexual revolution already experienced by Berg's hippie followers, a more radical step was taken when Berg and his young consort, Maria, launched the "Flirty Fishing Ministry" in the mid-1970s. This new evangelical strategy involved using women's beauty and sexual favors to win souls for Jesus, to attract new members, and, incidentally, to drum up financial support.

As the result of these cultural patterns, The Family's eschatology, which otherwise conforms to the classical premillennial drama of Protestant fundamentalism, has become startlingly feminized and sexualized. Sexy half-clad women dominate the group's iconography like a postmodernist collaboration between Hal Lindsey and Hugh Hefner. Apocalyptic landscapes illustrating the founder's *Mo Letters* and warning tracts like the *Endtimes News* feature topless Amazons waging war during the Tribulation (see girls' comic *Heaven's Girl*, 1984). Once the Antichrist is overthrown, Berg's vision of Heaven on Earth begins to resemble Gauguin's Tahiti. Ladies in loincloths continue to give birth, to nurse their babies and enjoy picnics with new lovers, for in Heaven "none are married nor given in marriage." Reminiscent of the old "Flirty Fishing" days, flying missionaries in bikinis distribute silver leaves of the gospel to those not yet "saved"—and even to (pagan) extraterrestrials on other planets.

Since Maria assumed the mantle of leadership in 1994, the gender equity established by Berg is veering toward a more radical romantic type of feminism (Reuther 1988). Maria married her secretary, "King Peter," and together they have launched a "flood of prophecy" that encourages members to cultivate a more sexual relationship with Jesus in their prayer life. She exhorts both men and women to work on "acquiring more female characteristics: gentleness, quietness, submission" that she predicts will be increasingly necessary as the Endtime draws near:

> In His spiritual relationship with us, the Lord doesn't look on these physical bodies . . . but accepts us all as His Bride, His Beloved, His chosen woman in whom He delights and longs to love. (*ML* 3029, paragraph 123)

In a prophecy published in the *Loving Jesus Revelation* (*ML* 3029, paragraph 109, October 1996), the Lord makes it quite clear that under Maria's rule Family women will be empowered as leaders in the Time of the End:

> Did I not say unto David that after he was gone, it would be a day of women? For I have foretold of this day, the day when the weaker vessel shall become strong. . . .

In this way "Mama Maria" continues to feminize, eroticize, and marginalize the faith of this new religious movement now in its second and third generation, in a manner consistent with the spirit of its founder whose mystical eroticism has evoked much controversy.

One notable feature of these "feminized" millennia is a tendency toward optimism and peaceful resolutions—what Stephen D. O'Leary (1994) would term the *comic* frame of apocalyptic discourse. He identifies two frames that interact, each dramatizing its own resolution of the problem of evil; the *tragic* (dualistic and anticipating a redemptive climax marked by catastrophic suffering), and the *comic*, which espouses an open-ended or cyclic view of the future that can be influenced by human agency. Feminist apocalyptic dramas appear to be reacting against what they perceive to be the male-generated *tragic* mode of narrative. Nevertheless, the widespread assumption that humanity can finally enjoy the fruits of peace with women in charge is belied by some prophetesses' fascination with weapons and the themes of war.

Elizabeth Clare Prophet of the Church Universal and Triumphant (CUT), a sect originating from Theosophy and the I AM movement (Lewis and Melton 1994) is one of the outstanding millenarian prophets of our age. After the death in 1973 of the original founder, her husband and "twin flame" Mark Prophet, she succeeded him as the Messenger. From the Church's headquarters in Montana, she delivers high-speed oral "dictations," relaying messages to humanity from the Ascended Masters. Some of these messages are apocalyptic in content, particularly the prophecies of Saint Germain, who is expected to succeed Christ when the Piscean Age moves into the Age of Aquarius. In a 1986 dictation, Saint Germain warned that the Soviet Union was planning a nuclear attack on America, and members should prepare by building bomb shelters. In 1989 he proclaimed nuclear war was more likely than having a death in the family. Again, on March 11, 1990, Saint Germain predicted that the Soviet attack was imminent, and urged members to withdraw their money from banks, move out of urban areas, stockpile food and weapons and move into underground tunnels to prepare for the Tribulation.

Despite these classic ingredients of a *tragic* survivalist midtribulationist agenda, Dehaas (1994) argues that CUT conforms rather to Wessinger's model (1993) of "progressive millennialism"—not unlike O'Leary's *comic* frame.

There have also been rare occasions of violent or criminal behavior perpetrated by female or profeminist charismatic leaders. In 1986, Rajneesh's personal secretary, Ma Anand Sheela, was sentenced in federal court to twenty years in prison after pleading guilty to a range of crimes and misdemeanors. These included wiretapping, immigration fraud, arson, the attempted murder of Rajneesh's physician, and deliberately infecting the townspeople of The Dalles with salmonella poisoning. She was also a suspect in the plot to bomb Attorney General Fruhnmayer's car (Milne 1986, 319–320).

The Order of the Solar Temple (OTS), notorious for their 1994 mass suicides/homicides staged in Quebec and Switzerland, espoused an ecofeminist apocalyptic theory. Luc Jouret, the Quebec Grand Master, claimed it was necessary to balance positive "feminine energies"—which they associated with the French culture, art, and nature—with the extant negative "male energies"—associated with the English, industrial powers, and materialism. To this esoteric end, the OTS imported eleven francophone members from Martinique to Quebec to combat the anglo influence (Palmer 1996). Joseph DiMambro, the OTS Grand Master in Switzerland, raised his daughter, Emmanuelle, to be the avatar, or "cosmic child" of the New Age. DiMambro's young mistress was immaculately impregnated by the Ascended Master Manatanus in a public "rite of conception" involving lazer beams, puppets, and special lighting effects staged in the underground crypt at Salvan.

DiMambro, however, had hoped for a male avatar, and compensated by bringing the child up as a boy, insisting she be referred to as "he." When ex-member, Tony Dutoit, the OTS' former electrical engineer who had stage managed their sound and light shows, had the effrontery to conceive a child against DiMambro's advice and then to name the boy "Emmanuel" and ask DiMambro to be his godfather, he may have unwittingly invited the Grand Master's ferocious reprisal. The Dutoit family were executed as "traitors" before the Quebec chalet was set on fire. Thus, a kind of gender war may have contributed to bringing on what the Swiss judge, André Piller, termed the OTS' "long-planned apocalypse."

That the apocalyptic imagination in America is resplendent with — or (depending upon one's perspective) alarmingly polluted by — feminine images, is a phenomenon easy to prove. To guess its meaning is a more difficult task.

Sexual imagery has always been a strong element in endtime narratives, as it is in the world's creation myths. Cosmogonies usually recount the origins of life from the union of the first Man and Woman, to their eventual separation through the Fall into mortality through infanticide, parricide, or incest. Millenarians through the ages seem to be particularly set on reconstructing the primordial drama in Eden and exonerating Eve. Norman Cohn (1970, 180) describes the Brothers of the Free Spirit movement (circa 1550), which attracted many wealthy unmarried women who emulated Eve in practicing ritual nudity, thus "asserting . . . that they were restored to the state of innocence which had existed before the Fall" (Cohn 1970, 180).

Apocalyptic narrations of destruction and regeneration must, of necessity, include the symbols of the creation myth common to its culture. Western monotheistic patriarchal religions tend to show a dearth of creation myths that depict woman's life-giving creativity or explicit images of the birth process. Judy Chicago, the feminist artist and sculptress, claims she could not find any adequate iconography of creation in Western art, only masculine images she found utterly unconvincing — "unless you believe in God touching Adam on the finger!"

Now that the prospect of mass destruction is a plausible reality and we confront the terrifying photographs of Hiroshima and other bomb experiments as they invade our collective consciousness through the media, there is a corresponding need to contemplate primal images of birth. Since the 1970s, there has been a trend to make childbirth a public event — to film it, invite friends into the labor room. The raw, uncensored photographs of birth have become acceptable, even sacred. At the same time, there has been a corresponding trend to hide the ugly intimate details of the deathbed — to "medicalize" death, as Phillippe Aries (1988) argues. Aries laments the decline of the traditional *artes moriendi*, the public deathbed scene, of farewells and religious testimonials. It might be argued that this lost art has been replaced by the art of birth, a new public ritual; and that when one contemplates the grim, "scientific" possibility of a global holocaust, earth goddesses presiding as midwives over a planet's *accouchment* are considerably less scary than sky gods in battle!

Today we find a profusion of feminine imagery and a strong female presence in the millennial dreams of the late twentieth century. As students of religion and culture we are aware that myths and symbols mirror society and its natural environment, and that a people's mythology will respond to changing social and ecological conditions. It appears reasonable, therefore, to assert that that millenarian movements today are feeling the impact of feminism, and that the contemporary eschatologies featuring cosmic interplay between polar forces, good versus evil, light versus dark, sky versus earth, will express our deep preoccupation with issues of gender, identity, and power.

REFERENCES

Aries, Philippe. 1988. *The Hour of Our Death*. New York: Oxford University Press.

Babb, Lawrence, ed. 1986. "History as Movie." In *Redemptive Encounters: Three Modern Styles in the Hindu Tradition*. Berkeley: University of California Press.

Balch, Robert. 1982. "Bo and Peep: A Case Study of the Origins of Messianic Leadership." In *Millennialism and Charisma*, edited by Roy Wallis. Belfast: Queen's University.

————. 1996. "How to Avoid Finding Evidence of Clergy Malfeasance: the AWARE Study of the Church Universal and Triumphant." Unpublished manuscript.

Chander, Jagdish. 1981. *Adi Dev, the First Man*. Prajapita Brahma Kumaris World Spiritual University. Singapore, Malaysia: Kim Hup Lee Printing.

Cohn, Norman. 1970. *The Pursuit of the Millennium*. London: Oxford University Press.

Daly, Mary. 1974. *Beyond God the Father: Toward a Philosophy of Women's Liberation*. Boston: Beacon Press.

————, (in cahoots with) Jane Caputi. 1987. *Websters' First New Intergalactic Wickedary of the English Language*. Boston: Beacon Press.

Dehaas, Jocelyn H. 1994. "Apocalyptic Prophecy and the Notion of Non-Linear Time in the Church Universal and Triumphant." Paper presented, 1994 meeting for the Society for the Scientific Study of Religion, Albuquerque, New Mexico.

Foster, Lawrence. 1981. *Religion and Sexuality: Three American Communal Experiments of the Nineteenth Century*. New York: Oxford University Press.

Grace, James. 1985. *Sexuality and Marriage in the Unification Church*. Toronto: Edwin Mellen Press.

Johnson, Sonia. 1989. *Wildfire: Igniting the She/Volution*. Albuquerque: Wildfire Books.

Kern, Louis. 1981. *An Ordered Love*. Chapel Hill: University of North Carolina Press.

Knshna Premg Swami, ed. 1984. *The Book: An Introduction to the Teachings of Bhagwan Shree Rajneesh*. Rajneeshpuram, OR: Rajneesh Foundation International.

Lee, Martha. 1995. *Earth First! Environmental Apocalypse*. New York: Syracuse University Press.

Lewis, James R., and J. Gordon Melton, eds. 1994. *Church Universal and Triumphant in Scholarly Perspective*. Stanford, CA: Center for Academic Publishing.

Marrs, Wanda. 1989. *New Age Lies to Women*. Austin, TX: Living Truth Publishers.

Melton, J. Gordon. 1995. "Sexuality and the Maturation of the Family." In *Sex, Slander, and Salvation*, edited by James R. Lewis and T. Gordon Melton. Goleta, CA: University Press of America.

―――. "Finding Enlightenment with Ramtha." Unpublished manuscript.

Milne, Hugh. 1986. *Bhagwan: The God That Failed*. New York: St. Martin's Press, Caliban Books.

Moore, Lawrence R. 1977. *In Search of White Crows: Spiritualism, Parapsychology and American Culture*. New York: Oxford University Press.

Palmer, Susan J. 1996. "Purity and Danger in the Solar Temple." *Journal of Contemporary Religion* 2 (3) (October).

Prophet, Elizabeth Clare. 1986. *Saint Germain on Prophecy*. Livingstone, MT: Summit University Press.

Rael. 1989. *The Message Given to Me by the Extraterrestrials*. Tokyo: Raelian Foundation.

Rajneesh, Bhagwan Shree. 1987. *A New Vision of Women's Liberation*. Poona, India: Rebel Press.

Ramtha. 1987. *Intensive Changes: The Days Yet to Come*. Yelm, WA: Eastsound.

Reuther, Rosemary Radford. 1988. *Women in Religion in America*, vol. I. New York: Beacon Press.

Rudolph, Kurt. 1987. *Gnosis: the Nature and History of Gnosticism*. San Francisco: Harper & Row.

Wessinger, Catherine ed. 1993. *Women Outside the Mainstream: Female Leaders in Marginal Religions in Nineteenth Century America*. Urbana: University of Illinois Press.

―――. 1993. "Annie Besant's Millennial Movement: Its History, Impact, and Implications Concerning Authority." *Syzygy: Journal of Alternative Religion and Culture* 2: 55–70.

Apocalypticism and the Churches

1000 YEARS OF PEACE!
—The Millennium!

22. THEN JESUS & ALL OF HIS BORN-AGAIN, SAVED CHILDREN WILL TAKE OVER THE WORLD & ORGANISE IT & RULE IT & RUN IT THE WAY IT SHOULD HAVE BEEN RUN if man had yielded to God! They're going to set up the Kingdom of Heaven on Earth & restore the Earth to the beauty of the Garden of Eden again! This amazing period will last for one thousand years & therefore it is known as The Millennium!

The Vengeful Virgin
Case Studies in Contemporary American Catholic Apocalypticism

9

Michael W. Cuneo

INTRODUCTION

When Veronica Lueken (or Veronica of the Cross, as she is sometimes referred to by her most loyal followers) died on August 3, 1995, American Catholicism lost probably its greatest native-born prophetess of the apocalypse. For more than twenty years, Veronica had regaled (and sometimes terrified) her followers with tales of sin and salvation, killer comets and bloodthirsty vampires, flying saucers from hell, and, perhaps most famously of all, an imposter pope from central casting. Some of this (the vampires and UFOs, for instance) was simply vintage Veronica, without any real precedent in Catholic tradition, but the driving theme behind all of her messages was something that Catholic mystics and seers had been preaching for generations: as punishment for its recalcitrant sinfulness, according to Veronica, virtually the entire world stood on the brink of a horrible chastisement. In just a matter of years (it is almost always just a matter of years) countless millions would be incinerated in a nuclear holocaust, and any sinners that still survived would then be swept away by a "cleansing ball of redemption."

Veronica, of course, is only part of the story here. Over the past thirty years or so, apocalyptic fantasies of this sort have circulated freely within some of the rather murkier regions of what may be described as the netherworld of American Catholicism. Especially among Catholics deeply aggrieved by the enormous changes that have befallen both their church and the wider society during this period, these fantasies have provided relief and consolation and also a powerful sense of spiritual vindication. For the most part, moreover, they have been composite creations—doomsday hybrids made up of elements taken from an almost bewildering variety of sources. Whatever else might be said of it, contemporary Catholic apocalypticism is a remarkably eclectic phenomenon.

THE SOURCES OF AMERICAN CATHOLIC APOCALYPTICISM

In general terms, Catholic apocalypticism in contemporary America has drawn its primary inspiration from five more or less distinct sources, and the most important of these by far has been the miraculous realm of Marian apparitions. During many of her earthly visitations over the course of the past two centuries, the Virgin Mary has warned of the horrible catastrophes that lie ahead unless women and men repent of evil and dedicate themselves to the pursuit of righteousness. In some cases, these warnings (such as those associated with the apparitions that presumably took place at La Salette, France, in 1846, and Fatima, Portugal, in 1917) have received the imprimatur of the institutional church, but church approval hasn't always been a decisive consideration. The apparitions that have been reported in recent decades at Garabandal, Spain; Necedah, Wisconsin; and Bayside, New York, for example, have failed to pass ecclesiastical tests of authenticity, but the messages connected with them have nevertheless been enormously influential within certain sectors of American Catholic apocalyticism.[1]

Second in importance to Marian apparitions are the endtime prophecies and private revelations that have been attributed over the centuries to a wide variety of Catholic mystics and visionaries, including the likes of Anna-Katarina Emmerick, the eighteenth-century German stigmatist; Michel de Notredame (or Nostradamus); and even Pope Pius X. With very few exceptions, these prophecies have been tantalizingly vague and open ended, and hence susceptible to an almost limitless range of interpretation. In 1936, for example, the visionary Teresa Neumann is reported to have said that "The furies of hell are now set loose. Divine punishment is inevitable." And Pius X, a couple of decades earlier, was only slightly less oracular: "I saw one of my successors taking to flight over the bodies of his brethren. He will take refuge in disguise somewhere; and after a short retirement he will die a cruel death. The present wickedness of the world is only the beginning of the sorrows which must take place before the end of the world." The malleability of prophetic utterances such as these—their ready adaptability to present circumstances—is precisely what gives them value. The divine retributions and disasters of which they speak are always looming just ahead, or lurking around the very next corner.[2]

And then, of course, there's also the so-called prophetic literature of the Old and New Testaments, and especially the Book of Revelation. While generally of subordinate importance to Catholic apocalypticism in America, biblical prophecy is sometimes invoked as a kind of legitimation or corroboration of the Marian messages and private revelations mentioned above.

Marian apparitions, mystical revelation, and scripture are the three most important *explicit* sources for Catholic apocalypticism in America, but there are also two rather important *implicit* (or less frankly acknowledged) sources. The first of these is Protestant millenarianism, particularly as it has been filtered through the popular media of televangelism, religious radio, and best-selling books such as Hal Lindsey's *The Late Great Planet Earth*. With their fondness for affixing precise dates to the approaching chastisement, their penchant for schematic interpretations of history, and their sensationalistic depictions of the suffering lying in wait for the unrighteous, Catholic apocalypticists have sometimes betrayed heavy indebtedness to themes more commonly associated with Protestant Adventism and fundamentalism. Occasionally, moreover, this indebtedness has bordered on outright plagiarism. In what appears to be a case of direct borrowing from Darbyite dispensationalism, for example, the followers of Veronica Lueken have been assured by their movement's leadership that they will be miraculously "raptured" to a place of safekeeping on the eve of the apocalypse.[3]

Almost as important as Protestant millenarianism, and by no means unrelated to it, is the conspiracy culture of America's extreme political right. In recent years, in fact, many Catholic apocalypticists have invested heavily in the ideology of the contemporary militia movement. Alongside their warnings of an impending chastisement, they have inveighed against the United Nations and the threat of one-world government, they have accused the Clinton administration of sabotaging constitutional freedoms, and, in the aftermath of Waco, they have persistently claimed that America is on the verge of declining into a repressive police state.[4]

IDEOLOGICAL CHARACTERISTICS

Although Catholic apocalypticism is quite often a belief system espoused by scattered individuals, or by small, relatively unstructured groups, it has sometimes also given rise to full-fledged social movements. And not surprisingly, considering their shared reliance upon the sources identified above, these movements have tended to hold a number of ideological characteristics in common.

1. *The approaching chastisement.* As punishment for its rampant infidelity and selfishness, according to Catholic apocalypticists, virtually the entire world stands on the brink of catastrophic damnation: the Virgin Mary has delivered the verdict personally through her specially appointed seers, and the chances of having the sentence either commuted or deferred must be considered exceedingly slim. (The precise timing and disposition of the approaching chastisement are matters upon which Catholic apocalypticists themselves are in serious disagreement.)

2. *Holy elites.* During her appearance at La Salette in 1846, the Virgin Mary apparently called for the creation of a special community that would be entrusted with preaching the necessity of conversion to the entire world and whose members would be known as the "apostles of the last times" (Zimdars-Swartz 1992, 184). This appellation (or its equivalent, "disciples of the latter

days") has been adopted by most Catholic apocalyptic movements in contemporary America. The members of these movements (or, at least, the full-fledged members) regard themselves as spiritual elites responsible for warning the world of the catastrophes that almost certainly lie ahead.

3. *Political passivity/premillennial fatalism.* Outside of preaching the necessity of conversion (or, in one notable case, the necessity of consecrating Russia to Mary's Immaculate Heart), Catholic apocalypticists have pursued a course of almost complete worldly withdrawal. Far from entering into strategic alliance with other right-wing Catholics (or right-wing Protestants) over issues such as abortion, they have mostly been content with cultivating their own salvation while awaiting the consummation of world history. It is only through divine intervention, in their view, that the affairs of the world might possibly be set straight.

4. *Anticommunism.* As is almost always the case with Marian-based movements, Catholic apocalyptic movements in contemporary America are fanatically anticommunist.[5] Despite popular impressions to the contrary, they insist, international communism is as dangerous and insidious a force today as ever before.

5. *Conspiracy mentality.* Hand in hand with their strident anticommunism, Catholic apocalypticists are positively drenched in conspiracy. Absolutely nothing, in their view, can be taken at face value; one must always probe far beneath the surface of events for their true meanings and hidden significance. (As often as not, moreover, this conspiracy-mongering has been cloaked in an anti-Semitic rhetoric.)[6]

6. *Catholicism-in-crisis.* Catholic apocalypticists, without exception, believe that the institutional church has fallen into a state of unprecedented crisis in the years following the Second Vatican Council. Its priesthood, its moral teaching, and its ritual life have all been deeply corrupted by secularism, and only through some miraculous stroke can the church be restored to its former glory.

7. *The papacy-in-crisis.* Since the Second Vatican Council, according to Catholic apocalypticists, the papal throne has been occupied either by exceedingly weak and vulnerable men—or by outright imposters.[7]

8. *Thaumaturgical authority.* In the final analysis, Catholic apocalypticists defer not to the papacy or the traditions of the Catholic past but rather to the sacred apparitions and seers upon which their movements are variously based.

9. *Sectarian impulse.* As a result of their spiritual elitism and several of the other tendencies enumerated above, Catholic apocalypticists have tended to

define themselves apart from the institutional church—and sometimes have broken away from it altogether.

Despite these shared characteristics, Catholic apocalyptic movements are by no means all of a single piece. As the following case studies should amply attest, they may vary widely in terms of both their systems of belief and their basic organizational structure.[8]

THE FATIMA CRUSADE

Of the dozens of Marian apparitions that have been reported worldwide over the past two centuries, none has been a richer resource for Catholic apocalypticism in America than Fatima. According to Catholic apparitional lore, the Virgin Mary made six miraculous appearances to three peasant children, Lucia dos Santos and her younger cousins Jacinta and Francisco Marto, in the small Portuguese village of Fatima over a five-month stretch in 1917. During one of these appearances, on July 13, the Virgin apparently communicated a three-part secret that the children refused to reveal to their interrogators. The so-called Fatima secret was kept under tight wraps for more than twenty years, but in a memoir she wrote at the request of her religious superiors in 1941, Lucia (who was by then a Carmelite nun) disclosed the contents of its first two parts. The first part of the secret, according to Lucia, consisted of a horrifying vision of hell, and in the second part the Virgin Mary requested (among other things) that Russia be consecrated to her Immaculate Heart. As the Virgin herself apparently put it to the three young seers: "If my requests are heeded, Russia will be converted, and there will be peace; if not, she will spread her errors throughout the world, causing wars and persecutions of the Church. The good will be martyred; the Holy Father will have much to suffer; various nations will be annihilated" (quoted in Zimdars-Swartz 1992, 199).

Lucia's memoir seems to have been taken quite seriously by church officials, and on October 31, 1942, Pope Pius XII consecrated not just Russia but the entire world to Mary's Immaculate Heart. While being interviewed by a Dutch priest named Father Jongen in 1946, however, Lucia indicated that Pius XII's consecration fell far short of what the Virgin had actually requested. "The exact petition of Our Lady," she reportedly told Father Jongen, "was for the Holy Father to make the consecration of Russia to Her Immaculate Heart, commanding that at the same time and in union with His Holiness, all the bishops

of the Catholic world should do it" (quoted in Alonso 1995, 13). At about the
same time, moreover, Lucia apparently committed the third part of the July
1917 secret to writing, and following a directive from the Virgin she sealed it in
an envelope and instructed that it not be released to the public until 1960.
Pope John XXIII apparently read the secret in 1959, but 1960 came and went
without it being made public. And in later years, John XXIII's papal successors
likewise elected to keep it under wraps. Finally, on May 13, 1982, and then
again (for good measure) on March 25, 1984, John Paul II became the second
pope to consecrate the world to Mary's Immaculate Heart, but like Pius XII
forty years earlier he neglected to make specific mention of Russia or to under-
take the consecration in absolute unison with all the bishops of the Catholic
world (Zimdars-Swartz 1992, 204–218).

Although the Fatima apparitions were pronounced authentic by the bishops of Portugal as early as 1930, it wasn't until the 1950s and the onset of the
cold war that the apparitions became the object of widespread devotion in the
United States. With its call for the consecration of Russia, in fact, Fatima was
regarded by many American Catholics in the 1950s and early 1960s as the
West's best hope for neutralizing the military might of the Soviet Union and
halting the spread of communism (Zimdars-Swartz 1992, 206–207). During this
time as well, the third part of Lucia's secret (now known simply as "the third
secret of Fatima") was a topic of feverish speculation within certain quarters of
the American church. Did the secret warn of an impending nuclear holocaust?
Or of a forthcoming period of tribulation for the papacy? Speculation of this
sort never really caught on within the broader Catholic world, however, and
during the mid- to late 1960s devotion to Fatima in general faded into the
woodwork of the American church. In the newly modernized Catholicism that
was emerging in the wake of the Second Vatican Council, Fatima and other
apparitional pieties were widely dismissed as relics of a benighted and best-
forgotten past.

Over the past ten years, no one has worked harder at restoring a sense of
relevancy to Fatima than Father Nicholas Gruner. Born in Montreal in 1942,
and ordained to the priesthood in Avellino, Italy, in 1976, Gruner made his initial foray onto the North American Fatima scene in 1978 when he launched a
new Marian ministry that was centered around a quarterly magazine called the
Fatima Crusader. At the outset, the *Crusader* was a blandly pious, small-circu-
lation affair, mostly taken up with articles on the spiritual benefits of the
rosary, but in the mid-1980s Gruner fastened upon the issue that would lift the

magazine to sudden prominence. However much the Vatican might want to deny it, Gruner advised his readers, the consecration of Russia requested by the Virgin Mary at Fatima was still waiting to be done. Both Pius XII and John Paul II had failed to carry out their consecrations in temporal unity with every bishop throughout the Catholic world, and both had neglected to make specific mention of Russia. In Pius XII's case, Gruner argued, this failure to comply with the Virgin's specific demands may simply have been an oversight, but in the case of John Paul II a far more insidious dynamic was at work. In the first place, a great many Catholic bishops had undergone secret (or not so secret) conversions to communism since the Second Vatican Council, and there was no way these bishops would agree to participate in a public consecration that seemed to single out communist Russia for special criticism. And in the second place, the Vatican was still bound to a secret agreement that Pope John XXIII had signed with Soviet leader Nikita Khrushchev on the eve of the council, with John XXIII promising to go soft on Soviet communism in return for Khrushchev's promise to go soft on Catholics living behind the Iron Curtain. This Vatican-Moscow accord might have made limited sense at the time, Gruner argued, but now, more than twenty-five years later, it was one of the chief factors holding back the consecration of Russia demanded by the Virgin at Fatima. And to make matters worse, communist sympathizers inside the Vatican, led by Secretary of State Agostino Cardinal Casaroli, were fully committed to keeping the accord in place.[9]

As Gruner and his *Crusader* staff railed against the Vatican-Moscow pact and other related evils throughout the late 1980s, they succeeded in giving the Fatima cause a new (and decidedly sexier) lease on life. Far from being the object of a merely grandmotherly piety, Fatima was now fully caught up in the mysterious world of Vatican Ostpolitik, clandestine deal-making, and geopolitical brinkmanship. To many of the *Crusader's* readers, all of this was undoubtedly heady stuff: in return for their support of Gruner's ministry, they were being given a privileged window into the inner workings of the most critical historical developments of the age. And the most critical development of all, as the *Crusader* consistently pointed out to its readers, was the mounting military might of the Soviet Union. In an endless parade of articles bearing such red-banner headlines as "URGENT! COMMUNISIM IS ADVANCING" and "THE GREAT SOVIET DECEPTION," the magazine did everything possible to set the record straight: Perestroika was a hoax, Gorbachev was every bit as diabolical as Stalin, and, despite all the sweet talk coming out of Moscow, communist

Russia was assembling the pieces for a final military assault on the entire free world. Not that any of this should have been surprising. The Virgin Mary had warned at Fatima that Russia would spread error and misery throughout the world unless her requests were granted; and now, more than seventy years later, the Virgin was still waiting.[10]

Determined not to keep her waiting any longer, Gruner pursued vigorous action on several fronts simultaneously. In early 1988 he tried to pressure the pope into rescinding the iniquitous Vatican-Moscow accord by sponsoring a letter-writing campaign to the Vatican, and later the same year he unleashed a furious journalistic campaign against more moderate Fatima organizations such as the Blue Army. (Both the Blue Army and the Fatima Family Apostolate, Gruner's chief competitors on the North American Fatima scene, held that the consecration of Russia had already been properly carried out by Pope John Paul II and that the era of subsequent world peace promised by the Virgin Mary at Fatima was now in the process of being realized.) At roughly the same time, moreover, he launched a daily radio program, *Heaven's Peace Plan*, that was slotted on forty-three stations in the United States and Canada, and he followed this up with a weekly television show called *Fatima: The Moment Has Come*. All of these initiatives were enormously expensive, of course, and during the late 1980s Gruner began sending out personalized pitch letters that, for sheer chutzpah, would have caused even Oral Roberts to blush in appreciation. "You are so important," he assured each of his supporters (or potential supporters) in July 1989. "I am writing you today—as one of Our Lady's dearest ones—to plead urgently for your help. . . . Our bank account is now practically empty. . . . Please say a Hail Mary with me now that you and all of Our Lady's children will respond generously FROM THE HEART to this desperate appeal. . . . Our Lady's FULL Fatima message is our only hope. If She is not heard in time then the whole world including the United States will be enslaved by Communist Russia and many entire nations will be annihilated. PLEASE HELP NOW. It is almost too late."

To the chagrin of his competitors, this high-pressure salesmanship helped Gruner make significant inroads into the North American Fatima market, and by the early 1990s the *Crusader*'s circulation had increased exponentially to more than four hundred thousand, and his overall ministry had grown into a $5 million a year enterprise. As time went on, moreover, Gruner demonstrated impressive rhetorical resiliency. When the Soviet Union disintegrated, and much of the former communist world embraced the principles of free markets and open elections, he insisted that nothing had changed except the color of the uniforms. Despite all the fanfare over the emergence of a new and gentler world order, communism remained a force of apocalyptic reckoning and Fatima was still the free world's only defense against enslavement and eventual annihilation. And when he came under attack from the Vatican for suggesting that John Paul II was either too weak or too afraid to carry out the consecration of Russia according to the precise terms requested by the Virgin, Gruner defended himself by invoking the famous Third Secret of Fatima. Although the Third Secret had still not been formally revealed, he told his readers, the very best evidence indicated that it referred to a horrible apostasy that would strike the church toward the close of the century. And as the mounting attacks against his ministry from the institutional church made vividly clear, this period of apostasy was already well underway. When Sister Lucia herself, moreover, suggested in a 1992 interview that the consecration of Russia had in fact been properly carried out by John Paul II in 1984, Gruner's second-in-command, a freelance priest named Paul Leonard, raised the specter of brainwashing. "Why has Sister Lucia made such a fool of herself?" Father Leonard wrote in the Winter 1993 issue of the *Crusader*. "Her present state of mind is in itself a strong indication that Sister Lucia has been mentally abused by her superiors who have subjected her to mind control. She has been 'trained' to say that the consecration of Russia is already accomplished, that Russia is converted and whatever else the Ostpolitik-minded officials of the Vatican want her to say."

To this point at least, the great majority of Gruner's supporters (most of whom seem to be women, middle-aged and older) have elected to stay with him throughout all of this frantic maneuvering. Of course, all things considered, Gruner offers his supporters a relatively cheap ride. Not much more is expected of them beyond making financial contributions and attending the occasional public lecture, and in return they're given the satisfaction of participating, however vicariously, in a spiritual struggle of cosmic importance. As Gruner himself told me during an interview at his ministry's headquarters in the Buffalo/Fort Erie area: "The peace of the world and the salvation of millions of souls hinges on the truths of Fatima. What we're doing is a matter of life and death."

THE APOSTLES OF INFINITE LOVE

In comparison with the Apostles of Infinite Love, a radical monastic community based in St. Jovite, Quebec, Gruner's Fatima ministry seems almost boringly mainstream. Founded in 1962 by an itinerant preacher named Brother John (née Gaston Tremblay), the Infinite Love community has long been one of the most widely vilified (and abidingly controversial) Catholic groups in North America. Practically since its inception, the community has been plagued by accusations of sexual abuse and brainwashing. It has been the target of police raids and media exposés, and at one point its leader actually spent six months in jail after being convicted of illegal sequestration and contempt of court. For more than twenty years now, the community has ordained married men and both married and single women, and yet on most other counts it has been time-stoppingly conservative. And on September 10, 1968, in what may have been the most controversial development of all, the community announced that its founder had been mystically elevated to the papacy under the name of Gregory XVII (Gregory XVII 1989; Côté 1991).

Despite its French-Canadian roots, the Infinite Love community warrants inclusion in any discussion of contemporary American Catholic apocalypticism. Slightly more than two-thirds of its three hundred full-fledged members and roughly the same proportion of its several thousand lay supporters (or tertiaries) are American, and since the late 1970s the community has operated mission centers in Brooklyn, New York, and Paterson, New Jersey. Even more important than this, however, is the symbolic significance of the community for the broader Catholic right. Since 1968 and the mystical coronation of Brother John, the Apostles of Infinite Love have defined the outer limits of right-wing dissent for Catholic apocalypticists and traditionalists of every imaginable stripe—in the United States no less than in Canada. While other apocalyptic groups have been openly critical of the institutional church, the Apostles have repudiated it altogether and opted for outright separatism. And while other groups have invested their guiding mystics and seers with varying degrees of supernatural authority, only the Apostles have gone so far as to declare theirs the supreme ruler of the universal church of the endtimes.

In a 270-page encyclical entitled *Peter Speaks to the World*, which he issued in 1975, Brother John (or Gregory XVII) reminded his readers that the Virgin Mary, during her miraculous appearance at La Salette, had warned that the day was coming when "Rome will lose the Faith and become the seat of Antichrist." And with the rise of theological liberalism and promiscuous ecumenism after the Second Vatican Council, he said, this day has now arrived. The entire institutional church has fallen into apostasy, and a new church, headed by Gregory XVII, has been brought into being to preserve authentic

Catholicism. Regardless of how small this new church might be, or how fiercely persecuted, Brother John wrote, it will persevere in truth until the very end.

> When God chastised the world by the Flood, only a tiny portion of humanity was spared by entering Noah's Ark. Thus, the True Church of Jesus Christ, which God has charged Us to direct, is the Ark of the new times raised up by Providence to save a portion of Christendom. "Fight, children of light," said Our Lady of La Salette, "you little number who see; for behold the time of times, the end of ends." (Gregory XVII 1993, 211–212)

In conjunction with its spiritual elitism, the Infinite Love community subscribes to a full-blown theology of doomsday. When the very best prophetic evidence is taken into account, the community claims, there seems little question that the final drama of world history will be played out according to the following three-stage scenario: (1) *The first chastisement*. In this opening stage, which is already underway, an anti-pope is installed in Rome and the authentic Catholic Church is reduced to a small and persecuted remnant. Following a series of wars and natural disasters, which will result in billions of deaths, communism (or some functionally equivalent force) will assume ironfisted control of almost the entire world. Eventually, however, a Great Pontiff (Gregory XVII or his divinely appointed successor) will lead a Catholic counterforce into battle and succeed in establishing a new Christendom on earth. (2) *Period of peace and virtue*. With the establishment of a renewed Christendom, there will be a brief period of peace and prosperity on earth. The church will receive millions of new converts, and its religious authority will be uncontested. (3) *The second chastisement*. This Catholic utopia, however, will prove short-lived. Over time, there will be a widespread return to infidelity and wickedness, and a second period of war and calamity will bring a final end to world history.[11]

Considering the salvific stakes involved, it's little wonder that the Infinite Love community has placed inordinately heavy demands upon its members. In addition to taking mandatory vows of celibacy, all full-fledged brother and sister Apostles are required to swear absolute and unflinching allegiance to Gregory XVII, and all newcomers are required to turn over their worldly possessions to the larger community. Although the Apostles of Infinite Love haven't succeeded in reaching as wide an audience as Gruner's Fatima Crusade ministry, they remain the most commitment-intensive and frankly sectarian Catholic apocalyptic movement, and also the most deeply threatening to both the religious and secular establishments.

VERONICA LUEKEN'S BAYSIDE MOVEMENT

For the most entertainingly eclectic of Catholic apocalyptic movements, one need look no farther than the Our Lady of the Roses ministry of Bayside (Queens), New York. During the summer of 1970, as the story goes, the Virgin Mary began making regular appearances to a working-class housewife named Veronica Lueken on the grounds of St. Robert Bellarmine's parish church in Bayside. Despite opposition from the resident pastor, the apparitions were soon drawing anywhere from 500 to 2,000 pilgrims at a time, and Veronica was well on her way to becoming a major celebrity within American Catholicism's Marian underground. In the summer of 1973 the Roman Catholic diocese of Brooklyn investigated the apparitions and concluded that they were the product, at the very most, of a "highly fertile imagination," and later the same year the parish staff of St. Robert's fenced off the church property and forced the pilgrims onto the street. Still undeterred, Veronica and her followers conducted their vigils for a year or so at a nearby traffic mall, and then, in May 1975, they negotiated a permanent meeting place on the grounds of the 1964–65 World's Fair in Flushing Meadow Park (Nobile 1978; Grant 1980; Donovan 1988).

Over the next twenty years, the Our Lady of the Roses vigils (as they were christened by the Virgin Mary) followed a familiar pattern. Upon arriving at a makeshift shrine set up on the vigil site, Veronica would fall like clockwork into an ecstatic trance and begin receiving messages from the Virgin and sometimes also from Jesus and other heavenly beings. (The messages would be tape-recorded on the spot and then later transcribed and sent out to Veronica's growing legion of followers across North America.) Most of the pilgrims would pray the rosary constantly throughout the vigils, with some occasionally taking time out to snap Polaroid pictures in the hope of capturing some sign or token of the Virgin's presence. These so-called miraculous photographs, which generally featured (at least to the uninitiated) indecipherable streaks of light or splotches of color, would sometimes afterward be taken to Veronica for an authoritative interpretation (Wojcik 1992, 181–220).

The highlight of the vigils, of course, were the sacred messages that the Virgin Mary communicated directly to Veronica. And throughout her extended engagement at the old World's Fair grounds the Virgin proved surprisingly voluble. In addition to condemning abortion and homosexuality and modern biblical criticism and a host of other evils, she found time to pontificate on everything from zombies and UFOs (which she described as "transport ships from hell") to the United Nations and the threat of one-world government.[12] The Virgin was particularly distressed by the upheaval within the Catholic Church after the council, and on September 27, 1975, in what may have been her most startling scoop of all, she informed Veronica that the real Pope Paul VI was being held prisoner in the Vatican while an imposter Paul VI, who was the beneficiary of acting lessons and cosmetic surgery, ruled in his place on the papal throne. It was this imposter pope, operating at the behest of a traitorous clique of modernist cardinals, who was responsible for banishing the beloved Tridentine Mass and throwing the church into disarray. As outrageous as the imposter theory might seem, it went a long way toward helping Veronica's followers make sense of some of the more disturbing changes that were unfolding in the church in the wake of the council. And what's more, it gave them both incentive and justification for staying in the church and fighting these changes rather than following the Infinite Love community's path into outright schism. It wasn't the real Pope Paul VI, after all, who was presiding over the dismantlement of traditional Catholicism but rather the cosmetically enhanced stooge who had taken his place on the papal throne (Our Lady of the Roses Shrine 1993, 116–29).

As the years passed, the topic that the Virgin turned to with increasing frequency was the approaching chastisement. In the very near future, she told Veronica on at least a dozen occasions, there will be a Great Warning, in the form of some horrible natural catastrophe, that will result in immense suffering throughout the world. The warning will be of short duration, and will be followed by a celestial miracle that will provide added inducement for people to surrender their hearts to God. In all likelihood, however, the great majority of people will persist in wickedness, and God in turn will unleash a furious chastisement upon the world. The chastisement will take place in two distinct stages. First, there will be a major global conflict (World War III) in which countless people will perish, and then virtually the entire world will be destroyed by a great comet, or Ball of Redemption (Our Lady of the Roses Shrine 1993, 36–46).

As the Virgin took pains to emphasize, however, there was still a slight chance that the chastisement might be averted, or its severity mitigated. And in this respect, Veronica and her followers had been given a momentous role. They were the Disciples of the Latter Days, the chosen few who had been charged with the responsibility of preaching the necessity of conversion to the entire world. And if (as should be expected) the world turned a deaf ear to their preaching, the Virgin told Veronica, the Disciples would be miraculously raptured to a place of safekeeping on the eve of the apocalypse. "I give you great grace of heart, My children, to know that many shall be taken from your earth before the great Chastisement. It will be of great mirth, My child, to reveal to you that there will be much consternation and conflicting thought when these beloved children disappear from the earth. Many of your news medias [sic] shall state that they have been carried off by flying saucers. Oh no, My children, they were carried off into a supernatural realm of the Eternal Father to await the return of My Son upon earth" (Our Lady of the Roses Shrine 1993, 40).

As is normally the case with long-running enterprises of this sort, Veronica's ministry eventually developed a fairly rigid hierarchy of both status and authority. At the top were Veronica, her husband Arthur, and several of her closest confidants—the so-called inner circle. Next in line came a dozen or so young men known as full-time workers who lived together in a community called the Lay Order of St. Michael and who were responsible for both promoting the ministry and safeguarding its orthodoxy. (The sacred messages were supposed to mean exactly what Veronica said they meant—nothing more, nothing less.) After the workers were the people known as organizers. These were especially dedicated devotees of Veronica from outside the New York City area who were responsible for organizing prayer vigils in their local communities and also arranging pilgrimages to the old World's Fair grounds. And finally, there were the rank-and-file adherents who supported the ministry through their prayers and their (mostly) modest financial donations.

Over the years, it has mainly been the full-time workers and organizers who have upheld what Veronica sometimes referred to as "the total Bayside gospel," while most rank-and-file supporters have tended toward a decidedly more selective commitment. In June 1995 (just two months prior to Veronica's death) I interviewed a dozen Bayside supporters in New York City, and while all of them seemed convinced that Veronica was a holy woman, and that she was truly in touch with divine and redemptive forces, none seemed to think that this meant accepting everything she said with absolute literalness. During a time of unsettling change within their church, Veronica had given them spiritual consolation and reassurance of salvation, and for this they were enormously grateful. Even if some of Veronica's rather more exotic teachings (such as those dealing with UFOs and killer comets and imposter popes) were not strictly true, the supporters suggested to me, they were at least an excellent source of religious entertainment.[13]

DISCUSSION

As these three case studies indicate, Catholic apocalypticism may assume strikingly different forms. Of the three cases, Gruner's Fatima Crusade ministry is the most closely wedded to a church-approved apparitional tradition, and is also the most outwardly conformist to established church authority. Even here, however, the sectarian impulse has never been far from the surface. In assigning ultimate religious authority to the Fatima apparitions and their chief seeress, and in positioning himself as an impresario of sorts of the three-part Fatima Secret, Gruner has left little doubt as to where his true allegiance lies. If it were ever to come down to a choice between Fatima and Rome, Fatima would almost certainly win out.

The Infinite Love community is a hybrid case. The community bases itself simultaneously on the famous (and church-approved) La Salette apparition and on the mystical-hieratic authority of its founder and made-to-order pope. And over the years, as we've seen, this combination has proved highly subversive. In addition to ordaining women to the priesthood, the Infinite Love community has rejected the legitimacy of the post-conciliar Catholic hierarchy and broken away entirely from the institutional church. Veronica Lueken's Bayside movement, for its part, has operated almost entirely outside of the church's approved apparitional traditions while somehow managing to avoid (at least to this point) outright schism.

In terms of concrete organizational structure, the picture is equally one of diversity. With its entrepreneurial, pay-as-you-please approach, Gruner's Fatima Crusade ministry has thus far functioned as a model *audience cult* (Stark and Bainbridge 1985, 27–28). For a modest admission price, its supporters have been given front-row seats to an ongoing performance that Gruner has billed as the greatest apocalyptic drama of the century. The Infinite Love community, in contrast, by virtue of both its radical withdrawal from the broader culture and its intensive membership requirements, has operated very much as a classic *introversionist sect* (Wilson 1959). And for much of its history, the Bayside movement has been characterized by an organizational split personality. Whereas its hard-core devotees (namely, the workers and organizers) have demonstrated an extraordinary level of personal commitment to Veronica's messages, the great majority of its supporters have been primarily concerned with covering their eschatological bets and supplementing their thaumaturgical diets.

At one point or another, all three of these movements have incorporated elements from secular apocalypticism into their belief systems, and today they are almost as likely to be found expatiating on the debacle at Waco or the machinations of the FBI or the specter of one-world government as on the woes of the contemporary church. Much of this, however, is nothing more than ideological riffing, and it would be wrong to regard these particular movements (or any others within the Catholic apocalyptic fold) as Catholic militias-in-the-making. With their premillennial fatalism, political revolution is the last thing on their minds, and stockpiling rosaries is their preferred way of preparing for the coming storm.

The dominant image of the Virgin Mary within popular (or colloquial) Catholicism is generally assumed to be that of the marvelously munificent mother, eternally solicitous of her children's welfare and never reluctant to intercede on their behalf. But there is another side to Mary in the popular Catholic imagination—one that has rarely received notice and that would surely repay concentrated psychological scrutiny. For Catholic apocalypticists in contemporary America, the Virgin Mary is certainly maternal and certainly loving, but she's also stern and reproachful and vengeful. Rather than simply offering words of comfort and condolence, she imparts messages of unspeakable catastrophe and punishment. Mundane history is on the verge of crashing to an apocalyptic end, this vengeful Virgin promises, and women and men have no one to blame but themselves.

NOTES

1. For splendid scholarly accounts of these various apparitions, see Zimdars-Swartz (1992) and Carroll (1986).
2. For the Teresa Neumann and Pius X prophecies cited above, see Dupont (1973, 14, 22). Dupont's volume is probably the most useful anthology of Catholic endtime prophecy currently available in English.

3. On the notion of a "miraculous rapture" from a Protestant millenarian perspective, see Sandeen (1970, 62–64).

4. To this point, Catholic apocalypticists have mainly invoked secular or "outsider" themes such as these as a kind of second-order legitimation of their catastrophic worldview. For a provocative discussion of the contemporary militia movement, see Wills (1995).

5. On the deployment of Marian piety in general for right-wing political purposes, see Perry and Echeverría (1988). And for an attempt at constructing a more liberationist Mariology, see Gebara and Bingemer (1989).

6. Virtually everything that distresses them, from the decline of the Tridentine Mass to the rise of moral permissiveness within the broader culture, Catholic apocalypticists tend to blame (at least in part) on a Jewish-Masonic conspiracy.

7. As Norman Cohn (1970) has made vividly clear, conspiratorial fantasies centered upon the papacy have a venerable tradition within the mystical and millenarian undergrounds of Roman Catholicism.

8. The following three accounts are based in large measure on field research I conducted over a ten-month period in 1995. For a much lengthier (but differently focused) discussion of the three movements in question, see Cuneo (1996).

9. The so-called Vatican-Moscow accord had been a leading bête noire of the extreme Catholic right in Europe since the mid-1970s, and Gruner's initial contact with it was through the reactionary Scottish-Catholic *Approaches* magazine. According to some accounts, the accord was also negotiated in order to clear the way for Russian Orthodox observers to attend the Second Vatican Council. In his landmark study of the church's political entanglements, it might be noted, Hanson (1987) makes no mention of a clandestine Vatican-Moscow pact. For samples of the *Crusader*'s rather fevered approach to the issue, see Leonard (1986, 1987).

10. Gruner hasn't been at all hesitant over the years about tapping into the broader (and frequently secular) anticommunist literature. In addition to printing excerpts from the *McAlvany Intelligence Advisor*, he has given full play in the *Crusader*'s pages to such right-wing screeds as Conquest and White (1984).

11. I have distilled this three-stage scenario from Barette (1988) and St.-Pierre (1994), which are the two most important volumes of prophecy produced by the Infinite Love community. For a similar endtimes prospectus, see Dupont (1973, 1–2).

12. For a fairly comprehensive compilation of the earlier messages, see Our Lady of the Roses Shrine (1990).

13. At the time of Veronica's death, her ministry's mailing list consisted of 35,000 names in the United States, and roughly 55,000 worldwide. About 30 percent of this total actually supported the shrine with financial donations. Shrine

officials estimate that at least 60 percent of these active supporters were women.

REFERENCES

Alonso, Joaquin Maria. 1995. "Meaning of the 'Consecration' of Russia." *Fatima Crusader* Victory Issue (Autumn): 10–15.

Barette, Jean-Marie. 1988. *The Prophecy of the Apostles of the Latter Times*. St. Jovite, Quebec: Editions Magnificat.

Carroll, Michael P. 1986. *The Cult of the Virgin Mary: Psychological Origins*. Princeton: Princeton University Press.

Cohn, Norman. 1970. *The Pursuit of the Millennium*. New York: Oxford University Press.

Conquest, Robert, and Jon Manchip White. 1984. *What To Do When the Russians Come: A Survivor's Guide*. Briarcliff Manor, NY: White, Stein and Day Publishers.

Côté, Jean. 1991. *Prophet Without Permit: Father John of the Trinity*. Montreal: Pro Manuscripto.

Cuneo, Michael W. 1996. *The Smoke of Satan: Profiles of Right-Wing Dissent in Contemporary American Catholicism*. New York: Oxford University Press.

Donovan, James. 1988. "Bayside Unveiled: The Blessed Mother Takes a Beating from Her 'Friends.' " *Fidelity* 7 (March): 34–42.

Dupont, Yves. 1973. *Catholic Prophecy: The Coming Chastisement*. Rockford, IL: TAN Books.

Gebara, Ivone, and Maria Bingemer. 1989. *Mary: Mother of God, Mother of the Poor,* translated by P. Berryman. Maryknoll, NY: Orbis Books.

Grant, Roberta. 1980. "War of the Roses." *Rolling Stone* (February 21): 43–46.

Gregory XVII. 1989. *Questions and Answers*. St. Jovite, Quebec: Monastery of the Magnificat of the Mother of God.

———. 1993. *Peter Speaks to the World*, 2nd ed. St. Jovite, Quebec: Editions Magnificat.

Hanson, Eric O. 1987. *The Catholic Church in World Politics*. Princeton: Princeton University Press.

Leonard, Paul. 1986. "The Plot to Silence Our Lady." *Fatima Crusader* 20 (June–July): 9–13, 24–25, 27.

———. 1987. "Up To Now—The Vatican Moscow Agreement Has Silenced Our Lady." *Fatima Crusader* 22 (April–May): 12–15.

Nobile, Philip. 1978. "Our Lady of Bayside." *New York* 11 (December 11): 57–60.

Our Lady of the Roses Shrine. 1990. *Roses from Heaven*. Orange, TX: Children of Mary, Inc.

————. 1993. *Our Lady of the Roses, Mary Help of Mothers: A Book about the Heav-enly Apparitions to Veronica Lueken at Bayside, New York*. Lansing, MI: Apostles of Our Lady, Inc.

Perry, Nicholas, and Loreto Echeverría. 1988. *Under the Heel of Mary*. London: Routledge.

Sandeen, Ernest R. 1970. *The Roots of Fundamentalism: British and American Mil-lenarianism, 1800-1930*. Chicago: University of Chicago Press.

Stark, Rodney, and William Sims Bainbridge. 1985. *The Future of Religion*. Berke-ley: University of California Press.

St.-Pierre, Catherine. 1994. *Thou Art Peter*. St. Jovite, Quebec: Editions Magnificat.

Wills, Garry. 1995. "The New Revolutionaries." *New York Review of Books* 42 (August 10): 50–55.

Wilson, Bryan R. 1959. "An Analysis of Sect Development." *American Sociological Review* 24 (Winter): 3–15.

Wojcik, Daniel Noel. 1992. "Approaching Doomsday: Fatalism in Contemporary American Apocalyptic Beliefs." Unpublished Ph.D. dissertation, University of California at Los Angeles.

Zimdars-Swartz, Sandra L. 1992. *Encountering Mary*. New York: Avon Books.

Christian Reconstructionism and the Angry Rhetoric of Neo-postmillennialism

10 Anson Shupe

Christian Reconstructionism (CR) represents a wing of the Christian right that militantly believes conservative (Protestant) Christians can transform North American society (and ultimately the world) according to biblical principles found in the books of the Pentateuch and thereby create the basis for Christ's millennial kingdom on earth. In the words of one CR spokesperson, "the Bible presents mankind with a God-mandated set of social, economic, and educational, political, and legal principles that God expects His people to use as permanent blueprints for the total reconstruction of every society on earth" (North 1990, 3). Moreover, Jesus Christ's "new covenant" is alleged to have surpassed only the ceremonial sections of Old Testament law, leaving its moral and civil guidelines intact (Barron 1992, 25). Thus, a total reanalysis of America's socioeconomic-political infrastructure, termed *theonomics*, or *theonomy*, is necessary to plan for this bold reorientation of secular society.

Postmillennialist CR has sparked a burgeoning literature of debate that features CR's strident, contentious refutations of premillennialist Christianity as a biblically unsound "cop-out" surrendering the world to Satan versus premillennialist countercharges that CR is a heresy running counter to revealed prophecy.

The essential difference between the two theological positions, of course, deals with their proponents' biblically inferred expectations about the literal Second Coming of Jesus Christ to Earth (see Introvigne, this volume). Premillennialists anticipate a sudden return of Christ without warning. His return will be prefaced by war, pestilence, misery, and widespread social breakdown. Since Christ will come "as a thief in the night," Christians must conduct their lives constantly as if His arrival could occur at any minute. But besides keeping the faith and converting as many others as possible, true Christians have little to do with influencing the timing of Christ's arrival. The millennium or 1000 year reign of Christ must be brought about by Jesus, who alone can vanquish Satan.

Like premillennialists, postmillennialists believe that Christ is to return to Earth and that they are living in the figurative last days of a sinful world. But they hold to the idea that they must actively prepare the way for Christ's Second Coming and may even be able to alter the scheduling of the millennium. And this millennium may arrive quietly, settling in around the globe in a triumphant gradualism that matches God's will with human effort. By implication Christians must be political activists and will eventually establish a theocracy.

Today's neo-postmillennialists such as Christian Reconstructionists can thus be seen as confident optimists who are prepared to build the millennial kingdom. In contrast, twentieth-century fundamentalist premillennialism has been grounded in pessimistic fatalism about the world. Culture has been presumed to be degenerating and falling into the realm of Satan. Christians have not been thought capable of preventing the coming of Antichrist and the Great Tribulation. Yet many premillennialists, like conservative evangelicals generally, have become more committed to political activism in recent decades. The possible contradiction between political activism and the eschatological fatalism of traditional fundamentalism is a key part of the context of the rise of Christian Reconstructionism.

The present essay offers an analysis of this acrimonious post-premillennial debate and the rhetorical tactics that CR spokespersons have used in their return to what Campolo (1995, 140–141) has termed a "growing *triumphalism*."

What is Christian Reconstructionism?

CR has been described in detail elsewhere (Barron 1992; Barron and Shupe 1992). Essentially it is an intellectual movement within a larger field of New Christian Right thought known as *dominion theology*. Both dominion theology and CR are unabashedly postmillennial, endorsing a reinfusion of biblical values into American culture and institutions. Barron (1992, 14) delineates the broader perspective of dominionism as "a commitment to defining and carrying out an approach to building a society that is *self-consciously defined as exclusively Christian*, and dependent specifically on the work of Christians, rather than based on a broader consensus." Barron claims that dominionists aim for "sweeping fundamental change, not just readjustments, in the social system." The Christian Coalition, for examples, falls within this category in statements to "reclaim America for Christ" or to restore the United States to the status of a Christian nation.

CR, however, can be viewed as an even stricter persuasion within dominion theology, premising more of its "blueprints" on literal directions of the Pentateuch than other versions.[1] With its Calvinist Reformed Church tradition, CR writers have created an impressive literature elaborating "an emphasis on the Old Testament law." They "stress . . . the continued normativity not only of the moral law but also of the judicial law of Old Testament Israel, including its penal sanctions." They believe "that the Old Testament judicial law applies not only to Israel, but also to Gentile nations, including modern America, so that it is the duty of the civil government to enforce that law and execute its penalties" (Barker and Godfrey 1990, 9–10).

Thus, in 1973 when his *Institutes of Biblical Law* was first published, Reconstructionist patriarch Rousas John Rushdoony (1973, 14) wrote

> The creation mandate was precisely the requirement that man subdue the earth and exercise dominion over it. There is not one word of Scripture to indicate or imply that this mandate was ever revoked.

In short, a reconstructed Western civilization would not be merely "amended but rather razed and rebuilt" totally (Shupe 1989, 88).

Reconstructionists, like dominionists, are a diverse sectarian lot (Barron 1992). Rousas John Rushdoony has been turning out imposing tomes on the relevance of biblical law to every facet of human society since the late 1950s (Rushdoony 1986, 1973). Rushdoony can indeed be considered the modern catalyst of this Calvinist-based movement. Currently there are a number of CR organizations, geographically disparate and at times not in correspondence or fellowship with one another. Among their key centers are Rushdoony's Chalcedon Foundation in Vallecito, California; his son-in-law Gary North's Institute for Christian Economics in Tyler, Texas (in 1992 and thereafter, North seriously contemplated a move of ICE to either South Carolina or San Marcos, Texas); and Gary DeMar's American Vision organization in Atlanta, Georgia. If dominionism is not monolithic, neither is CR. It is more an alliance of like-minded crusaders, differentiated by temperament, polemical style, and levels of dogmatism, than a tightly knit movement.

CR is also a "top-down" intellectual movement. Rushdoony once generously estimated during the late 1980s that there are approximately 20 million charismatic Christians worldwide who would be (naturally, he reasoned) part of CR (Clapp 1987, 17−23). Gary North, however, has more realistically estimated that there are between 20,000 and 40,000 different subscribers to CR materials plus fundamentalist and conservative readers of various CR books (North 1989d); many of these are merely readers of newsletters and are sometimes organized into local discussion groups.

THE DEBATE: STYLE AND ISSUES

In addition to prodigiously publishing books and newsletters that sort through and flesh out the implications of applying the case law of Exodus, Deuteronomy, and Leviticus to modern urban society, Reconstructionists aim a good many salvos at two targets: purported secular humanists and premillennial Christians. Reconstructionists' outrage and disgust with secular humanists is probably greater compared to the criticisms reserved for their premillennialist cousins. Gary North's *Backward, Christian Soldiers?* (1984), for example, or his *The Hoax of Higher Criticism* (1989b), or *Unconditional Surrender* (1988a) can easily match evangelical writer Tim LaHaye's (1980) claims that virtually every social ill plaguing modern society, from drug abuse to abortion to falling SAT scores, can be explained by creeping humanism. And LaHaye's assertion that a conspiracy of several hundred thousand humanists can be held responsible for perpetuating these problems through their moral laxitude and political liberalism is closely paralleled by CR's own conspiratorial rhetoric (e.g., North 1989a, 1986b).

Religious pluralism is a heresy to Reconstructionists. In their view non-Christians as well as agnostics, atheists, and even "liberal" denominational Christians will get short shrift in a reconstructed society when Jesus Christ returns to rule it. Gary North (1982, 39) coldly writes

> Let the God-despisers get back in their closets and keep silent. They will be silent on that final day; they should be practicing early.

But most humanists, self-proclaimed or otherwise labeled, have probably never heard of CR, and even if they had, Reconstructionist writers' shrill accusations would sound little different from those of popular premillennialist spokespersons. As a result, this part of the debate continues to be largely one-sided.

Premillennialist Christians, however, have much more in common with postmillennialist Christians than do atheistic immoral humanists. From a social conflict standpoint of constructing movement identity, therefore, a good deal of opprobrium is directed at premillenialists by Reconstructionist authors to accentuate their respective differences. Premillennialists (particularly dispensationalists) are regularly castigated for being fatalistic pessimists and defeatists who believe in an "eschatology of shipwreck" and display "theological schizophrenia" (North 1984, 17, 29). Writes Gary North (1990, 1), "Protestant fundamentalist Christians have their eyes on the sky, their heads in the clouds, their hearts in Egypt, and their children in the government's schools." Like humanists, premillennialists are blamed for a wide range of current social ills. Writes one Canadian Reconstructionist:

> This [dispensationalist] rejection of the whole law of God, the adoption of a pessimistic eschatology, and a lack of understanding of God's covenant and purposes in history has led to a withdrawal of Christianity from the marketplace of ideas which govern a civilization. This vacuum created in our society by the withdrawal of Christian principles of government has given us widespread abortion, pornography, drug abuse, divorce, oppressive taxation, and other social ills which continue to plague our land. (Duncan 1990, 1)

Reconstructionists accuse premillennialists of "psyching themselves out," that is, of taking their rightful kingdom inheritance from God and creating an unbiblically based world order due largely to a false (catastrophic) eschatology now in "exegetical crisis." (This term is Gary North's [1988c, xvii]). DeMar and Leithart (1988, 50) opine:

> We suggest that the present preoccupation with the end of the world may be a false alarm pulled by the devil to keep the church from working at its full mission. The devil leads Christians to believe that changing the world is hopeless. (DeMar and Leithart 1988, 50)

Premillennialists have responded to CR negatively if only because Reconstructionists are fond of portraying themselves as an inexorably spreading Christian movement (because of the attraction of their truth claims) *and* because Reconstructionists claim that premillennial (particularly dispensationalist) Christianity is breaking up (e.g., Bahnsen and Gentry 1989). Popular evangelical writer Hal Lindsey, among others, has characterized CR as possessing an anti-Semitic streak (Duncan 1990, 1), while Hunt and McMahon (1985, 221) indict dominion theology's postmillennial emphasis as suspiciously close to New Age and Human Potential ideas:

> Although their basic beliefs differ, those who expect to establish a perfect kingdom on earth prior to the return of Christ have a goal that bears much resemblance to humanistic plans for uniting the world in love, peace, and brotherhood.[2]

In the foreword to DeMar's *Debate over Christian Reconstruction* (1988, xiv), Greg Bahnsen laments, "Over the last decade I have witnessed more slurs and misrepresentations of Reconstructionist thought than I have the heart or ability to count. . . ." Overall, however, from the standpoint of one who is not a Reconstructionist, dominionist, or premillennialist, the writings of CR's critics carry a noticeably less caustic tone than those of the representatives of the movement they critique. True, House and Ice, in *Dominion Theology: Blessing or Curse?* (1988), take Reconstructionists to task for (in their view) perverting theology and being unbiblical, link the movement's postmillennial assumptions to humanism and New Age, accuse it of deemphasizing human depravity, and condemn its anti-Semitic potential. Ice, in his preface, even maintains that many Christians attracted to CR and dominionism generally come with a Social Gospel–like hidden humanist agenda of political or social reform that actually fuels their participation. But there is little of the anger, arrogance, and downright contempt for their theological opponents in either House and Ice or Dager that is prevalent in Reconstructionist texts.

Similarly, a thoughtful collection of sixteen essays on CR and theonomy by faculty members of Westminster Theological Seminary (from which Reconstructionist author Greg Bahnsen obtained Master of Divinity and Master of Theology degrees) dispassionately examines CR's claims, interpretations, and hermeneutic style. The most harsh conclusion drawn by the volume's editors is rather tepid compared to the discernable rage found in CR books and articles. Referring to the Westminster Confessional Standards of Reformed and Presbyterian tradition as well as their Calvinist heritage, the essayists accuse theonomy of having in numerous ways represented a "distorted view" of that tradition. They contend that it overemphasizes continuities and neglects discontinuities between the Pentateuch and modern times (Barker and Godfrey 1990, 11).

One author (Longman 1990, 54) in that volume even suggests that theonomy and CR have made a useful contribution to such issues as "just" punishments, *"if one can see through the bombast"* (italics mine). The style of such critics is traditional academic, not junkyard dog. The above author, for example, questions CR by pointing out logical difficulties in operationalizing Mosaic laws to modern society rather than simply denouncing it as heresy:

> Now, according to Exodus 22:1, a thief must restore four sheep for one he has stolen and disposed of but five oxen for an ox. Why the difference? The Bible never says. How do we apply the principle today? If a thief steals my car, do I get four cars in return, or five? Rushdoony provides a wonderful example of modern midrash to argue that the victim gets fewer sheep because they reproduce so fast but how does this apply to my car? (Longman 1990, 51)

One recurrent problem for Reconstructionists is that they operate from an underdog mentality that leads them aggressively to posture contempt and an unmistakable air of superiority in their writings. One of the best examples is Gary North. In his 1990 1287-page tome *Tools of Dominion*, North not-so-subtly implies that his book is in the genre of such classics of Western Christianity as Augustine's *City of God*, Calvin's *Institutes of the Christian Religion*, Hobbes' *Leviathan*, and Kant's *Critique of Pure Reason* (among others). He openly gloats over what he claims to be the ineptitude of CR's detractors:

> Those few critics who have gone into print against us have generally been amateur theologians and imitation scholars. They have read a few of our newsletters and a couple of our books (if that), and then have invented the rest. . . . Meanwhile, we keep publishing. The longer a competent critic waits to produce a comprehensive, detailed attack on us, the more difficult his job becomes. No

intelligent critic wants to become a sacrificial lamb who is subsequently exposed publicly as someone who failed to do his homework. This is why time is on our side. (North 1990, 13)

The worst offender in the arrogance category, however, is John Lofton, a colleague of Rushdoony's and sometimes journalist for the *Washington Times*, a conservative newspaper in the nation's capital owned by Unification Church founder Reverend Sun Myung Moon. One of Lofton's favorite techniques is to telephone a secular or religious critic of CR who has offended theonomists and proceed to interview the unsuspecting person with leading and double-barreled questions that begin cordially enough but turn insulting and preachy. Then he publishes a vindictive account of the interview in the *Chalcedon Report* (a newsletter published by Rushdoony's think tank in Vallecito, California). The person thus interviewed is made to look the fool in the manner of the "straw men" that North criticized non-Reconstructionists for setting up.

Indeed, the underdog position of Reconstructionists not only accounts for their pugilistic belligerence but also for their exaggerated claims of "besting" premillennialists in what they consider to be bellwether debates and charge-countercharge exchanges but that otherwise are obscure events of which most theologians are virtually unaware. For example, Gary DeMar's *The Debate over Christian Reconstruction* (1988), a discussion of a public debate on theonomy between reconstructionists Gary DeMar and Peter Leithart (both of the Atlanta-based CR group American Vision) and premillennialists Tommy Ice and Dave Hunt, gleefully touts a *Rocky*-style "knockout" of premillennialism. The book jacket, with no small amount of hyperbole, asserts that this particular debate was more than just "another chapter" in the perennial debate among Christians over what constitutes genuine orthodoxy. Rather, it claims, this confrontation was a turning point in the history of Western Christendom:

> At stake was the future of the Reformation movement begun nearly half a millennium ago by Martin Luther and John Calvin. At stake was the integrity of American evangelicalism. At stake was the very nature of Western culture and civilization.

Such puffery is not lost on premillennialist Christians who are affronted by attacks on themselves as a category of losers and on prominent individuals such as Dave Hunt. House and Ice, for example, criticize North and others for their smug boasting, characterize it as "churlish," and wonder at Reconstructionists' lack of compassion for their allegedly misguided fellow Christians. They even cite an ex-Reconstructionist pastor, Doug Wilson, who grew fed up with certain of the movement's writers' mean-spirited attacks and lack of humility. Wilson observes that "the law of God cannot be kept by people who think that arrogant boasting is a virtue" (cited in House and Ice 1988, 347).

WILL THE PENDULUM SWING TOWARD CIVILITY?

Speech and communication specialists Pearce, Barnett, Littlejohn, and Alexander (1989) analyzed a series of debates between the Reverend Jerry Falwell (social-political conservative, Independent Baptist minister, and founder of the now-defunct Moral Majority, Inc.) and Massachusetts U.S. Senator Ted Kennedy (a well-known liberal Democrat) during the mid-1980s. Content analyses of the debates reveals how each man attempted to keep his exchanges civil and respectful, but despite this surface congeniality there was a nonbridgeable "split between incompatible worldviews." Only the personalities of the two speakers prevented the debates from degenerating into what Pearce et al. termed *reciprocated diatribe* (which before the debates had been the standard rhetorical style of mutual critiquing between antagonists such as Jerry Falwell and Tim LaHaye, on the one hand, and People for the American Way's Norman Lear, on the other).

The Reconstructionist-premillennialist debate is currently at the level of reciprocal diatribe. The Reconstructionists boast of their exegetical certainty as well as their sure eschatological vindication (no matter how far off that may be). Moreover, they seemingly gloat with a religiously ruthless "take-no-prisoners" imperiousness. The premillennialist Christians, for their part, have struggled since the humiliating Scopes Monkey Trial of 1925 to regain a sense that they are once again safely ensconced within mainstream American culture, only to have an upstart postmillennialist movement claim that they are the betrayers of the true Christian tradition. This offends them.

Thus, there will be little opportunity for genuine constructive dialogue that has either side seriously listening to the other until Christian Reconstructionists decide to change their style and tactics, if not their overall educational strategy, and produce a situation in which premillennialists can thereby feel less threatened. There seems to be little chance of that happening soon in the current generation of theonomists, however, given the top-down nature of CR "knowledge production," with its limited mass membership base and most activities at the intellectual level controlled by a relatively few persons who seem to delight in their own contentious rhetoric. Civility is not yet established. The Reconstructionists are still more interested in war cries than meaningful dialogue.

Notes

1. One alternative version of dominion theology growing within charismatics and Pentecostals is the Restoration Movement. Here the emphasis is on a return to what is envisioned as literal biblical history (Holy Ghost experiences, tongues, miracles, and so forth) embodied in more sectarian parts of the modern church. It is both heavily experiential and "progressive" in its belief that many current denominational churches have been left behind by the work of the Holy Spirit while others are progressing. Dominion theology, in many respects, has roots in the earlier "Latter-Rain" movement of the late 1940s and 1950s (Nation 1992; Darrand and Shupe 1983).

2. Reconstructionists have spent a lot of words on criticizing Hunt in particular, who in reply has singled out dominion theology as a New Age heresy (Hunt 1985; North 1988c). After considering the actual implications of living in a world in which violations of strict Mosaic law were prosecuted in the way that Rushdoony, Bahnsen, North, or DeMar have suggested, Dager (1990, 188) concludes, "I'm afraid we'd end up with a bloodbath that would virtually wipe out the next generation of humanity were these penalties instituted today."

References

Bahnsen, Greg L., and Kenneth L. Gentry, Jr. 1989. *House Divided: the Break-up of Dispensational Theology*. Tyler, TX: Institute for Christian Economics.

Barker, William S., and W. Robert Godfrey, eds. 1990. *Theonomy: A Reformed Critique*. Grand Rapids, MI: Zondervan.

Barron, Bruce. 1992. *Heaven on Earth? The Social and Political Agendas of Dominion Theology*. Grand Rapids, MI: Zondervan.

————, and Anson Shupe. 1992. "Reasons for the Growing Popularity of Christian Reconstructionism: The Determination to Attain Dominion." In *Religion and Politics in Comparative Perspective: Revival of Religious Fundamentalism in East and West*, edited by Bronislaw Misztal and Anson Shupe. Westport, CT: Praeger Publishers.

Campolo, Tony. 1995. *Is Jesus a Republican or a Democrat?* Dallas, TX: Word.

Chilton, David. 1987a. *Paradise Restored.* Ft. Worth, TX: Dominion Press.

———. 1987b. *The Great Tribulation.* Ft. Worth, TX: Dominion Press.

Clapp, Rodney. 1987. "Democracy as Heresy." *Christianity Today* (February 20): 17–23.

Dager, Albert James. 1990. *Vengeance is Ours.* Redmond, WA: Sword.

Darrand, Tom Craig, and Anson Shupe. 1983. *Metaphors of Social Control in a Pentecostal Sect.* Lewiston, NY: The Edwin Mellen Press.

DeMar, Gary. 1988. *The Debate over Christian Reconstruction.* Atlanta, GA: American Vision.

———. 1987. *Ruler of the Nations.* Ft. Worth, TX: Dominion Press.

———, and Peter Leithart. 1988. *The Reduction of Christianity.* Atlanta, GA: American Vision.

Duncan, Mark. 1990. *The Five Points of Christian Reconstructionism from the Lips of our Lord.* St. Edmonton, BC, Canada: Still Waters Revival Books.

House, H. Wayne, and Thomas Ice. 1988. *Dominion Theology: Blessing or Curse?* Portland, OR: Multnomah Press.

Hunt, Dave, and T. A. McMahon. 1985. *The Seduction of Christianity.* Eugene, OR: Harvest House.

LaHaye, Tim. 1980. *Battle for the Mind.* Old Talppan, NJ: Fleming H. Revell.

Longman III, Tremper. 1990. "God's Law and Mosaic Punishments Today." In *Theonomy: A Reformed Critique*, edited by William S. Barker and W. Robert Godfrey. Grand Rapids, MI: Zondervan.

Nation, Gary D. 1992. "The Restoration Movement." *Christianity Today* (May 18): 27–31.

North, Gary. 1990. *Tools of Dominion.* Tyler, TX: Institute for Christian Economics.

———. 1982. "The Intellectual Schizophrenia of the New Christian Right." In *The Failure of the American Baptist Culture*, edited by James B. Jordan. Tyler, TX: Geneval Divinity School.

———. 1984. *Backward, Christian Soldiers?* Tyler, TX: Institute for Christian Economics.

———. 1986a. *Honest Money.* Ft. Worth, TX: Dominion Press.

———. 1986b. *Conspiracy: A Biblical View.* Ft. Worth, TX: Dominion Press.

———. 1987a. *Ruler of the Nations.* Ft. Worth, TX: Dominion Press.

———. 1987b. *Dominion & Common Grace.* Tyler, TX: Institute for Christian Economics.

———. 1987c. *Liberating Planet Earth.* Ft. Worth, TX: Dominion Press.

———. 1988a. *Unconditional Surrender.* 3rd ed. Tyler, TX: Institute for Christian Economics.

———. 1988b. *Unholy Spirits.* Ft. Worth, TX: Dominion Press.

———. 1988c. *Is the World Running Down?* Tyler, TX: Institute for Christian Economics.

———. 1988d. Foreword to *The Reduction of Christianity* by Gary DeMar and Peter Leithart. Atlanta, GA: American Vision.

———. 1989a. *Political Polytheism: The Myth of Pluralism*. Tyler, TX: Institute for Christian Economics.

———. 1989b. *The Hoax of Higher Criticism*. Tyler, TX: Institute for Christian Economics.

———. 1989c. *When Justice is Aborted*. Ft. Worth, TX: Dominion Press.

———. 1989d. Personal written communication to author, April 12, 1989.

Pearce, W. Barnett, Stephen W. Littlejohn, and Alison Alexander. 1989. "The Quixotic Quest for Civility: Patterns of Interaction between the New Christian Right and Secular Humanists." In *Secularization and Fundamentalism Reconsidered*, edited by Jeffrey K. Hadden and Anson Shupe. New York: Paragon House.

Rushdoony, Rousas John. 1986. *Law and Society: Volume II of the Institutes of Biblical Law*. Vallecito, CA: Ross House.

———. 1973. *The Institutes of Biblical Law*. Vallecito, CA: The Presbyterian and Reformed Publishing Company.

Shupe, Anson. 1989. "The Reconstructionist Movement on the New Christian Right." *Christian Century* (October 4): 880–882.

The Persistence of Apocalypticism Within a Denominationalizing Sect

The Apocalyptic Fringe Groups of Seventh-day Adventism

11 Ronald Lawson

INTRODUCTION

The origins of Seventh-day Adventism were urgently apocalyptic. Its founders had all been disciples of William Miller, whose proclamation throughout the American Northeast that the Second Coming of Christ would occur on October 22, 1844, had spawned the "Millerite Movement." Although grief-stricken and humiliated by the "Great Disappointment," this segment of the movement continued to anticipate the imminent return of Jesus. Its leaders regarded this belief as so central to their faith that they enshrined it in the name they adopted: Seventh-day *Adventist*.

October 1994 marked the 150th anniversary of the failure of Miller's prophecy—and a further century and a half of preaching that Jesus would soon return. However, during this period American Adventism has been transformed: Adventists have grown in number, put down roots in the society, and experienced prosperity. This paper investigates the extent to which an urgent apocalypticism continues to be taught and believed within Adventism today.

THEORETICAL FOCUS

This question is explored with the help of church-sect theory. Developed first in Europe (Troeltsch 1931 [1911]), this theory proved especially stimulating once Niebuhr applied it to the religious situation in the United States (1957 [1929]). The religious pluralism and absence of an established church here caused researchers to alter the theory's nomenclature, as they now compared *sects* with *denominations* rather than *churches*, and tested Niebuhr's claim that all *sects* would inevitably be transformed into *denominations* (Yinger 1957, 54). Eventually Stark and Bainbridge, responding to confusion caused by differences among researchers in the lists of characteristics used to define *sect* and *denomination*, put forward a single dimension, "the degree to which a religious group is in a *state of tension* with its surrounding sociocultural environment" (1985, 23). According to this definition, sects are in high tension with their environments while denominations have low tension (49–51).

Although research has shown that not all sects become denominations,[1] as generations pass most of those that survive and grow compromise with the world, thus reducing tension and moving toward denominational status (Wilson 1969 [1963], 371, 372). This usually occurs as they increase their participation in the wider society and as influential members experience upward mobility and then find that the tension between their religious group and society is inconsistent with their interests (Stark and Bainbridge 1985, 134, 99, 103). Since an urgent apocalyptic position anticipates "the end of the world"—the sudden destruction of society—a group holding such a position is, by definition, in high tension with its environment. However, intense apocalypticism is difficult to maintain: "The expectation that the world is to overturn through supernatural action is necessarily subject to repeated postponement" (Wilson 1973, 36).

As a religious group begins to move from *sect* toward *denomination*, its membership is likely to become more diverse. For example, Niebuhr realized that some members would become uneasy with change and compromise, and would hold fast to the traditional teachings, thus creating theological diversity within the ranks and risking, ultimately, a new sectarian schism (1957 [1929], 19–20, 54).

RESEARCH METHODS

This paper is a product of a large study of international Seventh-day Adventism, whose data include more than 3,000 in-depth interviews from fifty-four countries and questionnaires from interviewees (who are mostly church employees) and samples of college students and laity. It focuses on the North American Division of the Adventist Church (the United States and Canada), drawing on data from interviews, questionnaires, and books, periodicals, and tapes published by the official Adventist publishing houses, independent organizations of conservative and liberal Adventists, and "independent ministries" on the fringes of Adventism. It also utilizes data from four other relevant surveys of North American Adventists.

APOCALYPTIC URGENCY AMONG EARLY ADVENTISTS

William Miller had concluded from his study of the apocalyptic visions of the biblical books of Daniel and Revelation that "the time of the end" had begun in 1798 and that the Second Coming of Christ would occur in 1844 (Numbers and Butler 1987). Although he withdrew after the failure of his prediction and most of his followers dispersed, a small group reinterpreted the key prophecy: October 22, 1844, was the beginning of the pre-advent judgment in heaven and was the final date singled out by time prophecy; the return of Jesus would follow quickly. A young visionary, Ellen White, played an important role in confirming this interpretation. Since they initially held that with the beginning of judgment the "door of mercy" had been shut, they made no efforts to evangelize. Even after they came to believe that they were called to share their message with others, they avoided formal organization and foreign evangelism, believing that insufficient time remained.

Miller's prophecies had portrayed governments as wild beasts that hurt God's people. Adventists elaborated on these prophecies as they developed their eschatology further. They adopted a unique interpretation when some members were arrested for violating state "blue laws" following their adoption of the Saturday Sabbath: beginning in 1851, they denounced the American Republic, identifying it with the second beast of Revelation 13, which "had two horns like a lamb" and spoke "like a dragon." They saw the early days of the U.S., when it had adopted its Constitution and Bill of Rights, positively—as symbolized by the beast's lamb-like appearance, with the two horns representing the principles of political and religious freedom. But, pointing to slavery and to the religious intolerance they had experienced, they held that it had betrayed both principles—it was a dragon in lamb's clothing, and was destined to play a persecuting role in the world's final events (Morgan 1994, 238). That is, Adventist eschatology invoked tension with the state: it was highly sectarian at this point.

EXTENDING THE TIME

The new sect finally created a formal organization and chose a name for itself in the early 1860s. Having organized, Adventists then began to build institutions and, in 1874, they sent their first foreign missionary to Europe. Many more missionaries followed—and more institutions were built abroad. The building spree between 1860 and 1901 included 16 colleges and high schools, a medical school, 75 "sanitariums" or hospitals, 13 publishing houses, and 31 miscellaneous institutions (such as health food factories). Although these institutions were created in order to facilitate Adventists in their goals of spreading their "last warning message" and thereby ushering in Christ's kingdom, the result was gradual goal displacement: there was an inevitable tension between longer-term building and organizing and the urgency of their message.

Meanwhile, Ellen White had elaborated on Adventist eschatology, with special attention to the final events just before the Second Coming. The main players would be Satan[2] and his henchmen—the Roman Catholic Church,[3] "Apostate Protestantism,"[4] "Spiritualism,"[5] and the U.S. government. These would persecute God's "remnant"—the loyal Adventists—beginning in the United States:

When Protestantism shall stretch her hand across the gulf to grasp the hand of
the Roman power, when she shall reach over the abyss to clasp hands with spiritualism, when, under the influence of the threefold union, our country shall
repudiate every principle of its Constitution as a Protestant and republican government . . . then we may know that the time has come for the marvelous working of Satan and that the end is near. (White 1885, 451)

White's eschatology was published in final form in 1888 in *The Great Controversy between Christ and Satan*. The details of the eschatology reflected the
times in which White wrote—spiritualism was in vogue, and a Protestant
establishment was trying to shore up its position by, among other things,
introducing a "national Sunday law" that would protect and codify the state
blue laws. Although White declared that "the final events" would be "rapid,"
her detailed list of future events created an impression that the end was somewhat more distant—especially when the national Sunday law failed to pass in
both 1888 and 1889. Adventists had a part in this outcome—they had chosen
to work against the fulfillment of their own sign of the eschaton.

The elaboration of Adventist eschatology had involved some reshaping,
especially of their view of the United States. While they continued to identify
America with the two-horned beast, it was no longer portrayed as already in
the dragon phase, but as still lamb-like, and its demise was thus seen as less
imminent. That is, the time believed to be remaining before the Second Coming of Christ was lengthening, and tension with the state was beginning to
relax. Moreover, Ellen White now counseled rapprochement with civil authorities in order to facilitate missionary work, urging Adventists to help prolong
the future of America "so the Adventist message could go forth and flourish"
(Butler 1974, 193). Adventists thus found themselves in an anomalous situation
where they wished to delay the end of the world in order to have greater
opportunity to preach that it was at hand. Consequently, although their
rehoned eschatology saw the passage of a national Sunday law as the culmination of the prophecy concerning the two-horned beast, and thus a sure signal
that the end was at hand, they felt obliged by Ellen White's counsel to "extend
the time" to respond boldly to this threat (Butler 1974, 196–198; Morgan 1994,
241–42). A flurry of political activity culminated in the creation of what
became the Public Affairs and Religious Liberty Department within the General Conference,[6] which institutionalized the Adventist Church's role as a
watchdog of the First Amendment.

During the following decades, Adventism continued to accommodate the state. It altered its stance on military service, pursued accreditation for its colleges, and accepted government aid for its schools and hospitals (Lawson 1996a,1996b). In order to gain accreditation, it exposed its academics to graduate study at major universities, which inevitably made the content of their courses less sectarian, and thus also impacted their students. Meanwhile, accreditation prepared the way for widespread upward mobility among graduates of Adventist colleges (Lawson 1995).

Adventism also began to adjust to the religious economy. In the 1950s church leaders participated in a series of meetings with two well-known Evangelical scholars, Walter R. Martin and Donald Grey Barnhouse, who, in the process of writing a series of studies on Christian "cults," had begun researching Seventh-day Adventism. When Adventists published their answers to the Evangelicals' questions, it was revealed that they had denied three doctrines that had been widely held among them but were offensive to Evangelicals (QOD 1957). All were relevant to the specialness of Adventism and its endtime message.[7] Although some members expressed a sense of betrayal over the new formulation of belief, there was widespread relief when Martin's book declared that Adventists were not a cult but were "bretheren" of the Christian Evangelicals (Martin 1960).

Adventists were putting down roots in society and, in the process, becoming world-affirming. The apocalypse was less imminent. Adventist spokespersons sometimes recognized this explicitly. For example, when, during World War II, Supreme Court decisions strengthened religious liberty and Roosevelt included freedom of religion as one of his four basic freedoms, the editor of the official church paper commented that what Adventists had prophesied clearly lay further in the future (Editorial 1943). Seventh-day Adventism had become a denominationalizing sect.

EXPECTANCY AND DELAY

This does not mean that Adventists had abandoned their eschatology. They continued to believe that Jesus was returning soon and to look expectantly for signs of the fulfillment of Ellen White's whole eschatological scenario. Consequently, they remained prone to excitement whenever they found evidence that the return of the Lord might be near. Although the Adventist Church, as a corporate religious body, learned the lesson of 1844 and has never set or endorsed a date for the Second Coming, groups of Adventists have focused on particular dates for that event more than twenty times in the past 150 years (Paulien 1994, 24). Their attention was often drawn to these "signs of the times" by Adventist evangelists, for eschatology remained at the center of Adventist evangelism—it attracted crowds and gained conversions, especially during times of crisis. Adventist evangelists made much of both world wars, the great depression, the election of John F. Kennedy, the first Catholic, as president; the Cuban missile crisis; the first expedition to the moon;[8] the sexual revolution of the 1960s and rise of the gay movement; and the cold war.[9] The Adventist Church also used the expectation of the return of Jesus—and fear of not being ready—to maintain the commitment of its members and to control their behavior.

However, there was considerable burnout on the issue over time as the extended delay made its impact: it proved increasingly difficult to maintain a high level of expectation. Most Adventists settled into a state of chronic fretfulness about the Second Coming. While they have "held onto the Sabbath," members of the baby-boomer generation, in particular, "are frankly embarrassed by those wild, apocalyptic books on which this church was founded" (Fagal 1992, 3; Branson 1991, 2).

As Adventists have buried generations of forebears who believed that they would live to see Jesus return, they have tried to find reasons for the delay. Two main explanations have been put forward, each of which is associated with a response:

(1) The delay has been caused because members' characters are not yet ready for translation. The response is to somehow attain fully sanctified lives (Douglass 1975). Interviewees who hold this position admitted that they experience a lot of stress, for most feel that they have not "arrived," and are therefore responsible for the delay—or in danger of being lost.

(2) Since Jesus had stated that the gospel would be preached in all the world and then the end would come, the problem must be that Adventists have failed to complete this task. This is the explanation espoused most strongly by the administrators who address the issue. Their response has been to pour more energy and resources into evangelism and other forms of spreading the "Advent message."

THE FRAGMENTING OF THE ADVENTIST APOCALYPTIC

The data suggest that the doctrine of the Second Advent, as taught and believed within American Adventism today, is fragmenting:

(1) *Church administrators.* Church administrators deliver mixed messages. On the one hand, they make strong affirmations of the traditional doctrine. Adventism's creed, the list of twenty-seven "fundamental beliefs," passed at the 1980 General Conference Session with strong administrative backing, continues the expectation that the return of Jesus will be soon. A book by the current president of the General Conference, published to coincide with the 150th anniversary of the Great Disappointment, notes that the unexpected delay is causing some to question, but affirms that "WE STILL BELIEVE!" (Folkenberg 1994, 9).

On the other hand, when an Adventist publishing house was sued by the Equal Employment Opportunity Commission because of its discrimination against women in salaries and promotions, the defense brief, which must have been written with the input and approval of church leaders, distanced present-day Adventism from its "earlier" anti-Catholicism as "nothing more" than a manifestation of an attitude common among conservative Protestant denominations in earlier decades "which has now been consigned to the historical trash heap so far as the Seventh-day Adventist Church is concerned" (Pacific Press Case 1975, 4). Was this mere opportunism, or a straw in the wind?

Adventist leaders preside over a strongly centralized, hierarchical organizational structure. Its institutions root it strongly in this world: for example, the finances of its massive U.S. hospital system dwarf the budget of the General Conference, and its hospitals are currently eagerly engaged in mergers with non-Adventist hospitals—sometimes with Catholic hospitals—in order to strengthen their positions.

(2) *Adventist evangelism.* Adventist evangelism—whether it adopts the form of blockbuster public meetings making full use of multimedia, "Revelation Seminars," magazines such as the *Signs of the Times*, "soul-winning" books, or television and radio programs—still focuses strongly on "endtime events." Adventist evangelists typically invoked the timeline prophecies to show that the "time of the end" began in 1798 and that 1844 was the last pinpointed date, which left the Second Coming as the next major event—and would then point to whatever current events seemed appropriate to suggest that the denouement was very near. However, many evangelists and writers have eagerly updated their eschatological content since the collapse of the Soviet empire in 1989, for they now claim to see a convergence of trends preparing the way for the fulfillment of Ellen White's predictions. These "trends" include the following: (i) papal influence has grown dramatically, coming to the fore in the role played by Pope John Paul II in the collapse of

communism; (ii) the U.S., having emerged as the sole superpower, is finally in a position where it could, in alliance with the papacy, press the whole world into conformity with an attack on God's elect; (iii) the New Christian Right has emerged as a political force in the U.S. and has built an alliance with the Catholic Church over abortion and other social issues, and both are attacking church-state separation and receiving some cooperation in this from the Supreme Court; (iv) a resurgence of spiritualism is occurring in several guises—in the New Age movement and the widespread interest in "near-death experiences" and appearances of the Virgin Mary (Finley 1992a, 1992b; Moore 1992, 1995; Goldstein 1993, 1996).

Although the grim Adventist eschatological scenario is portrayed as close to culmination, it is still future for Adventist evangelists. With their unhindered access to meeting spaces, advertising, publishing, and the airwaves, their utilization of modern conveniences, and their satisfaction with the image that Adventism and its institutions project to society, they are clearly personally comfortable in America today.

(3) *Pastors*. Since Adventist evangelism emphasizes eschatology, converts are usually those attracted by this topic. However, when they join Adventist congregations, they find that their pastors typically give far less emphasis to eschatological subjects than the evangelists. When I asked 115 North American pastors what themes they stressed in their sermons, only 7 percent mentioned eschatological subjects as their prime theme.

These data should not be interpreted as suggesting that Adventist pastors in North America are ignoring the topic of the apocalypse. When 296 pastors responding to another survey were asked how many sermons they had preached over the preceding twelve months "where the Second Coming had been the sole subject," the median response was three (Rosado 1991).[10] More than half (50.3 percent) of 1,988 North American members included within a survey of the world membership of the Adventist Church sponsored by the General Conference reported hearing a sermon on "the Second Coming or last day events" "more than once" during the preceding year. On the other hand, only 23.8 percent had heard a sermon dealing with "the 2,300 years or other prophetic events"—topics that were likely to have been more urgent in tone (World Survey). That is, most of the pastors who choose to address the topic of the Second Coming in their sermons approach it as a doctrine, without a great deal of urgency.

When the responses of interviewees to a block of questions asking to what extent they agreed with statements rooted in Adventist eschatology were cross-tabulated with age, a sharp age break emerged. Those who had entered the ministry before the mid-1960s—when a seminary degree was not the norm and very few of the college religion teachers had doctorates—were much more likely to answer that they "strongly agree" or "agree" with these statements; on the other hand, those who had entered the ministry later were more prone to "disagree" or "strongly disagree." Since a seminary degree was the norm for the latter, they had been exposed to scholars with advanced degrees from the finest universities and also, increasingly, in the Adventist colleges during their baccalaureate programs. This interpretation is confirmed by cross-tabulations between "years of education" and the same block of eschatologically rooted statements: those with only sixteen years education tended to agree with the statements, while those with higher degrees tended to disagree. That is, the key to understanding the relatively low priority accorded to apocalyptic preaching by pastors lies in what is taught in the seminary and by the religion departments of Adventist colleges.

(4) *The seminary and departments of religion* in general avoid the traditional Adventist approach to eschatology. Several of the forty-nine such teachers interviewed mentioned that they would not teach a course on Daniel and Revelation or that no one was willing to do so. Interview excerpts illustrate the tone of these comments:

> The Second Advent is not now an important part of Adventist faith and life. . . . Daniel and Revelation has not been really important in Adventist scholarship during my career. There have always been courses on them, but the area has not been terribly important to the intellectual life of the church. We've had a collective subliminal awareness that traditional interpretations don't make a lot of sense. We have over-interpreted these pictures, which really say that there is a struggle between good and evil which God will win. We've tried to interpret each detail, to do left-brain analysis to what is really a right-brain piece of art.
>
> I preach the Second Coming, but differently—my emphasis is not on time, but on its influence on ethics. . . . I am having difficulty preaching the signs of the coming in the old way—they are ordinary historical events, so that every generation could see them in their time—so many periods expected His return. . . .
>
> My course, "Apocalyptic Studies," presents apocalyptics as a literary genre, as just another way of writing theology.

These attitudes are confirmed in seven recent books where theologians have addressed apocalyptic themes. The following quote is representative of them all:

My purpose . . . is to highlight the text of the Bible rather than comment on the continuing swirl of current events. . . . The safest course is to understand the Bible's view of the end on its own terms, rather than expecting direct answers to the kinds of questions that only people in our day could have asked. Our Bible is the product of God speaking to people in another time and place. . . . The purpose of the Bible's teaching about the end is not to satisfy our curiosity about the future but to teach us how to live as we await the end. . . . When will the Son of Man come? There is nothing in the current scene that gives us the absolute certainty that the end is immediately before us—or a long time in the future. (Paulien 1994, 13, 34, 89, 159)

(5) *Laypersons*. In surveys of 785 church members and 1305 students at Adventist colleges, I asked to what extent they agreed with the statement "Christ will return in your lifetime." One-seventh (14.7 percent) of the members and one-fifth (21.1 percent) of the students agreed strongly. More than three-fifths of the members and half the students answered "uncertain," which is theologically technically correct since Jesus said "no man knows the day. . . ." As expected, cross-tabulations showed converts to be significantly more urgently apocalyptic than members raised by Adventist parents.

A survey of more than 13,000 students in Adventist high schools found that 31.3 percent worried "very much" "about not being ready for Christ's return," and 21.3 percent "about not being faithful during the Time of Trouble." (Another 28.4 percent and 22.5 percent respectively worry "quite a bit.") Urgency engenders fear among this age group (Valuegenesis Study). When these same questions were asked in a survey targeted at 3,300 Hispanic students, the proportion admitting to being fearful proved to be higher still: 59.5 percent worried "very much" about not being ready for Christ's return and 45.1 percent about possibly proving unfaithful during the Time of Trouble (AVANCE Study). (Another 17.9 percent and 20.1 percent respectively worried "quite a bit.")

That is, while large majorities of laypersons show a belief in the doctrine of the Second Coming, urgent apocalypticism seems to be much less widespread, being concentrated among converts and, often fearfully, among younger students exposed to indoctrination in Adventist schools.

MOVEMENTS ON THE FRINGES OF ADVENTISM

Urgently apocalyptic "independent ministries" on the fringes of Adventism have multiplied in recent years. Their growth is associated with the frustration of many converts who, having been attracted by the eschatological preaching of the Adventist evangelists, are disappointed to find far less of this in the churches they join after their baptisms. These ministries have so disturbed church leaders as a result of the flow of their outspoken literature around the globe and the perception that they are diverting considerable amounts of income from the denominational conduit, that the Annual Council of the church in 1991 voted to condemn them as "producing distrust and division that hinder the work of God" ("Perth Declaration" 1991, 7). In 1992 the North American Division of the church published a large book, *Issues: The Seventh-day Adventist Church and Certain Private Ministries*, laying out its grievances with some of the ministries as a warning to members. Like the early Christians, who continued to think of themselves as Jewish and therefore focused their evangelism on Jews—initially in Jerusalem, and then in the cities to which they had scattered—the leaders of these groups continue to identify with Adventism, even if they have been disfellowshipped, and to focus their efforts on reaching Adventists. (The best known of these ministries was David Koresh's Branch Davidians.)

The fringe apocalyptic ministries are much more urgent in their apocalypticism than most mainstream Adventists. They generally differ from the latter (who have themselves been shown to be very diverse on this issue) in at least one of two main ways. First, many of them are so impatient with the long delay in the Second Coming since 1844 that merely pointing to recent world events as new evidence that the general Adventist eschatological scenario is on track (as the leading evangelists have done) is unsatisfactory to them: they want more direct proof that these are the very last days and Jesus is about to come. To accomplish this they often develop some kind of timeline prophecy that focuses on the current period. Second, they often see the Adventist church leadership as so compromised with the "world" and the members as so "lukewarm" in their spirituality that the church is unready to receive Christ and as such is responsible for his delay. Some of them portray the official church as having shifted positions on beliefs and behavioral standards, so that it has obscured the "last warning message" bequeathed to it through Ellen White, and present their own group as the true "historic Adventists." When criticisms of church leadership are met, in turn, with charges of heresy and attempts to subject them to church discipline, the rancor escalates.

My analysis divides these urgently apocalyptic groups into five categories.[11] The attempts to apply time prophecies to the present differ considerably from one category to another.

(1) *The 6,000 year umbrella time prophecy.* The argument here is that, according to Bishop Ussher's biblical chronology, the creation took place about 4004 B.C., so that the sixth millennium is closing. If each millennium is symbolized by one day, the seventh, or Sabbath, millennium—what the book of Revelation calls THE millennium—is about to open. Premillennialists believe that Christ returns before then.

One of the authors who falls into this category, G. Edward Reid, is an unusual case, for he is a lone writer rather than the head of a ministry, and he holds a departmental position at the headquarters of the Adventist North American Division. He submitted his book manuscript, which suggests that Christ will return by the year 2000, to the Review and Herald (R&H), an Adventist publishing house, but it was rejected because the editors saw it as too apocalyptic and irresponsible in its biblical interpretation. However, he was able to gain the support of the marketing staff, which is made up of old hands from the Adventist Book Centers (ABCs), one of the havens of Adventist fundamentalists. When he was able to raise money to self-publish the book, he arranged for the R&H job-printing division to print the book; this erroneously leaves the impression with many readers that it has the "imprimatur" of the publisher, especially since its marketing division signed up to distribute it through the ABCs and it carries, on the back cover, an endorsement from the chair of the religion department at Southern College, the most conservative of the Adventist colleges in the United States (Reid 1994).

A. Jan Marcussen is best known as the author of *National Sunday Law* (1983), a simplified rehash of the position put forward by Ellen White in the *Great Controversy*, with no attempt to link it to current events. He has struck a chord among a segment of Adventists, for they have provided him with the funds to print and distribute 7.8 million copies of the book in nineteen languages since 1983. His newsletters attempt, with poor documentation, to show that the law is about to be enacted. He also puts forward other evidence that the end is upon us, and in his newsletter of mid-November 1995, he used the 6,000-year theory to cement his case, claiming that this period would culminate in 1996.

(2) *The Jubilee Cycle.* This approach takes the Levitical Jubilee year, based on seven "sabbatical years" for a total of forty-nine years, through seventy cycles—a symbolic number—and thus to our day. However, although the dates of some sabbatical years are known, there is disagreement about the dating of jubilee years in biblical times.[12] Consequently, various proponents disagree

about the ending of the seventieth cycle. An earlier group in the Pacific Northwest settled on the year 1987, and expected the Second Coming that year. The person best known for this timeline, Larry Wilson of Wake Up America Seminars, initially announced that the cycle ended in 1992, before settling on 1994. For him this is the beginning of the final period, during which the usual timeline prophecies, such as the 1,335 days of the book of Daniel, are applied as literal rather than symbolic (a day for a year) days. He expected the events accompanying the Great Tribulation to begin in 1994 or 1995, and that this would include a large asteroid hitting the earth. These events would culminate in the Second Coming of Jesus "around 1998" (Wilson 1994, 1). In a defensive "addendum" inserted in the fifth edition of his most widely circulated book after the close of 1995, he states that he does not regard the delay as a failure of his interpretation. He continues to preach and to publish—the number of copies of this book in circulation has passed 500,000 (Wilson 1994).

(3) *Applications of the timeline prophecies of Daniel and Revelation to the present.* This has been done by several ministries, usually as literal days. Some of them see this as a second (dual) fulfillment, others as the prime application. They look for clues in current events, and link them to the prophecies—a method that gives them a great deal of scope, and therefore also room for disagreement with one another. The best known of these is Charles Wheeling of Countdown Ministries in Alabama—perhaps because he has been active over a long period. He saw the Iran-Iraq War (beginning in 1980) as the harbinger of the Battle of Armageddon; more recently, he has found the Persian Gulf War in prophecy. He looks for an international crisis in the banking system, and is currently very interested in the actions and sayings of the pope. Because he rejects the earlier applications of the timeline prophecies, the year 1844 has no special significance for him. Even though this would seem to put him at odds with the writings of Ellen White, he has been extraordinarily active in publishing and distributing millions of copies of the *Great Controversy*—both in whole and in part—in many countries (Wheeling 1995).

(4) *The status of Jerusalem.* William Grothier of the Adventist Laymen's Foundation and Bible Prophecy Seminars, and editor of the monthly paper *Watchman, What of the Night?*, stands apart from the other ministries in his focus on the status of Jerusalem as a sign of the end of time.[13] He sees the unification of Jerusalem in 1967 as the "beginning of the end of time," and its appointment as capital of Israel in 1980 as the close of probation for nations—and also, because of its illegitimate changes in its doctrine, of that of

the corporate Adventist Church; individuals have a little extra time, but that too is now petering out (Grothier 1995; 1994). In a switch, he focused his paper during 1995 on the aims of the papacy as given in recent encyclicals.

(5) *Those who "sigh and cry" over the apostasy of the Adventist Church.* Several prominent ministries—Hope International (publisher of *Our Firm Foundation*), the Hartland Institute (a college without accreditation and publisher of *The Last Generation*), Cherrystone Press (the personal vehicle of Dr. Ralph Larson), and Prophecy Countdown (a television and shortwave radio ministry) fall into this category. Their key complaint is about changes in Adventist doctrine, such as in the nature of Christ (from sinful—like ours—to sinless—like pre-fall Adam's) as a result of the Bible conferences with Evangelicals Martin and Barnhouse during the 1950s. Because these changes impact on Adventist eschatology (such as the belief that the final generation must overcome as Jesus overcame and stand perfect at the close of probation) and apostasy within the church was predicted by Ellen White, the latter is therefore seen as a clear sign that the end is imminent (Larson 1993, 180).

Although most of the ministries in this category may be counted as doctrinally orthodox, they have drawn much more fire from Adventist leadership than the other categories: the condemning book *Issues* was aimed directly at them—by name—by church leadership, and most of their leaders have been disfellowshipped since its publication in 1992. They have come under attack because their orthodoxy makes them more attractive to unsettled Adventists, they appear to attract considerable sums from their supporters that might otherwise have gone into denominational coffers, their criticism of the official church and its leadership is constant and uncompromising, and their influence is being felt among Adventists in the developing world because of the widespread distribution of their publications there. (Because it comes without cost to recipients there, the circulation of *Our Firm Foundation* is said to exceed that of the official church paper.)

A CONTROVERSY THAT HIGHLIGHTED THE ADVENTIST DILEMMA

The media attention to the Branch Davidian crisis showed church leaders how dangerous such fringe groups could be to the reputation of Adventists, for in the first hours after the ATF raid on the Davidian compound there were many news reports that revealed that Koresh's followers had been drawn from among Adventists,[14] and that identified the Branch Davidians as Adventists. Since Adventist leaders place high priority on projecting a positive image of their church, they regarded this as a crisis of major proportions. They were successful in having the Branch Davidians' connection to Adventism removed from later media reports through the help of costly media consultants (Lawson 1995).

The Branch Davidians were not the only case of a ministry's causing public embarrassment for Adventists at that time—and the other example was much more perplexing. In November 1992, forty-two billboards appeared in Orlando, Florida. Half of these stated "When Church & State Unite, What Do You Lose?" and the rest "Just How Secure is Our Constitution?" These "teasers" were followed by twelve huge billboards featuring a facial photograph of the pope: "Why is the Vatican Trying to Change Our Constitution?" They also offered the opportunity, via an 800 number, to buy copies of Ellen White's *Great Controversy*. The advertisers spent $80,000 on billboard space, $25,000 on newspaper advertisements, $35,000 on radio spots, and $100,000 on television time—a total of $240,000. Similar billboards were also erected in several West Coast cities. David Mould, an active Adventist originally from the Caribbean and head of Laymen for Religious Liberty, claimed responsibility. He explained that he had been angered because of what he saw as the silence of the Adventist Church on these issues at a time when he felt that it was clear that the prophecies of Ellen White were being fulfilled. (That is, his ministry is another example of category 5, above.) He announced that his organization would also sponsor a massive protest demonstration when the pope visited Denver in the fall of 1993, which would hopefully draw international attention (Knittel 1993, 53; Coffin 1993a, 4; 1993b, 8).

The initial billboard campaign presented a problem for the Adventist Church. Adventists are extremely well known in Orlando, which is the location of the church's largest hospital. Local talk shows and the press covered the campaign extensively. Florida Adventist Hospital was deluged with calls, and Adventist staff there were reported to be angry and embarrassed. Because of the decentralized nature of the campaign, the international headquarters of the church in Maryland chose to leave the local church administrators with responsibility for responding to the media. Yet how to respond posed a perplexing problem. While Laymen for Religious Liberty was a conservative independent ministry, it was not doctrinally at variance with the church. It was promoting a book that Adventists regard as divinely inspired and that is the benchmark of historic Adventist eschatology, and had apparently stimulated thousands of orders for it; the billboards highlighted positions often taught by Adventist evangelists and Revelation Seminars. Nevertheless, these were positions that mainstream Adventists had abandoned to such an extent that many of them became very ill at ease when they were publicly identified with them. Mainstream Adventists have become so comfortable with society that they found the conflict implied in the billboards threatening and intensely embarrassing.

The leaders of the Florida Conference were no exception. However, "they could not denounce [the billboards] in terms of the message, for doing so would have taken a position relative to Ellen White that would induce tremendous negative fallout from many devout Adventists." Eventually they wrote a letter to the local newspaper dissociating the Conference from Mould's actions but not from the *Great Controversy*; and they published a special edition of the conference newsletter that praised God for the sales of the book, but that then quoted a number of statements by Ellen White "cautioning church members not to present Adventist beliefs in denunciatory and injudicious manners" (Knittel 1993, 54).

Because of its potential national and international impact, church leaders chose to become involved directly in trying to deflect the negative media impact of the promised campaign during the pope's planned visit to Denver (Patterson 1994). This was ultimately not arranged by Mould, who had fallen into financial and legal difficulties, but by another independent group based in Montana, which contracted to rent billboards from the Gannett Corporation. Church leaders responded by working with the Adventist hospital in Denver to organize an advance media blitz and a religious liberty rally to present the Adventist Church positively. They also developed contacts with the media: "We told them what might happen, and explained that we were not responsible for it, and that we could not stop those who were responsible from doing it. We explained the same thing to religious leaders, including Catholics" (Patterson 1994).

Gary Patterson, the administrator who had been the media contact during the Branch Davidian crisis, was again placed on call, ready to go with a presentation once the billboards started to appear and the media focused on a press conference. When, shortly before the pope's visit, it became known that the billboards were imminent, a press conference was called. Patterson explained that the boards did not represent Adventism, and that doing something like this was against the advice of the author of the very book they were trying to distribute. While Adventists were Protestant, and therefore had their disagreements with Roman Catholics, they did not want to fight, and this was not the right time and place to address the differences. When reporters raised potentially embarrassing questions, Patterson found that he was able to fob them off with limited replies because of their lack of knowledge (Patterson 1994).

To the surprise and relief of the church leaders, the press conference had the unintended consequence of persuading the Gannett Corporation to abandon the billboard contract. That is, the church's media campaign aborted the crisis. However, the issue highlighted the dilemma of Adventism: "[The billboard issue raised] an urgent question: Did Ellen White's nineteenth-century knowledge and experience significantly influence her end-time scenario? Fundamentalists say no. Progressives say yes" (Walters 1993, 13). To many progressive Adventists, the crisis was rooted in the contradiction that the church had continued to pay lip service to the present relevance of all the writings of their prophet three-quarters of a century after her death, but were in fact acting differently. However, to conservatives, the reason why the *Great Controversy* now seems dated, bigoted, and likely to cause embarrassment to some Adventists is that it is coming true (Goldstein 1993, 5–7).

These experiences led church leaders to worry whether some of the other independent ministries could prove equally embarrassing with time. In an issue of the official church paper headlined "Are We Sitting Ducks for Cults?," published soon after the Davidian compound burned, an Adventist sociologist discussed "Why are some Adventists vulnerable to fatal fanaticism?" (Rosado 1993, 16). There is ample evidence of the relevance of this question in the conspiracy theories burgeoning among some segments of the Adventist membership where there is an urgent yearning for the fulfillment of their apocalyptic expectations. Some theories that have received wide currency in recent years are that a Sunday law has been secretly drafted and will be sprung upon the nation; that there is a scheme afoot to use computers, Social Security numbers, and credit card numbers to prevent Sabbath-keepers from being able "to buy or sell" and thus impose "the mark of the beast"; and that Jesuits have infiltrated the General Conference, which has subsequently become part of a conspiracy to keep Adventists in the dark about these threats.

CONCLUSION

The doctrine that the Second Coming of Christ is near continues to be affirmed in Adventist credal statements primarily because church leaders fear that any attempt to update the prophetic teachings of Ellen White would result in unmanageable fallout, and it continues to find expression in evangelistic preaching and writing because it still attracts potential converts. However, as American Adventism has put down roots in society and prospered, and has thus moved from near the sect pole toward the denomination pole of the sect-denomination continuum, the doctrine has lost a great deal of its urgency. However, as one might predict from the theory, considerable urgency continues on the fringes of Adventism, among the much more sectarian "independent ministries." These continue to attract a following because of the frustration of first-generation members, who were initially attracted to Adventism by its apocalyptic message, with the de-emphasis of the doctrine in Adventist churches.

Notes

1. Yinger, for example, introduced the concept of *established sect* (1946, 22–23).
2. The dragon of Revelation.
3. This interpretation was first made by European Protestant reformers.
4. By this White meant all the Protestant church organizations together with those members who failed to accept the Adventist message.
5. Since Adventists believed in "soul sleep"—that is, that the dead were dead until resurrected—any attempt to contact the dead was, by definition, of the devil.
6. Church headquarters.
7. These doctrines were that Christ was born with a sinful nature (this change disowned the bulwark of last-generation perfectionism), that the writings of Ellen White were free of error and equal to the Scriptures, and that Adventists alone comprised the biblical Remnant.
8. It was argued that surely God would step in to prevent sinful man's landing on a place without sin.
9. While Evangelicals generally saw the creation of the state of Israel as of cosmic significance, this was not part of Adventist eschatology.
10. This survey was introduced in a manner that was likely to encourage exaggerated reporting of attention to that topic.
11. Not all fringe groups are urgently apocalyptic. Some focus on health issues, others on the nature of God, etc. However, such groups are not within the scope of this paper.

12. Indeed, there is no direct evidence that the jubilees were observed at all after their initial explanation.

13. He also stands apart from the Evangelicals, who are concerned with the nation of Israel rather than Jerusalem.

14. Indeed, most of them were still on church rolls, for, following Davidian policy, they had not withdrawn their membership.

REFERENCES

Branson, Roy. 1991. "The Power of Apocalypse." *Spectrum* 21 (3): 2.

Butler, Jonathan. 1974. "Adventism and the American Experience." In *The Rise of Adventism: Religion and Society in Mid-Nineteenth-Century America*, edited by Edwin S. Gaustad. New York: Harper and Row.

Coffin, James. 1993a. "Media Campaign Heats up in Orlando." *Adventist Today* 1 (2): 4–6.

———. 1993b. " 'I will not be Quiet': Profile of David Mould." *Adventist Today* 1 (2): 8, 18.

Douglass, Herbert E. 1975. *Perfection: The Impossible Possibility*. Nashville: Southern Publishing Assoc.

Editorial. 1943. *Review and Herald*, July 22.

Fagal, William. 1992. "The New Awakening." *Adventists Affirm* 6 (1): 3–4.

Finley, Mark. 1992a. *Confidence Amid Chaos*. Boise: Pacific Press.

———. 1992b. "How Near is Near?" *Adventists Affirm* 6 (1): 12–24, 40.

Folkenberg, Robert S. 1994. *We Still Believe*. Boise: Pacific Press.

Goldstein, Clifford. 1996. *One Nation under God?* Boise: Pacific Press.

———. 1993. *Day of the Dragon*. Boise: Pacific Press.

Grothier, William H. 1995. *The Sign of the End of Time*. Ozone, AR: Bible Prophecy Seminars.

———. 1994. *Jerusalem in Bible Prophecy*. Ozone, AR: Bible Prophecy Seminars.

Knittel, Frank A. 1993. "The Great Billboard Controversy." *Spectrum* 23 (1): 53–56.

Larson, Ralph. 1993. *Apostasy is the Issue*. Cherry Valley, CA: Cherrystone Press.

Lawson, Ronald. 1996a. "Church and State at Home and Abroad: The Evolution of Seventh-day Adventist Relations with Governments." *Journal of the American Academy of Religion*. Forthcoming.

———. 1996b. "Onward Christian Soldiers?: Seventh-day Adventists and the Issue of Military Service." *Review of Religious Research*, 37 (3): 97–122.

———. 1995. "Seventh-day Adventist Responses to Branch Davidian Notoriety: Patterns of Diversity within a Sect Reducing Tension with Society." *Journal for the Scientific Study of Religion* 34 (3): 323–341.

Marcussen, A. Jan. 1983. *National Sunday Law*. Thompsonville, IL: Amazing Truth.

Martin, Walter. 1960. *The Truth about Seventh-day Adventism*. Grand Rapids, MI: Zondervan.

Moore, Marvin. 1995. *Armageddon: The Devil's Payday*. Boise: Pacific Press.

———. 1992. *The Crisis of the End Time*. Boise: Pacific Press.

Morgan, Douglas. 1994. "Adventism, Apocalyptic, and the Cause of Liberty." *Church History* 63 (June): 235–249.

Niebuhr, H. Richard. 1957 (1929). *The Social Sources of Denominationalism*. Cleveland: Meridian.

North American Division. n.d. *Issues: The Seventh-day Adventist Church and Certain Private Ministries*. Silver Spring, MD: North American Division.

Numbers, Ronald L., and Jonathan M. Butler. 1987. *The Disappointed: Millerism and Millenarianism in the Nineteenth Century*. Bloomington: Indiana University Press.

Pacific Press Case. 1975. "Reply Brief for Defendants in Support of their Motion for Summary Judgment." *Equal Employment Opportunity Commission, et al., vs. Pacific Press Publishing Association, et al*. March 3.

Patterson, Gary. 1994. "The General Conference and the Branch Davidian Crisis." Talk at the New York Adventist Forum, June 11.

Paulien, Jon. 1994. *What the Bible Says about the End-Time*. Hagerstown, MD: Review and Herald.

"Perth Declaration." 1991. Minutes of Annual Council. *Adventist Review* 168 (45): 7.

QOD. 1957. *Seventh-day Adventists Answer Questions on Doctrine*. Washington, DC: Review and Herald.

Reid, G. Edward. 1994. *Even at the Door*. Self-published.

Rosado, Caleb. 1991. Data from a survey of pastors from five U.S. conferences.

———. 1993. "The Appeal of Cults." *Adventist Review* 170 (30): 16–20.

Stark, Rodney, and William Sims Bainbridge. 1985. *The Future of Religion*. Berkeley: University of California Press.

Troeltsch, Ernst. 1931 (1911). *The Social Teaching of the Christian Churches*, translated by Olive Wyon. New York: Macmillan.

Walters, James. 1993. "The Great Controversy: Ambivalence Won't Wash Today." *Adventist Today* 1 (2): 13.

Wheeling, Charles. 1995. "The Time has Come." Tapes of meetings recorded at Henderson, NC, November 3–4. Jemison, AL: Countdown Ministries.

White, Ellen. 1885. *Testimonies for the Church*, vol. 5. Oakland: Pacific Press.

———. 1888. *The Great Controversy between Christ and Satan*. Oakland: Pacific Press.

Wilson, Bryan R. 1969 (1963). "A Typology of Sects." In *Sociology of Religion*, edited by Roland Robertson. Baltimore: Penguin.

————. 1973. *Magic and the Millennium*. New York: Harper and Row.

Wilson, Larry. 1994. *Warning! Revelation is about to be Fulfilled*, fifth ed. Brushton, NY: Teach Services.

Yinger, J. M. 1946. *Religion in the Struggle for Power*. Durham, NC: Duke University Press.

————. 1957. *Religion, Society and the Individual*. New York: Macmillan.

Latter Day Revisited
Contemporary Mormon Millenarianism

12 Massimo Introvigne

TRADITIONAL MORMON MILLENARIANISM

Millenarianism is not only about when this world will end. It also has to do with *how* the end will take place. Millenarianism is best defined as a knowledge, normally of religious origin, about both the imminence and the immanence (i.e., the this-worldliness) of the end (see Olson 1982). Contemporary millennial rhetoric insists mostly on the imminence ("the end is at hand": see

O'Leary 1994). But in the eighteenth and nineteenth centuries immanence and knowledge of the precise details of the eagerly awaited millennial kingdom were at times much more important than date setting for a number of religious groups (see Weber 1987). And the prevalence of the *how* rather than the *when* of the end of the world was evident in early Protestant millenarianism, in the first century after the Lutheran Reformation (Burns 1988, 31). Scholarship of millenarianism has long concentrated on distinguishing between premillenni-alism and postmillennialism. Both believe in a millennial kingdom—a thou-sand years of peace before the Final Judgment. Premillennialists, however, rely on a pessimistic interpretation of human history, believing that events on earth will go from bad to worse until Jesus Christ personally comes to inaugu-rate the millennium. The postmillennialist view is, on the other hand, opti-mistic: the saints' efforts will succeed in establishing the millennium, and Jesus will come only at the end of this human effort. Postmillennialism was a typical eighteenth-century ideology, rooted in an optimistic faith in progress, equally present in Lutheran, Presbyterian, and Episcopalian theologies (Tuve-son 1949, 29–30). After the French Revolution, a more pessimistic mood pre-vailed among millenarian Protestants, and premillennialism gradually replaced postmillennialism (Weber 1987). Most premillennialists, influenced by British revivalists Edward Irving (1792–1834) and (later) John Nelson Darby (1800–1882), also believed in a literal rapture of the saints to heaven in order to preserve the faithful from the suffering of the Antichrist's kingdom and of the Great Tribulation. The premillennialists, however, differed on when the rapture would exactly take place (before, during, or at the end of the Great Tribulation) and they divided accordingly into pretribulationists, midtribula-tionists, and posttribulationists. The divisions persist to this day (Reiter 1984, 41–44). Eventually, pretribulationist premillennialism emerged to become the dominant position among evangelical and fundamentalist Protestants, in the United States and elsewhere, and also inspired a number of new religious movements.

The Church of Jesus Christ of Latter-day Saints, established by Joseph Smith (1805–1844) in 1830, was obviously a millennialist church insofar as it believed in a coming kingdom of literally one thousand years. It was also mil-lenarian in the prevailing sociological sense of the term, since—as its very name announced—it was persuaded it lived in the latter days of human his-tory. Whether, however, early Mormons were postmillennialist or premillenni-alist has long been a matter of debate among historians. Early Mormonism was, above all, restorationist, concentrating on the gathering of Israel and the building of Zion on earth. The very notion of restoration has been, however, interpreted differently by scholars of Mormon history. Marvin Hill (1989) and, particularly, Jan Shipps (1985), have described Mormonism as a "new religious tradition" looking toward the past, to the true Church of old now restored through the prophetic mission of Joseph Smith. Klaus J. Hansen (1967) and a number of scholars drawing on his research on the secret Council of Fifty established by Joseph Smith have described the Mormon restoration as turned to the future, focused on the forging of a political and economic kingdom of God in Nauvoo, Illinois, and later in the intermountain West. Although few scholars ventured to settle the question in definitive terms, the "Kingdom school" led by Hansen mostly regarded early Mormonism as postmillennialist, while interpreting Mormonism as one among a number of America's nineteenth-century new religions devoted to the restoration of the primitive Church that may favor a classification in the premillennialist group. The question is complicated by the fact that early Mormon authors, although prolific in their writings on the end of the world, rarely bothered to compare their views with those of other millennialists. Ernest Lee Tuveson, who in *Millennium and Utopia* (1949) had insisted on the peculiarities of postmillennialism, discussed Mormon millennialism specifically in *Redeemer Nation* (1968, 175–186), and placed it at the cutting edge between premillennialism and postmillennialism. Early Mormons were premillennialists in their eager expectation of apocalyptic events leading to the end of the world, but at the same time exhibited postmillennialist trends in the restorationist theme of the building of the kingdom. Hansen (1967) and Hill (1989) remarked on the same ambiguity, pointing to what has been called a "qualified postmillennialism" (Brooke 1996).

That early Mormons were postmillennialists (however "qualified") is, understandably, argued by authors like John L. Brooke, who insists on the hermetic and Masonic influences on Joseph Smith (see Brooke 1994), since the hermetic and Masonic thought of the eighteenth and early nineteenth centuries was generally optimistic and looked forward to a postmillennialist golden age. Brooke's theory about hermetic influences on the Mormon prophets has, however, been criticized as speculative, while Michael W. Homer (1994, 105–113), in his almost definitive treatment of the relationship between early Mormonism and Freemasonry, has noted that the Masonic influence affected symbol and ritual but not the general Mormon view of history and the world. In an important series of articles later collected and expanded in a book, Grant Underwood (1993) has revised the traditional understanding of Mormon millennialism, arguing that early Mormons were typical, if moderate, premillennialists who awaited "the literal, personal, return of Christ to inaugurate the millennium" (Underwood 1993, 118). Apostles Orson Hyde (1805–1878) and Parley P. Pratt (1807–1857) are mentioned by Underwood as clear examples of Mormon premillennialist rhetoric. Directly criticizing the Hansen thesis, Underwood maintains that Mormon politics were not radical but moderate, and that the idea of building a kingdom on earth was not incompatible with the prevailing American premillennialism of the 1840s. Underwood concludes that early Mormons were by no means particularly original in their premillennialism, and in fact, as far as their ideas on the millennium were concerned, were rather typical of the prevailing Protestant evangelical attitude of mid-nineteenth-century English-speaking evangelical Protestantism. The fact that Mormon missionaries spoke a familiar premillennialist language explains, according to Underwood, why conversions were comparatively easy in the country where modern premillennialism was born and more widespread, the United Kingdom. In short, Joseph Smith's millennialism was not part of a fringe but mainline. He eagerly awaited the end of the world, the premillennial Second Coming and the advent of the millennium, but so did countless evangelical Protestants of his time. Predictably, Underwood's thesis has not convinced the staunchest tenants of the "qualified postmillennialism" thesis (see critical review by Brooke 1996); and others have noted that, unlike Joseph Smith, his successor Brigham Young (1801–1887) easily identified the millennium with Zion and the gathered city of the saints. Young's rhetorical question to an assembled Mormon conference in 1845, "Know ye not that the millennium has commenced?", was hardly compatible with mainline evangelical premillennialism (Quinn 1994, 178 and 403). However, even granting that a different emphasis prevailed during Young's presidency and for some decades after his death among Utah Mormons, Underwood makes a strong case for early Mormons as mainline premillennialists, taking seriously their name of Latter-day Saints and eagerly awaiting an imminent end of the world.

THE TALMUDIC PHASE

William E. McLellin (1806–1883) was ordained an apostle in the Mormon Church in 1835. He was excommunicated in 1838 but, in the meantime, had

kept detailed journals noting the missionary emphasis and the sermons typically preached in different periods. These journals have been recently published (Shipps and Welch 1994). They show that between 1831 and 1836
strictly millenarian themes already experienced a decline. The assassination of
Joseph Smith of 1844 and the loss of the sacred site of Independence, Missouri—tied to millenarian Mormon expectations in Smith's prophecies—further diminished the emphasis on the imminent Second Coming. In the early
Utah sermons, millennial rhetoric is still prevalent but date setting for an
imminent Second Coming is not frequent. Joseph Smith had announced that,
had he lived until his eighty-fifth year—1890—he would have seen the Second Coming. The most current interpretation of the prophecy was that it was
contingent on Smith being alive in 1890; since he was murdered in 1844, the
end of this world was not to be expected for 1890. However, folk expectations
for a Second Coming in 1890 existed at a popular level, and it has been argued
that these Mormon expectations even influenced the Native American Ghost
Dance religion—whose Mormon connections have been often noted (Barney
1986)—and the tragic conclusion of this experience at Wounded Knee (Coates
1985). In fact, rather than the end of the world, 1890 marked the "American-
ization" of the Mormon Church with the Manifesto of president Wilford
Woodruff (1807–1898) that officially ended the practice of polygamy.
Although, ironically, Woodruff was personally persuaded that the end of the
world was imminent, his Manifesto (to be understood as part of a complex
transition going beyond the mere problem of polygamy) symbolized a new era
where millenarian rhetoric and new revelations became rare. Mormonism had
entered a "Talmudic phase," in which the prophetic role of the president is
still considered theologically the same as it was at the time of Joseph Smith,
but in practice revelations are no longer received frequently by the prophet
(Walton 1980, 19) and, at any rate, do not concern an imminent end of the
world. Perhaps the most skilled observer of this development was Ephraim
Edward Ericksen (1882–1967), a noted Mormon philosopher and a liberal often
in disagreement with some authorities of the Mormon Church. In 1922 he
noticed the emergence of a "Mormon scholasticism" that tended to formalize
Mormon doctrine in a creed or dogma, which diminished the dynamic spon-
taneity of continuous revelation and downplayed the millenarian theme
(Ericksen 1922, 98; see Kenney 1987).

If Mormonism has indeed entered into a Talmudic phase involving a routinization of the millenarian charisma, some sort of countermovements should

be expected. After all, the millenarian theme is still present in Mormon scriptures and nineteenth-century classics familiar to many members. Because of the decline in public emphasis, the membership's thirst for millenarianism must be quenched in private. Of course, one of the ways the need is satisfied is the growing interest in early Mormon millenarianism. Underwood's book was granted the Best Book Award by the Mormon History Association in 1995. The discussion on hermetic and Masonic themes influencing alleged Mormon post-millennialism is also lively and, at times, heated among the community of Mormon scholars and history buffs (the second category is quite important in a religious community shaped and motivated by history), particularly after the publication of Brooke's 1994 *The Refiner's Fire*. While this phenomenon concerns the important but numically limited Mormon intellectual community, other phenomena are more widespread. I will discuss six manifestations of contemporary Mormon millenarianism, moving from the mainline membership of the Church toward fringe or splinter groups (without examining directly the latter): (1) folk beliefs within the mainline Church; (2) millennialist fiction; (3) metaphysical literature on a New/Golden Age; (4) conservative biblical and Book of Mormon scholarship; (5) political fundamentalism; and (6) religious "fundamentalism" and schism.

FOLK BELIEFS WITHIN THE MAINLINE MORMON CHURCH

Among the Mormons, "fundamentalist" has a peculiar meaning and usually identifies polygamous splinter Mormon groups. Fundamentalist splinter groups (to be discussed later in this chapter) are millennialists in a peculiar sense, and do not share the usual premillennialism so common among American evangelical fundamentalists (see Strozier 1994). Fundamentalism in the usual sense, as a specific subculture of Protestant evangelicalism, was certainly not popular with Mormons in the nineteenth and early twentieth centuries. Philip L. Barlow (1991) has demonstrated that by limiting the authority of the Bible and "promulgating an extra-Biblical canon" Mormonism could only be very far from American fundamentalism, whose key beliefs were the sufficiency and inerrancy of the Bible (see Mauss and Barlow 1991, 406). Only later in our century, the Mormons' changing use of the King James Version of the Bible exhibited all the features of a Mormon "assimilation" to the evangelical and at times fundamentalist establishment (Mauss and Barlow 1991, 410–411). D. Michael Quinn has emphasized the importance of the "fundamentalist" attitudes (and the association with the conservative Protestant lobby during his diplomatic career) of J. Reuben Clark (1871–1961), who served as a member of the Mormon First Presidency from 1933 to 1961. Clark was instrumental in importing fundamentalist attitudes on the Bible into Mormonism, including a predisposition toward classical premillennialist (pretribulationist) interpretations (Quinn 1983). According to Armand L. Mauss, a Mormon "retrenchment" took place between 1960–1990, including an increased "susceptibility to fundamentalist 'scare' scenarios." Stories about demonic possession, rampant Satanism, and the imminent end of the world, although never officially supported by the Mormon Church leaders, constituted a corpus of "folk fundamentalism" that got "disseminated upward into the leadership echelons and then back downward to the folk with an authoritative aura." The lack in the late years of the Ezra T. Benson (1899–1994) administration of a "full and vigorous First Presidency," according to Mauss, made it very difficult to rein in the "folk fundamentalist" preferences of individual Mormon authorities, but this does not necessarily mean that these preferences were shared by the majority of the presiding brethren (Mauss 1994a, 129–149; see also Mauss 1994b, 185–188). The kind of premillennialist scenarios suggested by Mauss are not specific to Mormon folk culture, but are part of the general evangelical lore, whose general appeal (disseminated through national novels, movies, and TV preaching) has penetrated the Mormon subculture, notwithstanding its peculiarities. It may be expected that the Gordon B. Hinckley administration, with its reemphasis on peculiar Mormon themes, will be less vulnerable to upward dissemination into leadership echelons of forms of Protestant folk premillennialism.

On the other hand, folk beliefs peculiar to the Mormon subculture (not to be confused with those assimilated from the larger evangelical world) will probably remain alive. Mormonism has always maintained a rich folklore in which miraculous manifestations and revelations occur, are communicated by word of mouth, and are eventually modified and amplified until they finally gain credence and exercise a widespread influence on local communities. Professional folklorists have studied these phenomena for years. One principal cycle of stories in this genre refers to the Three Nephites—three of the apostles called by Jesus during his mission to America described in the *Book of Mormon*—who received permission from the Savior to remain on earth to provide help for mankind until the Second Coming. The appearance of the Three

Nephites to pioneers of Utah, and their counsel, is one of the most popular types of Mormon folk stories involving private revelations. Modern Mormons do not have to rely solely on oral traditions told by grandmothers or the students of folklore. Folklorist William A. Wilson demonstrated that stories of the Three Nephites continue to circulate today: only, the three apostles no longer appear at Indian raids but rather at automobile accidents (Wilson 1988, 23). And it is not uncommon for stories about the Three Nephites to include prophecies about the end of the world.

Another interesting source of millennialist folklore is a special type of private revelation given to every Mormon: the blessing, which is customarily given when youngsters reach the age of twelve by a patriarch, who is a local leader called to give blessings, in which he tells the youngster what tribe of Israel he or she is descended from and something about his or her future life. These blessings are transcribed and, in most cases, kept by the beneficiary of the blessing as a guide for his or her life and, although this is not encouraged by general authorities, may include allusions to the end of the world and other apocalyptic events. Until 1979 the Mormon Church had a Presiding Patriarch. The fact that this office was terminated in 1979 has been interpreted as "a classical example" of Weber's routinization of charisma and of the desire of Mormon presiding hierarchy not to emphasize "extraordinary times and persons" and prophecies about apocalyptic times (Bates and Smith 1996, 230). There is little doubt, however, that with or without a Presiding Patriarch, patriarchal blessings have continued to contribute to the underground stream of Mormon folk beliefs, often a repository of unofficial millenarian ideas.

MORMON MILLENARIAN FICTION

One of the conservative Mormon critics who have warned against folk millenarianism and prophecies and their potential danger to the integrity of the Mormon faith is the nationally acclaimed Mormon science fiction and fantasy writer Orson Scott Card. He publishes a conservative Mormon newsletter, *Vigor*, where a strict adherence to the teaching of Mormon general authorities is recommended, and folk millennial prophecies are often criticized with great severity. This is, in a sense, ironic, since Card's own fiction may be regarded as an alternative way in which Mormon people (and, of course, many non-Mormon Americans) quench their thirst for a lost millenarian innocence. In Card's books, Mormon motives have always been present and in recent works, if anything, they have become even more obvious. Although, of course, regarding science fiction as a secularization of millenarian literature is not uncommon among literary critics, the case of Card is peculiar and the concept of secularization could hardly be applied, since the Mormon writer does not in any way conceal his religious affiliation. A Mormon literary critic, Michael R. Collings, argued in 1984 that Mormonism and science fiction are incompatible, since they direct their followers to different revelatory experiences and are therefore in competition with one another (Collings 1984, 115). By 1987, however, Collings had apparently changed his mind after having read some of Card's science fiction. "Card"—according to Collings—"in fact, goes where no Mormon has gone before," having approached directly the question of religious faith in the context of science fictional extrapolation, or, in other words, having applied rational extrapolation to a universe of revealed truth, thus creating a new "religious allegory" (Collings 1987, 7–11). To a more limited extent, similar phenomena could be recognized in Mormon visual arts, particularly in the work of fantasy artist (and professor at Brigham Young University) James C. Christensen. Of course, one could argue that in science fiction or fantasy art and literature, millenarianism also gets sanitized, since it does not claim to be more than fiction (although a fiction that could be significant and inspirational for the readers' lives), thus minimizing the risk of a conflict with official teachings.

MORMON METAPHYSICAL LITERATURE

A different kind of literature, claiming *not* to be fictional, deals with psychic experiences. Believing in the preexistence of human souls and in the possibility of communications with angels and other heavenly beings, Mormons are of course open to psychic experiences. Leading authority in psychic research Raymond Moody noted that Mormons are more open than other religious people to take seriously near-death experiences (Moody and Perry 1988, 88–89), and collections of near-death experiences with a specific faith-promoting Mormon content have been collected by pious Mormon editors (see for example Top and Top 1993). Near-death experiences and earlier psychic journeys often draw on the American reservoir of popular occult-metaphysical themes, announcing a Golden Age (or, more recently, the New Age) with postmillennialist (but not necessarily Christian) emphasis. This kind of announcement of a

Golden Age is likely to conflict with specific Mormon ideas about the millennium (grounded, after all, in the Protestant biblical tradition) and to cause
problems with general authorities. In the 1950s Annalee Skarin (1899–1988), a
Mormon housewife, obtained a significant success with books describing
metaphysical experiences grounded in both Mormonism and themes of the
occult subculture, and hinting to a coming Golden Age. Due to personal action
taken by Apostle Mark Petersen (1900–1984), a staunch defender of the faith,
Skarin was excommunicated in 1952 (see Taylor 1991, 46). Despite her followers' persistent claim that Skarin did not die but inaugurated the Golden Age
by being "translated" into heaven such as Enoch in biblical days, evidence
exists that she in fact died in 1988 in Red Bluff, California.

   While devotees of Skarin constitute a still existing loosely affiliated religious
movement, another Mormon housewife who has acquired national prominence
with her psychic experiences, Betty Jean Eadie, is apparently still a member in
good standing of her Church. Eadie had her (second and most important, after
one as a young girl) near-death experience in November 1973 in a Seattle hospital. After different manuscript versions, the story of her experience was
rearranged by professional writer Curtis Taylor and published in 1992, becoming a national (and later international) bestseller with the title *Embraced By The
Light* (Eadie and Taylor 1992). Eadie presents a complex structure of the afterlife
and the spirit world that she claims to have visited during her 1973 experience,
and hints at a coming new age of peace and hope. Not unlike Skarin, Eadie
combines themes taken from Mormonism and from the metaphysical tradition
(now, of course, also including a rich New Age literature). Like Skarin, Eadie
has been criticized by conservative Mormons, including Apostle Boyd K.
Packer and (interestingly enough) novelist Orson Scott Card (Card 1994, 1,
4–12). So far, however, Eadie has not been excommunicated, and claims to
enjoy the support at least of her local Mormon leaders (Fletcher Stack 1993).

CONSERVATIVE SCHOLARSHIP AND DOCTRINES

Mormons generally avoid the word "theology," regarding it as contradictory
with their doctrine of continuous revelation, but in fact theological speculations have never been rare in the Mormon community both at a scholarly and at
a popular level. It is not uncommon to see works, also published by one or
another mainline Mormon press, going far beyond recommended Church doctrine

on millenarian themes, including setting dates for a possible imminent end of the world or speculating on the Antichrist. Such themes appear in works by authors such as W. Cleon Skousen and Duane Crowther (neither of them a professional scholar), published by Mormon presses and distributed through Church-owned Deseret bookstores without apparent objections or problems. A more serious incident involved biblical scholar Avraham A. Gileadi, who in 1991 published a highly speculative (and millenarian) book on the last days (Gileadi 1991). Although the book was published by the Church-owned Deseret Book Company, Gileadi was caught in the wave of excommunications that hit the independent Mormon intellectual community in 1993 and was excommunicated, the only conservative among a number of liberals. Gileadi has since published a more moderate comment on Isaiah (1994), which was received with favorable comments in some Mormon conservative circles close to the general authorities. Gileadi did not participate in the protests organized by other intellectuals excommunicated in 1993, and remained close to the Church. In February 1996 he was rebaptized into the Latter-day Saints Church.

What message Gileadi's 1993 excommunication was supposed to convey is unclear. Authors with millenarian views more extreme than Gileadi have not been excommunicated. His sin may have been to associate with certain liberal Mormon intellectuals, or he may have been hand-picked as an example for others. Armand Mauss has noted, at any rate, that the excommunication policies in matters doctrinal appear at times to be contradictory, mentioning *inter alia* the non-excommunication of Duane Crowther and Betty Eadie. Mauss comments: "I would prefer not to see *any* of these authors disciplined, but if there is to be Church discipline for . . . espousing unofficial or unauthorized doctrines, then we need to have clear instructions about *which* kinds of doctrines and/or which kinds of publications must be avoided" (Mauss 1996, 23–24).

POLITICAL FUNDAMENTALISM

The 1993 excommunication of Gileadi may be tied with earlier excommunications of many "ultraconservative followers." National newspapers reported in late 1992 that "hundreds of dissidents have been expelled in Arizona, Idaho, Nevada, and Utah, perhaps the largest wave of excommunications in the Church since the 1850s" (Johnson 1992). Those excommunicated belonged to apocalyptic groups awaiting "political and economic chaos" with ties to right-wing organizations. Unlike typical Mormon "fundamentalists" (who do not recognize the authority of the Mormon Church, have established splinter groups, and often practice polygamy), these "ultraconservatives" belong to the mainline Mormon Church and have no desire to leave it unless and until they are excommunicated. They could be called political, rather than religious, fundamentalists. Most of them advocate a pastiche of antigovernment sentiment and apocalyptic oldtime Mormonism. W. Cleon Skousen, a former Salt Lake City police chief, established the ultraconservative Freemen Institute, later renamed the Center for Constitutional Studies (in order to distance itself from the militia-style "Freemen"). Although Skousen—mentioned earlier as a prolific author of doctrinal books on Mormon eschatology and prophecy—is in no way an advocate of violence, some of his students have associated with the militia movement. Among those is N. Samuel Sherwood, described as "a Mormon and perhaps one of the most high-profile militia advocates in the United States" (Carter 1995, 50). Sherwood abandoned the Constitutional Militia Association that he had founded in Idaho because of what he described as a radical infiltration. He claims to be an advocate of nonviolent militias and has reorganized a U.S. Militia Association. However, he advocates the death penalty for, among others, "homosexuals" and "any criminal who can't prove rehabilitation in seven years" (Carter 1995, 50). Colonel Bo Gritz, presidential candidate of the ultraconservative Populist Party, obtained 28,602 votes in Utah, more than anywhere else in America. Gritz himself converted to Mormonism, and after his 1992 campaign purchased 228 acres of land near Kamiah, Idaho, hoping to build a Mormon millenarian community. In 1994, however, Gritz left the Mormon Church when he was told by his local leaders that a Mormon is supposed to obey the laws of the land (twelfth Article of faith), and that includes paying taxes. Gritz, threatened with excommunication, declared that the Mormon Church now "appears to be more controlled by the government than God" and asked to have his name removed from Church membership roles ("Gritz Quits the Church" 1995, 89).

While it is clear that political fundamentalists include millenarian scenarios in their beliefs, it is debatable to what extent, as it is often argued, "Mormon millennialism is the catalyst" (Carter 1995, 48) for a widespread presence of militias in Mormon-dominated countries of the intermountain West (see also Karl 1995; Stern 1996). One veteran ATF agent who claims to be a specialist of militias told reporter Mike Carter in 1995 that "the Mormon religion is fertile ground for those kinds of anti-government, we-can-take-care-of-ourselves beliefs. There are groups all over Utah waiting for Armageddon. . . . Some of these groups are seeing evidence and signs of the last days in all that is happening around us. They are coming to the idea that government is the Anti-Christ" (Carter 1995, 48). When it comes to specific examples, however, most of the groups cited are not part of the mainline Mormon Church but of splinter groups, in some cases practicing polygamy or separated from the mainline Church for decades. They should certainly not be confused with the Church of Jesus Christ of Latter-day Saints. Carter argues that a number of political millenarian fundamentalists remain in the Mormon Church, trying not to disclose their true beliefs to their local leaders. When discovered, they are invariably excommunicated. The notoriety brought to the militia movement by the Oklahoma City 1995 bombing will certainly induce the Mormon Church to act still more quickly when violence or illegal activities are advocated under millenarian pretexts.

SPLINTER GROUPS—RELIGIOUS FUNDAMENTALISTS

Excommunicated right-wing militiamen or other political fundamentalists may easily end up joining one of the many splinter groups that often continue the practice of polygamy and are called "fundamentalists" in the current Mormon jargon. Since the purpose of this chapter is to discuss Mormon millenarianism in the mainline Church of Jesus Christ of Latter-day Saints, I will not specifically discuss fundamentalist splinter groups: excellent works on this matter have been published in recent years (see for example Quinn 1993; Bradley 1993). It is, at any rate, important to emphasize the following: (1) by no means are all fundamentalist groups engaged in violent activities; most of them are composed of peaceful and generally law-abiding citizens (with the obvious exception of the illegal practice of polygamy), a point emphasized by Bradley (1993), although armed and dangerous groups responsible for considerable bloodshed also exist in the fundamentalist community; and (2) polygamy is not the only reason that the fundamentalist community exists (according to some estimates, there are 40,000 fundamentalist members in the different groups in the United States, Canada, and Mexico); for some groups millenarianism and a scare scenario of the imminent end of the world are even more important than polygamy. Quinn (1993, 277) has speculated that even in the (unlikely) case that the mainline Mormon Church will allow polygamy in the future (perhaps in order to gain more African converts) "many Mormon fundamentalists may realize that their fundamentalist identity is more important to them that even a polygamous LDS Church" and not come back to the fold.

Although related to a very specific topic, this observation may be a fit conclusion for this chapter. Mormon millenarianism has had a complicated history, and radical millenarianism is currently allowed by the Church only in metaphorical forms (such as fiction) or within limited boundaries. Millenarianism, the very idea of being a *latter-day* saint, is however so crucial to Mormon identity that an underground—and occasionally, above-ground—millenarian stream will continue to run parallel to mainline Mormonism even in the twenty-first century. Any attempts by the general authorities to suppress it entirely (as opposed to the occasional disciplining of the lunatic fringe) will probably not be very popular within the larger Mormon community, and is at any rate unlikely to succeed.

References

Barlow, Philip L. 1991. *Mormons and the Bible: The Place of the Latter-day Saints in American Religion*. New York: Oxford University Press.

Barney, Garold D. 1986. *Mormons, Indians, and the Ghost Dance Religion of 1890*. Lanham, MD: University Press of America.

Bates, Irene M., and E. Gary Smith. 1996. *Lost Legacy: The Mormon Office of Presiding Patriarch*. Urbana and Chicago: University of Illinois Press.

Bradley, Martha Sonntag. 1993. *Kidnapped from That Land: The Government Raids on the Short Creek Polygamists*. Salt Lake City: University of Utah Press.

Brooke, John L. 1994. *The Refiner's Fire: The Making of Mormon Cosmology, 1644-1844*. Cambridge: Cambridge University Press.

———. 1996. "A Course Correction in Mormon Historiography." *Sunstone* 19 (1) (March): 61–64.

Card, Orson Scott. 1994. "A New Age Testament: A Mormon Reader Looks at 'Embraced By The Light'." *Vigor: Advice & Commentary on Mormon Life* 6 (August): 1, 4–12.

Carter, Mike. 1995. "Militias' Intent: A Fight for the Right." *Salt Lake City: Utah at Its Best* 6 (4) (July–August): 44–51, 123.

Coates, Lawrence G. 1985. "The Mormons, the Ghost Dance Religion, and the Massacre at Wounded Knee." *Dialogue: A Journal of Mormon Thought* 18 (4) (Winter): 89–111.

Collings, Michael R. 1984. "Refracted Visions and Future Worlds: Mormonism and Science Fiction." *Dialogue: A Journal of Mormon Thought* 21 (3) (Fall): 106–116.

———. 1987. "The Rational and the Revelatory in the Science Fiction of Orson Scott Card." *Sunstone* 11 (5) (May): 7–11.

Eadie, Betty, with Curtis Taylor. 1992. *Embraced By The Light*. Placerville, CA: Gold Leaf Press.

Ericksen, Ephraim Edward. 1922. *The Psychological and Ethical Aspects of Mormon Group Life*. Chicago: University of Chicago Press.

Fletcher Stack, Peggy. 1993. "Mormon's Book On Afterlife Gains National Response." *Salt Lake Tribune*, October 23.

Gileadi, Avraham A. 1991. *The Last Days: Types and Shadows from the Bible and the Book of Mormon*. Salt Lake City: Deseret Book Company.

———. 1994. *The Literary Message of Isaiah*. New York: Hebraeus Press.

"Gritz Quits the Church." 1995. *Sunstone* 18 (2) (August): 89.

Hansen, Klaus J. 1967. *Quest for Empire: The Political Kingdom of God and the Council of Fifty in Mormon History*. East Lansing, MI: Michigan State University Press.

Hill, Marvin S. 1989. *Quest for Refuge: The Mormon Flight from American Pluralism*. Salt Lake City: Signature Books.

Homer, Michael W. 1994. " 'Similarity of Priesthood in Masonry': The Relationship between Freemasonry and Mormonism." *Dialogue: A Journal of Mormon Thought* 27 (3) (Fall): 1–113.

Johnson, Dirk. 1992. "Mormon Church Has Begun To Expel Many Extremists." *New York Times*, December 21.

Karl, Jonathan. 1995. *The Right to Bear Arms: The Rise of America's New Militias*. New York: Harper Paperbacks.

Kenney, Scott G., ed. 1987. *Memories and Reflections: The Autobiography of E.E. Ericksen*. Salt Lake City: Signature Books.

Mauss, Armand L. 1994a. "The Mormon Struggle with Assimilation and Identity: Trends and Developments since Midcentury." *Dialogue: A Journal of Mormon Thought* 27 (1) (Spring): 129–149.

———. 1994b. *The Angel and the Beehive: The Mormon Struggle with Assimilation*. Urbana and Chicago: University of Illinois Press.

———. 1996. "Authority, Agency & Ambiguity: The Elusive Boundaries of Required Obedience to Priesthood Leaders." *Sunstone* 19 (1) (March): 20–31.

———, and Philip L. Barlow. 1991. "Church, Sect, and Scripture: The Protestant Bible and Mormon Sectarian Retrenchment." *Sociological Analysis: A Journal in the Sociology of Religion* 52 (4) (Winter): 397–414.

Moody, Raymond A., with Paul Perry. 1988. *The Light Beyond*. New York: Bantam Books.

O'Leary, Stephen D. 1994. *Arguing the Apocalypse: A Theory of Millennial Rhetoric*. New York-Oxford: Oxford University Press.

Olson, Theodore. 1982. *Millennialism, Utopianism, and Progress*. Toronto, Buffalo and London: University of Toronto Press.

Quinn, D. Michael. 1983. *J. Reuben Clark: The Church Years*. Provo, UT: Brigham Young University Press.

———. 1993. "Plural Marriage and Mormon Fundamentalism." In *Fundamentalists and Society: Reclaiming the Sciences, the Family, and Education*, edited by Martin E. Marty and R. Scott Appleby. Chicago and London: University of Chicago Press, 240–293.

———. 1994. *The Mormon Hierarchy: Origins of Power*. Salt Lake City: Signature Books.

Reiter, Richard R. 1984. "A History of the Development of the Rapture Positions." In *The Rapture: Pre-, Mid-, or Post-Tribulational?*, edited by Richard R. Reiter, Paul D. Feinberg, Gleason Lee Archer, and Douglas J. Moo. Grand Rapids, MI: Academie Books, 11–44.

Shipps, Jan. 1985. *Mormonism: The Story of a New Religious Tradition*. Urbana and Chicago: University of Illinois Press.

Shipps, Jan, and John W. Welch, eds. 1994. *The Journals of William E. McLellin, 1831-1836*. Provo: Brigham Young University Studies, and Urbana: University of Illinois Press.

Stern, Kenneth S. 1996. *A Force Upon the Plains: The American Militia Movement and the Politics of Hate*. New York: Simon & Schuster.

Strozier, Charles D. 1994. *Apocalypse: On the Psychology of Fundamentalism in America*. Boston: Beacon Press.

Taylor, Samuel W. 1991. "The Puzzle of Annalee Skarin: Was She Translated Correctly?" *Sunstone* 15 (1) (April): 42–46.

Top, Brent L., and Wendy C. Top. 1993. *Beyond Death's Door: Understanding Near-Death Experiences in Light of the Restored Gospel*. Salt Lake City: Bookcraft.

Tuveson, Ernest L. 1949. *Millennium and Utopia*. Berkeley: University of California Press.

———. 1968. *Redeemer Nation: The Idea of America's Millennial Role*. Chicago and London: University of Chicago Press.

Underwood, Grant. 1993. *The Millenarian World of Early Mormonism*. Urbana and Chicago: University of Illinois Press.

Walton, Michael D. 1980. "Mormonism: The Talmudic Phase?" *Sunstone* 5 (5) (September–October): 18–20.

Weber, Timothy P. 1987. *Living in the Shadow of the Second Coming: American Premillennialism, 1875-1982*, 2nd ed. Chicago and London: University of Chicago Press.

Wilson, William A. 1988. "Freeways, Parking Lots, and Ice-Cream Stands: The Three Nephites in Contemporary Society." *Dialogue: A Journal of Mormon Thought* 21 (3) (Fall): 13–26.

Violence and Confrontation

PERSECUTION!
13. A NUMBER OF WARS, ALONG WITH THE ANTICHRIST'S WORLDWIDE SUPPRESSION & PERSECUTION OF ALL WHO REFUSE TO WORSHIP HIM, will make this Great Tribulation period a time of _trouble_ such as the World has never known! But God, in His Word, repeatedly tells us how _long_ this time of Great Tribulation will last—exactly 3-1/2 _years_, or 42 _months_, or 1260 _days_, from the time that the Antichrist sets up his image at the Temple—to _encourage_ us to hang on & keep going for Jesus!

Millenarians and Violence
The Case of the Christian Identity Movement

Michael Barkun

Millenarian movements have grown in contemporary America as in a hot-house, but few of the growths have been stranger or more unsettling than that of Christian Identity. Neither a denomination nor a sect, it is a movement composed of independent churches, Bible study groups, political organizations, and communal settlements tied together by shared religious beliefs. At its core lie three convictions: first, that white "Aryans" are direct descendants of the biblical tribes of Israel; second, that Jews are the biological descendants of Satan, having their origin in Satan's seduction of Eve in the garden of Eden; and third, that the Last Days, when history reaches its consummation, are about to begin (Barkun 1990; Barkun 1994b).

The first proposition, linking "Aryans" with Israelites, elaborates upon the beliefs of British-Israelism, the eccentric English movement that began in the mid-1800s. British-Israelism argued that the origin of the British peoples lay in the wanderings of the "ten lost tribes" of Israel, who allegedly found their way from Near Eastern exile to the British Isles. Identity has altered and extended this belief, making all persons of northwestern European origin ("Aryans") descendants of Israelite forebears. By implication, then, "Aryans" are to function as God's chosen instrument in the world.

The second central belief, which attributes satanic paternity to Jews, is Identity's strangest characteristic. Cobbled together from a variety of sources in deviant religion and crank scholarship, it has two major implications: it divests the Jewish people of any connection with Israelite origins or biblical prophecy, and instead turns them into literal, not merely metaphoric, extensions of Satan. Hence Identity anti-Semitism rest on a putatively genetic foundation that is symmetrical with its myth of the religious status of "Aryans": just as "Aryans" are presumed to be divinely exalted because of Israelite ancestry, so Jews are deemed to be comparably degraded because of their diabolical paternity. By extension, therefore, in Identity's view, the relationship between "Aryans" and Jews has been and will continue to be one of unremitting conflict, a war of the forces of light against the forces of darkness.

This Manichean strain informs Identity's third principle, its emphasis upon an imminent apocalypse. As premillennialists, Identity believers might on the surface appear to bear some resemblance to mainstream Protestant fundamentalists. In fact, Identity possesses an eschatology all its own, for the endtimes are seen in racial terms, the final struggles between white "Aryans" and their impure adversaries. The enemy will be led by Jews but will include all those nonwhite, racially "inferior" peoples who must be destroyed before Identity's millennium can be realized. Chilling in its uncompromising racism, the Identity vision of the end has sometimes propelled it into violent confrontations with the state, a point to which we shall shortly return.

Since the movement has neither an authority structure nor a coordinating mechanism, its size cannot be accurately determined. Estimates have ranged from as few as 2,000 to as many as 100,000. The task of determining size is made more difficult by the suspiciousness of many Identity organizations and the fact that Identity beliefs have permeated many groups not overtly linked to the movement, notably much of the Ku Klux Klan and Posse Comitatus. It is safe to assume, however, that Identity has a followership at least in the low five figures. As in most groups linked to political violence, the majority of Identity adherents seem to live unexceptional lives that appear to be as law-abiding as those of their neighbors. There is within identity membership, however, a core with a significant potential for violence. They find in Identity theology justifications for the use of force against groups identified as God's enemies—Jews, nonwhites,[1] and government above the local level (often referred to as "ZOG," the "Zionist Occupation Government").

Such an association with violence is not merely speculative. Three examples must suffice. One Identity group with substantial paramilitary capabilities, the Covenant, Sword and Arm of the Lord, established a fortified communal settlement, called Zarephath-Horeb, in southern Missouri, where it held military training programs, acquired and modified weapons, and published guerrilla warfare manuals. The community disbanded after a raid by federal forces in 1985, narrowly averting violence on the scale of the Waco episode eight years later. Better known than CSA was the Idaho-based group, The Order (sometimes referred to as Bruders Schweigen or the Silent Brotherhood). Seeking to stimulate what it saw as an inevitable, apocalyptic race war, The Order began a campaign of violence in 1983 that included armed robberies, counterfeiting, arson, and the assassination of Denver radio personality Alan Berg. Half of The Order's approximately forty members were Identity believers, and several had associations with two major Identity churches, Richard Girnt Butler's Church of Jesus Christ Christian, affiliated with Aryan Nations, in Hayden Lake, Idaho, and Pete Peters's Church of LaPorte in Colorado. Finally, in August 1992, a standoff between federal officers and the armed Identity family of Randy Weaver resulted in the deaths of two family members and a U.S. marshall on an Idaho mountaintop, in an affair that anticipated the Branch Davidian debacle the following year. Weaver's trial was in progress even as events were unfolding in Waco.

Such incidents could be multiplied. For present purposes what matters is their shared characteristics. They involved groups of religiously committed Identity believers, well armed, with a sense of being beset by the forces of evil, standing at the edge of what they believed to be the final struggle between light and darkness. While many groups, particularly on the extreme right, have fostered paramilitary organization (Bennett 1988, 325), Identity is set apart by its linkage of the paramilitary with religious imperatives. Arms, training, and military preparedness are necessary, they say, because God's plan for the end of history requires it.

This follows in part because Identity believers are posttribulationists, a distinction that requires a brief theological digression. One-quarter to one-third of American Protestants are endtime believers,[2] and virtually all of these believe that the end of history will be preceded by a seven-year period of tumult, the Tribulation, during which violence will intensify, Antichrist will extend his rule, and vast armies will move toward Armageddon (Boyer 1992). However, the majority of those who take the Tribulation seriously do not believe that they themselves are in any danger of having to endure it, for most Fundamentalists also accept the doctrine of the Rapture—the belief that as the Tribulation begins, the saved will be physically lifted off the earth to dwell with Jesus for the seven years of the Tribulation and will return to earth with him at the time of the Second Coming. Believers in the Rapture are hence pretribulationists, because for them the Rapture will provide rescue before the Tribulation begins. Small numbers of contemporary millennialists, however, are posttribulationists, who reject the idea of the Rapture and are convinced that the saved will have to remain on earth through the violence and persecution of the Tribulation until Jesus rescues them at the Second Coming (Weber 1983, 11). Identity lies firmly in the posttribulationist camp.

More concretely, Identity posttribulationism is a characteristically racist variation. According to it, the violence of the Tribulation will take the form of race war, in which nonwhite peoples will attack and seek to destroy the white population. Antichrist will be a Jew, and his rule will represent the climax of the Jewish conspiracy's attempt to take control of the world, one of the last episodes in the long struggle between God and Satan.

The more seriously Identity takes its posttribulationism, the more that commitment leads to self-fulfilling prophecies. Identity's strident verbal attacks on Jews and nonwhites produce responses in the form of verbal counterattacks and, occasionally, attempts to silence Identity advocates. The greater these pressures, the more they confirm Identity belief that the Tribulation is indeed at hand, for the responses of Identity targets and opposition to Identity teachings are taken as evidence that the rule of Antichrist is about to begin. The result is a form of pseudo-validation. Identity believers, as it were, "manufacture" the events required to "prove" that they are the persecuted elect. They do so by goading others into behaving in ways believers can treat as proof that their scenario for the end of history is correct. This simultaneously gives Identity the appearance of an empirically grounded theory of history, while preserving its essentially nonfalsifiable character. The rhetorical thrusts of believers can always be counted on to elicit an appropriately hostile response.

Nonfalsifiability is strongly reinforced by Identity's conspiratorial view of the world. The drama of salvation is built around Satan's conspiracy to defeat God, while the drama of worldly politics is alleged to revolve around the Jews' conspiracy to rule the world. Since Identity imputes to its adversary unlimited cunning and stealth, no evidence against the existence of what some Identity writers have called "the Great Conspiracy" is regarded as credible. Whenever opposing views are presented, they are dismissed; or, rather, they are recast as further proof of the conspiracy's cunning. For only plotters with unnatural skill could conceal themselves so brilliantly.

Pseudo-validation, in which Identity believers stimulate the very opposition they have predicted, pushes them toward more and more radical forms of withdrawal from the larger society. For if the rule of Antichrist is indeed imminent, and if Identity Christians must somehow survive it, then they must disconnect themselves from an environment seen as simultaneously corrupt and perilous. At this point, Christian Identity intersects with what is often referred to as "survivalism": that is, a lifestyle predicated on the belief that an impending catastrophe (in this case, race war) requires the cultivation of maximum self-sufficiency, so that the individual is no longer dependent upon traditional institutions. The goal is to be self-sufficient in food, energy, health care, security, and all the other services and resources traditionally supplied by others. Not all survivalists are Identity believers. Indeed, Kurt Saxon, who claims to have coined the term "survivalist," derides Identity believers as "a bunch of kids in adult bodies" (Zellner 1995, 62).[3] Nonetheless, as posttribulationists are convinced they will be caught up in an endtime racial Armageddon, Identity believers are drawn to survivalism. With the commitment to survivalism comes withdrawal, always psychological and often physical, which partially explains the clustering of Identity groups in rural areas, particularly in the American West.

Withdrawal, in turn, is closely related to paramilitary activities: the acquisition of arms, the development of military skills, and the formulation of plans for the defense of Identity enclaves. If ordinary society is about to collapse or (worse yet) be taken over by satanic forces, then security, like food and shelter, must be provided by those who consume it. If Antichrist is around the corner, the world becomes an ever more dangerous place. As William V. Fowler puts it: "If GET YOUR GUNS AND AMMUNITION NOW and prepare for war, you have nothing to lose" (Fowler 1977, 10, emphasis in original). Law enforcement agencies, instead of being seen as sources of security, are instead perceived as sources of danger, the spearhead of the enemy's campaign, a view that, as we shall see, the actions of these agencies often seem to confirm.

As these fears engender withdrawal into armed encampments, the result can only be yet greater suspiciousness and more inflammatory rhetoric directed at those outside. Those who view Identity as dangerous respond in kind, with verbal attacks, monitoring, and surveillance, which as before, is taken to confirm Identity's original apocalyptic fears. For Identity, the perceived enemy is a monolith, in which the Anti-Defamation League, the FBI, and the news media are construed as different manifestations of the same shape-changing adversary.[4]

The logic of posttribulationist survivalism suggests separation and insularity, animated by a desire to be left alone. In fact, the relationship between Identity rightists and the society they despise is far more complex. In this sense, the fate of the Branch Davidians is instructive, for although the Davidians were certainly not an Identity group, their confrontation with government arose out of a similar dynamic, a complex and reciprocal relationship between withdrawal and engagement. The very factors that stimulate withdrawal — belief in the imminence of the Last Days and fear that the world is about to fall into the hands of primal evil — make it impossible for that withdrawal to be complete. Paradoxically, the very efforts to cut themselves off bind communally based millenarians to the environment they detest.

For Identity, efforts to withdraw confirm a boundary between the pure and the impure, a distinction that extends from religion and politics to such domains as food and health. In a little-noted parallel to New Age groups, Identity believers are preoccupied with similar fears of processed and chemically contaminated food, and dangerous or ineffective drugs and medical treatments. All that is outside is contaminated and contaminating; all that is within the circle of believers is pure and purifying. The realm of the impure extends to the state as well, since "ZOG" is seen as already under the control of the Jewish conspiracy and its allies.

Ironically, however, the very act of withdrawal increases the likelihood of pressure from the state. For the more radical the withdrawal, the greater the probability that those who withdraw will ignore, circumvent, or violate the complex network of laws and regulations the state has put in place. Such areas as firearms, tax payments, and the treatment of children have been particularly productive of conflicts between withdrawing millenarians on the one hand and the administrative state on the other.

By contrast, such clashes occurred far less frequently among the communitarians of the 1830s and 1840s. Groups such as the Shakers and the Oneida Perfectionists had to deal with occasional local hostility but did not find themselves targets of significant federal action. Only the Mormons—rapidly growing and politically active—felt the weight of the state's hostility (Weisbrod 1980). Antebellum communitarians fared better than Identity counterparts for a number of reasons: the governments they faced were weaker and less intrusive; the groups saw themselves as models for the larger society and hence sought to present a sympathetic face to the outside world; and they viewed that world as corrupt yet salvageable. They certainly entertained no fantasies of violent overthrow or insurrection.

Among those on the contemporary ultraright, however, withdrawal may stimulate the very confrontations with the state that it is ostensibly designed to avert. Waco in 1993 was prefigured by the Randy Weaver case the preceding year. Weaver, too, was accused of firearms violations. His isolated, survivalist lifestyle and the arms he possessed were believed to require a massive, heavily armed federal presence. In this case, only three deaths resulted rather than the more than eighty that occurred outside Waco. The dynamics, however, were the same. Withdrawal begat violent engagement.[5]

The dialectic of withdrawal and engagement is paralleled by the dialectic within Identity of optimism and pessimism. This is not an abstract distinction, for those who believe in the imminence of the "final battle" between good and evil cannot avoid predictions of the battle's outcome. Like other millenarians, Identity believers exude optimism and confidence. They are historical determinists who believe God has a timetable for secular and sacred history that makes the triumph of the elect inevitable. Identity believes itself to constitute the divinely appointed elite, the saints who will rule with Jesus over the millennial kingdom. This status flows directly from their assertion that they, not the Jewish people, are the true Israelites to whom divine prophecy is addressed. As God's only legitimate representatives on earth, they constitute the spearhead of His forces in their war with a satanic enemy. Finally, the racist/anti-Semitic subculture in which Christian Identity is embedded fosters representations of military victory by a small, divinely empowered elite. The most famous of these representations, which has circulated widely on the racist right, is William Pierce's pseudonymously authored novel, *The Turner Diaries*, in which a clandestine racist organization seizes control of the United States and eventually the world. Pierce, ironically, is not only not an Identity believer; he views Identity, along with other supernatural religions, with contempt, a position not in evidence in *The Turner Diaries*, but clear in Pierce's second novel, *Hunter*. Nonetheless, *The Turner Diaries'* sales appear to have included many Identity readers, and The Order in the 1980s was almost certainly explicitly modeled on the organization in Pierce's book (Macdonald 1980, 1989; Flynn and Gerhardt 1989, 81, 93, 140, 194).

Despite the commitment to historical determinism, the self-identification as a religious elite, and the fantasies of military triumph, Christian Identity also harbors a suppressed but powerful pessimistic strain. Motifs of hopelessness and despair coexist uneasily with millenarian triumphalism. In part, this pessimism is the other side of the sense of elite chosenness. As already noted, Identity numbers are exceedingly small. In addition, there seems no likelihood of a significant increase in the foreseeable future. While some individuals with Identity associations have enjoyed transient political success (notably David Duke), Identity beliefs lie so far outside conventional American religion that the possibility of a mass following appears remote indeed. Identity enhances its sense of chosenness by contrasting the purity of its own motives and beliefs with what it sees as the softness of most American whites, whom it portrays as debased by a consumer society and led by clerics who have been coopted by a Jewish-controlled "establishment." Thus, not only does Identity lack a mass following; it dismisses as unworthy its only available recruiting pool, concentrating instead on such marginal groups as prison inmates and skinheads.

These considerations are in turn linked to Identity's frequently articulated belief that the white race is the object of "genocide" through a campaign of deliberate race mixing (*Calling Our Nation* 1989, 25). Bizarre though this may sound, it is a frequent and serious theme on the racist right, further reinforcing the sense of being besieged. It is also consistent with Identity's view of itself as the true Israelites and of Jews as usurpers. "Aryans" are the real targets of genocide while Jewish claims to being genocidal victims are fraudulent (Identity, like other segments of the far right, accepts the claims of Holocaust revisionism).

Hence millenarian and apocalyptic strains are in constant tension within the Identity belief system, and the explicit fantasy scenarios of victory compete with implicit nightmare visions of defeat and obliteration. The sense of pessimism has tended to increase over the last decade, largely as a result of increasingly intense government surveillance and more aggressive prosecutions in the post-Order period. While Identity defendants have sometimes been acquitted (notably after a trial for seditious conspiracy in 1988),[6] actual and potential legal proceedings have taken both an economic and psychological toll. In addition, Morris Dees has pioneered the use of civil damage suits against racist organizations. No Identity groups have yet been defendants in such cases, but the fear of private litigation has added yet another threat.

What effects will such factors have on Identity's violent propensities? On the one hand, revolutionary millenarians have often lapsed into permanent political passivity, as was the case with the Anabaptists. Such quiescence, with its refocusing upon otherworldly concerns, has usually come, however, only after defeats so crushing that any further armed challenge to the existing order appeared utterly futile. While Identity has suffered many defeats in both armed and courtroom confrontations, none has been definitive enough to stimulate a fundamental reorientation. The movement still appears to regard itself as the embattled remnant of God's forces on earth, with the final outcome precariously balanced between victory and defeat.

Whatever hopes once existed among Identity followers for a mass uprising were frustrated by The Order's defeat and the successful prosecution of its members. Identity's disdain for the white population conveniently rationalizes its abandonment of mass insurrection. There was brief enthusiasm for David Duke's political ambitions, for Duke, although never an Identity follower, has maintained close ties with Identity figures since his days as a Ku Klux Klan leader. With Duke's failure to win the Louisiana governorship, and his inability to mobilize significant numbers of the Republican electorate in primary contests, the electoral arena too has ceased to be attractive.

What seems likely to continue is the cultivation of a separate lifestyle in small groups that are in American society but not of it. The openly expressed political position associated with Identity is a form of territorial separation, in which the Pacific Northwest would be detached to form an "Aryan homeland." Eschewing talk of civil war, Identity literature remains vague about the means for effecting this secessionist option and equally vague about why the United States government would permit it. The argument most frequently raised, however, is that the growth of Identity pockets within such states as Washington and Idaho would lead naturally toward the creation of an autonomous polity.

To the extent that groups either within the Northwest or elsewhere are armed, feel threatened, and harbor frustrated political ambitions, conditions exist for future Wacos. Identity, like the Branch Davidians, is a millenarian movement convinced that it stands on the threshold of a cosmic battle in which it is destined to enact a central role. As Waco has taught us, individuals so situated do not necessarily make decisions based on what outsiders might regard as appropriate cost-benefit calculations. Such groups possess "scenarios" that lay out the expected sequence of endtime events, and however they assess their immediate prospects for victory or defeat, they may choose to let the scenario play itself out. (For this reason, the deaths at the Branch Davidian compound should not be classified as "suicides," regardless of how the fire may have started [Barkun 1993, 1994a].) The immense imbalance between the resources of Christian Identity and those of the government thus does not ensure that Identity groups will not violently confront the authorities. The self-fulfilling character of posttribulationist predictions, and the dialectic of withdrawal and engagement already discussed, suggest that confrontations will continue. The government's overwhelming power, far from deterring a violent response, may well provoke it, for the millenarian "script" has two leading roles, not merely one, and the determination of how and whether Identity groups play their role in a violent manner may well depend upon the actions of the authorities.

The dynamic described here, in which deviant acts and societal responses chase one another in a spiral, is not limited to Christian Identity. Indeed, it is a well-described process, most often referred to as deviance-amplification. It was first noted by Leslie T. Wilkins (1965, 87–92) in connection with young gang violence, and elaborated upon by Stanley Cohen (1972) in his study of youth disorders at British seaside resorts in the mid-1960s. The connection with new religious movements was finally made by Roy Wallis (1977) in his study of the Church of Scientology.

Wallis's model of deviance-amplification lays out the following stages:

1. Initial deviation from valued norms lead to
2. Punitive reaction which leads to
3. Further alienation of the deviants which leads to
4. Further deviation which leads to

5. Increased punitive reaction which leads to (3) . . . etc., in an amplifying
   spiral. (Wallis 1977, 208)

This is precisely the process described above for Christian Identity, in
which withdrawal, hostility toward minorities, and a sense of being besieged
stimulate the responses from governmental and private organizations that are
most likely to reinforce the original behavior. By the same token, just as the
process, seen from the perspectives of the deviant group, increases the likelihood of more deviant behavior, so the process of reinforcement exists on the
other side. That is to say, seen from the standpoint of the sanctioning institutions (law enforcement agencies and civil rights groups, for example), the continued deviant behavior of groups like Christian Identity reinforces *their*
propensity to continue to apply sanctions. The process is consequently symmetrical. Not only does the spiral increase the likelihood of harsher and more
violent confrontations between deviants and sanctioners; it also freezes each
side in its role. Deviants become more disruptive and provocative, while sanctioners become more vigilant and repressive.

Can the spiral be broken? Deviance-amplification theory suggests that it can,
in either of two ways. The most commonly noted type of *de*amplification occurs
when the sanctions become so severe that the deviants no longer find it in their
interest to continue former patterns of behavior. A less common form of deamplification occurs when the sanctioning organizations cease to apply the sanctions. Thus, if we think of sanctions arrayed in order of severity along a
continuum from tolerance to repression, deamplification is most likely at the
extremes, while amplification is most likely in the mid-range (Wallis 1977, 22–24).

If we now look again at Christian Identity, the picture becomes at once
clearer and more complex. The degree to which Identity might respond to
extremely severe sanctions is limited by the fact that, unlike youth gangs, for
example, Identity believers are committed to what they conceive as ultimate,
noncompromisable values. They see at stake nothing less than the fate of the
world, with God as their ally. This clearly complicates what might ordinarily
be seen simply as a process of ratcheting up the sanctions until pain exceeds
pleasure. The futility of this in the context of millenarian religious groups was
tragically demonstrated outside Waco. By the same token, it may still be possible to use sanctions for the purpose of getting such groups to alter their tactics.
Federal and state prosecutions of Identity and non-Identity rightists after the
suppression of The Order is a case in point, since it greatly diminished the

willingness of Identity groups to initiate direct confrontations with the state. Such pressure has not, however, been so intense as to convince believers that they ought not to defend themselves against it. One of the most pressing analytic problems, therefore, is distinguishing more precisely those applications of pressure likely to reduce deviance from those likely to provoke self-destructive outbursts of violence.

Deamplification through tolerance is also complex in the case of Christian Identity, for the issue is defined in terms of First Amendment law. While this is not the place to lay out the convoluted issues associated with the free exercise clause, sanctioning a religious group requires a delicate balancing of the believers' right to freedom of belief and practice, and the state's right to limit practice when a compelling interest requires it. Increasingly, Supreme Court opinions in this area have had to address nonmainstream religious groups, such as the Native American peyote cult and the santeria churches of Hispanic south Florida. The Court's ability to maneuver in this area has now been circumscribed by the Religious Freedom Restoration Act (1993), which, as a matter of statute law, requires that limitation of free exercise be justified only by a compelling state interest, and be accomplished through the least restrictive means. (The U.S. Supreme Court is presently reviewing the RFRA.) Unlike other deviant groups, therefore, Christian Identity can confront the state on a relatively level legal playing field, where state action can be challenged on both constitutional and statutory grounds. This may help to induce sanctioning agencies to exercise restraint. In addition, excessive use of force may backfire in subsequent criminal trials. Thus, Randy Weaver was acquitted of all but minor charges, in large measure because jurors believed the government had acted improperly. The ability of the FBI to bring the standoff with the Identity-influenced Montana Freemen to a peaceful conclusion in June 1996 suggests that federal authorities have acquired a more sophisticated understanding of such situations.

The risk of deviance-amplification remains, however. As long as Identity continues to hold a posttribulationist position, it will continue to nurture survivalist lifestyles, with all of their potential for arousing suspicion in others. As long as Identity continues to identify Jews and nonwhites with demonic conspiracy and racial inferiority, organizations devoted to combating prejudice will continue to monitor their activities. For the state's part, the ingrained stereotypes law enforcement officials hold about exotic religious groups, along with the bureaucratic turf wars that often inspire dramatic shows of force, remain significant obstacles in handling new religious movements.

Consequently, there is only slight cause for optimism in assessing the potential for violence involving Christian Identity. There is no evidence that Identity itself has reached that point of quiescence in which millenarians sublimate their eschatological yearnings in nonviolent ways. Nor is there reason to believe that the authorities fully understand the difference between provocative and nonprovocative tactics. Identity appears caught in a cycle in which its own expressions of hostility toward others provoke the animosity it expects. As the cycle forces Identity deeper into communal and paramilitary stances against the world, explosions of violence directed against symbols of public authority are more likely to occur. Although the rapid collapse of The Order has for the moment laid to rest dreams of a popularly based white-supremacist insurrection, there remains the very real possibility of scattered "Götterdämmerungs" as Identity coteries play out their scripts of the last days.

NOTES

1. Identity in fact classifies Jews as nonwhites. For purposes of clarity, I maintain the conventional distinction here.
2. In the absence of a national religious census, only rough estimates are possible. This is particularly so in the case of Protestant fundamentalists, many of whom do not belong to centrally administered denominations.
3. Saxon has defined a survivalist as "one who anticipates the collapse of civilization and wants to save himself and his loved ones and bring something to the movement, if you would, which will contribute to the advancement of the next generation."
4. The concept of the "the Great Conspiracy," in which all lesser plots are nested, permits explanations that are simultaneously parsimonious (since all evil effects are attributed to a single cause) and nonfalsifiable (since no evidence that contradicts the theory is regarded as credible).
5. On July 8, 1993, the jury in the Randy Weaver trial acquitted him and his codefendant of all major charges growing out of the standoff. Initial reports suggest that the jury was strongly influenced by the belief that the government had used excessive force in attempting to effect Weaver's arrest. This is in line with the strong support the Weaver family received from non-Identity local residents during the standoff.
6. The federal government prosecuted a group of fourteen right-wing figures for conspiring to overthrow the federal government. The trial at Ft. Smith, Arkansas,

ended on April 7, 1988, in the acquittal of thirteen defendants (charges against one were dropped). While several defendants were not Identity believers, a number were, including Louis Beam and Richard Girnt Butler. In a movement with significant internal strife, it was not altogether surprising that two major Identity figures, Dan Gayman and James Ellison, testified against the defendants. They have taken the position that violence can only be employed in self-defense against the representative of Antichrist.

REFERENCES

Barkun, Michael. 1990. "Racist Apocalypse: Millennialism on the Far Right." *American Studies* 31: 121–140.

———. 1993. "Reflections After Waco: Millennialists and the State." *Christian Century* (June 2–9): 596–600.

———. 1994a. "Millenarian Groups and Law Enforcement Agencies: The Lessons of Waco." *Terrorism and Political Violence* 6: 75–95.

———. 1994b. *Religion and the Racist Right: The Origins of the Christian Identity Movement.* Chapel Hill: University of North Carolina Press.

Bennett, David H. 1988. *The Party of Fear: From Nativist Movements to the New Right in American History.* Chapel Hill: University of North Carolina Press.

Boyer, Paul. 1992. *When Time Shall Be No More: Prophecy Belief in Modern American Culture.* Cambridge, MA: Harvard University Press.

Calling Our Nation. 1989. "Last Days of ZOG." Number 59.

Cohen, Stanley. 1972. *Folk Devils and Moral Panics.* London: MacGibbon & Kee.

Flynn, Kevin, and Gary Gerhardt. 1989. *The Silent Brotherhood: Inside America's Racist Underground.* New York: The Free Press.

Fowler, William V. 1977. "Who Is the Anti-Christ King Today?" *End Time Revelation Newsletter* 2 (7): 10.

Macdonald, Andrew (pseud. William Pierce). 1980. *The Turner Diaries.* Washington, DC: National Alliance.

———. 1989. *Hunter.* Hillsboro, WV: National Vanguard Books.

Wallis, Roy. 1977. *The Road to Total Freedom: A Sociological Analysis of Scientology.* New York: Columbia University Press.

Weber, Timothy P. 1983. *Living in the Shadow of the Second Coming: American Premillennialism 1975-1982.* Grand Rapids, MI: Academie Books.

Weisbrod, Carol. 1980. *The Boundaries of Utopia.* New York: Pantheon.

Wilkins, Leslie T. 1965. *Countercultures: A Sociological Analysis.* New York: St. Martin's Press.

Zellner, William W. 1995. *Countercultures: A Sociological Analysis.* New York: St. Martin's.

Religious Totalism, Exemplary Dualism, and the Waco Tragedy

14 Dick Anthony, Thomas Robbins

INTRODUCTION

This paper looks at "totalistic" movements of a particular kind. We are concerned with groups that are characterized by apocalyptic worldviews, highly dualistic (quasi-Manichean) and absolutist beliefs, and charismatic leadership. Such movements are often communal and may tend to exhibit intense solidarity and authoritarian control by the leadership over the lives of participants.

What is particularly interesting about such "totalistic cults" is that they some-times tend to be rather volatile; indeed some groups that appear to be of this type, such as the Branch Davidians, Peoples Temple, Hare Krishna, Aum Shin-rikyō, and the Order of the Solar Temple, have become involved in confronta-tional violence with authorities and/or intramural factional violence.[1] A number of other groups of this nature, such as the Unification Church of Rev-erend Moon, have not exhibited major violent altercations but have neverthe-less become highly controversial and have been widely (if possibly unfairly) stigmatized as "destructive cults."

To some degree the volatility of these authoritarian movements can be explained in terms of the intrinsic instability of charismatic leadership (Rob-bins and Anthony 1995; Wallis and Bruce 1986), which interacts with those elements of apocalyptic and millenarian outlooks that clearly tend to facilitate volatility (Robbins and Anthony 1995).[2] However, from a psychological stand-point, the most widely discussed model, which purports to explain the hold totalistic movements have over their members as well as the proclivity of such groups to extreme behavior, is the "brainwashing," "coercive persuasion," or "mind control" model (Appel 1983; Conway and Siegelman 1978; Delgado 1977; Singer and West 1980). Reviewing models of conversion, sociologists Snow and Machlek note that according to a number of writers in this genre, "Induced physiological dysfunctioning of the brain is . . . seen as the key to conversion. . . . [W]e have a picture of the convert as an individual who has been made receptive to new ideas because his or her critical faculties and ego strength had been eroded by information control, overstimulation of the ner-vous system, forced confessions and ego destruction, among other factors" (Snow and Machalek 1984, 179). Some writers have emphasized the manipula-tions of psycho-physiological processes that produce brain or nervous system dysfunctions such as "snapping" (Conway and Siegelman 1978). Violence is said to be facilitated by the overpowering quality of cultist indoctrination, which, as one writer notes, "results in increased suggestibility, dependency, and a willingness to obey orders without reflection" (Appel 1983, 169). In essence, what the present writers have termed "the extrinsic model" (Anthony and Robbins 1995) envisions an ego-alien "false self" being externally imposed on "cult victims" through psychologically coercive conditioning processes and induced hypnotic states. Participation in these groups is seen from this stand-point as essentially *involuntary* (Delgado 1977).[3]

Though not incompatible with all aspects of the extrinsic model, the approach taken here is formulated as an *alternative* to the mind control approach and affirms the basically voluntary nature of recruitment to all or most totalist groups (in nontotalitarian societies) and of conversion to totalistic ideologies.[4] It is interesting that alleged cultic brainwashing is conceived as something very sinister, and those (like the present authors) who evince skepticism are sometimes seen as naive or complacent. In our view, the idea of brainwashing is less disturbing than the possibility that persons can become neo-Nazis, terrorists, or ritual murderers *voluntarily*, without being hypnotized or "snapping." What seems complacent, in our view, is the premise that were it not for pernicious brainwashing, all persons would share one's own putatively decent values and that destructive fanaticism is mainly a product of an arcane psychotechnology. In other words, a natural hegemony of our own values seems to be presupposed by some assertions about brainwashing.

The Appeal of Contemporary Totalism

"In an age of anxiety any 'totalist' creed exerts a powerful attraction," writes E. R. Dodds (1963, 134) in *Pagan and Christian in an Age of Anxiety.*[5] Although Christianity in its early centuries was militantly apocalyptic (O'Leary 1994), we won't belabor the early Christian analogy with contemporary "cults." Robert Lifton envisions totalism offering a person, at a high cost and in an authoritarian and manipulative context, "an intense peak experience: a sense of transcending all that is ordinary and prosaic, and of freeing himself from the encumbrances of human ambivalence, of entering a sphere of truth, reality, trust and sincerity beyond any he had ever known or even imagined" (Lifton 1961, 439).

In this chapter we suggest that contemporary cultural fragmentation exacerbates patterns of identity confusion to which young persons are particularly susceptible. Erik Erikson (1953) maintains that young persons with certain psychological conflicts may develop a fragmented personal identity that is polarized between unrealistically positive and negative self-images that compete for priority within the individual's self-definition. Totalitarian movements appeal to such conflicted individuals by reinforcing a grandiose self-conception linked to an idealized leader or absolutist doctrine. At the same time totalistic movements and mystiques also provide the foundation for participants' projection of negative elements of their polarized self-image onto scapegoats. According to Erikson, young persons who experience difficulties in evolving a total self-image as a continuous, unitary individual may be tempted to effect "a total immersion in a synthetic identity" through apparent total commitment to a strident movement affirming "extreme nationalism, racism or class consciousness" and highlighting a "collective condemnation of a totally stereotyped enemy" (Erikson 1953, 170).

Thus Erikson affirms that under stress, some persons may temporarily develop what might be considered a sort of "proto-totalist" personality pattern. Some youths develop "negative identities" in which there is a reversal of polarized "good" and "bad" selves such that one's previously disvalued "bad self" is affirmed as one's true identity. A negative identity may be "acted out" through involvement in socially stigmatized pursuits such as drugs, crime, promiscuity, or by participation in delinquent subcultures.[6] However, sometimes such a negative identity may be refined or reconstructed as a *contrast identity* (our term) in which the individual defines himself or herself in terms of some esoteric or radical subculture that is apotheosized as the fountain of redemptive purity and goodness while the divergent mainstream is demonized as totally evil, corrupt, or doomed. Thus, given a self-concept that is polarized between a good self and a bad self, involvement in a totalist movement with an idealized charismatic leader and an absolutist apocalyptic outlook creates a basis for affirming a pure, heroic self through identification with the exalted virtues of the movement, its compelling vision, and extraordinary leader, while incompatible feelings and weaknesses are projected onto denigrated *contrast groups* such as reds, Jews, blacks, liberals, authorities, or nonbelievers. A sense of wholeness and purpose may thereby be gained, but it will be dependent on an ideological context of extreme dualism.

When these psychodynamics are played out in totalist groups, the authoritarian charismatic leader may be experienced as an idealized father figure for participants as well as a foundation for their self-idealization. With "parental" authority, the leader may sanction disruptive or violent behavior (Wright and Wright 1980). Part of this dynamic is illustrated by an interesting report on the racist Christian Identity movement (Young 1990). According to the author, "Identity members engage in self-idealization" (1990, 151) and project weaknesses and defects onto outsiders, thereby illustrating the principle that "To perceive oneself as pure, impure feelings and impulses must be projected into the world where they become embodied in others" (Young 1990, 157). A charismatic racist leader can "empower" alienated, rebellious, or conflicted followers by legitimating their pent-up hostility and directing it toward scape-goats designated by the leader and movement ideology. "As a transitional object, the cult leader helps members express hostile impulses. . . . [W]hen the cult leader initiates an antisocial act . . . members become free to act in a guilt-less and violent way" (Young 1990, 157).[7]

We emphasize at this point that we do not view young persons experiencing identity confusion or "split self" patterns as necessarily afflicted with some kind of major disturbance, "sickness," or serious mental illness (although a small minority of members of authoritarian extremist groups might qualify). We would rather emphasize the role of *sociocultural factors*. If it is assumed that coherent selves may require a coherent culture, then contemporary cultural fragmentation and what Robert Bellah (1981) calls America's "Broken Covenant" might be expected to provide a context for the pervasiveness of "narcissistic" syndromes, "borderline" personality disorders, and "dissociative" disorders of self-fragmentation, which in fact have been observed by clinicians (Eagle 1984).[8] Presently, "a greater frequency of self-disorders may occur because of certain social factors which are not mediated by mothering and child-rearing experi-ences. For example, the lack of stable ideologies and values . . . or an atmosphere of disillusionment and cynicism in the surrounding society may be potent fac-tors contributing to experiences of emptiness and meaninglessness and may be most operative not in our young childhood but in the period from pre-adoles-cence to young adulthood" (Eagle 1984, 73, n. 92). In a fragmented culture, per-sons with fully holistic and integrated selves may even be in the minority.

An example of a posited nexus involving sociocultural patterns, psychody-namics, and authoritarian movements can be found in Erik Erikson's pioneer-ing early paper, "Hitler's Imagery and German Youth" (1942). Sociocultural dislocation in the Weimar period undercut traditional patriarchal and authori-tarian child-rearing patterns and encouraged the antinomian rebellion of youth against fathers perceived as weak. The credibility of authoritarian fathers was undermined by the German humiliation at the close of the Great War and the subsequent disorder of the Weimar period. Many children devel-oped a deep ambivalence about authority. While rejecting the authority of their fathers, who were seen as inwardly uncertain of their values and thus arbitrary and hypocritical in their assertions of authority, they nevertheless yearned for a strong, consistent, and value-oriented authority figure. They were therefore more receptive to the appeal of a dynamic ideologue, a self-confident and forceful "Fuehrer."

More recently, Janet Jacobs (1987) has suggested that participants in patriarchal guru and Jesus groups that flourished in the late 1960s and 1970s were
influenced by the moderately patriarchal "Father Knows Best" mystique of the
1950s and early 1960s, although actual fathers during the period in which they
grew up were often weak and unable to exercise authority effectively. Charismatic patriarchal gurus and quasi-fundamentalist prophets were initially
adopted as surrogate strong fathers often associated with overt "familial" mystiques. Ambiguities and ambivalence regarding parental authority have also
been implicated in narcissistic and authoritarian personality patterns identified in samples of student radicals and antinomian counterculturalists in the
late 1960s and early 1970s (Rothman and Lichter 1982).

The American social "covenant," according to Robert Bellah (1981), has
become "an empty and broken shell." The absence of an integrative social
ethic tends to diminish the capacity of parents—who are themselves contending with self-fragmentation—to operate as compelling identity figures for
their children and thereby to transmit coherent values. This situation may
result in a tendency for parents to "objectify" their children in the sense of
evaluating them largely in terms of tangible and "objective" extrinsic standards such as those related to their "success" in social and career venues. Anxiety over competence, power, and success are thus heightened among the
children, who become more likely to develop a "narcissistic" psychological
pattern entailing a polarized self-image in which a grandiose image of a mas-
terful, omnicompetent self is split off from an image of a weak and pathetic
failure. Psychological volatility, identity confusion, narcissistic syndromes,
split selves, problems with relationships, and strong ambivalence toward
authority render some (generally young) persons susceptible to the appeal of
absolutist movements with authoritarian charismatic leaders preaching stri-
dently dualist ideologies linked to visions of apocalypse.[9]

Exemplary Dualism

A vision of the apocalypse "provides a mechanism for shifting evil outside of
the self," notes Peter Gardella (1995, 196; see also Strozier 1994). "Apocalyptic
is always about ego; its violence derives from projecting rejected aspects of the
self onto enemies" (Gardella 1995, 200). Dualistic apocalypticism generally
deals with the creation of sociomoral *boundaries*. In the Christian tradition,

millenarian excitation has been associated with the demonic figure of Antichrist, whose alleged servants, allies, and sociohistorical objectifications highlight the perceived ultimacy of certain moral, doctrinal, and sociopolitical distinctions (Fuller 1995).

It will readily be seen that this perspective on apocalypticism is consistent with our analysis of totalist movements. Extrapolating Erik Erikson's psychology of totalism, we have referred above to *contrast identities* characterizing many members of totalist groups with distinctly apocalyptic and dualist worldviews. Through contrast identities, movement participants may provisionally heal identity fragmentation by identifying with an idealized image (embodied in the group leader and absolutist group values) and projecting negative traits and weaknesses onto disvalued scapegoats. Absolutist groups may thus selectively recruit persons who are experiencing identity fragmentation and are predisposed toward the crystallization of contrast identities. However, movements and their leaders may reinforce and intensify these patterns through socialization, ideology, and encouragement of members to channel hostilities toward contrast symbols and designated demons (Wright and Wright 1980; Young 1990; Hasselbach and Reiss 1996).

We have elsewhere identified the particular kind of apocalyptic-dualist ideology that we feel is closely related to contrast identities as *exemplary dualism* (Anthony and Robbins 1978, 1995; Robbins and Anthony 1995). In exemplary dualist worldviews, contemporary sociopolitical or socioreligious forces are transmogrified into absolute contrast categories embodying moral, eschatological, and cosmic polarities upon which hinge the millennial destiny of humankind. We originally applied our concept to the ideology of the Unification Church (Anthony and Robbins 1978), which at the time exhibited a vehement, anticommunist worldview that was integrated with a highly dualistic theology elaborated around the interrelated polarities of God-centered versus anti-God, and Abel versus Cain forces (Anthony and Robbins 1978; Robbins et al. 1976). Subsequently, Constance Jones, a participant at a seminar at which Dr. Anthony presented the concept of exemplary dualism, applied it to the worldview of Jim Jones and his ill-fated Peoples Temple Movement, in which

> Themes of destruction, redemption, flight and deliverance taken from the book of Isaiah were used to justify a prophecy of the destruction of the fattened nations and escape of the righteousness into a new nation. . . . The United States, its institutions and even its standards of beauty were portrayed as the "beast"—totally irredeemable. Well-versed in both doctrinal and operational aspects of the oppos-

ing forces of good and evil, members of the Peoples Temple were prepared for sacrifice, struggle and an apocalyptic "final showdown." (Jones 1989, 212)

Although they diverged sharply in terms of their orientations toward American civic symbolism, Marxism, capitalism, and Judeo-Christian scripture, in the late 1970s the Peoples Temple and the Unification Church both manifested distinctive exemplary dualist worldviews, and both "claimed to play a central role in the eschatological battle between good and evil" (Chidester 1988, 137). According to Galanter (1989, 248–249), the confrontational violence that might have erupted during the period in the early 1980s in which the Unification Church experienced its greatest tension with its American social environment was inhibited in part by the bureaucratization and spatial decentralization of the Church such that layers of "middle management" mediated the relationship between devotees and the charismatic "Father Moon" and operated as a stabilizing factor.[10]

Although in initially introducing the concept of exemplary dualism we have emphasized the demonization of disvalued sociohistorical entities, e.g., the papacy as the "Whore of Babylon" in Protestant millenarianism (Robbins and Anthony 1995) or world communism as Satan's vehicle, the term can be generalized (Anthony and Robbins 1995) to refer to quasi-Manichean movements and ideologies. An elect group is specified whose members are encouraged to define their collective and personal identities in terms of absolute contrasts with radically disvalued individuals, groups, or cultures outside of and presumptively hostile to the group. The group envisions itself as an enclave of truth, purity, and virtue in a corrupt, evil, and doomed world, and it may anticipate or even welcome the world's hostility.[11] Participants may acquire a sense of wholeness, purpose, and purity, and, moreover, *may experience relief from anxiety or depression* (Galanter 1989), which, however, may depend upon continuing loyalty to and solidarity with the movement and adherence to group beliefs (Galanter 1989).[12]

VOLATILITY OF TOTALIST GROUPS

We have discussed the psychological sources of volatile totalist movements in contemporary society and their linkage of exemplary dualist apocalypticism to the crystallization of contrast identities on the part of devotees. The essential

focus of the exemplary dualism/contrast identity pattern on demonized contrast symbols may, in a context of apocalyptic expectations, become associated
with themes of violence and persecution and occasionally with paramilitarist
activities. Such movements may then become distinctly volatile and potentially violent.

Ideological and religious groups with highly dualistic worldviews may provide effective milieux within which split selves may be provisionally healed
through the projection of negativity and rejected elements of self onto ideolog-
ically designated scapegoats. Such movements may also provide structured
contexts for gratifying interpersonal relationships among persons who have
difficulty establishing stable relationships. Personality types manifesting self-
splitting often have difficulties with stable, intimate relationships, because
they tend to alternate compulsively between idealization and denigration of
prospective partners. Narcissists may obsessively focus on short-term status
and approval rewards in relationships and are often perceived as selfish and
manipulative, a judgment of which they may sometimes be uncomfortably
aware. Absorption in a "cause" can provide an offsetting sense of selflessness
and self-sacrifice.[13] Communal and quasi-communal movements may provide a
structured setting for interpersonal relationships combined with an ideological
foundation for intimacy in the sense of constructing mutuality through shared
repudiation of contrast symbols and the delineation of sharp sociomoral
boundaries. Finally, persons with fragmented selves may often manifest a
strong *dependency* on others and may even appear to become "addicted" to
some social involvements (Simmonds 1978). They also may become dependent
on positive external feedback and reinforcement, which close-knit ideological
groups may easily provide. Such persons may persistently seek to develop relationships with father surrogates, idealized nurturers, or, in the case of narcissistic personality types, powerful leaders who embody strength and "success."
Positive traits evocative of power, strength, integrity, heroism, warmth, and
compassion may be projected onto movement leaders, while feelings of worth-
lessness, helplessness, deviousness, and lack of human feeling can be projected onto contrast symbols perceived as alien or hostile to the system of
idealized values and heroic leadership.

Unfortunately from the standpoint of the convert, many of the close-knit
ideological "cults" that may seem so initially attractive tend to be unstable and
sometimes ephemeral. Charismatic authority is inherently precarious (Robbins
and Anthony 1995; Wallis and Bruce 1986) and would-be messiahs and prophets

may experience difficulties in sustaining role-identities involving idealized characteristics attributed to flawed individuals.[14] Devotees who make substantial sacrifices for high-demand totalist movements will likely develop a latent resentment against the group and its idealized leader, which may surface under stressful conditions (including coercive deprogramming). The whole symbolic identification system may then be quickly *reversed* such that the heroic exemplar of absolute values and virtues metamorphoses into a demonized contrast symbol. The volatility of various forms of split-self personalities whose relationships are often superficial and transient contributes to the instability of the groups that depend upon such participants. As a result, many of these movements exhibit high defection rates and are prone to continual schisms and disruptions.

These various sources of instability are augmented by the fact that narcissistic personalities and other split-self personality systems, as well as dualistic contrast identities, are founded upon what contemporary psychoanalysts call *projective identifications* (Kernberg 1987, 93–115). Standard "projection" distances the subject from the object on which disvalued feelings or traits are projected, whereas in projective identification, the subject identifies with the projective object and experiences *a psychological dependency on the recipient of projected attributes*. This represents a disruptive factor in the interpersonal relations of narcissists and other personality types with fragmented identities, who become continually anxious over reciprocity from positive projective identity figures and are thereby prone to resentment and projective reversal. This dynamic may carry over and destabilize the leader-follower relationship in close-knit movements depending upon such personality types. More interesting is the psychological dependency of both the leaders and participants on their *negative* projective objects—their "enemies" who symbolize evil. Fundamentalists, Robert Lifton (1993, 168) maintains, "remain haunted by the specter of evil. Satan is a necessary construct as is Jesus or God."

The consequence of this dependency pattern is that outsiders—particularly demonized scapegoats—*can influence the evolution and behavior of an exemplary dualist movement*. Apocalyptic totalist movements may feel compelled to reinforce and reify their systems of symbolic meaning by actively *confronting evil* (Lifton 1993; Strozier 1994). This is a potentially dangerous situation; e.g., Robert Lifton maintains that fundamentalist totalism is "always on the edge of violence, because it ever mobilizes for an absolute confrontation with designated evil, thereby justifying any action taken to eliminate the evil"

(Lifton 1993, 202). This confrontational impulse is mitigated somewhat by *proselytization,* which provides a manageable, nonviolent mode of "confronting" outsiders. There may be other modes of confrontation, such as pentecostal "prayer warrior" mystiques, that allow the group actively to contend with evil without violence while sustaining the rigid boundaries of the totalist self. Radical separatism or retreatist imperatives (e.g., Jim Jones's transplanting his movement from California to Guyana to preserve autonomy) may cut off proselytization, which can isolate a group and render any threatened penetration of its boundaries traumatic (Galanter 1989).[15] The persisting need for the symbolic reinforcement of confrontation may render violence more likely (particularly if there actually are some hostile outsiders).

The dynamic of psychological dependence on contrast symbols is especially salient with regard to totalist groups whose beliefs highlight apocalyptic scenarios, and particularly in the case of movements whose belief system entails an expectation that *the movement itself will have a key role in the unfolding of the endtimes scenario.* To valorize such a conception, it may be essential that the human symbols of evil forces "play their part," or at least not act in a manner that contravenes their assigned roles. Charles Strozier notes that "survivalist groups in Idaho . . . tend to believe that God will rapture them into the clouds only in the middle or at the end of Tribulation, because they first want to experience the violence directly and fight it out with the beast" (Strozier 1994, 10). Such an anticipation highlights the psychological dependency of exemplary dualists on their perceived evil antagonists, who must appear capable of being either ultimately won over or vanquished. They can appear hostile to the vanguard movement, but they must not seem capable of destroying the latter, at least not prematurely (before the final apocalypse) and not *under circumstances so humiliating and trivializing that the movement's grandiose apocalyptic scenario appears discredited.*

In the remainder of this chapter we will look at how this dynamic played out cataclysmically through the fatal confrontation between the Branch Davidian sect and federal agents at the Mt. Carmel settlement of the sect in Waco, Texas.[16]

TRAGEDY AT WACO

Like Jim Jones's Peoples Temple movement in its later years, the Branch Davidians at the Mt. Carmel settlement in Waco, Texas, under the leadership of

David Koresh clearly represents what we term exemplary dualism (Robbins and Anthony 1995; Anthony and Robbins 1995). Vernon Howell (later David Koresh) was originally a Seventh-day Adventist and was captivated by the grim apocalyptic message of church-sponsored "Revelation Seminars," which featured "dramatic, even frightening images in a multimedia portrayal of Armageddon" (McGee and Clairborne 1993, 10). In 1981 he joined the "Branch Davidians," an offshoot of the schismatic "Davidian Seventh Day Adventists" begun by Victor Houteff (who originally founded Mt. Carmel) in 1935. Howell became fascinated with the prophetic realm of the imminent "last days" of endtimes, which in the Book of Revelation is mystically represented by the "Seven Seals," which Howell believed could only be opened by a new prophet.

Howell was "intelligent, mechanically adept, a capable guitarist, and the possessor of an immense store of memorized passages of Scripture" (Kelley 1995, 23). His charisma was situated in the context of an Adventist-Davidian subculture whose members were intensely concerned with endtimes prophecy. Through various vicissitudes and altercations (including a shoot-out), Howell seized the leadership of the movement from his visibly disturbed predecessor, George Roden, and ultimately became David Koresh.[17] Mt. Carmel was renamed "Ranch Apocalypse."

"Howell radicalized the movement's millennial teaching," which became re-oriented around a vision of "a titanic struggle between the forces of good and evil" (Pitts 1994, 36–37). In developing his message, Koresh decoded cryptic apocalyptic passages from Scripture, which he, like many fundamentalists, interpreted as referring to the present. For Koresh, "the inbreaking of God's will into history was about to occur, with a cosmic struggle between good and evil; the forces of evil would be concentrated in the present center of earthly power, the government of the United States, whose Babylonian power would be brought to bear against The Lamb [Koresh] and his elect" (Kelley 1995a, 23). Koresh and his followers "must therefore build and fortify a compound and amass weapons to prepare for the inevitable war with [state] agents. . . . Under Koresh the government is evil personified and battle with the government was necessary to bring in God's Kingdom" (Pitts 1994, 37). The desperate struggle between The Lamb et al. and the Babylonians[18] will bring down a heavenly host to decisively win the battle of Armageddon and inaugurate the Kingdom of God.

The Branch Davidians accumulated guns and also sold them commercially. However, in expanding his arsenal, Koresh was influenced not only by commerce and grim apocalyptic vision but also by the unfortunate coincidence of SWAT maneuvers by local law enforcement teams transpiring on March 5–9, 1992. "Koresh saw this three-day episode of noisy police maneuvers within ear-range of Mt. Carmel as brazen intimidation by the Babylonians, and he responded with strong defensive measures" (Kelley 1995a, 23), which in turn brought him to the attention of the Bureau of Alcohol, Tobacco and Firearms (ATF). Koresh was also being investigated by Texas child protection workers for possibly engaging in statutory rape and child abuse while "spreading the seed of the Messiah."

It is worth noting that the Koreshians were a kind of *midtribulationists* who, unlike most fundamentalists, did not believe that the True Faithful would be raptured up to heaven *before* the horrible seven-year Tribulation and reign of Antichrist (which all premillennialists believe will precede the final Battle of Armageddon and subsequent Second Coming of Jesus Christ). In contrast, the Branch Davidians anticipated that they would struggle to survive the early years of Tribulation, be eventually slain by demonic forces during the Tribulation, and return with the Heavenly Host to vanquish Satan's minions at Armageddon (Strozier 1994, 91). This expectation, like the "survivalist" *posttribulationist* vision which sees the embattled Saints somehow surviving the Tribulation to fight at Armageddon, entails a greater anticipation of conflict and persecution compared to the expectations of the *pretribulationists*, who believe they will depart the planet right before the bad times commence.[19] The Davidians anticipated a struggle to death with the Babylonians, but they expected the final conflict to unfold probably in 1995.

It is easy to presume that the apocalyptic and exemplary dualist Branch Davidians were more or less foaming at their collective mouth in violence-prone volatility. Nevertheless, David Koresh et al. at Mt. Carmel required more external provocation to act violently compared to Jim Jones et al. at Jonestown, Guyana (Robbins and Anthony 1995). It took an actual air-and-ground military assault by government forces to elicit the first violent response from the Davidians, whereas at Jonestown, the mere visitation of an unarmed congressperson and his party, who were about to return to the United States with a handful of voluntary defectors, produced a murderous assault on the visitors followed by an orgy of murder-suicide among more than 900 persons. In contrast to what appears to be the case with respect to the Aum Shinrikyō sect in Japan (Mullins, this volume), there is no evidence that the Davidians intended to turn their weapons against private citizens outside of Mt. Carmel (in the absence of armed provocation), although this scary possibility was raised by the Treasury Department report on the Waco tragedy (quoted in Kelley 1995a, 28). The role of dualist-apocalyptic Davidian ideology at Waco was played out primarily in terms of rendering Koresh et al. psychologically primed to interpret a military confrontation (or "dynamic entry") initiated on February 28, 1993, by about ninety federal agents (supported by helicopters) as the anticipated strike of the Babylonians against The Lamb in the last days! In contrast, most citizens faced with such a confrontation (e.g., drug enforcement agents sometimes accidentally raiding the wrong address) would not respond violently, because they would interpret the situation as a "terrible mistake" rather than a demonic onslaught at the apocalypse. This apocalyptic interpretive proclivity does represent an authentic source of volatility; moreover, other exemplary dualist leaders and groups (e.g., Peoples Temple, Aum Shinrikyō) may be rather more aggressive than Koresh and his followers.

In this connection, Koresh and the Davidians are accused of plotting and perpetrating, with a maximum of firepower, a vicious "ambush" directed at the ninety or so ATF personnel advancing supposedly to serve a warrant. It has been argued (Kelley 1995a, 1995b) that the Texas jury that acquitted some Davidians of charges of murder and conspiracy (but convicted them of manslaughter and use of a deadly weapon in commission of a felony) thereby rejected the "ambush" model. In contrast to the claim of the Treasury report that the Davidians "knew the Babylonians were coming and decided to kill them" (quoted in Kelley 1995b, 375), Dean Kelley maintains that "a more accurate description would be 'decided to fend them off' " (Kelley 1995b, 375). Dr. Alan Stone, one of the behavioral scientists hired by the Justice Department to evaluate the action at Waco, noted in his report that the Koreshians were "willing to kill but not cold-blooded killers" (quoted in Kelley 1995b, 375). Dr. Lawrence Cancro, another psychiatrist on the Justice Department panel, seemed to maintain that the issue of "who shot first" is beside the point. "Certainly an armed assault by 100 agents had to be seen as an attack independent of who fired the first shot" (Cancro 1993, 3).

"To a religious group nourished on apocalyptic images from the Book of Revelation, the [ATF] assault must have seemed like the first skirmish of Armageddon" (Lewis 1994, 93). Indeed the ATF action had obvious implications for appearing to dramatically confirm the Davidians' apocalyptic vision of persecution and final Babylonian depredation at endtimes. Koresh, who frequently quoted the Second Psalm, "The Kings of the Earth set themselves, and the rulers take counsel against the Lord and his anointed" (quoted in Boyer 1993, 30), did anticipate a government assault, though probably in 1995. The actual military-style raid that the ATF directed at Mt. Carmel in late February 1993 "seemed to those inside to validate at least part of Koresh's prophecy. The Branch Davidians and their leader began preparing for the end" (McGee and Clairborne 1993, 11).

After the shoot-out with the ATF and during the subsequent 51-day standoff with the FBI, Koresh and his subleaders may well have wished to find a peaceful solution to the confrontation.[20] However, the shoot-out with the FBI had no doubt enhanced the salience and immediacy of Koresh's midtribulationist apocalyptic vision. He may well have been inhibited from surrendering to the ATF in part because his prophetic vision would be compromised if the dramatic confrontation ended "not with a bang but with a whimper." By definition *an apocalypse does not peter out*!

When dealing with exemplary dualists and fervent apocalyptics,[21] danger may arise if their apocalyptic vision appears to be dramatically *confirmed*, or, conversely, if circumstances are threatening to *disconfirm* prophecy in an oppressively trivializing manner, e.g., the Messiah meekly surrenders to authorities and is removed to prison to serve time on firearms charges or for statutory rape. What needs renewed emphasis here is the psychological dependence of exemplary dualists with contrast identities grounded in projective identifications on their scorned "enemies." The latter may thus be inadvertently "empowered" to exert substantial influence on the apocalyptic group. Although he does not make our psychodynamic argument, Dr. James Tabor, who negotiated indirectly with Koresh (see below), maintains that, in the context of the circumstantial flexibility built into the Davidian's prophecy, *"The F.B.I. actually held within its control the ability to influence Koresh's interpretations, and thus, his actions"* (Tabor 1995, 271, our emphasis). But the FBI consistently acted in such a way as to appear to confirm Koresh's apocalyptic expectations. As they followed "the standard negotiation strategies and tactical maneuvers associated with the Hostage Rescue Barricade situations . . . the FBI inadvertently played the part of the Babylonian forces" and thereby confirmed a "chiliastic interpretation of the standoff" (Tabor 1995, 271). By employing massive force, the ATF in February 1993 and the FBI in April (see below) appeared, according to Michael Barkun, to validate Koresh's catastrophic, apocalyptic script. "He wanted and needed their opposition, which they obligingly provided in the form of the initial assault, the nationally publicized siege and the final tank and gas attack. When viewed from a millenarian perspective, these actions, intended as pressure, were the fulfillment of prophecy" (Barkun 1994, 44).

Two religion scholars, Dr. Tabor and Dr. Phillip Arnold, were able to make indirect contact with Koresh (Tabor 1994, 1995; Kelley 1995a) through a radio show and subsequent taped messages. They attempted to convince the Davidian leader that the scripture from the Book of Revelation can be reinterpreted such that the opening of the "Sixth Seal" (which produces the destruction of humankind) would be delayed, thus allowing the Messiah to complete his work. In effect Koresh was being offered a "way out" involving a shift of his messianic role from the sacrificial Lamb whose death triggers the Apocalypse, to the Great Messenger who would reveal the new meaning of prophetic scripture to the world. Koresh appeared to acquiesce and sent out a message claiming a new revelation and promising to surrender after he wrote an exposition of the meaning of the Seven Seals to be presented to the world.

"The FBI saw this as just another in a long series of delaying tactics and went ahead with their plans to use tear gas" (Kelley 1995a, 26). They did send in writing materials, but they were skeptical about Koresh actually doing any writing. Apparently Koresh did write more than twelve initial pages. James Tabor asserts, "There is not the slightest doubt in my mind that David Koresh would have surrendered peacefully when he finished his manuscript" (Tabor 1994, 21); however, most of the FBI agents were equally certain that Koresh would never have emerged. In any case, the FBI lost patience and advanced with armored vehicles with rams. They punctured the compound walls and inserted CS gas. Fires erupted and most of the Davidians, including the children, perished. Whether the fires were deliberately set by the (putatively suicidal) Davidians or reflected the flammability of the gas inserted by the FBI is in dispute, but collective suicide is a distinct possibility considering that Koresh et al. would have interpreted the seeming "tank attack" by the FBI as the final murderous assault of the Babylonians.[21]

Totalist movements with exemplary dualist worldviews and vivid apocalyptic expectations are potentially volatile, particularly if led by charismatic leaders with messianic self-conceptions (Robbins and Anthony 1995). This potential volatility may not be actualized unless officials (or other "enemies" of the group) act hastily and clumsily, and, moreover, fail to appreciate the leverage that their position as the recipients of projective identifications may give them over apocalyptics who are actually somewhat psychologically dependent upon them. There will be more Wacos, warns Michael Barkun, if law enforcement officials "naively become co-participants in millenarians' end-time scripts" (Barkun 1994, 49).[22]

NOTES

1. It is not our view that all "cults" or even most close-knit authoritarian and "totalistic" movements with apocalyptic and dualistic worldviews are prone to violence. On the other hand, most of the American "cults" such as Peoples Temple or the Branch Davidians that have become involved in confrontational violence with authorities appear to fit this description (Robbins and Anthony 1995).

2. The instability of charismatic leadership is related to the absence, more or less by definition, of both institutionalized restraints on and institutionalized supports for the authority of the leader. Elements of apocalyptic and dualistic worldviews that enhance volatility include the presumed imminent extinction (and hence diminished salience) of conventional norms, the anticipation of extreme persecution and violence to be directed against the group in the imminent endtimes (i.e., a heightened sense of threat and urgency of self-defense), and the demonization of outsiders as unregenerate exemplars of evil forces opposing the promise of redemption and determined to destroy the group (Robbins and Anthony 1995).

3. Although the work of Robert Lifton is cited by contemporary crusaders against cults (and although Dr. Lifton may have or have had some sympathy for the anticult crusade), Lifton's seminal early volume on Maoist "thought reform" (1961) analyzes the conversions of several respondents to partial sympathy with Maoism in terms of their proto-totalist, *predisposing personality traits*. "Ideological totalism," states Lifton, entails "the coming together of immoderate ideology with equally immoderate character traits—an extremist meeting ground between people and ideas" (Lifton 1961, 419).

4. Free will and the issue of what is "voluntary" and what is "coerced" and thus "involuntary" is a complicated question that we do not wish to go into at length here. See Anthony and Robbins 1992.

5. In his 1953 article on "Wholeness and Totality—A Psychiatric Contribution [to the study of totalitarianism]" Erik Erikson originated the concept of "totalism," which he defines as more or less of an individual "inclination" to convert to a totalitarian ideology under certain conditions (Erikson 1953, 159). In the well-known book *Chinese Thought Reform and the Psychology of Totalism*, Robert Lifton (1961) partly shifted the emphasis of the concept from an individual to a

group and/or doctrinal proclivity. For Lifton "Ideological Totalism" is said to have eight basic dimensions: "Milieux Control," "Mystical Manipulation" (of powerful symbols), "the Cult of Confession," "the Sacred Science" (of absolutist, unchallengeable dogma that is supposedly precisely applicable to concrete situations), "The Demand for Purity," "Loading the Language" (with clichés and verbal formulas that inhibit thought), "Doctrine Over Person" (the subordination of human experience to doctrinal claims), and "The Dispensing of Existence" (the rights and claims of nonbelievers needn't be considered). In our view, most of these elements can be derived from a conception of a close-knit, authoritarian movement with intense solidarity and adherence to distinctly apocalyptic and dualistic ideology, which will tend to recruit persons who are "totalist" in Erikson's sense.

6. Anthony and Robbins (1995) review a number of studies indicating that a large proportion of participants in authoritarian "cults" in the 1970s and 1980s had previously experienced phases of "alienation" from conventional normative expectations and heavy involvement in drugs. (See also Richardson 1995.) One researcher who studied an authoritarian and communal fundamentalist group concluded that many of the converts were basically "switching addictions," such that they had found in this fairly regimented group a stable and secure setting that could facilitate a continuation of their basic preconversion psychological patterns (Simmonds 1978). See also the recent confessional essay by a former German neo-Nazi leader who appears to depict the emergence of totalist neo-Nazi identities as a process of doctrinaire elaboration of existing alienated and antisocial hippie, punk, and skinhead identities initially articulating a stylistic rebellion against the rigid "anti-Fascist" conformity promoted by the communist East German regime (Hasselbach and Reiss 1996, 45).

7. According to one theory, as "transitional objects," leaders of "cults" help young converts manage their hostilities; but violent cult leaders teach converts to channel hostility (Wright and Wright 1980). A former German neo-Nazi leader recollects, "We also spent a lot of time indoctrinating beginners—not necessarily to make them more violent but to take the violence that was already in them and channel it in a politically useful manner" (Hasselbach and Reiss 1996, 51).

8. It has become a cliché of social criticism that in the context of cultural fragmentation and the absence of a compelling social ethic, American society has itself become "narcissistic" in the sense that the Protestant ethic and "inner directed" values have been replaced by a superficial "success ethic" that evaluates persons in terms of superficial tangible and material criteria. The resulting pervasiveness of egoistic individualism is said to be linked to a deficit of community (Bellah et al. 1985; Lasch 1978). Narcissistic personalities are said to

experience oscillation of their self from between a grandiose, exalted self-image and a radically devalued self. Narcissists tend to have difficulty crystallizing stable bonds based on empathy and mutuality. They tend toward manipulativeness in their relationships and seek short-term rewards of praise and status. They cannot easily sustain long-term commitments. Proliferating "narcissistic," "borderline," and "schizoid" disorders are all characterized by central interrelated elements of self-fragmentation, "splitting," and "projective identification" (Eagle 1984; Kernberg 1975; Rothman and Lichter 1982; Wright and Wright 1980).

9. It will be apparent to some readers that some of the characteristics that we attribute to totalist movements, their devotees, and susceptible personalities correspond to the elements of the well-known "Authoritarian Personality Syndrome" (Adorno et al. 1950; Altemeyer 1988) or the "Dogmatic" cognitive style (Rokeach 1960). Some empirical research has correlated "authoritarian" and "dogmatic" personality elements with religious fundamentalism (Altemeyer 1988; Kirkpatrick et al. 1991). In their study of student radicals and counterculturalists, Rothman and Lichter (1982) identify a pattern of *inverse authoritarianism* characterizing activists who have hang-ups with authority and who share some elements of the authoritarian personality syndrome, but who rebel against traditional authority, and who, moreover, perceive their parents' values as ambiguous, hypocritical, or insecure. Instead of manifesting traditional "right-wing authoritarianism," some young persons with deep ambivalence toward authority may overtly turn against their parents' values and received institutions; however, their rebellion may conceal some elements of polarized selves, ambivalence, and contrast identities that characterize classic right-wing authoritarians. A "protean" subtype of the inverse authoritarian tended to act out antinomian, antiauthority patterns and to manifest a low tolerance for any kind of hierarchical authority. Anthony and Robbins (1995) examine the findings of studies of the personalities of controversial cults, including various studies reported by Richardson (1995) and Galanter (1989). Evidence of the presence of certain elements associated with either traditional or inverse authoritarianism was identified, including dogmatism (Rokeach's "D" Scale), social conformity, compulsivity, rigid superego controls on latent hostilities, and impulsivity and antinomian predilections. There was a general absence of serious psychopathology.

10. Reverend Moon and his wife are referred to by devotees as "Our True Parents." According to one ex-convert, participants in indoctrination-recruitment seminars are encouraged to assume "a childlike, dependent role in the group" (Edwards 1982, 36). The devotee "lives to be a good boy or girl in daily life with the hope that by believing the parents and following the rules, they will

learn to completely internalize their perfect parent [Reverend Moon] and become an adult" (Edwards 1982, 37). Jacobs (1987) discusses the multiple identifications of female devotees with the leaders (as father, as lover, and as one's ideal self) of patriarchal guru and prophetic Jesus groups in the 1970s and the gradual dissolution of these identifications in the process of disaffiliation.

11. There is a substantial critical literature—of variable quality and involving scholars, journalists, and apostates—that identifies within movements such as Hare Krishna, the Bhagwan movement, and Scientology attitudes involving antinomianism, spiritual elitism, contempt for outsiders, as well as exploitative orientations toward nondevotees, paranoia, and anticipations of future violent conflicts.

12. In his study of individuals being converted to the Unification Church, Marc Galanter (1989) found many troubled or alienated persons. Compared to a matched control sample, converts had high levels of self-reported psychological distress. Subsequently, converts' "decline in feelings of psychological distress was directly proportional to the degree of cohesiveness they felt toward the group" (Galanter 1989, 35). This effect did make leaving the group or losing faith somewhat stressful.

13. On the appeal of the Unification Church in the 1970s to persons who desired to see themselves as self-sacrificing, see Robbins et al. (1976).

14. See Jacobs (1987) for a pertinent discussion of the dissolution of leader-follower identifications among female defectors from patriarchal guru and Jesus movements in the 1970s.

15. Galanter (1989, 98–128) argues that active proselytization has a stabilizing effect on movements because the need to appeal to outsiders as prospective converts inhibits the symbolic isolation of a movement in its own "separate reality." Terminating outreach shifts systemic energies from conversion to internal surveillance and monitoring. Negative feedback is suppressed and preventing penetration of system boundaries becomes imperative, such that enhanced boundary tension is likely.

16. Space will not permit a very detailed exposition of the sequence of (sometimes disputed) events. We have depended primarily on two collections: Lewis (1994) and Wright (1995) plus a number of other articles, particularly Kelley (1995).

17. "Koresh" denotes Cyrus, the Persian king who conquered the Babylonians. The Messiah of the Jews is expected to be descended from the biblical King David.

18. The ancient city of Babylon is depicted in scripture as wicked, pagan, and degenerate. It figures symbolically in various contemporary prophetic visions in which it often represents contemporary (degenerate) culture, society, polity, or religion.

19. A key characteristic of American Protestant fundamentalism is *premillennialism*, a variation of apocalyptic prophecy in which the reign of Antichrist and the Great Tribulation will *precede* the Second Coming of Christ. Christ and his

host will defeat Antichrist at Armageddon and usher in the 1,000-year reign of Christ, or the millennium. This is a "pessimistic" and "catastrophic" model in the sense that humankind is viewed as too depraved to be capable of ushering in the millennium by itself. This view contrasts the more traditional *postmillennial* view in which the church gradually Christianizes the world to bring in the millennium.

For most fundamentalists, the grim catastrophism of the premillennial vision is mitigated by the expectation that the faithful will be raptured to Heaven before the Tribulation begins, i.e., *pretribulationism*. In contrast, posttribulationists envision the faithful having to endure the Tribulation and hide out from demonic gendarmes. *Midtribulationists* will have to survive part of Antichrist's rule. Barkun (1994) maintains that posttribulationism leads to a truculent "survivalist mentality," in which there is an expectation of and preparation for violence and persecution—which may also apply to "midtribs" such as the Branch Davidians.

20. The tape of influential Davidian Wayne Martin (played on *Nightline*) calling 911 and pleading for a cease-fire might indicate some Davidian inclination to find a "way out." If Koresh was determined on a holocaust, why not just keep shooting until everyone was killed? We envision the Davidian leader as *vacillating* and subject to crosspressures, including pressure exerted by his catastrophic apocalyptic commitment.

21. From the Davidians' standpoint, they would not be choosing to die but *choosing the manner of their deaths*, since the final assault of the demonic Babylonians would slaughter The Lamb and followers anyway. Some of the children and others were apparently shot in the head, which may indicate intended mercy killings, perhaps after the fire had mounted. Four Christian critics of cults (Samples et al. 1994, 77–96) maintain that Koresh was intimately familiar with apocalyptic biblical passages involving references to a wrathful, "devouring," "purifying," "cleansing," or "consuming" fire. They suggest that Koresh believed that a fiery conflagration was necessary to bring on the ultimate apocalypse and Armageddon. Koresh, it is argued, initially opposed suicide but could accept deaths in a fiery holocaust associated with a physical assault initiated by outside forces. "Koresh may have felt that the government agents (part of the 'world order' the Davidians identified with Babylon) were merely acting out their prophesied roles. They were playing their parts perfectly and didn't even realize it. All that remained was for the Lord (Koresh himself) to 'kindle a fire' that would 'devour all round about him' " (Samples et al. 1994, 81; "kindling a devouring fire" quotes from Jeremiah 50:24, 32).

22. The possibility needs to be examined that the federal agents were also thinking and acting in a dualistic and apocalyptic mode such that extreme inflexibility and Machiavellian subtlety was attributed to the stressed sect leader, who was

actually vacillating and confused. "In the end," suggests Stephen O'Leary, "the government's agents were probably motivated by the same sense of ending that governs the logic of apocalyptic drama: the need to control the script by seizing the initiative and seeking some form of narrative closure" (O'Leary 1994, 228).

References

Adorno, Theodor, Else Frenkel-Brunswick, Daniel Levinson, and R. Nevitt Sanford. 1950. *The Authoritarian Personality*. New York: Norton.

Altemeyer, Bob. 1988. *Enemies of Freedom*. New York: Jossey-Bass.

Anthony, Dick, and Thomas Robbins. 1978. "The Effect of Detente on the Growth of New Religions: Reverend Moon and the Unification Church." In *Understanding New Religions*, edited by Jacob Needleman and George Baker. New York: Seabury.

———. 1992. "Law, Social Science and the 'Brainwashing' Exception to the First Amendment." *Behavioral Science and the Law* 10 (1): 5–30.

———. 1995. "Religious Totalism, Violence and Exemplary Dualism." *Terrorism and Political Violence* 7 (3): 10–50.

Appel, Willa. 1983. *Cults in America*. New York: Holt, Rinehart and Winston.

Barkun, Michael. 1994. "Reflections After Waco: Millennialism and the State." In *From the Ashes*, edited by James Lewis. Lanham, MD: Rowman and Littlefield.

Bellah, Robert. 1981. *The Broken Covenant*. New York: Seabury.

Bellah, Robert N., Richard Madsen, William M. Sullivan, Ann Swidler, and Steven M. Tipton. 1985. *Habits of the Heart*. New York: Harper and Row.

Boyer, Paul 1993. "A Brief History of the End of Time." *New Republic* (May 17): 30–33.

Cancro, Robert. 1993. Letter to Phillip Heymann, Deputy Attorney General (Aug. 30). In *Recommendations of Experts for Improvements in Federal Law Enforcement After Waco*. Washington, DC: U.S. Department of Justice.

Chidester, David. 1988. "Stealing the Sacred Symbols: Biblical Interpretation in the Peoples Temple and the Unification Church." *Religion* 18: 137–152.

Conway, Florence, and Jim Siegelman. 1978. *Snapping: America's Epidemic of Sudden Personality Change*. Philadelphia: Lippincott.

Delgado, Richard. 1977. "Religious Totalism." *Southern California Law Review* 51: 1–99.

Dodds, E. R. 1963. *Pagans and Christians in an Age of Anxiety*. New York: Norton.

Eagle, Morris. 1984. *Recent Developments in Psychoanalysis: A Critical Evaluation*. New York: McGraw-Hill.

Edwards, Christopher. 1982. "The Dynamics of Mass Conversion." In *Cults and the Family*, edited by Florence Kaslow and Marvin Sussman. New York: Haworth.

Erikson, Erik. 1942. "Hitler's Imagery and German Youth." *Psychiatry* 5: 475–493.

————. 1953. "Wholeness and Totality—A Psychiatric Contribution." In *Totalism*, edited by Carl Friederich. Cambridge, MA: Harvard.

Fuller, Robert C. 1995. *Naming the Antichrist: The History of an American Obsession.* New York: Oxford University Press.

Galanter, Marc. 1989. *Cults: Faith, Healing and Coercion.* New York: Oxford.

Gardella, Peter. 1995. "Ego and Apocalypse in America." *Religious Studies Review* 21 (3): 196–201.

Hasselbach, Ingo, and Tom Reiss. 1996. "How Nazis Are Made." *New Yorker* 71 (43) (Jan. 8): 36–57.

Jacobs, Janet. 1987. *Divine Disenchantment.* Bloomington, IN: Indiana University.

Jones, Constance H. 1989. "Exemplary Dualism and Authoritarianism in Jonestown." In *New Religions, Mass Suicide and the Peoples Temple,* edited by Rebecca Moore and Fielding McGehee. Lewiston, NY: Edwin Mellen.

Kelley, Dean M. 1995a. "Waco: A Massacre and its Aftermath." *First Things* 52 (May 18): 22-37.

————. 1995b. "The Implosion of Mt. Carmel and its Aftermath." In *Armageddon in Waco,* edited by Stuart Wright. Chicago: University of Chicago.

Kernberg, Otto. 1975. *Borderline Conditions and Pathological Narcissism.* New York: Aronson.

————. 1987. "Projection and Projective Identification." In *Projection, Identification, and Projective Identification,* edited by J. Sandler. Madison, CT: International University Press.

Kirkpatrick, Lee, Ralph Hood, and Gary Patrick. 1991. "Fundamentalist Religion Conceptualized in Terms of Rokeach's Theory of the Open and Closed Mind." *Research in the Social Scientific Study of Religion* 3: 157–180.

Lasch, Christopher. 1978. *The Culture of Narcissism.* New York: Norton.

Lewis, James R., ed. 1994. *From the Ashes: Making Sense of Waco.* Lanham, MD: Rowman and Littlefield.

Lifton, Robert. 1961. *Chinese Thought Reform and the Psychology of Totalism.* Revised ed. 1989. Chapel Hill, NC: University of North Carolina.

————. 1993. *The Protean Self.* New York: Basic Books.

McGee, Jim, and William Clairborne. 1993. "The Waco Messiah." *Washington Post National Weekly Edition* (May 17–23): 10–11.

O'Leary, Stephen. 1994. *Arguing the Apocalypse.* New York: Oxford.

Pitts, Bill. 1994. "The Davidian Tradition." In *From the Ashes,* edited by James Lewis. Lanham, MD: Rowman and Littlefield.

Richardson, James R. 1995. "Clinical and Personality Assessment of Participants in New Religions." *International Journal for the Psychology of Religion* 5 (3): 145–170.

Robbins, Thomas, and Dick Anthony. 1995. "Sects and Violence." In *Armageddon in Waco,* edited by Stuart Wright. Chicago: University of Chicago.

Robbins, Thomas, Dick Anthony, Madalyn Doucas, and Thomas Curtis. 1976. "The Last Civil Religion: The Unification Church of Reverend Sun Myung Moon." *Sociological Analysis* 37 (2): 111–125.

Rokeach, Milton. 1960. *The Open and Closed Mind.* New York: Basic Books.

Rothman, Stanley, and S. Robert Lichter. 1982. *Roots of Radicalism: Jews, Christians and the New Left.* New York: Oxford.

Samples, Kenneth, Erwin DeCastro, Richard Arbunes, and Robert Lyle. 1994. *Prophets of the Apocalypse: David Koresh and Other American Messiahs.* Grand Rapids: Baker.

Simmonds, Robert H. 1978. "Conversion or Addiction: Consequences of Joining a Jesus Movement Group." In *Conversion Careers,* edited by James Richardson. Beverly Hills: Sage.

Singer, Margaret, and Louis J. West. 1980. "Cults, Quacks and Non-professional Therapies." In *Comprehensive Textbook of Psychiatry 3,* edited by H. Kaplan, A Freedman, and B. Sadock. Baltimore: Williams and Wilkins.

Snow, David, and Richard Machalek. 1984. "The Sociology of Conversion." *Annual Review of Sociology* 10: 167–190.

Strozier, Charles. 1994. *Apocalypse: A Theory of Fundamentalism in America.* Boston: Beacon Press.

Tabor, James D. 1994. "The Waco Tragedy: An Autographical Account of One Attempt to Avert Disaster." In *From the Ashes,* edited by James Lewis. Lanham, MD: Rowman and Littlefield.

———. 1995. "Religious Discourse and Failed Negotiations." In *Armageddon in Waco,* edited by Stuart Wright. Chicago: University of Chicago.

Wallis, Roy, and Steven Bruce. 1986. "Sex, Violence and Religion." In *Sociological Theory, Religion and Collective Action,* edited by Roy Wallis and Steven Bruce. Belfast: Queens University.

Wright, Fred, and Phyllis Wright. 1980. "The Charismatic Leader and the Violent Surrogate Family." *Annals of the N.Y. Academy of Science* 347: 266–276.

Wright, Stuart, ed. 1995. *Armageddon in Waco.* Chicago: University of Chicago.

Young, Thomas. 1990. "Cult Violence and the Identity Movement." *Cultic Studies Journal* 7 (2): 150–157.

The Mystical Apocalypse of the Solar Temple

John R. Hall, Philip Schuyler

At one o'clock in the morning on October 5, 1994, police telephoned investigating judge André Piller in his office in Fribourg, Switzerland. "Your intervention is requested at Cheiry for a fire," Piller was told. Half an hour later, he arrived in Cheiry, a hamlet southwest of Fribourg. On a hill overlooking the village, the barn of La Rochette farm stood engulfed in flames. While firemen tried to save the structure, Piller and his colleagues entered the farmhouse, where they discovered canisters of propane and garbage bags full of gasoline hooked up to detonation devices that hadn't gone off—yet. Then, Piller reported, "We saw this Monsieur with a plastic bag over his head. Albert Giacobino. We said to ourselves at first that this could be—could be! Conditional!—a suicide with a fire." There were only two problems with this hypothesis: although Giacobino had a bullet wound in the head, there was no gun near the body, and no hole in the plastic bag.

Searching further, police eventually discovered a hidden salon. In briefcases on the floor, papers mentioned a group called the Order of the Solar Temple. The room looked as though a meeting had been in progress. "But that raised a question," Piller noted. "Where are these people?" Finally, around four in the morning, at the end of a narrow corridor with more incendiary devices, Piller and his colleagues found a secret room. There lay eighteen bodies dressed in silk capes, arranged in a circle, radiating outward like the spokes of a broken wheel. Beyond the circle, a door opened into a small, octagonal chamber with mirrors on the walls and three more bodies on the floor. In a connecting room, yet another body lay alone. Altogether, there were twenty-three dead, twenty-one of them shot with a gun, ten with plastic bags over their heads.

Piller and his colleagues had barely absorbed the shock when they learned that a similar fire had broken out in a complex of three vacation villas in Granges-sur-Salvan, a resort town about sixty kilometers away. The houses belonged to Camille Pilet, a retired sales director of the Piaget watch company; a shadowy figure named Joseph DiMambro, and Luc Jouret, a homeopathic doctor and former Grand Master of the Ordre du Temple Solaire (OTS). When the flames died down, investigators found twenty-five bodies scattered around two of the Salvan villas; most of them were beyond recognition. In a parking area above the villas, police found a car registered to Joel Egger, a resident of the torched Cheiry farmhouse.

Hearing about the Swiss fires the next day, police in Quebec connected them to a strange fire that had broken out on the morning of October 4 in Morin Heights, a resort town in the Laurentian Mountains near Montreal. Only hours before the events in Switzerland, the blaze swept through a complex of luxury condominiums owned by the same men—Camille Pilet, Jo DiMambro, and Luc Jouret—and a woman named Dominique Bellaton. A Swiss couple, Gerry and Colette Genoud, had perished in the fire with no obvious signs of violence. But after the news from Switzerland, police returned to the condos and found three more bodies, hidden in a storage closet. Antonio Dutoit, a Swiss citizen, had fifty stab wounds in the back, and his British wife, Nicky, had eight wounds in the back, four in the throat, and one in each breast. Their three-month-old baby, Christopher Emmanuel, had been stabbed six times in the chest, resulting in twenty gashes to his heart.

News analysts were quick to compare the deathly tableaux to the murders and mass suicide at Jonestown in 1978 and the fiery carnage at Waco in 1993. Much the same connection was made by the anonymous writer of four letters that were mailed to journalists, scholars, and government officials the morning after the fires. One letter, addressed "To Those Who Love Justice," claimed the group had been subjected to "systematic persecution" by authorities on three continents and noted "a particularly troubling coincidence" between the Waco standoff and a 1993 operation by the Sûreté du Quebec that targeted Luc Jouret. Nevertheless the letter defined the deaths in the fires as a "Transit, which is in no way a suicide in the human sense of the term."

The Ordre du Temple Solaire was hardly a sect of the dispossessed. It appealed mostly to the affluent bourgeoisie and people of the new middle classes. Among the dead in the so-called Transit were a mayor of a Quebec town, a journalist, an official in the Quebec Ministry of Finance, and a French nuclear engineer. The roster of known associates included Edith and Patrick Vuarnet, the wife and son of Jean Vuarnet, the French skier and sportswear manufacturer. Michel Tabachnik, a distinguished orchestra conductor and student of Pierre Boulez, had lectured to the group. Such people could easily fit in at the Chamber of Commerce, a ski club, or a yoga class, but they don't seem like the types for Armageddon.

Initially, the Swiss police suspected that the leaders of the group might not be found among the dead. In this scenario, the cult became a gang, and the deaths, part of a plot to make off with the loot. Patrick Vuarnet, who had mailed the Transit letters on Jo DiMambro's instructions from the Eaux-Vives post office in Geneva, was detained for questioning. Two days after the fires, André Piller issued warrants for the arrest of Luc Jouret, the charismatic master of the group, and DiMambro, the presumed financial director. News reports began to portray the two as international racketeers who had amassed an enormous fortune—$93 million in Australian banks alone—through spiritual confidence games, money laundering, and gun running. But within a week, Swiss authorities announced that the gang suspects were all indeed dead. At a lurid press conference the next month, a Sûreté du Quebec spokesman concluded that

Joel Egger and Dominique Bellaton had perpetrated the Morin Heights killings and then boarded a flight for Switzerland. From there, he said, Jouret and company had intended to depart for Sirius, the Dog Star.

For many observers, the people who died under Temple auspices must have been either selfish cynics or hapless postmodern fools. Others believe one or another clandestine plot led to the tragedy. From a third direction, the deaths are seen as the product of "cults" enacting some vision of the millennium. But these possibilities are not necessarily contradictory. They all stem from the ambiguous relations between an established social order and countercultural religious movements. Many countercultural groups offer mystical association or quietistic community. But the most volatile ones, "apocalyptic sects," prophetically reveal a cataclysmic end of the world as we know it (Hall 1978).

Today's affluent, mostly post-Catholic society of francophone Europe hardly seems like the place where "religious" anxieties could take hold, especially among people like those associated with the Solar Temple. This anomaly raises rich questions of cultural analysis that cannot be fully addressed in a short essay. But considering *l'affaire Temple Solaire* in apocalyptic terms does yield a revealing, albeit provisional, understanding of the group's demise. This understanding can be developed by way of three theses about countercultural religious movements more generally. The trajectory of any such movement, we maintain, depends upon (1) formulae for "salvation" drawn from countercultural resources; (2) struggles over "cultural legitimacy" between the movement and an established social order; and (3) tensions between different constructions of reality within the movement itself.

THESIS ONE: COUNTERCULTURAL RESONANCE

To succeed even modestly, a religious movement must resonate with the existential "salvation" concerns of its audiences. Typically, a decline in the relevance of previous salvation formulae is coupled with new "salvation" concerns among audiences from emergent or changing social strata. This, in broad strokes, is the story that Max Weber told of the Protestant reformation in Europe, where an ethic of self-regulation resonated deeply with the spiritual and worldly anxieties of diverse classes participating in emerging urban capitalism. The Solar Temple hardly bears the significance for the postmodern world that Protestantism held for modernity. But neither will it suffice to describe OTS participants as victims of an elaborate con game, for charlatanism does not necessarily distinguish flash-in-the-pan cults from movements that attain a world historical significance. As Weber (1978, 242) remarked, Joseph Smith, the founder of Mormonism, "may have been a very sophisticated swindler (although this cannot definitely be established)." Con game or no, what was the Solar Temple's appeal?

To address this question is to pinpoint the predicament of today's Catholic Church. Through the Vatican II reforms of the 1960s, the Church sought to coax back the disaffected, notably by jettisoning the Latin mass. In Europe, not only has this strategy failed, it has driven some conservative followers to schismatic sects where they can still experience the mystery of the traditional mass. On the other side of the Atlantic, a similar bifurcation occurred. Quebec, once as Catholic as the pope, underwent *la révolution tranquille* in the early 1960s. "People left the church massively," remembers Montreal social scientist Daniel Latouche. Today, the Quebecois are still culturally Catholic. But given the exodus thirty years ago, argues Bertrand Ouellet, the director of Montreal's Centre D'Information sur les Nouvelles Réligions (CINR), "they only have memories of the Catholic church before Vatican II. And when they arrive at the period of life where the great questions come out again, they have nothing, zero, zip for an answer, and they search elsewhere." Often, they look to new religions. "Formerly," Ouellet muses, "there was one great religion, like a garden that was fully cultivated. Well, we chopped down the garden, and now things sprout up everywhere. It's not a spiritual desert, it's a forest. A jungle." CINR has files on some three thousand (overwhelmingly peaceful) sectarian religious groups in Quebec—Eastern, New Age, fundamentalist, mystical, worshippers of extraterrestrial life, the whole gamut.

Among manifold possibilities, the Solar Temple fixed its roots in European traditions of the Knights Templar and Rosicrucian mysticism. A surviving member in Quebec goes so far as to claim that the contemporary group met the same fate as the original Knights Templar. "What's the difference between the Middle Ages and now?" asks Louis-Marie Bélanger. "None. Maybe the way it's done is a little more subtle. The result is the same. We had to close too, because we were publicly banished."

The medieval Templars' fabled story is well told by Peter Partner (1982). Formed in the twelfth century, the Order of Poor Knights of the Temple of Solomon guarded pilgrimage routes to Jerusalem. Its soldiers took Christian vows, and the Church of Rome sanctified the order through the efforts of St.

Bernard de Clairvaux—the man whom Dante, in *The Divine Comedy*, had intercede with the Virgin Mary on behalf of the pilgrim who arrived in heaven seeking God. The Templars took up wearing the white mantle (symbolizing innocence) with a red cross (affirming readiness for Christian martyrdom). Led by a Grand Master, they established cohesive military units and helped finance the crusades with donations from feudal nobility. By the end of the thirteenth century, the Templar organization was a hybrid. Flourishing outside the existing religious and feudal orders, it combined military and security operations with banking, money lending, and the dispensing of salvation. Left unchallenged, the group conceivably could have shifted the nascent European power complex toward a religiously sanctioned capitalistic military socialism.

This possibility evaporated, however, after infidels defeated the Templars at Acre, on the coast of Galilee, in 1291. Many martyrs attained Christ in the last battle, but the defeat raised a thorny theological question. Why had the forces of God failed? The secretive Templars became suspect. "Atrocity tales" began to describe them as greedy, corrupt in matters of honor, foolishly heroic in military strategy, and possibly even guilty of sodomy. The king of France, Philip the Fair, had agents infiltrate the group, and in 1307 he and Pope Clement V ordered mass arrests of all known Templars in Europe. Accused of organized heresy, some Templars committed suicide rather than repudiate their vows. But hundreds broke down and confessed. On May 12, 1310, fifty-four knights who had recanted their confessions were burned alive at the stake. Four years later, their Grand Master, Jacques de Molay, denied all charges against the order, and he was burned at the stake in Paris. Within the year, Philip the Fair and Clement V died too, victims, legend has it, of the curse placed on them by the Grand Master. Dante's pilgrim later found Philip the Fair in purgatory, in the place devoted to avarice.

In addition to invoking the medieval Knights Templar, the Solar Temple of today also embraced the longstanding Rose-and-Cross heresy that claims, as one seventeenth-century French poster put it, to "rescue our fellow men from the error of death." There is nothing particularly original here. Over the last four centuries, hundreds of neo-Templar and Rosicrucian orders have been formed by a series of mystics, prophets, and charlatans who took up the mantle of the Knights Templar or claimed contact with the "Unknown Superiors" reputed to make revelations to Grand Masters of the Rosy Cross. Eventually, masonic fraternities began to claim descent from these "invented traditions," the better to legitimate their own odd mix of esoteric lore and enlightenment philosophy, egalitarian conviviality, and "aristocratic" status-graded member-ship. But secret organizations also became venues of political intrigue. By the nineteenth century, conservatives facing the unruly popular classes began to use the lodges to reaffirm the old order—virtue, authority, and the aristocracy of a master race. Just as readily, radicals drew on the esoteric traditions to invoke reason, community, and "synarchy"—a revolutionary utopian plan to establish a technocratic oligarchy of Templar initiates. Today, this hidden world of intrigue feeds both the semiotic fantasy of Umberto Eco's novel, *Foucault's Pendulum*, and the populist paranoia of Pat Robertson's *The New World Order*. In these books, clandestine struggles unfold between vast but sub-merged apparatuses of secret organizations, from the conservative Catholic lay organization, Opus Dei, to the Trilateral Commission. And whatever their truth, as legends they enjoy a certain public currency.

Jo DiMambro moved in this murky world for forty years. At one time or another he was associated with the Rosicrucian order, AMORC, and the Sover-eign and Military Order of the Temple of Jerusalem, a neo-Templar society. (Both groups deny he was a member.) Tracing a genealogy of the Solar Temple by Massimo Introvigne (1995), one can easily imagine DiMambro rubbing shoulders with the Mafia, the Italian Masonic lodge P2, and the private Gaullist police organization, Service d'Action Civique. But the significance of such connections—if they existed at all—remains in doubt. There is, in fact, very little solid information about DiMambro's life. Born in the south of France in 1924, he is known to have been convicted of fraud in 1972 for impersonat-ing a psychologist and passing bad checks. Around that time, he established a communal group, La Pyramide, near Geneva. When the commune's farmhouse caught fire in 1979 (a rumored insurance swindle), he started another group in Geneva, the Fondation Golden Way.

At some time, DiMambro had become quite friendly with Julien Origas, a reputed former Gestapo agent who had founded the Renewed Order of the Temple (ORT), a group that combined Templar and Rosicrucian ideas. DiMam-bro also came under the influence of Jacques Breyer, a French alchemist. The main ideas of the Solar Temple trace to these lineages.

Julien Origas had participated in the broadly Rosicrucian post-World War II milieu of French mysticism, where stories circulated about "Ascended Mas-ters" who possess the gift of eternal life, moving in and out of historical exis-tence either in material bodies or as spectres. As for Jacques Breyer, he was an active participant in French freemasonry circles during the 1950s, where he met Maxime de Roquemaure, who claimed to carry the true esoteric legacy of the medieval Knights Templar through a branch of the order that had survived over the centuries in far-off Ethiopia. Together they founded the Sovereign Order of the Solar Temple, based on ideas about a "solar Christ" (Introvigne 1995, 271–272). Breyer even published a book on the relation between alchemy and *The Divine Comedy*, Dante's famous poem in which, at the very end, the pilgrim arrived in heaven finally glimpses "the Love that moves the Sun."

Dr. Luc Jouret entered the DiMambro-Origas-Breyer orbit in 1980. Born in the then Belgian Congo in 1947, Jouret received a medical degree from the Free University of Brussels in 1974, practiced conventional medicine in Belgium, and discovered homeopathic medicine in India while on a journey to learn the medicines of the world. In the late 1970s and early 1980s, he began to practice homeopathy and give lectures about it in Belgium and in France, just across the border from Geneva. There, Jo DiMambro invited him to speak at Golden Way.

In turn, DiMambro arranged for Jouret to meet Julien Origas, and in 1981, Jouret joined the Renewed Order of the Temple. At some point, following the path of Origas, Jouret was ordained as a "priest," in his case by a dissident Roman Catholic self-proclaimed "bishop." When Origas died in 1983, Jouret took over ORT as Grand Master. Forced out in a schism within a year, he took more than half the membership with him. By that time, Jouret had tied his fate to DiMambro. In 1984 they founded the Ordre Internationale Chevalresque Tradition Solaire, later called the Ordre du Temple Solaire, again with Jouret as Grand Master.

The alliance opened a new world of possibilities. In effect, Jouret operated as a front man, projecting an integrated, holistic, homeopathic vision of the new age that opened into a secret Templar- and Rosicrucian-inspired society. Under the sponsorship of Club Amenta and Club Archédia—organizations that Jouret helped found in the early 1980s—he traveled a lecture circuit in France, Belgium, Switzerland, Martinique, and Quebec, making presentations to audiences with as many as 600 people on topics like "Love and Biology," "Christ, the Sphinx, and the New Man," and "Old Age: The Doorway to Eternal Youth."

Herman Delorme, for one, was tremendously impressed when a girlfriend invited him to attend a 1990 lecture in Montreal. "You start listening," he claims, "and by God, you know, you just all of a sudden feel so attracted to what he is saying. You talk about the universe, you talk about how man is made of four ingredients and how the stars are made of these same four ingredients. Then you go back to Egypt and Egyptology, and then somewhere along the line comes the possibility of extraterrestrials. And it goes on and it goes on like that." Anyone interested in learning more about the "art of living" could join one of Jouret's clubs; each specialized in a different area, such as nutrition and organic gardening, or music and theater. But Jouret also had something else to offer. Herman Delorme was called on stage after his second seminar, and Jouret told him, "If you make the first steps, I'll make sure that you make the other ones." "Well," Herman said, "I had no idea what he meant, but it sounded so great, you know, coming from him. I felt like I had been singled out."

With his deep, soothing voice and dark, penetrating eyes, Jouret was, by all accounts, a riveting speaker. "In the interior of the physical body," he would announce, "there blooms a force, a vital energy which was there before Man's physical appearance on earth." In Jouret's homeopathic vision, every pathology results from a disruption of vital energy. But what really matters is the Sick Being. As he concluded one cassette, "You are not sick because you have a disease; you have a disease because you are sick." It was an easy jump from homeopathy to environmentalism, and from there to ecological apocalypse. Pollution, Jouret warned, affects the earth in the same way that a bad diet affects the human body—it disrupts the vital energy. In fact, pollution is not merely "the exterior degradation of the Planet, of Life as such," it is "an exterior reflection of a pollution much deeper inside Man—mental pollution, emotional pollution, and, at the extreme, an authentically spiritual pollution." The transition from the Age of Pisces to the Age of Aquarius would bring us out of this pollution, Jouret asserted. However, the passage would not be as peaceful as the 1960s vision of it. We face "a kingdom of fire, in which everything will be consumed." For those who cross over, the Age of Aquarius will bring new vibratory harmonies. And, Jouret intimated, harnessing the vital force will not only assure victory over disease and pollution in this world, it can completely liberate us from the human condition.

Liberation or no, the Ordre du Temple Solaire was hardly begun when the homeopathic physician began to feel that Europe was too constricted. According to Swiss religious historian Jean-François Mayer, Jouret was quite upset that a French anticult organization—the Center for Documentation, Education, and Action Against Mental Manipulation—mentioned his name in connection with Origas's Renewed Order of the Temple, a group they identified as "very dangerous" in a 1984 publication. That same year, talking to Montreal reporter Mario Pelletier, Jouret announced that Europe was old and worn out, its land filled with millions and millions of bodies, all the vibrations of war and violence. On the other side of the Atlantic, however, Quebec was blessed with a broad granite plate and a strong magnetic field that would protect his followers in the coming cataclysm. By 1984, Jouret and DiMambro had decided to establish a base in North America.

It was around this time that Rose-Marie and Bruno Klaus met Luc Jouret, when Bruno consulted the doctor on the advice of a friend. Bruno thought he had a bad earache, but Jouret found something far worse, a "cancer" that he proceeded to cure. Soon thereafter, the Temple astrologer, a onetime hair-dresser named Marie-Louise Rebaudo, found major changes in Bruno's chart. The planetary alignments revealed that he was to move to Quebec to help start a 350-acre "ark of survival." "We were leaving Pisces and going toward Aquarius," Rose-Marie recalled. "Europe was going to be burnt up, and we needed to escape to another continent. They said they wanted one hundred people, enough to repopulate the world afterward."

The chosen survival farm was located at the edge of the little town of Ste. Anne-de-la-Pérade, on the north shore of the Saint Lawrence River, between Montreal and the city of Quebec. The group bought an old orphanage, where they established a New Age retreat they called Le Centre Culturel du Domaine du Sacré-Coeur. Advertising flyers from the late 1980s announced programs on "the science of life," along with chamber-music concerts and "spectacles." Half a dozen members of the group lived in the house, and others who had moved to town took their meals there nearly every day. Once a month, members of the Ordre du Temple Solaire came from all over Quebec for a meeting on the night of the full moon. Gatherings also marked the transits of the earth around the sun. Jean-François Mayer recalls attending a similar celebration—a bonfire held in the French Savoie countryside to mark the 1987 summer solstice. "The only ceremonial part was the fire, and people came from several sides, each with a torch, and put it in. And there were also some instructions: we had always to turn around the fire only clockwise." During the event, Mayer remarked to a Temple representative, "Oh, this is ritual." "Well, no," the man replied. "Real ritual, it's something much more."

By 1990, the Rule of the Solar Temple described an order under the absolute authority of a secret inner group called the Synarchy of the Temple. There were three major degrees—Brothers of the Court, Chevaliers of the Alliance, and Brothers of Former Times. Deemed worthy, the Temple seeker gained access to deeper and deeper spiritual truths. But enlightenment came not through meditation, as in Buddhism, nor in the form of personal prayer that the Protestant reformers had championed. Like traditional Catholicism, the Order of the Solar Temple produced its core religious experience of the divine mysteries through ritual, a device that worked even for people who were not, as Max Weber once put it, "musical" in matters of transcendental illumination. The Order offered a mystical *mood* available to anyone they initiated, not just the spiritually gifted.

On the occasion of one ritual, a videotaped initiation ceremony, men and women wearing white mantles with a red cross file slowly, two by two, into a round room. Each couple bows before a candle that sits on a mirrored triangular pedestal in the center of the chamber, and then the pairs split to form two lines along the wall. Suddenly, from beneath their robes, the chevaliers raise swords in unison, pointing the blades toward the light. As the video's sound track switches from *Lohengrin* to Gregorian chant, two Templars lead in a man in a business suit. The escorts carefully place a new robe and surplice around the shoulders of the initiate, who then kneels before a priest, his hands on the altar next to a red rose and a Bible held open by a sword. The priest picks up the sword and dubs the initiate on his right shoulder, his left shoulder, and the top of his head. After the ceremony ends, the members file out of the sanctuary, two by two. At the end of a long corridor, one can barely see a mirrored door slide open as the video ends.

Behind the mirrored door would lie the inner sanctum, a small round room just large enough for a handful of people. There, the chosen few saw and heard the Ascended Masters, emanations of eternal life who dispensed Gnostic wisdom and practical advice. At a ceremony with forty people, perhaps only three or four would be admitted to the room, leaving others to wait outside, sometimes for hours. Temple survivor Thierry Huguenin talks of "montages" in the crypts. Police in Quebec and Switzerland have mentioned holographic projections. Whatever they were, the spectres, together with the robes, candles, incense and music, created a powerful sacred event where initiates joined an eternal chain of life.

"Whether or not one believes in reincarnation," Huguenin told us, "you have to admit that man lives with emotions, and you know that one can have an experience as a child and remember it at eighty. And you can imagine, if you do believe in reincarnation, that there is a memory, a cellular memory, which, across time and space, comes back home to live in man." Jo DiMambro "made me believe that I was a great reincarnation of Bernard de Clairvaux," Huguenin revealed. Everyone seems to have been inhabited by a famous soul;

perhaps we all are and simply don't know it. Thierry knew the last Grand Master of the Knights Templar, Jacques de Molay, and almost all the apostles of Jesus. "And then, Egypt, well, there we had a lot. Akhnaton, of course, was DiMambro. DiMambro was Akhnaton, Moses, Cagliostro, Osiris. He used to say, 'You understand, in all my incarnations I always had to fight, because my spiritual development was always so far in advance of the time when I was living.'" Inside the Order, according to Huguenin, Luc Jouret had no special status; he simply had a job to do, like everyone else. As for Jo DiMambro, according to Louis-Marie Bélanger, he "was one of the last on earth. Maybe one of the last conscious persons on earth. It's that simple." He didn't preach, he didn't lecture. He was a mystagogue who listened to his followers, listened to the Masters, and spoke for them all. Unknown to the outside world, Jo DiMambro was the secret master.

The Solar Temple appealed almost entirely to francophone people of Catholic background. With the skill of alchemists, the Solar Temple's practitioners transcended neat modern distinctions between reason and faith. They mixed homeopathy, astrology, numerology and Christian symbols into a hybrid neo-traditional Catholic countercultural worldview that eliminated any sharp distinction between life and death and extended the spirit world of the Saints to encompass Ascended Masters who visit this world. Although the Solar Temple is probably not the avatar of an overall cultural reordering, its worldview traffics in broader New Age reconstructions of religious meanings that bear observation. With the Catholic Church itself beset by secular influences, the Solar Temple resurrected ritualistic enchantment for a postmodern world.

THESIS TWO: THE STRUGGLE OVER CULTURAL LEGITIMACY

However marginal countercultural religious movements may appear, they must have a certain power in wider society, for they are alternately subjected to ridicule and repression. Like the medieval Knights Templar, such groups are "utopian." That is, their ascendancy on a wide scale would dramatically reorder society. To dismiss them as bizarre, manipulative, and irrational simply confirms their utopian status, and underscores the threat that organized deviance can pose to an existing social order. Tacit recognition of this potential can be found in many times and places. In our era, a loosely institutionalized movement to control "cults" is often manifested in an alliance among (1) cultural opponents of deviant groups, including former participants and distraught relatives of members; (2) news reporters who frame cult stories in terms of moral deviance; and (3) modern states that have absorbed the "religious" function of enforcing cultural legitimacy. In the most extreme cases, conflicts between such alliances and countercultural movements result in violence (Hall 1987; 1995, 205–235). Given this potential, it is important to ask whether the extreme violence of the Solar Temple was somehow connected to what a Transit letter called "systematic persecution."

The leaders of the Solar Temple worked assiduously to promote a public image of high cultural legitimacy, holding seminars in the best hotels, lecturing at rented halls in universities. Yet the public facade protected a secret world, and it turned out to be a fragile construction. The single person who opposed the group most doggedly, Rose-Marie Klaus, was the Protestant exception who proves the rule of the group's appeal to a culturally Catholic audience. "Mysticism," says Klaus with considerable distaste. "All this tra-la-la and all those robes. It's a thing very far from Protestantism. Luc Jouret depended on the Masters, but they didn't exist. I never believed in that. I am too Protestant for anyone to tell me that there's something else besides God."

Six months after arriving in Ste. Anne-de-la-Pérade, as her lapsed Catholic husband Bruno grew ever more involved, Rose-Marie pulled back from the order, though she continued to live with Bruno in a house just down the street from Sacré-Coeur. One day, as Rose-Marie remembers it, Bruno came home and announced, "The Masters have decided. I am going to live with another woman." Upset, Rose-Marie called upon Luc Jouret to mediate, but his solution followed a Temple formula of "cosmic" coupling that ignored the boundaries of earthly marriage. Luc set Rose-Marie up with another man. "But, ouf, it didn't work," she says. "Six weeks. Because I saw later that this man went with other women, the women had other men. It was very mixed up."

In most instances, a husband and wife participated in the Temple together— as a couple or in "cosmic" rearrangements—or else they divorced. But for years, Rose-Marie neither followed her husband nor left Ste. Anne-de-la-Pérade. "I had a foot inside, but always one outside," she says. Eventually, however, for reasons that remain disputed, Rose-Marie became completely alienated: "I said, 'I won't do it any more. I can't. I'll be ruined.' " Sometime in 1990, she began discussing her troubles with friends, including a police officer whom she had met through her daughter's school.

One friend suggested that Rose-Marie contact Info-Secte (or Info-Cult, as they call themselves in English). The private organization, based in Montreal, defines a "cult" as "a highly manipulative group that exploits its members and can cause psychological, financial, and physical harm." Working, its flyer says, "to help families of cult members and ex-members of cults," Info-Secte has close ties with the larger Cult Awareness Network (CAN) in the United States. A similar group, l'Association pour la Défense des Familles et de l'Individu (ADFI) has branches around France and on the Caribbean island of Martinique, but not in Quebec. "We are the equivalent," says Yves Casgrain, the research director at Info-Secte at the time.

When Rose-Marie Klaus came to their offices around 1991, Info-Secte already knew about the Solar Temple from scattered, unsubstantiated complaints. Klaus told Casgrain about her separation from her husband and her troubled efforts to recoup her investment in the farm at Ste. Anne. Casgrain also recalls Rose-Marie Klaus telling him of "problems." The farm was going bankrupt, investors were losing money, and Robert Falardeau, an official at the Quebec ministry of finance, had replaced Luc Jouret as Grand Master at Sacré-Coeur. Whatever Casgrain made of Klaus's account, he took no public action. She was pursuing a lawsuit at the time, he says, so "she would never unpack her bags for us." Casgrain soon learned more, however, from another source. On September 10, 1991, the president of ADFI in Martinique, Lucién Zécler, sent a circular about the Solar Temple to Info-Secte and other organizations in Quebec.

Zécler's letter cited the 1984 anticult publication connecting Jouret to the Renewed Order of the Temple and Julien Origas, "former head of the Gestapo at Brest." The leaders of OTS, Zécler inferred, "sit at the extreme right of God." He described the Order's message of planetary catastrophe and he quoted a 1991 Temple bulletin announcing, "the countdown is locked in." The immediate threat, as Zécler saw it, was proselytizing. Jouret had persuaded certain wealthy and influential Martiniquans to sell their possessions and depart the island for Quebec. "We have come to the conviction," Zécler's letter concluded, "that the only way to save the relatives of our friends and stop the hemorrhage is to unmask this organization in its noxious practices."

This letter did not get many responses from Quebec, but it got one from Rose-Marie Klaus. On October 20, 1991, she composed a four-page handwritten letter. Addressing herself "to all [in] this beautiful world who hope to have a better life here in Canada, believing in Luc Jouret, Grand Spiritual Master of the Order of Templars," Klaus sarcastically suggested how "urgent" it was for her readers to invest in "this 'monument' of manipulation, deception and mystification," and closed by offering to "give you other information, or to meet you."

"It was Casgrain who said to us that if we got in touch with Mme. Klaus, she was ready to give us a lot of information," Zécler recalls. Rose-Marie received a typed letter from Zécler dated July 17, 1992. "Dear Madame," it read. "In October, 1991, Info-Sectes provided our association against sectes with a photocopy of a letter that you were willing to write to denounce the swindle in which you and your family were victimized by the Solar Temple." Public opinion in the Antilles and metropolitan France would benefit from learning more about the "actual machinations" of Jouret and the order, Zécler wrote, and he asked Klaus for written permission "before undertaking the necessary steps." By the end of 1992, Rose-Marie had completed her divorce from Bruno. OTS had provided a $150,000 settlement, amounting, in the court's reckoning, to half the money that the couple originally had put into the project. But Rose-Marie still asserted that the Solar Temple owed her money, and the settlement freed her to amplify her denunciations. With ADFI-Martinique paying for the plane ticket, she traveled to the Caribbean island in December of 1992. During a stay of about two weeks, Rose-Marie spoke to the Rotary Club, and stories about her appeared in the island's newspaper, Frances Antilles. "After the visit of Mme. Klaus," says Zécler, "there was a film that we produced, and the Templars calmed down." From what Zécler heard, some Martiniquans "went to Canada to demand the money that they had invested in the project. Because they realized finally that Jouret had fooled them."

In Canada, Jouret had indeed been replaced by Falardeau as Grand Master at Sacré-Coeur, as Klaus told Info-Secte. The change occurred in 1990, when Jouret began to put what some members found to be too much urgency into his already apocalyptic message. Jouret responded by founding a new group, called l'Académie de Recherche et Connaissance des Hautes Sciences, ARCHS, a pun on Jouret's favorite images of an ark of survival and a bridge arching to the future. Just as in the 1983 ORT schism, Jouret took a number of loyalists with him. His key ally, Jean-Pierre Vinet, a vice president at the state-run Hydro-Quebec power company, then helped him become a "management guru" in both senses of the term. In 1991 and 1992, Dr. Jouret lectured on topics like "Business and Chaos," and "The Real Meaning of Work."

Vinet and Jouret drafted Herman Delorme to become president of ARCHS, but by Herman's account, the title carried few responsibilities and no authority.

"One day I managed to get a little private session with Jouret," Herman recalls, "and he says, 'Herman,' he says, 'You're where you're supposed to be, so just do what you're supposed to do without question.' " In November 1992, Jean-Pierre Vinet tested that allegiance, asking Delorme to get him a pistol with a silencer. Vinet explained that he needed protection, but he didn't know how to shoot and he wanted to practice without disturbing neighbors. Taught to obey, Herman took the request to Daniel Tougas, a policeman whose wife had attended several of Jouret's lectures. Tougas could provide guns but not silencers, so Herman turned to a fellow student in his karate course, "who had done some time on a drug charge or something." That man, Bernard Gilot, turned out to be a police informant.

At about the same time, the Sûreté du Quebec later reported, a man identifying himself as "André Massé" began calling government offices, threatening to assassinate the Minister of Public Security, Claude Ryan, and several Parliamentary deputies. The Sûreté du Quebec has never been able to find out anything about "André" or the organization he claimed to represent, "Q-37" (supposedly named for the thirty-seven Quebecers who made up the group). However, SQ asserts that at the time, investigators saw a possible connection between Q-37's threats and Herman's interest in buying guns. Following this slim lead, the SQ obtained a warrant to tap Herman's phone, and then Vinet's. In turn, they searched a villa in St. Sauveur owned by Temple member Camille Pilet. Pilet and Luc Jouret got wind of the search during a trip to Switzerland, and they engaged a Montreal attorney, Jean-Claude Hébert, to get to the bottom of the matter, but Hébert was able to learn nothing.

News of the investigation never got back from Pilet and Jouret to Vinet and Delorme, who continued to pursue the plan to buy weapons. Gilot, the police informant, strung them along until the police arranged for him to approach Herman with a sting. Herman recalled: "He showed me pictures of AK-47s and tanks and Isuzus—what do you call them?—Uzis. And I was telling myself, what do I have to tell these people to get a simple little handgun with a silencer? And here they are, asking me all sorts of questions. 'How big a group are you?' Of course, you know, we're about thirty. 'You serious?' Of course we're serious, we're all business people. 'Do you have any political ideology?' " Herman chuckled. "I hate politics! But then you can interpret that as I hate politicians, or I'm gonna shoot politicians. They would interpret everything that I said according to what they *thought* was going to happen."

Herman finally settled on a set of three pistols and a vague agreement to "buy a ton" later. He made the pickup on Nun's Island in Montreal on the afternoon of March 8, 1993. Forty-five minutes later, as he was pulling off Highway 74 near his home, he was ambushed by a SWAT team and forcibly arrested. Within hours after police nabbed Delorme, they took Jean-Pierre Vinet into custody and issued a warrant for the arrest of Luc Jouret, who was in Europe at the time.

Three days after the arrests, less than three months after her return from Martinique, Rose-Marie Klaus was on the front page of the tabloid *Journal de Montreal*, scowling and holding up a white robe with a red cross. "I Lost One Million," the headline declared. A week later, Quebec's *Photo Police* had a picture of Rose-Marie in the same pose, the headline promising "What They Haven't Told You About the HORROR OF THE ORDRE DU TEMPLE SOLAIRE." These stories—and interviews with other newspapers, radio, and television stations—turned out to be repetitions, with some elaboration, of Rose-Marie's allegations to Info-Secte in 1991.

Some of the news coverage over the next month was less tendentious. Active members defended OTS in several articles, and the citizens of Ste. Anne said that they had no objections at all to the group. Claude Ryan himself appealed for public "prudence" on the subject of sects. But some newspapers routinely characterized OTS as a doomsday cult involved in an "arms-trafficking plot." Among other commentators, Yves Casgrain of Info-Secte could not resist making comparisons with Waco, where the FBI siege of the heavily armed Branch Davidians had just begun.

The arrests and media scrutiny led to Jean-Pierre Vinet's dismissal from Hydro-Quebec, and they touched off an investigation within the state-owned utility. The examiner's report confirmed that Jouret had given lectures at Hydro-Quebec facilities. Fifteen employees had been members of OTS or l'ARCHS, he concluded, and other employees had attended meetings. (OTS and Hydro-Quebec were linked again in March 1994, when someone blew up two power line transmission towers. The SQ released a letter that claimed responsibility on behalf of OTS. The writer, however, betrayed an ignorance of both OTS style and the details of the bombings, and the police dismissed the letter as a prank.)

In 1993, Jean-Claude Hébert thought he could win acquittal on the weapons charges, and afterward he continued to question the legality of the phone taps and warrants. Jouret, however, didn't want any publicity. "They were very preoccupied by a question of image," Hébert said of Jouret and Pilet, whom he visited in Switzerland. "At that period, they had the wind in their sails, and I could understand that the negative publicity put out in Canada might come down in France, in Switzerland, in Martinique, and spoil his whole network of activities." At a brief trial in July 1993, the Crown Prosecutor accepted a plea bargain, and the judge reasoned that the weapons had been purchased for defensive purposes and that the defendants had already been abundantly penalized by the media. He sentenced Jouret, Vinet, and Delorme each to one year of unsupervised probation and a fine of $1,000, to be donated to the Red Cross.

In law enforcement circles, however, the gun incident was categorized as illegal arms trafficking, and it triggered a chain reaction of investigations. Within two days after the arrests, SQ publicly announced an inquiry into financial aspects of OTS. Australian police opened a parallel inquiry later in 1993. A bulletin went out from the international police organization, Interpol, alleging that Jo DiMambro and a woman confidant, Odile Dancet, had taken part in two banking transactions in Australia of $93 million each. French authorities initiated a separate investigation in 1994, putting a temporary delay on reissuing the passport belonging to DiMambro's wife, Jocelyne. By March 1994, the Royal Canadian Mounted Police were cooperating with Australian Federal Police inquiries concerning possible money laundering.

Temple principals never fully understood the extent of these investigations, but they had their suspicions. Jo DiMambro learned about the delay in renewing Jocelyne's French passport, and on the last day of his life he gave Patrick Vuarnet both his and Jocelyne's passports and a bitter letter of complaint addressed to the French interior minister, "Very dear Charlie" Pasqua (who himself has been associated with Interpol and Service d'Action Civique). One of the Transit letters sent the same day, "To Those Who Value Justice," did not mention the rumors of money laundering that circulated on the Interpol network. But it did claim that OTS had been the target of a "pseudoplot" concocted by connecting the order with Q-37, a supposed terrorist group that had never been publicly mentioned before the gun arrests. By 1995, SQ sergeant Robert Poeti would say, "Q-37, as far as we're concerned, never existed. It was a joke, a guy who called. There are people who are deranged, who do this. We are convinced that the one who made the calls had nothing to do with the Ordre du Temple Solaire. Nothing at all." If so, we are left with an irony of history—that a mere coincidence should have drawn together police action, the Temple's most formidable dissident, and cultural opposition in the mass media.

We do not know the complete genesis of the cultural denunciations chan-
neled through ADFI-Martinique, Info-Secte, Rose-Marie Klaus, and the media.
Nor do we know exactly how the Sûreté du Quebec and other law enforcement
agencies around the globe came to unleash full-scale arms-trafficking investigations of individuals seeking to buy several pistols with silencers. At present,
it seems that these events converged in an elective affinity rather than through
direct collusion among law enforcement and cultural opponents. Whatever the
connections, those who sought to harmonize the transition to the new era *construed* the scandals as the results of persecution.

THESIS THREE: THE MULTIPLE CONSTRUCTIONS OF TEMPLAR REALITY

The tensions that countercultural religious movements often engender can be
especially volatile in the case of apocalyptic sects. Among typical orientations
of such groups, the *warring sect* is engaged in a struggle between the forces of
good and evil that amounts to the apocalypse enacted, whereas the postapocalyptic *otherworldly sect* seeks to escape "this" world to establish a tableau of
"heaven on earth" beyond the evils of the secular world. *Mysticism* brings a
third construction of reality into play—eternal transcendence from the his-
toricity of this world (Hall 1978). In these terms, perceiving an apocalyptic
"war" of persecution by opponents in addition to an imminent ecological
apocalypse, the leaders of the Temple ultimately shifted the destination of
their escape from the granite bedrock of Quebec to a mystically achieved
colony "beyond" the "old" or the "new" world.

   The Sûreté de Quebec has argued that if they had not stumbled on the plan
to buy guns, the murders and suicides would have taken place in Quebec in
the spring of 1993, with perhaps twice as many participants. But this thesis
does not exactly accord with their other explanation—for the murder of the
Dutoits in Quebec just before the deaths in Switzerland. In this SQ account, the
Dutoits' fate was not sealed until well after the gun incident. In the summer of
1994, Tony and Nicky had the temerity to name their newborn baby Christopher Emmanuel, even though Jo DiMambro had reserved the name
Emmanuelle for his own daughter. (The girl was said to be a "cosmic child,"
supposedly conceived when Jo pointed a magical sword—with a battery-pow-
ered light—at Dominique Bellaton's throat). "She was the Avatar who was

going to rebuild the Temple and prevent the Apocalypse," according to Lt. Richard St. Denis. The SQ reports having discovered a written ritual according to which "the Anti-Christ had to be killed by two knights with a stake." They insist that the Dutoit baby was the Antichrist, pierced with knife blows that each had a symbolic significance. With the baby's body, investigators claim to have found a stake.

In evaluating this ritually saturated account, it is worth recalling that, from the Temple viewpoint, the SQ was part of the plot against the group. The Transit letter that denounces government agencies—in league with the Mafia and Opus Dei—for pushing them to leave this earth, reserves its most bitter venom for the Sûreté du Quebec and the Q-37 tie-in. "We accuse them of collective assassination," the letter concludes. Small wonder that Quebec authorities prefer a mystical interpretation of the Transit.

No one now is in a position to conduct the experiment with history to reveal what would have happened if the followers of the Ascended Masters had not believed themselves to be the target of a conspiracy. As Casaubon, the Templar scholar and narrator, remarks in Umberto Eco's novel, *Foucault's Pendulum,* "Counterfactual conditionals are always true, because the premise is false." However, some evidence suggests that the firearms arrests in 1993 actually hastened, rather than delayed, the Transit. Not only are the Transit letters laced with the rhetoric of persecution, one letter calls the departure of the Order "premature." But this raises the question, premature in relation to what?

The most esoteric of Temple doctrines is based on Jacques Breyer's 1959 book, *Arcanes Solaire, or the Secrets of the Solar Temple.* There, complex charts and alchemical formulations unveil the relation between eternity and history, and how enlightened spirits can move from historical incarnations to disincarnation and back, carrying the Solar Depository in and out of time, *if* they align their actions with epochal moments of harmonic energy.

"Fire!" Breyer enthuses, "Ask God: that Israel (among others) convert to Christianity, now that we have reached *the End of Time,*" which one chart calculates as 1999.8. On another chart, Breyer asserts that Jesus was born four years before the year 1 M.E., and concludes, "The Grand Monarchy ought to Leave this world around 1995–96." According to this calculation of the apocalypse, the 1994 Transit *was* premature. The clock was ticking, but there was still time before the End of Time. (Even at the end, it should be noted, other religious sects, seeing their long-anticipated and precisely dated apocalypses come and go, have simply revised their calendars.) The dates in Breyer's charts, the author himself noted, were based on mere mundane calculation, and are therefore approximate. They left considerable room for revisionist flexibility. Indeed, by one of Breyer's calculations, the last phase of the Age of Pisces, beginning with the revolutions of 1848, is divided in half, with the first half ending in the year 2002 and the final end not coming until sometime in the twenty-second century.

"October the 4th, 1994," mused Herman Delorme. "Add up the numbers, one by one, and see what we come out to. The fourth, okay, and the tenth month. Four plus one is five plus zero is still five, plus one is six, plus nine is fifteen, and nine is twenty-four. Twenty-four plus four is twenty-eight, two and eight is ten, one and zero is—one. One is a new beginning." A new moon came into phase that night, just as the planet Mars entered the house of Leo, the polar opposite of Aquarius.

In the early 1990s, Delorme reminds us, "There was talk of this 'departure' for Sirius"—the location of the "Great White Lodge" mentioned in one Transit letter. Another letter, "Transit for the Future," tells of a brotherhood of thirty-three Rosicrucian Elder Brothers who used "assumed bodies" in order "to accomplish the Divine Plans." Now that they had found their message rejected at the end of the twentieth century, the letter asserts, the Elder Brothers had decided to leave this historical period of existence. But before departing, they gathered together people enlightened enough to cross beyond the Apocalypse of our era "with the end of producing the embryo of our future Generation."

Two widespread and mutually contradictory myths have fueled speculations about this self-proclaimed Transit—that its perpetrators were rolling in money from arms trafficking and that they faced a financial crisis. In the true Templar tradition, television miniseries, movies, and pulp books are spinning conspiracy theories based upon both. The first myth, initiated in October 1994 by the Swiss weekly *l'Hebdo* and the Canadian Broadcasting Company, drew together recycled press reports about the 1993 gun incident and the Interpol memo about the $93 million. In April 1996, after an eighteen-month investigation, Swiss authorities reported no evidence of either money laundering or anything remotely approaching $93 million. No doubt the search for the fabled wealth will continue. The second myth is that the group around DiMambro and Jouret took their own and others' lives because of imminent financial disaster. To be sure, the gun incident precipitated a wider defection of members (already begun with the schism in 1991), and the example of Rose-Marie Klaus encouraged both followers from Martinique and other disaffected members to try to get their money back. However, even after settling a number of financial claims in the summer of 1994, the core group still held enough property and cash to have continued a lavish life for some time to come.

What the Solar Temple did lose in March 1993 was something they had worked obsessively to protect—the good name necessary to continue their enterprises. The SQ investigation yielded only three handguns with silencers, but it precipitated a public crisis of legitimacy. Under the glaring spotlight of the bad publicity in Martinique and Quebec, the lucrative career of a charismatic New Age lecturer itself became a scandal, closing off recruitment and new sources of money. (The growing bubble of an expansionary momentum ground to a halt.) Jean-Claude Hébert remembers going to visit Jouret in Switzerland after the gun raid. "That's what started to destroy his pedestal. And he experienced it as an enormous anguish," says Hébert. "I *think* that in his mind, it was perhaps the beginning of the end." The Swiss authorities reached a parallel conclusion: although the *idea* of a Transit dates from at least 1990, psychological preparation did not begin until 1993.

As for DiMambro, there are rumors that his health was failing. He had cancer, people say, of a sort that Jouret could not cure. Whether these rumors are true, DiMambro may have believed his life to be near its end. Perhaps he orchestrated murders and suicides as an effort to salvage personal and collective honor in the face of personal death and an earthly organizational future that promised only further decline, and at the very time that the apocalypse approached.

The distribution of the bodies and their manner of death suggests that this explanation is incomplete, for DiMambro hardly acted alone. Thousands of miles away, in Quebec, the Dutoits obviously were murdered, but probably not because their son was the Antichrist. According to several sources, Tony Dutoit had become disillusioned with the Temple in the early 1990s, and began to reveal backstage secrets about the crypt electronics that he had installed. That betrayal may have resulted in his murder as a traitor. Collette and Gerry Genoud just as obviously committed suicide on their own. According to the Sûreté du Quebec, they assisted Joel Egger and Dominique Bellaton in the murder of the Dutoits. Over the next four days they cleaned up after the murders, prepared incendiary devices, set the timers on the devices, and then laid themselves out on their beds, dressed in their robes and medals, ready to make the Transit in the fire that ensued.

Legally, ethically, and emotionally, the four children and three teenagers who died in Switzerland—including the cosmic DiMambro girl—were murdered.

The question that remains is whether their parents knowingly included them. That happened in seventeenth-century Russia, when entire families of Old Believers locked themselves in churches and set them on fire, and it happened again in 1978, when women brought their babies up to receive the cyanide poison that killed 913 members of Jim Jones's Peoples Temple in Jonestown, Guyana (Hall 1987).

As at Jonestown, evidence also suggests that many of the twenty-five people dead at Salvan were not unwilling participants. Evident loyalists or long-time members included DiMambro's wife, mistresses, and secretaries, Luc Jouret and his Canadian ally, Jean-Pierre Vinet, and Joel Egger and Dominque Bellaton, the presumed Morin Heights murderers. Herman Delorme recalls the last time he saw Vinet. "I'm leaving definitely," Jean-Pierre told him in July 1994. "You probably will never see me again. You don't have anything left to accomplish, but I do." Others made similar foreboding comments before their deaths. A surviving daughter reports that her mother once told her, "One day they were going to depart for Venus, and there was no reason to be sad when they disappeared." On the other hand, if reports are correct, Jo DiMambro's 25-year-old son had distanced himself from his father, and he may have been murdered for appearance's sake, to bring the family back together in death.

On the last day of his life, Jo DiMambro gave Patrick Vuarnet a short fifth letter printed in the same computer font as the other Transit letters. "Following the tragic Transit at Cheiry," the letter says, "we insist on specifying, in the name of the Rose + Cross, that we deplore and totally disassociate ourselves from the barbarous, incompetent and aberrant conduct of Doctor Luc Jouret." It continues, "He is the cause of a veritable carnage." At Cheiry, two people died of suffocation. The other twenty-one had received powerful sleeping pills before being shot to death; some had three or more bullets to the head. Ten bodies total were found with plastic bags over their heads. Some had died much earlier than others and their bodies were moved after death. Several showed signs of struggle. Three of them, Swiss authorities concluded, were murdered for revenge. Among these may have been Albert Giacobino, the principal investor in the Cheiry farm, and Marie-Louise Rebaudo, the group astrologer, who were both reportedly trying to recover their investments. Jouret's ex-wife, Marie-Christine Pertué, may have been brought to Cheiry for personal reasons (she and Jouret had married in the early 1980s, but they divorced after their only child died in infancy). A group of Canadians, including Robert Falardeau, may have come to represent the group in Ste. Anne, perhaps seeking reconciliation with Luc Jouret without knowing what they were get-ting into. But it is also evident that some who died at Cheiry had close or enduring ties to the core group. One of the Canadians, Jocelyne Grand'Maison, had been a member of the Renewed Temple before the Solar Temple was started. Camille Pilet, the organization's chief financier, was there, as was 70-year-old Renée Pfaehler, one of the founding members of Golden Way and a vigorous recruiter for the group. And several of the dead had direct family ties to individuals who died at Salvan.

All those who died at Cheiry were killed by someone else, but we cannot be sure whether the deaths were assassinations or assisted suicide. Friends and relatives rightly remain incredulous that anyone could ever have wittingly participated in something as farfetched as the Transit plan to effect a transmi-gration of living souls. Some small dignity might be salvaged by declaring a judgment of wholesale deceit, trickery, and murder. But it seems likely that people died at Cheiry under a variety of circumstances, from murder to sui-cide, with shadings in between. Some were murdered "traitors." Some who willingly embarked on the spectacular Transit could have been surprised by the bullet to the brain. Yet others may have participated in their own deaths, as the Transit letters claim, "in all lucidity and all liberty." During the Swiss investigation into the deaths, an elegant woman in her forties came into inves-tigating judge André Piller's office, dressed in a dark red cape, draped in neck-laces and little crosses. She was devastated, she told Piller, that she had not been summoned to the Transit. Piller replied, "Transit? Twenty out of twenty-three with bullets in their heads? What kind of a Transit is that?" The woman answered, "Listen. They all wanted the Transit, but they didn't have the courage to go. I might not have had the courage either, and I would have been happy if someone had helped me. If it was necessary. Why not?"

In Transit

Like the fourteenth-century Templars, the visible Solar Temple disappeared in flames. But the Ascended Masters may continue to walk amongst us. As the Transit letters say, "The Rose + Cross has not finished surprising you." True, some former members are trying to move on. Thierry Huguenin has worked to recoup the financial losses of his Templar years by publishing his memoirs and consulting on a television film. Herman Delorme has considered joining

Creations, a multilevel marketing scheme with spiritual overtones. As for Louis-Marie Bélanger, he refuses to judge his fellow Templars. "Maybe they are a little more conscious than I am," he suggests, "and they knew things I didn't know." But Bélanger will follow his own path. "The thing is," he told us, "you don't need to be in an order, a templar order, to be a Templar."

Still, the Martinique anticult activist, Lucién Zécler, believes that OTS is reorganizing, quietly, under a new name. And why not? According to the Transit letters, "their name or the label of their organization matters little. We will say simply that they appear and disappear at a precise time, always at critical moments of civilization." The authors further claim that they will be able to "call back the last Servants capable of hearing this final message." The rest of us, trapped in mundane history, have their wishes of peace as we face "the terrible ordeals of the Apocalypse."

How many more Servants will be called back remains to be seen. After the 1995 winter solstice—the one closest to Breyer's date for the departure of the Grand Monarchy—French authorities found a circle of fourteen charred, bullet-ridden bodies in a mountain clearing near Grenoble. Three were children. The adults were associates of the Solar Temple who had not made the earlier Transit, including Patrick Vuarnet and his mother, Edith. Near the fourteen lay the bodies of two more Templars—a French immigration inspector and a French police official. Apparently they had shot the others before starting the fire that consumed the whole group after they shot themselves. Investigators later found notes in four homes of the dead describing wishes to "see another world."

Given that the leaders had all supposedly died in October 1994, this "Transit" produced strong public response. Both French and Hydro-Quebec officials voiced concerns that the secret order had infiltrated government agencies, and France formed a government watchdog group to "battle against the dangers of cults." Authorities temporarily removed a child from the home of her mother, a known Temple associate before 1994. In Quebec, Yves Casgrain of Info-Secte warned that the sect probably continued to operate underground, and Herman Delorme predicted that ten to twelve people might be caught up in a new suicide, at the summer solstice of 1996 (nothing happened). Police in France undertook preventive roundups involving scores of suspected Temple members, apparently fearing another collective suicide on each new moon, equinox, or anniversary of the dates when the fifty-four medieval Knights Templar and their Grand Master, Jacques de Molay, were burned alive at the stake at the beginning of the fourteenth century.

For all our own sciences and religions, we do not know what happened to the souls of these deceased. Atheist, agnostic, or believer, our attitudes toward death are matters of faith. Uncertain of the alternative, most of us do our best to prolong life. We may disagree about capital punishment and war, abortion and assisted suicide, but we find murder and suicide of the young and the healthy to be an unconscionable assault on religious and humanistic values alike. If the letters of Transit bear faithful witness, however, death for the believing Adepts was not the final frontier, but rather a ritualized journey to be undertaken when transcendent purpose called for it, willingly, with noble spirit, without remorse or fear. In choosing the Transit, the true believers among those who died affirmed their heresy by enacting a demonstration.

From the seventeenth century onwards, Rosicrucian societies have claimed to reverse the Fall, offering their secret knowledge to transform human existence from its presently mistaken paths, promising immortality as the reward for breaking through the mantles of illusion. This assault on modern religion and science offers people who feel alienated a ready explanation for their condition: they have no home in our world because they are really members of an eternal brotherhood. In turn, the disbelief they meet in the outer world sustains the boundaries that divide them from us. Rarely do deviant religions that recruit among the alienated provide their converts with such a tidy account of why they experience alienation or how, as an enlightened elite, to meet external challenges. The Transit letters reject the detractors who would label them as a cult, and they refuse to sully the wisdom of the ages with struggles against some latter-day inquisition. Yes, traitors were brutally murdered, but those responsible for these crimes will not allow themselves to be held accountable for their actions in our world. Martyrs, argued St. Bernard de Clairvaux, sacrifice their lives to a higher cause. Immortal mystics do not make such a sacrifice. They have no life to give. They simply return to eternity.

References

Breyer, Jacques. 1959. *Arcanes Solaire; ou, Les Secrets du Temple Solaire*. Paris: La Colombe.

Hall, John R. 1978. *The Ways Out: Utopian Communal Groups in an Age of Babylon*. New York: Routledge and Kegan Paul.

———. 1987. *Gone From the Promised Land: Jonestown in American Cultural History*. New Brunswick, NJ: Transaction.

———. 1995. "Public Narratives and the Apocalyptic Sect." In *Armageddon in Mount Carmel*, edited by Stuart A. Wright. Chicago: University of Chicago Press.

Introvigne, Massimo. 1995. "Ordeal by Fire: The Tragedy of the Solar Temple." *Religion* 25: 267–283.

Partner, Peter. 1982. *The Murdered Magicians: The Templars and Their Myth*. New York: Oxford University Press.

Weber, Max. 1978. *Economy and Society*. Berkeley: University of California Press.

Selected Periodicals and Newspapers:

24 Heures (Lausanne, Switzerland)
l'Actualité (Montreal)
Agence France Presse
Le Devoir (Montreal)
Gazette (Montreal)
L'Hebdo (Geneva)
L'Illustré (Lausanne, Switzerland)
Le Journal de Genève
Le Journal de Montreal
Le Matin (Lausanne, Switzerland)
Le Monde
Photo Police (Montreal)
La Presse (Montreal)
Le Soleil (Quebec)
Toronto Sun

Aum Shinrikyō as an Apocalyptic Movement

16 Mark R. Mullins

INTRODUCTION

Just as 1923 is etched in the historical consciousness of the Japanese as the year of the Great Kanto (Tokyo) Earthquake, 1995 will undoubtedly be remembered as another year of terrible disaster. A nation that was still reeling from the shock of the January 17 Kobe-Osaka earthquake had to take another major jolt on March 20, 1995, when the deadly nerve gas sarin was released on the

Tokyo subway system. Shortly after 8 A.M., thousands of rush-hour com-
muters and scores of subway workers began stumbling out of some sixteen stations in central Tokyo coughing, vomiting, and collapsing. All told, the nerve
gas attack on the Chiyoda, Hibiya, and Marunouchi subway lines left 12 people dead and more than 5,000 injured. As the TV stations broadcast their live
coverage of the subway chaos, disbelief, and fear spread across the nation
again as it had only two months earlier following the Kobe earthquake.

Two days after the subway gas attack, the Tokyo Metropolitan Police
Department launched a nationwide investigation of Aum Shinrikyō, a new
religious movement still in its first decade. Since it was a young and small
movement, it had not yet been the focus of serious research and was relatively
unknown. When the police investigation of Aum began, everyone began scram-
bling for information. At the time, Aum was barely a blip on the computer
screen for most scholars of new religious movements. In a situation where many
new religious movements boast millions of members, a group of approximately
10,000 seemed to warrant little attention.

When the subway incident occurred, about the only information available
were Aum publications, a few articles by journalists who had covered the
conflict between Aum members and residents in several local communities,
and a brief description of Aum in a standard reference work on new religions
in Japan (Inoue 1990). Since the "Aum Affair" began in March 1995, scholars
and journalists have been forced to give serious attention to this movement in
order to make sense of the ongoing police investigation and the trials of Shoko
Asahara and other leading members. Over the past year scores of books, magazines, and journals devoted to Aum have been published. While a definitive
analysis will be difficult to achieve for some years, this paper will briefly locate
Aum Shinrikyō on the larger map of Japanese religion and sketch its development as an apocalyptic movement over the past decade.

Scholars working in the field of Japanese new religions often group movements historically in four periods. Over the course of Japan's modernization,
new religious movements have flourished on a number of occasions. The fourth
and most recent period is widely regarded to have begun in the mid- to late
1970s. Movements that developed since that time are often grouped together
under the umbrella term *shin shin shukyo* or "neo-new religions" to distinguish them from the established new religions (*kisei shin shukyo*) that developed in earlier periods.[1] This period is characterized by a growing interest in
the occult, mysticism, supernatural powers, and various New Age phenomena.

Apocalyptic ideas and literature have also been a prominent feature of this most recent period. New religions in Japan have long been regarded as syncretistic as they draw on beliefs and practices from various religious traditions. Those groups that have emerged since the late 1970s are even more eclectic, since modern forms of communication and travel have made it possible to draw on many more imported sources of ideas and beliefs. This is the larger context for understanding the development of Aum Shinrikyō.

THE BEGINNINGS OF AUM SHINRIKYŌ

The founder of Aum Shinrikyō, Chizuo Matsumoto, was born in 1955 on the southern island of Kyushu. From the age of five he attended a boarding school for the blind, moving to Tokyo after graduation with hopes of entering the University of Tokyo. Unable to pursue university studies, he studied acupuncture and traditional Chinese medicine in order to make a living. Following marriage in 1978, he and his wife sold Chinese medicine and natural foods and practiced acupuncture. Over the years he independently pursued studies of various Asian religious traditions and practiced ascetic disciplines such as yoga. In 1984, he and his wife began to hold regular yoga classes in Shibuya (an area in Tokyo). Two years later, he traveled to India with a few of his students to undergo more rigorous spiritual training and claimed to have achieved ultimate enlightenment in 1986 while training alone in the Himalayan mountains.

In 1987, he adopted the holy name Shoko Asahara and continued his religious activities, giving his group the name Aum Shinrikyō. According to Asahara, *Aum* is a Sanskrit term that refers to the creation, preservation, and destruction of the universe. *Shinri* is the Japanese word for truth and *kyo* refers to teaching. In short, Aum Shinrikyō is a religion claiming to teach the truth about the creative and destructive power in the universe. After considerable difficulties, Asahara was finally able to register Aum Shinrikyō with the government in 1989 as a religious juridical person (*shukyo hojin*). With official recognition and tax-exempt privileges, Asahara and his followers were able to pursue their religious activities in earnest.

Aum can best be viewed as an eclectic Buddhist movement that draws on various Asian traditions, such as yoga and Tibetan Buddhism. Aum Shinrikyō claims to offer its members liberation from illness and suffering and ultimate enlightenment. At least during the early years, the stress was on personal liberation and enlightenment. This emphasis may be seen in Asahara's earliest books, *Chonoryoku: Himitsu no kaihatsu ho* (Psychic power: A secret means of development) (1986) and *Seishi o koeru* (Transcending life and death) (1986).

THE EVOLUTION OF ASAHARA'S APOCALYPTIC VISION

A revelation from the Hindu deity Shiva, which became the primary deity in Aum, led Asahara to regard himself as a messianic figure who was to lead his followers in the establishment of an ideal society referred to as the Kingdom of Shambhala. Japan was to be transformed into this utopian kingdom through the establishment of independent communities, called the Lotus Village Plan.

To traditional Buddhist teachings, ascetic practices, and utopianism, Asahara added a number of apocalyptic ideas drawn from a variety of sources. The following list of Asahara's book titles from 1989 clearly reveals the increasing prominence of apocalyptic concerns: *Metsubo no hi* (The day of destruction) (1989); *Metsubo kara koku e: Zoku metsubo no hi* (From destruction to emptiness: A sequel of the day of destruction) (1989); *Jinrui metsubo no shinjitsu* (The truth of humanity's destruction) (1991); *Nosutoradamusu himitsu no daiyogen* (The secret prophecy of Nostradamus) (1991) (Asahara's interpretation of the sixteenth-century French astrologer's predictions regarding Armageddon); *Kirisuto sengen* (Proclamation as Christ) (1991); and *Kirisuto sengen Part 2* (Proclamation as Christ Part 2) (1992). Asahara's study of various apocalyptic visions, including the Book of Revelation and the Prophecy of Nostradamus, provided him with many key ideas and images that he freely adapted.

Asahara initially taught that evil energy is spreading throughout the world and we are headed toward a major catastrophe in 1999—mass destruction from nuclear war. To avoid this fate, 30,000 believers are needed to transfer the evil energy into positive energy (i.e., individuals who have achieved the liberation provided through the example, teaching, and methods advocated by Asahara). Only then can humankind avoid this major disaster. This early emphasis on prevention, however, disappears from his later apocalyptic writings. Armageddon is no longer avoidable, but the number who die at Armageddon can be limited through Aum's activities. The survival of a small number of chosen people, who will be able to build a new civilization, becomes the goal of Aum's activities. By 1990, the vision and ideals of the Lotus Village are overshadowed by the concern for mere survival. Asahara's remarks and various

Aum publications stress the need to build nuclear shelters in Aum communes to protect members from the unavoidable war and the nuclear and chemical weapons that are bound to be used.

The goal of self-sufficiency, noted in relation to the Lotus Village Plan above, becomes closely connected to Asahara's evolving apocalyptic vision. Since a major war or catastrophe is no longer avoidable, Aum must prepare for the inevitable disaster and build an alternative community that can survive without outside resources and provide the foundation for building a new civilization. This requires self-sufficiency not only in such basics as food and clothing, but also in fundamental scientific research and training.[2]

SOCIAL ORGANIZATION AND MEMBERSHIP

The idea of self-sufficient and holistic communities eventually gave birth to the administrative structure of Aum organized along the lines of a ministate with Asahara at the top. This organizational structure is one of Aum's features that distinguish it from most other new religions in Japan. While both traditional religious groups and new religions normally have divisions or departments for such areas as religious education, proselytization, and publications, Aum's administrative structure essentially duplicates that of the national government. Almost twenty different agencies or ministries exist under the command of Supreme Leader Asahara, including the Defense Agency, Construction Ministry, Health and Welfare Ministry, Public Relations, Science and Technology Ministry, Chemical Team, Education Ministry, and Telecommunications Ministry. Aum has clearly organized with the aim of creating a completely separate society.[3]

Another distinguishing feature of Aum Shinrikyō is related to the nature of its membership. The figures for Aum in early 1995 included approximately 10,000 members scattered among some twenty-five centers across Japan and another 30,000 members in Russia. The membership in Japan included 1,247 individuals who belonged to the special category of *shukkesha*, individuals who have renounced society and live in one of the centers or communities. These deeply committed members who form the core of the movement are quite young, with some 75 percent in their twenties or thirties. Almost 40 percent of the *shukkesha* are women (Yamashita 1995, 63; Shimazono 1995, 4).

Aum's increased emphasis on *shukke*, renouncing the world and living in the religious community, has been the focus of many criticisms and a major source of conflict between Aum and many families. With more than 10 percent of the movement cut off from regular employment and income, it has also been the cause of many financial concerns. The unusually high percentage of monastics in relation to regular members has made it extremely difficult to manage financial affairs and has placed a heavy burden on members working outside of the organization (see Inoue 1995, 36).

THE DESTRUCTIVE SIDE OF AUM REVEALED

The brief summary above provides a picture of Aum's "public" face as it was generally perceived until March 1995. While Aum had been suspected of illegal activities prior to the subway gas attack, police had been unable to gather the necessary evidence to pursue any of the cases. This all changed on March 22, two days after the subway gas attack, when the Tokyo Metropolitan Police Department mobilized some 2,500 officers in raids on twenty-five Aum centers across the country. The pretext for the investigation was the suspicion that Aum had been involved in the disappearance of Kiyoshi Kariya, a Tokyo notary public clerk, but it was widely known that the police were searching for evidence of sarin gas or other chemicals used in its production.[4] Aum representatives quickly responded with charges that the police were simply looking for a scapegoat and persecuting a religious minority. They maintained that this violation of human rights and religious freedom was nothing less than a repeat performance of what the Japanese Special Higher Police (Tokko) had done to new religions and other religious minorities during World War II.[5]

Three days after the gas attack, Asahara claimed via video message that he and his followers were in fact the victims and that hundreds of his followers were seriously sick from nerve gas sprayed on them by U.S. troops. A newspaper published by Aum shortly after this similarly claimed that all of the Aum facilities had been attacked by poison gas and many members, along with Asahara, were weak and suffering ill-health as a result. On a radio broadcast by the movement from Russia, however, Asahara exhorted his followers with the disconcerting words: "It is time for you to carry out the plan of salvation. Let us prepare to meet our death without any regrets."

Aum spokesmen continued to proclaim their innocence as investigators intensified their search for evidence and for Asahara. During the first several weeks, Aum found some public support from a few social commentators and scholars who felt the heavy-handed tactics of the police were unjustified. The police, for example, had been detaining a number of Aum members on suspicion of committing minor offenses, which provided them an opportunity to search for other kinds of evidence. As truckloads of chemicals and other materials were confiscated from Aum centers around the country, the evidence for Aum's involvement in the gas attack and other illegal activities accumulated. Most observers came to view the police crackdown as justified and long overdue.

The climax of the investigation came during the early morning hours of May 16, when approximately 2,000 police officers arrived in Kamikuishiki, a small village at the foot of Mount Fuji, which was home to Aum's key facilities. The police discovered Asahara hiding in a secret room inside the Satyam No. 6 building, sitting on considerable cash and gold bars. The police also discovered several comatose followers in the Kamikuishiki facilities. Medical tests subsequently revealed traces of several dangerous drugs in these followers, such as pentobarbital, an anesthetic known to cause convulsions, mental instability, and even death. According to the statements of various members, the drugs were not only used to confine and restrain individuals seeking to leave the group, but also administered in a number of religious rituals.[6]

Between March 22 and May 16, the police arrested some 200 Aum members. To date, Asahara and 104 of his followers have been indicted on various charges and the police are still seeking the whereabouts of four other Aum members suspected of involvement in the subway gas attack. The trial of Asahara is now underway and is expected to last several years. He has been indicted for murder in relation to the Tokyo subway sarin gas attack on March 20, 1995, which killed 12 people and injured another 5,500; another sarin gas attack in Matsumoto, Nagano Prefecture, which killed 7 and injured 600 in June 1994; the kidnapping and murder of Tsutsumi Sakamoto, a lawyer representing concerned parents of Aum members, along with his wife and son; the kidnapping and death of Kiyoshi Kariya, the Tokyo notary public, in February 1995; and the lynching of Kotara Ochida, an "uncooperative" Aum member, in February 1994. Asahara has also been charged with the illegal production of various drugs.

The prosecution is arguing that Asahara directed his followers to produce sarin gas and planned to use it to commit mass murders to make his prophecies regarding Armageddon come true. Under the guidance of the Science and Technology minister, Hideo Murai, Aum was allegedly trying to produce some seventy tons of sarin gas, which it planned to spray on a major metropolitan area (Tokyo) using spray devices on helicopters and various other vehicles. Asahara is pleading innocent of all charges, but many of his underlings have already confessed to their involvement in these crimes and stated that they acted on his direct orders. Asahara and five of his followers were charged with the murders of Sakamoto and Sakamoto's wife and son. Although Asahara denied any involvement, the other five members confessed to the kidnapping and murder of the Sakamoto family.[7] On the basis of information obtained in these confessions, the police were able to find the bodies in three separate mountain locations in early September. Similarly, Masami Tsuchiya, one of Aum's top chemists, has admitted to producing the sarin gas that was used in an earlier attack on a neighborhood in Matsumoto, Nagano Prefecture, on June 27, 1994. More than 200 people were injured and 7 died from this initial gas attack. The mounting evidence and numerous confessions make it difficult to believe that Asahara did not have a central role in all of these crimes.

CONCLUSION

It has been more than a year since the subway gas attack and it is still difficult to fathom how a rather loose association of yoga practitioners evolved into an authoritarian apocalyptic movement bent on destruction. Perhaps in time it will be possible to unravel the complex interaction of factors that led to the spiral of violence. It is apparent that Asahara's character became increasingly authoritarian as he elaborated an apocalyptic vision, with himself as a central character in the unfolding drama. Reader (1996, 93) has recently suggested that Asahara's "precarious prophecies" essentially "locked the religion into a scenario from which it had little way out unless something drastic happened in the period leading up to 1997, and specifically in 1995, which Asahara had marked out as the year when the slide to destruction would begin."

It is important to remember that Asahara did not begin with random mass violence. Initial acts of violence occurred within Aum against members who were wavering and about to abandon the movement. According to recent police reports, thirty-three Aum followers are believed to have been killed between October 1988 and March 1995. Several are believed to have been lynched, at least eight died while working or undergoing intensive ascetic training, and two committed suicide. Another twenty-one followers have been reported missing. The authorities suspect that a number were murdered, including some who contributed substantially to Aum, either financially or through the donation of valuable real estate. It seems that each act of violence made the next one easier and necessary to cover up the past. By the time of the subway gas attack, it is likely that Asahara and his inner circle knew the police were about to begin a serious investigation.

Some observers wonder what took the Japanese authorities so long to take decisive action. It seems apparent that enough serious concerns had been raised about various Aum activities to warrant a more serious police inquiry prior to the subway gas attack. There had been numerous complaints that Aum Shinrikyō was engaged in questionable activities for a religious organization. Seiichi Takeuchi, for example, a farmer and the vice-chairperson of the Aum Shinrikyō Task Force Committee of Kamikuishiki Village, has been particularly outspoken regarding the failure of the police to take appropriate action toward Aum (1995). His community struggled with Aum for several years as the organization built a major complex of facilities in the village, including the facilities that were eventually used in the production of sarin gas. As early as 1990, the citizens groups from the villages of Kamikuishiki, Tomizawa, and Namino went to Tokyo to formally request the government to revoke Aum's legal status as a religious organization. Their appeals were essentially ignored, Takeuchi claims, because Tokyo bureaucrats had little concern over the predicament of rural communities and no major incidents had yet occurred in the metropolitan area. In July 1994, residents of Kamikuishiki also notified authorities of nausea and eye and nose irritation due to mysterious fumes coming from Aum facilities. The authorities still took no decisive action against Aum.

The recent history of Aum Shinrikyō reveals how one small but determined group can manufacture chemicals, illegal drugs, and develop weapons of mass destruction. The violence carried out by Asahara and his inner circle constitutes a prime example of what the late French sociologist Jacques Ellul referred to as the "democratization of evil" in modern technological societies. As Ellul (1989, 60) explained, "an increasing number of people among us is acquiring instruments that can hurt our neighbors or unknown people who, whether we like it or not, are close to us. This is the democratization of evil. Means that were once reserved for the powerful, for the rich, for aristocrats, and which constituted their privilege, are now within the reach of all of us. These means were always means by which the rich and mighty could ensure their domination and do wrong to the rest. It is very important to realize that these privileged means are now within the reach of all of us." Aum may be one of the first new religious movements to try to achieve its goals with the tools of modern science and technology. We may hope that it will be the last. The difficult task ahead is to find a way to preserve the free practice of religion in modern societies, while at the same time keeping dangerous materials and technology out of the hands of those who would use it to bring on Armageddon and establish their particular version of the millennium.

Notes

1. See Omura (1988), Mullins (1992, 232–246), and Shimazono (1993, 221–230) for an overview of new religious movements and discussion of the "neo-new religions."

2. The need for self-sufficiency is discussed in the recently reprinted edition of *Vajrayana Sacca* (Tokyo: Aum Shinrikyō Publications), no. 9, 1995.

3. Inoue (1995, 36) suggests that this comprehensive form of religious organization is related both to the utopianism of the group and to the persecution complex that developed as a result of criticisms by the mass media and various conflicts with local communities.

4. Kariya had apparently been hiding his sister, a member of Aum who was seeking to leave the group because of disagreements regarding the donation of her assets to Aum. According to police reports, she had already donated 60 million yen (approximately $600,000) when she went into hiding. Subsequent investigations and confessions by arrested Aum members confirmed that Kariya had been abducted on February 28, 1995, and taken to one of the Aum facilities in Kamikuishiki. Kariya apparently died from an overdose of the truth drug thiopental and was cremated in a microwave incinerator.

5. Between 1935 and 1943, for example, the Special Police investigated and arrested leaders and members of seventeen different religious groups. Many remained in prison until the end of the war. For a discussion of this earlier police treatment of religious minorities see Mullins (1994).

6. According to recent information, Aum had produced its own LSD since February 1994, and used it in a ritual called the "Christ initiation" from May of that year.

7. Aum leaders apparently feared that Sakamoto's activities on behalf of the "Victims of Aum" association would create such bad publicity that their plans to run candidates in the February 1990 Tokyo elections would be undermined. Asahara's brief attempt to enter Japanese politics was a total failure. Aum's political party, the *Shinri to* (Truth Party), fielded Asahara and twenty-four

other Aum members as candidates in the 1990 Tokyo elections, but not one candidate received enough votes for election. Asahara's apocalyptic writings about the destruction of humanity began in 1989, but he nevertheless led Aum into politics in 1990. It is difficult to know whether this was simply a publicity stunt or an attempt to mislead the public and authorities about his real intentions.

REFERENCES

Arita Yoshifu. 1995. *Oitsumeru Aum Shinri Kyo* (Cornering Aum Shinrikyō). Tokyo: KK Besuto Sera-zu.

Asahara, Shoko. 1986. *Chonoryoku: Himitsu no kaihatsu ho* (Psychic power: A secret means of development). Tokyo: Aum Publishing Division.

———. 1986. *Seishi o koeru* (Transcending life and death). Tokyo: Aum Publishing Division

———. 1989. *Metsubo no hi* (The day of destruction). Tokyo: Aum Publishing Division.

———. 1989. *Metsubo kara koku e: Zoku metsubo no hi* (From destruction to emptiness: A sequel of the day of destruction). Tokyo: Aum Publishing Division.

———. 1991. *Jinrui metsubo no shinjitsu* (The truth of humanity's destruction). Tokyo: Aum Publishing Division.

———. 1991. *Kirisuto sengen* (Proclamation as Christ). Tokyo: Aum Publishing Division.

———. 1991. *Nosutoradamusu himitsu no daiyogen* (The secret prophecy of Nostradamus). Tokyo: Aum Publishing Division.

———. 1992. *Kirisuto sengen Part 2* (Proclamation as Christ Part 2). Tokyo: Aum Publishing Division.

Egawa, Shoko. 1995. *Aum Shinrikyō tsuiseki 2200 nichi* (The 2200-day pursuit of Aum Shinrikyō). Tokyo: Bungei Shunju.

Ellul, Jacques. 1989. *What I Believe*, trans. Geoffrey W. Bromiley. Grand Rapids, MI: William B. Eerdmans Publishing Company.

Inoue, Nobutaka., ed. 1990. *Shinshukyo jiten* (Dictionary of new religions) Tokyo: Kobundo.

———. 1995. "Gendai shakai no 'byo' to 'shinshukyo' toshite no Aum Shinri Kyo" [The "illness" of modern society and Aum Shinri Kyo as a "new religion"]. *Shukan Asahi* (May 30): 35–38.

Kisala, Robert. 1995. "Aum Alone in Japan: Religious Responses to the 'Aum Affair.'" *Nanzan Bulletin* 19: 6–34.

Mullins, Mark R. 1992. "Japan's New Age and Neo-New Religions: Sociological Interpretations." In *Perspectives on the New Age*, edited by James R. Lewis and J. Gordon Melton. Albany: State University of New York Press, 232–246.

————. 1994. "Ideology and Utopianism in Wartime Japan: An Essay on the Subversiveness of Christian Eschatology." *Japanese Journal of Religious Studies* 21 (2–3): 261–280.

Omura, Eisho. 1988. *"Gendaijin no shukyo"* (The Religion of People Today). In *Gendai jin no shukyo* (The religion of people today), edited by Eisho Omura and Shigeru Nishiyama. Tokyo: Yuhikaku.

Reader, Ian. 1996. *A Poisonous Cocktail? Aum Shinrikyō's Path to Violence.* Copenhagen: Nordic Institute for Asian Studies.

Robbins, Thomas, and Dick Anthony. 1995. "Sects and Violence." In *Armageddon in Waco,* edited by Stuart Wright. Chicago: University of Chicago.

Shimada, Hiromi. 1991. *Ima shukyo ni nani ga okotteiru no ka* (What is happening in religious organizations?). Tokyo: Kodansha.

Shimazono, Susumu. 1993. "New Religious Movements." In *Religion and Society in Modern Japan,* edited by Mark R. Mullins, Shimazono Susumu, and Paul Swanson. Berkeley: Asian Humanities Press.

————. 1995a. *Aum Shinrikyō no kiseki* (The tracks of Aum Shinrikyō). Tokyo: Iwanami Booklet, No. 379.

————. 1995b. "Tracing Aum Shinrikyō's Tracks: The Formation and Transformation of Its Faith Universe." *Japanese Journal of Religious Studies* 22 (3–4): 381–415.

Takeuchi, Seiichi. 1995. *Aum 2000 nichi senso* [Aum's 2,000-day war]. Tokyo: KK Besuto sera-zu.

Takimoto, Taro, and Nagaoka Tatsuya, eds. 1995. *Maindo contoro-ru kara nogarete—Aum Shinrikyō dakkaishatachi no taiken* (Escaping mind control—The experiences of ex-members of Aum Shinrikyō). Tokyo: Koyu Shuppan.

Yamashita, Etsuko. 1995. "Shukke suru onnatachi" [Women who renounce the world]. In *Are wa nan datta no ka? 'Aum' kaidoku manyuaru* (What in the world was it? A manual for de-coding "Aum"). Tokyo: Daiyamondo Sha.

Young, Richard Fox. 1995. "Lethal Achievements: Fragments of a Response to the Aum Shinrikyō Affair." *Japanese Religions* 20 (2): 230–245.

Contributors

JAMES A. AHO (Chapter 3) is Professor of Sociology at Idaho State University. His latest book, *This Thing of Darkness: A Sociology of the Enemy*, was given the Gustavus Myers Best Study of Human Rights in North America award and the Pacific Sociological Association annual book award in 1996. He is also author of *The Politics of Righteousness: The Idaho Patriot Movement*.

DICK ANTHONY (Chapter 14) is a forensic and research psychologist who has a private consulting practice in issues raised by new religious movements. He has published widely on the psychological and social effects of involvement in the new religions. He may be reached at 809 Evelyn Avenue, Albany, California, 94706. Telephone (510) 527-1712. Fax (510) 559-8712.

ROBERT W. BALCH (Chapter 4) is Professor of Sociology at the University of Montana in Missoula. Since 1975 he has been conducting ethnographic studies of unconventional religious movements, most recently the Christian Identity sect in Idaho known as Aryan Nations.

MICHAEL BARKUN (Ph.D., Northwestern) (Chapter 13) is Professor of Political Science in the Maxwell School of Citizenship and Public Affairs at Syracuse University. He is the author of numerous books, articles, book chapters, and papers on millennialism, including *Religion and the Racist Right: The Origins of the Christian Identity Movement* (University of North Carolina Press, 1994); *Crucible of the Millennium: The Burned-over District of New York State in the 1840s* (Syracuse University Press, 1986); and *Disaster and the Millennium* (Yale University Press, 1974). He has also written extensively on international law, including *Law Without Sanctions* (Yale University Press, 1968) and *International Law and the Social Sciences* (co-author, Princeton University Press, 1970). He served as editor of *Communal Societies*, the journal of the Communal Studies Association, from 1987 through 1994. He has held research fellowships from the Ford Foundation and the National Endowment for the Humanities.

JOHN M. BOZEMAN (Chapter 7) is a Ph.D. candidate in American religious history at the University of Virginia; he also holds a master's degree in environmental engineering science. His research interests include new religious movements and the religious implications of technological development.

DAVID G. BROMLEY (Chapter 1) received his Ph.D. in sociology from Duke University and is currently Professor of Sociology and an Affiliate Professor in the Department of Religious Studies at Virginia Commonwealth University. He is also an Affiliate Professor in the Department of Sociology at the University of Virginia. His research interests include sociology of religion, social movements, deviance, and political sociology. Among his recent books are *Anticult Movements in Cross-Cultural Perspective* (Garland Publishers, 1994, edited with Anson Shupe); *Handbook on Cults and Sects in America* (2 volumes; Association for the Sociology of Religion, Society for the Scientific Study of Religion, and JAI Press, 1993, edited with Jeffrey K. Hadden); and *The Satanism Scare* (Aldine de Gruyter, 1991, edited with James Richardson and Joel Best). He is former president of the Association for the Study of Religion; founding editor of the annual series, *Religion and the Social Order*, sponsored by the Association for the Sociology of Religion; and past editor of the *Journal for the Scientific Study of Religion*, published by the Society for the Scientific Study of Religion.

He is currently working on *Religion and Resistance: Prophetic Religion in a Secular Age,* to be published by Rutgers University Press.

MICHAEL W. CUNEO (Chapter 9) is in the Department of Sociology and Anthropology at Fordham University. Over the past several years, Dr. Cuneo has written primarily in the sociology of religion area, with particular emphasis on Roman Catholicism in Canada and the United States. In addition to several reference works and numerous articles, he has recently published a major book, *Catholics Against the Church* (University of Toronto Press, 1989, 1991), that has been widely and very favorably reviewed in both the popular and scholarly media. His forthcoming book on Roman Catholic fundamentalism in the United States, *The Smoke of Satan,* has already been featured in a front-page *New York Times* article by Gustav Niebuhr (January 9, 1995) and a *Newhouse News Service* article by Delia Rios (February 27, 1995). In recent years as well, Cuneo has served as the social sciences representative on the *Being Right* project, an ongoing research project funded by the Lilly Endowment and dedicated to the investigation of religious conservatism in contemporary America. He has appeared regularly on CBC radio in Canada, and recently appeared in a *Voice of America* documentary on abortion-related violence in the United States. Cuneo is currently undertaking research for a forthcoming book entitled *Bronx Blues.*

Cuneo was born in Toronto in 1954 and earned his doctorate at the University of Toronto in 1988. He spent 1989 as a Killam Postdoctoral Fellow at Dalhousie University in Halifax, Nova Scotia, and has taught for the past five years at Fordham University in New York City.

JOHN DOMITROVICH (Chapter 4) is a Ph.D. student at the University of Montana and an instructor in the Department of Human Services at Salish-Kootenai Community College in Pablo, Montana. He has a master's degree in Social Anthropology from the University of Montana.

JOHN R. HALL (Chapter 15) is the author of *The Ways Out—A Book on Utopian Communal Groups in the U.S. during the 1960s and 70s* and "The Apocalypse at Jonestown," one of the earliest scholarly analyses of Jonestown, as well as a sociological and cultural history of the Peoples Temple, *Gone from the Promised Land.* He has also written on a variety of other sociological topics including *Culture: Sociological Perspectives,* co-authored with Mary Jo Neitz. His essay,

"Public Narratives and the Apocalyptic Sect: From Jonestown to Mount Carmel," was recently published in *Armageddon in Waco*, edited by Stuart A. Wright. He is Professor of Sociology at the University of California at Davis.

MASSIMO INTROVIGNE (Chapter 12) (b. Rome, 1955) is managing director of CESNUR, the Center for Studies on New Religions in Torino, Italy, and a part-time professor of religious studies at the Regina Apostolorum University in Rome. He is the author of fifteen books in Italian and the editor of another five in the field of new religious movements and contemporary magic, three of them translated into French. He is international editor of *Syzygy: Journal of Alternative Religion and Culture*, published in California by CESNUR and by the Institute for the Study of American Religion.

PHILIP LAMY (Chapter 5) received both his M.A. in Anthropology (1983) and his Ph.D. in Sociology (1991) at Northeastern University, Boston, Massachusetts. He is currently Assistant Professor of Sociology and Anthropology at Castleton State College, Castleton, Vermont, and his research and teaching interests are in social movements, the sociology of culture, mass media and communications, and religion. He is currently reworking his 1991 dissertation on survivalism and the American millennial myth for publication. Also, as part of his work in media and cultural studies, he is pursuing an interest in visual sociology and documentary filmmaking. With his filmmaking colleagues, he is in the final editing stages of a documentary film on the history and sociology of Salem witchcraft, entitled "Witch City," to be released in the coming year.

His publications include: "Millennialism in the Mass Media: The Case of *Soldier of Fortune Magazine*" (*Journal for the Scientific Study of Religion*, 1992), which was the winner of the 1992 Marshall Fishwick Award given by the American Popular Culture Association for the best article on popular culture; "A Response to James Lewis's 'Shooting Holes in Monolithic Millennialism' " (*Journal for the Scientific Study of Religion*, 1993); and "Punk and Middle-Class Values: A Content Analysis" with Jack Levin (*Youth and Society*, 1985), reprinted in Sandra Ball-Rokeach and Muriel Cantor's *Media, Audience and Social Structure* (Sage, 1986).

RONALD LAWSON (Chapter 11) has written extensively on the urbanization of Australia, tenant-landlord conflict in New York, and international Seventh-day Adventism. His books include *Brisbane in the 1890s* and *The Tenant Movement in New York, 1904–1984*. A book on Seventh-day Adventism is in preparation.

He is Professor in the Department of Urban Studies, Queens College of the City University of New York, Flushing, NY 11367; email: rlawson@cloud9.net.

MARTHA F. LEE (Chapter 6) is Associate Professor of Political Science at the University of Windsor, Windsor, Ontario, Canada. She is the author of *Earth First! Environmental Apocalypse* (1995) and *The Nation of Islam* (1988, 1996). With T. E. Flanagan, she has written articles on the Alberta Social Credit Party, as well as on the Black Muslims. She is currently researching the role of women in the early British fascist movement.

BARBARA LYNN MAHNKE (Chapter 4) is Regional Program Officer for the Division of Senior and Long-Term Care Services in Bozeman, Montana. She has a bachelor of arts degree in Sociology from the University of Montana.

VANESSA MORRISON (Chapter 4) is an undergraduate student at the University of Montana, where she is majoring in Liberal Studies.

MARK R. MULLINS (Chapter 16) is Professor of Sociology of Religion and Christian Studies at Meiji Gakuin University, Tokyo/Yokohama, Japan. After spending his childhood in Japan, he returned to North America for higher education and received his Ph.D. in Sociology of Religion and East Asian Traditions from McMaster University (Hamilton, Ontario). He is the author of *Religious Minorities in Canada* (1989) and co-editor of *Japanese New Religions Abroad* (1991), *Religion and Society in Modern Japan* (1993), and *Perspectives on Christianity in Korea and Japan* (1995). His current research is focused on indigenous Christian movements in Japan.

SUSAN J. PALMER (Intro. Chapter & Chapter 8) teaches Religious Studies at Dawson College in Montreal and is an adjunct professor at Concordia University, Montreal. She is the author of *Moon Sister, Krishna Mothers, Rajneesh Lovers* (Syracuse, 1994), *AIDS as an Apocalyptic Metaphor*, and co-author of *The Rajneesh Papers* and *Children in New Religions* (with Charlotte Hardman) as well as many articles. She is Associate Producer on *The Endtime*, a documentary film on The Family.

THOMAS ROBBINS (Intro. Chapter & Chapter 14) is a sociologist of religion. He is the author of *Cults, Converts and Charisma* and co-editor of a number of volumes including *In Gods We Trust, Church-State Relations* and *Between the*

Sacred and the Secular. He has authored or co-authored numerous articles on various aspects of contemporary religious movements. He lives in Rochester, Minnesota.

PHILIP SCHUYLER (Chapter 15), Associate Professor of Music at the University of Maryland–Baltimore County, received his undergraduate degree from Yale and his Ph.D. from the University of Washington. An ethnomusicologist specializing in North Africa and Middle East, his special interests include the ethnography of performance and the inter-relationship of the arts. His research has resulted in numerous articles, field recordings, and an ethnographic film.

ANSON SHUPE (Chapter 10) is Professor of Sociology at the joint campuses of Indiana University and Purdue University at Fort Wayne and a member of the graduate faculties of both universities. He received his B.A. from the College of Wooster and both his M.A. and Ph.D. degrees from Indiana University. He has previously held positions at Alfred University and the University of Texas at Arlington.

He is author of more than six dozen professional journal articles and book chapters, twenty-four authored/co-authored/co-edited books, and numerous newspaper/magazine articles and editorials covering new religious movements, ministerial abuse, and family violence. He is now continuing research that combines the sociology of religion with criminology/deviance theory. His most recent publication in this area is *In the Name of All That's Holy: A Theory of Clergy Malfeasance* (1995, Praeger Publishers).

CATHERINE WESSINGER (Chapter 2) is Associate Professor of the History of Religions and Women's Studies at Loyola University, New Orleans. She is author of *Annie Besant and Progressive Messianism* (Edwin Mellen Press, 1988). She is editor of and contributor to *Women's Leadership in Marginal Religions: Explorations outside the Mainstream* (University of Illinois Press, 1993), and *Religious Institutions and Women's Leadership: New Roles inside the Main- stream* (University of South Carolina Press, 1996). She is currently writing a book comparing Jonestown, Aum Shinrikyō, Branch Davidians, and the Mon- tana Freemen, and editing a book examining the interacting dynamics of mil- lennial beliefs, persecution, and violence involving religious groups.

Index